DATE DUE

D1042156

GAYLORD   PRINTED IN U.S.A.

Cornered

Cornered

BIG TOBACCO AT THE BAR OF JUSTICE

Peter Pringle

A MARIAN WOOD BOOK

HENRY HOLT AND COMPANY   NEW YORK

Henry Holt and Company, Inc.
Publishers since 1866
115 West 18th Street
New York, New York 10011

Henry Holt® is a registered
trademark of Henry Holt and Company, Inc.

Published in Canada by Fitzhenry & Whiteside Ltd.,
195 Allstate Parkway, Markham, Ontario L3R 4T8.

Library of Congress Cataloging-in-Publication Data
Pringle, Peter.
Cornered : big tobacco at the bar of justice / Peter Pringle. —
1st ed.
p.   cm.
"A Marian Wood book."
Includes bibliographical references and index.
ISBN 0-8050-4292-X (hc : alk. paper)
1. Trials (Products liability)—United States.   2. Products
liability—Tobacco—United States.   3. Cigarette industry—
Law and legislation—United States.   I. Title.
KF226.P75 1998   97-47008
346.7303'8—dc21   CIP

Henry Holt books are available for special promotions and
premiums. For details contact: Director, Special Markets.

First Edition 1998

Designed by Kate Nichols

Printed in the United States of America
All first editions are printed on acid-free paper. ∞

1   3   5   7   9   10   8   6   4   2

For Victoria,
and her generation

ACKNOWLEDGMENTS

IN THE SUMMER of 1994, when a handful of American journalists were being sued for possession of stolen company documents by the British tobacco giant Brown & Williamson, I was given access to these papers for my reports to *The Independent* in London. When, finally, the U.S. courts ruled the documents were in the public domain and the unprecedented legal assault on the tobacco industry began, I found myself in the middle of the battle, and this book was born.

Nathan Abse was my invaluable researcher, who began in 1995 cataloging and annotating the vast amount of material that had suddenly become available. His inside knowledge of the medical-science libraries, his dissection of dense scientific argument, and his sharp analyses were outstanding contributions to this work. His ability to travel long distances on next to nothing, and still fulfill his goals, became legendary. After the first year of the project, *The Washington Post* lured him away to be their National News Researcher, but he gave the book his support until the end. His reading of drafts was most helpful, and I am grateful for his work and his friendship.

My hope, as always, was to talk to both sides in the war. Alas, this was not possible. The tobacco industry retreated into its bunker; rejecting repeated attempts over three years, during which I also made a documentary for British television, to discuss the view from the corner in which the industry had become trapped.

The anti-tobacco lawyers were only too eager to tell their story, of course; propaganda is one of their key weapons. But, even so, I could not have completed my task without hundreds of hours of interviews with members of the plaintiffs' bar; I shudder to think what the billable time would add up to, had it not been freely given.

In Mississippi, my thanks to Don Barrett, Dick Scruggs, Mike Moore, Charles Mikhail, Steve Bozeman, and Lee Young, and the staffs of the Barrett Law Offices in Lexington, the attorney general's office in Jackson, and of the Scruggs law firm in Pascagoula. Charlene Bosarge was magnificently patient with the demands of my film crew, as was Sally Barrett, who should have been a star in the documentary. In Lexington, thanks also to Ella Horton, Earline Hart, and the staff of the Lexington Courthouse, who gave up part of their weekend, and to Tom and Jerry Ann Gant, who gave up their shop for an afternoon. Morton Mintz kindly lent me his valuable file on the Horton case.

In New Orleans, Wendell Gauthier was especially helpful and, for some reason, spared me from being a victim of his practical jokes. Presumably, my turn will come. John Coale was so friendly as Castano's publicity chief I often forgot he was a lawyer. Elizabeth Cabraser always shared a special insight. Also in New Orleans, Suzy Foulds answered innumerable document questions, and Sherill Horndorff, Russ Herman, Calvin Fayard, Joseph Bruno, Walter Leger, Ken Carter, Danny Becnel, and Christine Cox went out of their way to help.

In Minneapolis, Roberta Walburn interrupted her own punishing schedule to answer a flow of queries about the Minnesota case, and Mike Ciresi made himself available on a trip to London. Attorney General Skip Humphrey took time to explain his position. David Phelps of the Minneapolis *Star Tribune* and David Shaffer of the *St. Paul Pioneer Press* provided background material.

In Charleston, South Carolina, Andy Berly probably now has more confidential documents on the British tobacco giant BAT Industries than the company has itself—at least in one place.

In Louisville, Kentucky, Jeff Wigand said whatever he was allowed to say without breaching his confidentiality agreement, and Fox DeMoisey helped disentangle the web the industry had spun around its troublesome dissenter, Merrell Williams. And Williams himself spoke at length of his curious odyssey.

In Washington, D.C., David Kessler gave two long interviews in the midst of his very personal battle with the industry, and FDA officials Jim O'Hara, Jeff Nesbitt, and Mitch Zeller filled in the blanks. Phil Barnett and Ripley Forbes (before they moved on) and Alison Waldman were extremely helpful in Congressman Henry Waxman's office.

Thanks to Susan Sherman at the Labor Department for help during the OSHA hearings; also to Sherri Watson of the American Lung Association and to Rhett and Suzanne Klok for their assistance with OSHA transcripts. Matt Myers gave me a long historical overview of the confrontation between the health groups and the industry.

At the Advocacy Institute, Karen Lewis opened the institute's files. Also in Washington, a special thanks to Claudia MacLachlan for guiding me to a variety of legal sources. Muriel Sanford at the University of Maine Library, Special Collections, and Douglas Macbeth at the Jackson Library were guides to the Clarence Cook Little papers. Karen Miller offered her excellent dissertation study on Hill & Knowlton.

At three Mealey Tobacco Conferences, Ron Motley, Andy Berly, Charles Mikhail, Susan Niall, Hugh McNeely, and Madelyn Chaber helped simplify the complexities of tort law in unusually palatable ways. Separately, so did Don Garner and Carl Bogus. Clifford Douglas invariably had new information. And it was always a pleasure to bump into Gary Black, of Sanford C. Bernstein & Co., and check the latest price of Philip Morris stock. Sam Crawford guided me on Wall Street investment procedures.

In Boston, Dick Daynard, Mark Gottlieb, and the staff of the Tobacco Products Liability Project invited me to their own invaluable conferences and gave me access to their files. At Harvard Law School, my thanks to Laurence Tribe and also to Jon Hanson, who put on the most useful post–June 20 settlement conference. Tom Sobol was very helpful on company law.

In Jacksonville, Florida, Woody Wilner and Ginny Steiger explained the intricacies of their guerrilla tactics. In San Francisco, Stan Glantz and Chris Patti documented the industry's assault on the University of California at San Francisco.

The staff at the Centers for Disease Control provided many reports.

The library staffs of the National Institutes of Health, the Library of Congress, *The Times-Picayune*, Minneapolis *Star Tribune*, Louisville *Courier-Journal*, and the National Formulary were most helpful, as were, especially, Edward Abse, Bryson Clevenger, Elizabeth Crocker, and Sajjad Yusuf at the Alderman Library in Charlottesville, and George Griffenhagen at the American Pharmaceutical Association.

In London, Martyn Day and Martin Jervis provided insights into the British civil action, and in Oxford, Sir Richard Doll recalled the strange beginnings of the scientific understanding of the harm smoking can do.

A few weeks before he died of smoking-related cancer, Victor Crawford, a former industry lobbyist in Maryland, told me how tobacco lobbyists work at the state level.

Julian Norridge, the producer of my television documentary, gave helpful advice for the book, as well.

For their hospitality, I am indebted to John and Barbara Pringle, Curtis Wilkie, John and Mary Acton, Alexander and Susanna Chancellor, and Philip and Ann Jacobson.

My agent, Robert Ducas, persevered when publishers told him either that they did not have the resources to take on the tobacco industry or that the Third Wave litigation would come to nothing.

My editor, Marian Wood, said neither of those things, and it was a pleasure to work with her again. She was as inspiring and progressive as ever, despite her eccentric boycott of computers. My thanks also to Nancy Clements, Kenn Russell, and Chuck Thompson for their professional calm during the accelerated production schedule.

My family put up with an apartment stuffed with documents for longer than was fair. Eleanor Randolph, as always, lent unwavering support throughout the project and read the first draft, inserting her magical touches. Whatever mistakes my small band of helpers missed are, of course, my own.

New York
November 19, 1997

CONTENTS

CORNERED

PROLOGUE

DINNER AT ANTOINE'S

BEFORE HE LEFT his native Marseilles in 1840 for the steamy New World on the mouth of Mississippi, Antoine Alciatore learned the secrets of such rich, buttery delights as *pommes de terre soufflées* from the great French chef Collinet. Armed with this knowledge, he opened a small pension on the Rue St. Louis in the French Quarter of New Orleans, which over the years became one of the South's most famous restaurants. A lush, extravagant place, run for the city's finest, richest, and most notorious citizens, the menu changed to suit the era and the clientele. At the turn of the century, when there was a shortage of snails from Europe, Antoine's son, Jules, introduced oysters Rockefeller; sometime later there appeared a new dessert called omelette Alaska Antoine, or baked Alaska. This wobbly mass of meringue, pound cake, and ice cream can be created in monstrous proportions, if the occasion warrants, up to two feet long by one foot wide— all served on a gleaming silver platter. Such an occasion occurred shortly before Christmas in 1994 when the tobacco lawyers came to dinner.

It was December 13, and Antoine's large open dining area was bulging with pre–Christmas party revelers. The private President's Room at the back had been booked by a local lawyer of Cajun descent named Wendell Gauthier, known to his friends as "the Goat." His list of some fifty guests included many of the most famous and feared members of the plaintiffs' bar, that despised group of personal injury lawyers who make their vast fortunes off human catastrophe. Gauthier's list included "the King of Torts" (Melvin Belli from San Francisco); Stanley Chesley, "the Master of Disaster," from Cincinnati; John "Bhopal" Coale of Washington, D.C.; Russ "the Girth" Herman of Louisiana; and "the Asbestos Avenger" (Ron Motley of Charleston, South Carolina).

Over cocktails in the President's Room the question was who from Gauthier's honors list of legal warriors was actually going to turn up.

Stanley never comes to dinners, they had said of Chesley. He's far too grand. He makes contributions to the Democratic Party, and he's always talking about his latest visit to the White House. Melvin Belli couldn't come. At the age of eighty-seven, he was too frail. Pity, they sighed. Belli had the big name, the flair, the memory. The irrepressible Ron Motley, who could sniff out a corporation causing harm to the citizenry from half a continent away, was coming in his private jet, but he would be late. He was busy arranging a party for his fiancée on his yacht in Florida.

"Who cares about them?" muttered "Bhopal" Coale, sipping his Diet Coke. "All of them basically hate each other."

Some of them hated him, too. Or they used to. Russ Herman had once called Coale a "cesspool." In print.

"I'm not a cesspool; I'm a pirate," Coale said, recalling that he had once sailed an ancient British sloop from England to Spain and had been shipwrecked in the Bay of Biscay. Now, appropriately, he was in the home of the notorious French pirates, New Orleans.

"He's not a real pirate, he's a buccaneer like Jean Lafitte," interrupted the robust Mr. Herman, whose jolly face would fit well on the quarterdeck of an old galleon.

The real wonder of the evening was that any of these powerful lawyers had agreed to meet under one roof. Such is the fiercely competitive nature of their business that under normal circumstances they never hunt together. But there had never been such circumstances.

The greatest tort prize of all time—the treasures of Big Tobacco—suddenly seemed to be within the grasp of these risk capitalists of adversity. (One of the nicer descriptions of how they make a living.) For forty years, the tobacco companies had repelled all claims for damages caused by cigarettes. A sad parade of smokers had filed into court, trying to extract compensation for their lung cancers and their heart disease, but one after another they had been beaten back by the industry's powerful legal machines, leaving the plaintiffs' lawyers shell-shocked and occasionally even broke. The wiser members of the bar had stayed away. Now, however, they smelled blood.

In Louisville, Kentucky, a $9-an-hour law clerk had brazenly lifted thousands of pages of confidential tobacco company documents and handed them over for use in court. In Washington, D.C., the Food and Drug Administration had launched an inquiry into the tobacco industry with the aim of regulating nicotine as a drug. The White House was in the hands of America's first antismoking president. In New York, ABC News had aired a program charging the tobacco companies with "spiking" cigarettes with nicotine to keep smokers hooked. The network had been immediately served with a libel writ—for $10 billion, the largest in history.

These events had created a new antismoking era and set off an explosion of lawsuits that became known as the Third Wave of tobacco litigation. The first, from 1954 to 1973, came after the big lung cancer scare of the early '50s, when laboratory research linking smoking to cancer in mice was first published. Sick smokers went to court, but proving their cancer was caused by cigarettes was much more difficult than their lawyers had imagined; the companies had little problem creating a doubt in the minds of the juries. In the Second Wave, from 1983 to 1992, the scientific evidence was more firmly established, but the industry still successfully beat back any claims for damages by persuading juries that a smoker chooses to smoke knowing the risks. By this time, the industry had built up the most sophisticated legal defenses of any U.S. commercial enterprise and wore down its opponents by outspending and outlasting them. A tobacco lawyer had once boasted, paraphrasing General Patton, that he won cases not by spending his company's money, but by "making the other son-of-a-bitch spend all of his." Even the most determined and wealthy members of the plaintiffs' bar were unable to sustain the costs of bringing a case.

But in recent years, the plaintiffs' bar had won a series of spectacular awards in cases involving the asbestos industry, silicone breast implants, and the makers of women's contraceptives. The lawyers had accumulated a war chest and were prepared to put it to good public use, intending no less than to bring the tobacco industry to its knees and stop its pollution of the hearts and lungs of Americans. They also expected to take their cut, of course; 25 percent of billions of dollars, or so they hoped.

Wendell Gauthier, a multimillionaire member of the plaintiffs' bar, was the first to file suit. He would eventually persuade sixty other members to pledge $100,000 a year each to launch the largest-ever class-action suit against the tobacco companies. It was open to tens of millions of American cigarette smokers addicted to nicotine. Under an unlikely flag of friendship and cooperation, Gauthier had invited his comrades to Antoine's to mark the beginning of hostilities. The next morning they were due in court to argue the worth of the class action that would become known as the "Mother of All Lawsuits."

"Yes, I think the moment has come," observed the earnest Boston law professor Richard Daynard, fingering his graying beard and giving his latest forecast of when the tobacco companies would be paying out money for their past misdeeds. He was a veteran antitobacco activist and had been made an honorary member of Gauthier's group because of his encyclopedic knowledge of tobacco litigation and his legendary steel-trap mind. His dinner was free. In return, he could always be relied upon for a prediction of when the industry would collapse under the weight of lawsuits.

"How about the spring of 1996?"

"How about 2001?"

"How about the date of Motley's next wedding?"

"Which one?"

"Fish or steak?" interrupted the waiters. No *pigeonneaux royaux sauce paradis* for this crowd. Not yet, anyway.

ON THE OTHER SIDE of the restaurant, by coincidence as it turned out, the Rex Room had been booked by a group of lawyers representing the tobacco companies. Wood-paneled and hung with portraits of the past kings of the Krewe of Rex of Mardi Gras, the room was an appropriate place for the blue bloods of the legal profession who had flown in for the court hearing: lawyers from Chadbourne & Parke of New York; Jones, Day of Cleveland; King & Spalding of Atlanta; and Shook, Hardy & Bacon of Kansas City, all old campaigners for the tobacco barons. In contrast to Gauthier's guests, they sat restrained and somber at a long pine table. They were war weary.

The First and Second Waves of the campaign had been hard fought. The figures spoke for themselves. Eight hundred and thirteen claims filed against the industry, twenty-three tried in court, two lost, both overturned on appeal. Not a penny paid in damages.

The tobacco barons showed no sign of compromise in the face of the new enemy. They had retreated into their bunkers, predicting the furor would pass and accused Gauthier and his followers of jumping on a "publicity bandwagon" created by the media. Victor Schwartz, of the Washington, D.C., law firm of Crowell & Moring, which advises clients on tobacco litigation, said, "It's déjà vu, except for very powerful attorneys whom I have great respect for."

A new element in the Third Wave was complicating old formulas, however. In four states—Mississippi, Minnesota, Florida, and West Virginia—an entirely fresh approach to tobacco litigation was being taken by the states' attorneys general. They were seeking to recoup billions of dollars the states had paid under the Medicaid program to care for poor people with smoking-related diseases. The idea was to treat the tobacco industry like any other commercial enterprise whose product had caused harm—like asbestos and toxic waste dumps—and make them pay for the cleanup. Though the tobacco industry quickly dismissed these claims as frivolous and having no chance of success, in time they would become even more of a legal threat than Gauthier's grand class action, providing the other half of the pincer movement that finally brought the industry to the negotiating table in 1997.

Tired though the industry lawyers had become and facing forces they had never before encountered, they still relished the looming conflict. Defending tobacco lawsuits was a lucrative business, one of the best, and they believed they could be victorious. They looked down on Gauthier's group as a lower caste—greedy, attention grabbing, and a disgrace to the profession. They would prevail, as they had always done, or so they thought. In the Rex Room that night, Phil Wittman, a local lawyer representing tobacco defendants, said of Gauthier's suit, "It's a lot of smoke and mirrors. It's stuff that's been out there a long time."

Wall Street didn't think so. The financial risk to the industry was "staggering," stock analysts had warned. Losing Gauthier's suit could result in damages of $100 billion—twice the industry's annual sales revenue.

In between the two groups of lawyers at Antoine's that night, at a table in the open dining room, sat a group of four investment analysts from New York. They had flown down to attend the court hearing. They were so nervous, they wouldn't talk. "We can't say anything," said the normally garrulous Gary Black, of Sanford C. Bernstein & Co. "There's too much at stake here."

In the President's Room, Gauthier was rallying his forces with self-deprecating Cajun jokes. As the meal was nearing completion, he announced the arrival of Santa Claus. "We are going to send the tobacco lawyers a little Christmas present," he said to loud applause. In walked a man in a red costume sporting a white flowing beard and carrying aloft on a silver platter one of Antoine's baked Alaskas. Its sides were covered with "No Smoking" signs in red icing. "Take the tobacco companies their present," ordered Gauthier, and the Santa walked out of the President's Room, passed the table with Gary Black and the Wall Street analysts, and burst through the pine doors of the Rex Room singing, "Ho, ho, ho, Merry Christmas to one and all." The company lawyers were appalled, refused to accept the gift, shoved the Santa out of the room, and left the restaurant in a huff, abandoning their brandies, and, of course, their cigars. The enemy had been engaged.

IN THE COMING MONTHS, New Orleans would be the headquarters of the antitobacco forces, a gathering place for the new challengers of Big Tobacco, whose ranks swelled with each new exposure of the industry's deceitful past. Confidential documents were found in archives and attics and unearthed from the basements of courtrooms where long-forgotten members of the plaintiffs' bar had lost contests with the industry. One cache of scientific reports came from a woman who sought revenge on her lover, a researcher from Philip Morris who had left boxes of company documents at her house. Each month, it seemed, brought fresh evidence of tobacco industry lies and deceptions; how they had hidden research into smoking and health, manipulated nicotine levels, and sneakily targeted children in their advertising and promotion.

The tobacco companies had finally met their match. Here for the first time was an enemy that showed no fear of their superior legal forces and unlimited funds. Here was an enemy that would play legal tricks and more besides. They turned company whistle-blowers into national heroes, put stolen industry files on the Internet, leaked protected court documents, and persuaded judges to release papers the tobacco industry had long hidden from public view. Finally, they did a secret deal with the smallest of the tobacco companies, dragging the bigger ones to the negotiating table.

The lawsuits against the industry would mushroom. The American legal system had never witnessed such a contest in civil actions as would unfold over the next three years. By the middle of 1997, at least 530 law firms and thousands of attorneys were engaged in the battle for the hearts and lungs of Americans. Half of the country's largest law firms, charging fees of up to $500 an hour, were working for the tobacco companies. Another 182 firms had joined the ranks of the antitobacco forces. The annual legal bill for the Big Six tobacco companies—Philip Morris, R. J. Reynolds, Brown & Williamson, Lorillard, American Tobacco Company, and Liggett & Myers—amounted to $600 million dollars. More than 300 lawsuits were pending against them with potential damages of hundreds of billions of dollars. The long arm of U.S. civil law had even drawn in Britain's biggest tobacco enterprise, BAT Industries.

America's one-hundred-year war against tobacco seemed set for a final battle in court. The traditional crusaders against smoking, the "Health Nazis," as the industry dubbed them—the American Cancer Society, the American Heart Association, the American Lung Association, Action on Smoking and Health, the Advocacy Institute, Ralph Nader's Public Citizen, Doctors Ought to Care, and a host of small, independent tobacco education and control groups—took a backseat while the liability lawyers poured their much greater resources into the battle. "The antismokers want to get their message out, but we just want to kill them," said "Bhopal" Coale of the tobacco companies. "If our methods work there won't be any need to get the message out."

Simultaneously, the Clinton administration would lead a sustained attack on the industry through the youthful commissioner of the Food and Drug Administration, David Kessler. For the first time in its ninety-year history, the FDA would be cleared by the courts to regulate tobacco as a drug.

In the end, neither side was anxious to go into court. A group of plaintiffs' lawyers from Mississippi launched negotiations with the industry that would climax, in the summer of 1997, with a congressional proposal to radically change the way the companies had been doing business. After four decades of denying that smoking causes cancer, the industry's leaders backed down and signed the biggest liability settlement in U.S. corporate history, promising to pay out $368.5 billion over twenty-five years.

NONE OF THE DINERS at Antoine's that December evening would have imagined such an ending. Yet the early signs were there. On one side was an undisciplined guerrilla force, armed with an array of untried legal theories but able to move with lightning speed, energetic, motivated, and mischievous. On the other side were the larger, better equipped, and more experienced lawyers of the tobacco companies whose invincibility in court over four decades was legendary, but whose success had become a handicap. They could move only in blocks, their tactics were well known, their weapons old, and their leaders exhausted. This is the story of three tumultuous years that led to an astonishing truce in the century-old tobacco wars.

A federal court would rule that Gauthier's class-action suit was too big to be managed in one trial and had to be broken up into smaller trials in state courts. But its effect, even out of court, was devastating to Big Tobacco. For two years, it generated a barrage of antismoking propaganda unprecedented in history. And it was this lawsuit that prepared the ground for the mass offensive by the states' attorneys general to recoup medical costs.

The results were a surprise, but the uprising was inevitable. Big

Tobacco had become so rich and powerful, no part of government at any level would take it on. Only the lawyers of the plaintiffs' bar had the wit, the strength, and the prospect of big rewards to make it worth their while. Like all uprisings, it had several small beginnings. One of them occurred in a tiny Mississippi town on the edge of the Delta at the end of the 1980s, during the final phase of the Second Wave.

1

A NOVEL

OBSERVATION

"MR. ROSS: I feel that in time an objective study should be made into . . . cigarette smoking . . . to make certain that people who use [cigarettes] do not place an overdue burden on the others that do not use them and that the payment they make should be equal to the costs they create.

MR. SATTERFIELD: That is a novel observation, I must confess."

—An exchange in 1969 between Arthur Ross, then chairman of the Franklin National Bank, and Congressman David Satterfield of Virginia during hearings to ban cigarette advertising on television

HOLMES COUNTY, Mississippi, is depressingly poor—fifth from the bottom on the federal poverty scale. One reason is the land. The county lies sixty miles to the north of Jackson, the state capital, on the edge of the Mississippi Delta. But, in contrast to the Delta's fertile floodplain, Holmes County's red clay is unworkable and barren. Small landowners raise a few cattle and a hog or two, but in high summer the land is abandoned, blanketed in great cascading sculptures of kudzu. The county seat is Lexington, a tiny town of 20,600 built around a central square. It has a handsome redbrick courthouse with a clock tower, a thirty-foot-high Civil War statue, and several stores doing a brisk trade in secondhand goods with advertisements such as "Used Tires Guaranteed 3 Months." A mobile-home factory provides employment for the lucky few, the size of their wage packet being dependent to a large extent on the damage wrought to the

Gulf Coast during hurricane season. A few miles outside Lexington, you could be in rural Central America. Poorly dressed children play in dirty backyards with underfed dogs.

INTO THIS SOUTHERN BACKWATER in the fall of 1987 rolled the frontline legal forces of the American Tobacco Company, maker of Lucky Strikes, Pall Malls, Tareytons, and Carltons. They were preparing to spend millions of dollars from the company's $1.5 billion in annual tobacco sales to defend a lawsuit brought by a black carpenter named Nathan Horton. Aged fifty, Horton had smoked two packs of Pall Malls a day for more than thirty years, and he blamed the American Tobacco Company for his inoperable lung cancer. The image of this huge international tobacco company descending on tiny Lexington to squash the claim of a dying carpenter was the best, and the worst, example of what those plaintiffs' lawyers who had been through a to-bacco lawsuit and survived to tell the tale called "the Wall of Flesh" — a legal machine made up of hundreds of attorneys, paralegals, research-ers, scientific advisers, and private investigators, not to mention public relations consultants, that form the defense team when any U.S. tobacco company is challenged in the courts. The American Tobacco Company was then owned by American Brands, which, like other tobacco giants, had diversified over the previous decade and also owned life insurance companies, a liquor company that included Jim Beam whiskey and Gilbey's gin, and various other manufacturing enterprises, including makers of office products, padlocks, and golf clubs. Nathan Horton was a self-employed carpenter who had served in the navy, where he'd be-gun smoking two packs a day. He'd saved enough money to build his own house for his second wife and their six children, a step up from trailers and cement-block duplexes.

In 1986, Horton was hired by a sharp-witted, personable local law-yer named Don Barrett to help build a duck-hunting camp on the nearby Yazoo River. Barrett runs a family firm known as the Barrett Law Offices across the road from the courthouse and if Lexington had a squire, it would be Don Barrett. His home is only a short walk from the courthouse square, past the police station and the county jail. It is a Southern mansion set in a salient of prosperity amid live oaks, neat lawns, and well-groomed family pets. A great Shumard oak, said to 350 years old, guards the main entrance to Barrett's house. The law practice was started in 1933 by his father, Pat, who still works there. Don Barrett is a graduate of the University of Mississippi Law School, class of '69. He started specializing in toxic waste cases and personal injury law in the seventies and became chairman of the toxic torts section of the Mississippi Trial Lawyers Association.

Like many of his colleagues in the torts business, he kept looking for a chance to take on the tobacco companies. Horton, then fifty years old, had been told by his doctor that he had two years to live. Barrett offered to represent him on a contingency fee.

To Barrett, Horton looked like a good case, perhaps the best opportunity in a while to confront the industry. Mississippi was one of ten states in the union with a tort statute of "pure" comparative fault, which means that a plaintiff can win damages if a jury decides the maker of the product bore even a fraction of the blame for an injury. In almost all the other states, a plaintiff could not recover damages unless the defendants were found to be more than 50 percent responsible. In Mississippi, in theory, a manufacturer who was held just 1 percent responsible for Horton's condition would be liable for a proportionate share of the actual damages awarded.

Horton's suit was unusual in another respect. He claimed that the tobacco company had knowingly sold cigarettes contaminated with pesticides. Barrett had obtained an American Tobacco internal memo from 1976 stating that residues of the bug killer known as DDVP were present in cigarettes, in some cases in amounts more than four times higher than the federal maximum permitted in foods. A second memo a year later reported that American Tobacco was still "exposing unprotected finished cigarettes and little cigars as well as open bulks of tobacco and wrapping materials to DDVP aerosols." The memo also said that the way the company was spraying DDVP was not in compliance with directions from the Environmental Protection Agency. It was not exactly a winning weapon, but Barrett was looking forward to using it in court.

Still another reason for Barrett's confidence was that Lexington is one of the worst places for a large, wealthy corporation to defend a case against an aggrieved individual—especially a tobacco company against a local black smoker. It takes nine of twelve jurors to decide such a case in Mississippi. Holmes County is 75 percent black and an all-black, anti–big business jury was anticipated. Mississippi is also a nontobacco state where the tobacco companies were seen as symbols of big-city corporate culture, white-run businesses manipulating poor blacks from afar. Barrett could also count on some resentment of tobacco company marketing practices. Of late, the tobacco companies had been increasing their advertising targeted to blacks, a group disproportionately affected by smoking-related diseases. Cigarette consumption was falling among whites but it had increased among blacks, with young black females accounting for the fastest growing group of new customers. Black men had a 58 percent higher incidence of lung cancer than white men and blacks lost twice as many years of life, 8.1 compared to 3.8, because of smoking-related disease. Even so, R. J. Reynolds was preparing to market a cigarette targeted at blacks directly. Called "Uptown," it was so roundly condemned by black leaders and doctors that it was eventually scrapped.

After looking at the American Tobacco Company's finances, Barrett decided to demand one of the largest-ever sums for Nathan Horton's illness: $2 million in actual damages and $15 million in exemplary or punitive damages, those intended to make an example of a company's wrongdoing. Adding together Mississippi's favorable law, the sympathy Horton could command from his peers, and the determination of Barrett and his colleagues, observers of tobacco litigation thought Barrett had the best chance yet. The veteran antitobacco campaigner Dick Daynard, of Northeastern University Law School in Boston, commented, "In Holmes County you have people who are not immediately going to assume the beneficence of established American institutions like tobacco companies."

Wall Street was taking the case seriously, too. Tobacco stocks were already heavily discounted—that is, undervalued compared with other blue-chip stocks—because of pending lawsuits. Stock analysts, intent on sending back instant reports, were preparing to descend on the little Lexington courthouse with its one public pay phone. Some analysts were predicting possible drops of 15 percent, which in the case of the biggest company, Philip Morris, meant several billion dollars of lost value.

Even as Barrett prepared the case for trial, Horton's lung cancer was steadily sapping his strength. Once a robust six feet, one inch and 185 pounds, he was now down to 137 pounds. He was bent and weak of voice, preserved by blood transfusions and dependent on powerful pain-killers and other medications. It became clear he would not survive to take part in the trial. Late in January, Morton Mintz of *The Washington Post* interviewed him at home. They talked about his son, who had studied pharmacy at Ole Miss, and about fishing, but also about death. Horton said, "I have some good days, and I have some days when I cry all day. Some nights," he said, he was "scared to go to sleep, because this will be the end of it." Other times, he had "nightmares about cigarettes. I get to dream about them, craving. If it were so that cigarettes did give me cancer, I wish people would know it. I would hate for anyone to be in the position that I'm in right now." He died a few days later. He was buried in a tiny cemetery down the dirt road from his house. The Veterans Administration picked up the bill for the funeral and gave him a military headstone. His wife, Ella, took up the case on his behalf.

The first sign of American Tobacco's extraordinary commitment to its defense in the Horton case came that fall. At the courthouse in Lexington, a team of private investigators arrived, having come all the way from Los Angeles to carry out a thorough examination of the five hundred names on the jury register and make background files on all of them. The staff at the courthouse was aghast. Earline Hart, a young black woman who was the deputy circuit clerk when the L.A. team arrived, particularly remembers a handsome surfer type named Steve. She never knew his surname. "They went through all the court dockets, civil and criminal," she recalled, "including copies of marriage records or any liens against property. When they were finished with our records, they went to the Tax Collector's Office to find out if they were property owners, and then they went to the Justice Court to see if they had any misdemeanors filed against them." The courthouse had never witnessed this kind of pretrial investigation.

The company also hired "consultants": local leaders of the community who could advise the defense lawyers on reactions of the jury members once the trial began. Their job was to sit in the courtroom each day and act as a "shadow jury." Earline Hart called them the "fan club" because they would turn up each day and sit on the tobacco company's side of the court. The courtroom, which holds about 150 people comfortably, had up to 300 spectators each day. Local people stood in line to be sure of getting a seat. About fifteen or twenty were members of the "fan club," and anyone who sat in one of "their" seats was promptly asked to move elsewhere. Dick Daynard, who came down from Boston to observe the trial, put his briefcase on one of the reserved seats, and went to get a drink of water. When he came back, his briefcase had been moved to the other side of the courtroom. He was told that this was where the defendant's trial consultants sat. The effect was to let the jury know they were being watched by community leaders who had control over the welfare and economy of the county. "They always began the day shaking hands with the defense lawyers in full view of the jury," he recalls. "I've been in lots of courtrooms in my life and nobody's ever moved my briefcase from one bench to another." Although the tobacco company never admitted paying them, some of the consultants received $50 an hour, more than many workers in Holmes County made in a week.

American Tobacco hired five Mississippi law firms to help defend the case. The leader of the team was James Upshaw of nearby Greenwood. The company's New York lawyers were also present in force. They rented a wing of the local motel and sectioned it off with security guards. Room service meals were provided by the restaurant next door. The out-of-state lawyers quickly discovered that Holmes County is dry and the only local liquor store in Lexington was the Beveridge Shop. For years, the store's supply of Bombay gin had been gathering dust on the shelves, since the locals preferred whiskey. Soon after the tobacco lawyers hit town, the gin disappeared. There also seemed no end to the company's expense account. In Lexington, the defense team rented a house to serve as office space. The Federal Express delivery man made frequent visits there. On his last trip after the trial, he picked up a load of 1,500 pounds of documents bound for New York, at a cost of $5,000.

Barrett's funds, by contrast, were severely limited and his operation was local. It included Fred Clark, a black lawyer from Greenwood, and Charles McTeer, another black lawyer, from Greenville. Clark had graduated from Ole Miss law school ten years earlier and had worked with

Barrett on toxic waste cases. McTeer had graduated from Rutgers in 1972 and was a well-known civil rights lawyer.

To bolster his case, Barrett had deposed the company's former chairman and CEO, Robert Heimann. During two hours of examination about his twenty-five years with the company, Heimann showed himself to be arrogant and uncaring. Among several arresting observations, Heimann claimed that the idea that smoking was hazardous to health had never occurred to him or to anyone else in the company and he could not recall his board of directors ever discussing the issue. Asked whether it had ever occurred to the company that one day researchers would establish that smoking was hazardous to health, Mr. Heimann simply said, "No." Although he had never studied medicine and was not a statistician, the former chairman claimed that he was more qualified than a medical doctor to pronounce on epidemiological findings. The 1964 Surgeon General's report that was the first to establish a causal link between lung cancer and smoking was based on "spurious statistics" and had been advocated in "a reprehensible propaganda campaign," he said. Asked whether the Surgeon General was more qualified than he to determine if smoking is hazardous to health, Heimann replied, "No." He said, "Most physicians have little or no knowledge of statistical nuances and would be easily taken in and misguided by their improper use."

"So, is it your opinion that you are more qualified than a medical doctor?" he was asked.

"In that area, yes," replied Heimann.

"Did any senior executive [of the company] ever consult with any professional medical association . . . to determine if there were health hazards associated with smoking?"

"Not that I know of," answered Heimann.

Nearly a year after Horton's death, the trial began on January 5, 1988. Barrett put up a brave front. "It won't be long," he said of the tobacco industry, "before the house of cards comes tumbling down . . . or we slink back into our little holes, never to be heard from again." In his opening remarks, Barrett told the jury of the toxic cocktail of substances in cigarette smoke—from radioactive polonium-210 to high-phosphate fertilizers, residues of pesticides, and even microscopic particles "similar to asbestos." How could Nathan Horton possibly have known all this? he asked. And, therefore, how could he be said to have accepted all the risks? Defusing the personal responsibility factor, Barrett admitted Horton had to some extent been negligent in smoking Pall Mall cigarettes. But so had the company for selling them. "We accept our responsibility. The American Tobacco Company refuses to accept theirs, and that's what this lawsuit is all about." The company's defense ran to the usual argument. Horton was a strong-willed man totally in control of his life. If he chose to smoke and continued despite the 1966 warnings on the cigarette packs, advice from his family, his friends, and even his high school football coach—whom the company had tracked down—then that was his decision.

For almost a month the arguments went back and forth. All the while, the "fan club" dutifully turned up and made their observations for the defense lawyers: the jury was clearly confused by some of the medical evidence, and the word around town was that some of them thought that Barrett had asked far too much in damages. It was an amount of money only dreamed of in Lexington. In its closing speeches, the company charged that the medical experts who testified for Horton were suspect because they were zealots on a crusade against the company and that the plaintiffs' lawyers were out to make big bucks from the industry and out of the controversy over smoking and health. Barrett retorted that he was "proud to be on a crusade to clean up the tobacco industry."

The jury retired on January 28 with a key instruction from the judge that the company could not be held responsible in comparative fault unless the jury agreed it had been selling cigarettes it knew to contain harmful contaminants. As to the $15 million punitive award, the judge told the members of the jury—eleven blacks and one white— that they would have to find that the company had a reckless disregard for the public health in failing to test their cigarettes properly if they wanted to award punitive damages.

On the first day of deliberations, the jury deadlocked, eight in favor of the plaintiff and four for the company. Agreement seemed a long way off, and they were sequestered for the night in a motel in Greenwood, fifteen miles away. By the afternoon of the next day, the jurors were split seven to five in favor of the company and told the judge they couldn't agree. The judge declared a mistrial. The company declared victory, and the plaintiffs cried foul.

Barrett tried to open a judicial inquiry into whether the company's consultants had tampered with the jury. The judge's finding was that one of the consultants had made an improper call to two of the jurors but there was no criminal wrongdoing. The judge also blocked Barrett's efforts to subpoena all the consultants to determine exactly why they had been hired and how much they had been paid. Such a process, the judge ruled, could have a "chilling effect" on their future efforts to take on consultant work—a job that was perfectly legitimate. The two sides dispersed—American Tobacco with a legal bill estimated to be around $10 million and the Barrett Law Offices with a debt of $260,000 in out-of-pocket expenses and $2 million in billable time. Don Barrett had taken out a second mortgage on his house to cover the costs, but he vowed to fight on. "We came so close," he said, "once you slap the bully in the bar . . . you're in for the whole fight." But he could not have imagined where that fight would eventually lead him. The retrial was moved to Oxford, the site of Ole Miss, his alma mater, because the judge ruled there had been so much publicity and so much public sniping between the two sides that a new Lexington jury would be prejudiced. After hearing eleven days of evidence in the Oxford trial, the jury decided that cigarette smoking had caused Nathan Horton's lung cancer but refused to award damages, saying both the company and Horton were at fault. Each side put its own spin on the verdict. Barrett claimed victory because the jury had found Pall Malls were dangerous and Horton had not been fully aware of the risks. A lawyer for the tobacco companies said that when a jury awards no damages the tort isn't complete, and he claimed victory, too.

DON BARRETT HAD NEVER SMOKED but during the Horton trial he developed what he called his "cigarette habit"; he became addicted to suing the tobacco companies. He was bitter about the $2 million he had lost on the trial and wanted revenge. But he also wanted justice. If you live in Lexington, Mississippi, you have a worm's-eye view of the capitalist state whatever your politics. Barrett is a mixture of Southern populist, traditional Republican, and devout Methodist. He had seen who was smoking cigarettes and who was being harmed by them, mostly poor working people. He believed the tobacco companies should be forced to be more socially responsible. Beating them up in court was one way to make them do their public duty.

The strength of his commitment to tobacco litigation was as sturdy as his roots in Lexington. One summer's day in 1996, Barrett and I were driving out of town to visit Ella Horton. When the kudzu vines are at their peak in high summer, the landscape is stifling and you long for the open plain of the Delta, and the cotton fields. I asked Barrett why someone such as himself, who was relatively wealthy, despite his loss to American Tobacco, would stay in tiny Lexington. He replied that he had never had any plans to leave. As Faulkner had said of his treasured native state, "You don't love because; you love despite." But there was something else. Barrett said he had come to believe that he was doing God's work. He thanked the Lord that he had been given this opportunity to fight the wrongdoings of the tobacco companies; he was a crusader, just as the tobacco company lawyers had painted him in the Horton trial. He didn't want to put the tobacco companies out of business; he wanted to hurt them—as they had hurt Nathan Horton, and as they had hurt him.

The image he portrayed was oddly out of place with the picture of the unscrupulous courtroom brawler that most often comes to mind when thinking of personal-injury trial lawyers. A similar religious fervor could be found in two other Mississippi lawyers who would join Barrett in his campaign against Big Tobacco and eventually become the prime movers in bringing the tobacco industry chiefs to the negotiating table in the spring of 1997.

One was Mike Moore, Mississippi's attorney general, whose youthful good looks and instant charm belie the rough and tumble politics of his office. The other was Dick Scruggs, a courtly, bespectacled country lawyer with a ready smile, who had been a navy pilot, otherwise living most of his fifty years in the port town of Pascagoula, on Mississippi's Gulf coast. Scruggs and Moore had grown up in Pascagoula, but six years apart. Scruggs, whose parents were divorced and whose mother was a secretary at the Ingalls Shipbuilding Company, learned early the meaning of money; the shipyards were booming in the '60s making vessels for the navy, and the owners were very rich. As a teenager, Scruggs would spend many days hanging out at one of their grand antebellum houses on the beachfront, which had been converted into a club for families of shipyard employees. When he later made his own fortune through asbestos lawsuits, Scruggs would buy two of those houses. He had wanted to turn one into a reception hall for the town, but the neighbors opposed the idea. "Some of them are concerned the bubbas will be down there peeing in the flower beds," Scruggs would tell *American Lawyer* in his first big media interview in the spring of 1996.

Mike Moore grew up in a strong Catholic family in a comfortable middle-class neighborhood. One small setback he mentions in an otherwise easy childhood was that it took him longer than most to grow to his full height of five feet, eleven inches. He was only five feet, three inches when he graduated from high school, with the result that he was pushed around by his peers more than he would have liked. The suggestion is that this in part accounts for his congeniality and his reluctance to say no to people; and that it also left him with an uncontrollable ambition to succeed and an irrepressible desire to look after the "little guy." Certainly, he has been a great cheerleader for his small state. When he talked about "li'l ole Mississippa takin' on Big Tobacca," it was said with deep feeling—from a Southerner who was determined to make his mark on the Northern Establishment and, if possible, on the rest of the world.

In 1974, Scruggs and Moore met at the law school of Ole Miss. Moore was a keyboard player in a rock band and a Little League coach. Scruggs, six years older and straight off the flight deck, was more mature. He never had much time for nonacademic pursuits. He continued to fly in the navy reserve to help pay his tuition. Of Moore in those days, he says, "We were friends, but not close." After law school they went their separate ways, Scruggs to a law office in Jackson, the state capital; Moore home to Pascagoula. Still only twenty-seven, Moore became a district attorney, stirring up the local community during his first year in office by pressing charges and winning corruption convictions against four of the five county supervisors. As he moved up to Jackson to seek wider political office, Scruggs returned to Pascagoula to set up his own business. They met infrequently.

By chance in the late seventies, Scruggs encountered Don Barrett, on opposite sides of the Lexington courthouse. Barrett was a plaintiff's lawyer seeking damages for a domestic electrical fire and Scruggs was representing the power company. Barrett won the case but they became friends and later, when Barrett took up Nathan Horton's smoking case, Scruggs encouraged him.

In 1984, Scruggs started handling asbestos cases. The Johns-Manville Corporation had already filed for bankruptcy, leaving 16,500 asbestos lawsuits pending and an estimated 130,000 claims yet to be litigated. For a decade, the plaintiffs' lawyers had been winning or settling virtually every asbestos case they filed. Pascagoula shipyard workers came knocking on Scruggs's door. They all had lung diseases of various types caused by asbestos. Scruggs had read up on pulmonary medicine and put up his own money, a few thousand dollars, for the men to have medical exams, an initial expense other local lawyers involved in asbestos cases had balked at. Scruggs started winning cases. The result: Scruggs got the most clients, about 4,000 of them in all.

With some deft footwork he also managed to try his cases more quickly than others. The asbestos companies had succeeded in transferring most of the local cases from state to federal court, where they would have to wait in a long line to be heard. But Scruggs seized on a Mississippi Supreme Court ruling on strict product liability that for the first time gave plaintiffs the chance to include local distributors in personal-injury claims. The big asbestos companies had headquarters elsewhere, but by naming a local distributor as a defendant, Scruggs was able to get his cases returned to the state court, a much quicker route to trial. Scruggs was lucky to have a local populist judge, Darwin Maples, in charge of his local court. Maples wanted to get the cases in and out of his court as fast as possible.

As it turned out, Scruggs was also a master at cutting deals. While his colleagues looked on and scoffed, Scruggs slipped through settlements for much lower awards—but clinched the deals before the companies declared bankruptcy. Scruggs also consolidated thousands of claims into a single trial—a type of class action that had been pursued before by two other trial lawyers prominent in asbestos litigation, Ron Motley of Charleston, South Carolina, and Walter Umphrey, of Beaumont, Texas (now both on Wendell Gauthier's class-action committee).

In Pascagoula, Scruggs left his colleagues standing on the courthouse steps, pockets empty. His average client received between $50,000 and $60,000 and Scruggs took his 25 percent.

Moore, meanwhile, was running hard for attorney general. He was elected in 1987 with a class of yuppies who had taken over state government. Energetic, bright, and charming, Moore was soon being spoken of as a future governor of the state, something he did not discourage. He would win reelection in 1991 with 75 percent of the vote. Scruggs was a major contributor to his campaigns.

One of Moore's first tasks as attorney general was to add the state of Mississippi to the nationwide lawsuits against the asbestos companies to recover the cost of removing asbestos from public buildings. The attorney general's office had no staff to do the litigation, so Moore hired Scruggs to represent the state. In five years, Mississippi recovered $20 million and Scruggs received his 25 percent fee.

From his modest beginnings, Scruggs had already become a Southern gentlemen of considerable means. "I happened to be in the right place at the right time," he acknowledges modestly. By the '90s, Scruggs had two yachts, a holiday home in Key West, and his own Learjet. But to meet him you wouldn't know that his take-home pay is over a million dollars a year. Unlike some of his more colorful brethren in the plaintiffs' bar, Scruggs works out of cramped, spartan headquarters in a bleak shopping mall in the middle of Pascagoula. He drives a dark-green, two-seater Mercedes convertible, but it's parked outside the back door because there's no room at the front. In place of the usual English barrister or hunting prints on his law office walls, there are pictures of sailing boats and of Scruggs piloting his navy jets. He is almost apologetic about his boats and jet plane, although he clearly enjoys both.

SCRUGGS HAD now become an elite member of the plaintiffs' bar. While many of its members promote themselves as private attorneys general righting civil wrongs, stepping in to help the common man through the court system when government either can't or won't be of assistance, actually they participate in a litigation lotto. How much they are motivated by money and how much by social conscience or even guilt is a question hard to answer. But in the spring of 1994, the fact is that as a group these self-made men and women had never been so well placed to conduct a crusade. In New Orleans, Gauthier would say of his class action, "I know the outside world thinks we're greedy hogs. As I see it, this is our chance to do some good for society and give something back." Scruggs felt it was time to "reinvest" his capital. "If we don't use a substantial part of that money to reinvest in our clients and reinvest in the people that we represent, then the criticisms of us are justified. . . . We had a war chest and it was our duty to reinvest it." To Scruggs, it was a straightforward equation; spend some of your money in a good cause or keep your money and be despised for how easily you made it. This did not mean a rush to "invest" without prospects of a return, but none of them, especially the trio that emerged in Mississippi—Scruggs, Barrett, and Moore—imagined how much would eventually be on the table.

Like the other liability lawyers, Scruggs had occasionally thought of suing the tobacco companies. He had discussed the possibility with Ron Motley after a collaboration on an asbestos settlement. "We were bored with asbestos," Motley recalled. But, like the others, Scruggs had been put off by Big Tobacco's unbeaten record—and by his own experience.

In the summer of 1993, Scruggs went to Greenville, a tugboat town on the Mississippi, to lend a hand to Don Barrett and his "tobacco habit." In the second Horton trial, the jury had found that smoking caused Nathan's lung cancer death but, believing that both the American Tobacco Company and Horton were at fault, had awarded no damages. The company had been successful in portraying Horton as "an unattractive person for Bible Belt jurors," as Barrett put it, introducing evidence of his gambling and drinking. Now Barrett had another lung cancer case and it looked more promising.

Anderson Smith had died of lung cancer and emphysema in 1986 after smoking heavily for forty-five years. His daughter Jeannette Wilks sued the American Tobacco Company, Barrett's old enemy. This time he thought he had them. Smith was mentally retarded; he had the mental age of a six-year-old and Barrett had forty years of psychological reports saying that he did not have the ability to make an informed decision about anything. "That is how we were going to get around the 'smokers deserve what they get defense,'" Barrett recalled. But the trial didn't quite work the way Barrett had hoped.

In a pretrial motion Barrett also asked Judge Eugene Bogen, of the Washington County Circuit Court in Greenville, to rule on whether cigarettes are "defective and unreasonably dangerous for human consumption . . . because they cause cancer, emphysema, heart disease and other illnesses" when used as the manufacturer intended. To everyone's surprise, Judge Bogen ruled that they were and he imposed absolute liability on the company if it could be shown that cigarettes caused Smith's death. He ruled that the tobacco company could not use the assumption of risk or comparative fault defenses that had so bolstered their cases in the past. But the company turned around and said, in that case, it was then irrelevant that Smith was a mental defective. None of that evidence was ever given to the jury. In the end, the jurors said they had been convinced by the tobacco company that Smith had several other ailments that could have contributed to his death, and dismissed the case. Barrett found out later by interviewing the jurors that, in fact, they thought that there was strong evidence that lung cancer had caused his death, but they recalled the old argument, that no one had made him smoke, and it made them lean in the company's favor. "They never knew that he was mentally defective and was unable to make such a decision for himself," said Barrett. "We outsmarted ourselves. Not the first time," he chuckled.

Despite the loss, Barrett vowed to continue his quest, and Scruggs was now also interested in finding the right tobacco case. In pursuing the asbestos companies, Scruggs had learned about lungs and the effects of tobacco smoke. Many of the victims of asbestosis also smoked, and the two agents work synergistically. A person exposed to asbestos dust increases the risk of contracting lung cancer by about five times, but if that person also smokes, the risk is fifty times greater. The asbestos lawyers had seen two types of the diseases. If the victim didn't smoke, the asbestosis was usually "restrictive"—that is, it attacked the functioning lung tissue and immobilized it, causing slow suffocation. In the case of a client who was exposed to asbestos and tobacco smoke, however, there was usually "obstructive" lung disease; the airways were blocked by tumors. The tobacco companies were never joined as defendants in the asbestosis cases, however, because the asbestos companies feared that tobacco's legal armies would turn against them in court to escape blame. Instead, the asbestos companies came up with the so-called empty chair defense, mentioning the part played by cigarette smoke without actually calling in the tobacco companies. For Scruggs, tobacco had always been a side issue since the asbestos injuries were easily proved without the additional evidence. Whenever he thought about suing the tobacco companies, Scruggs came to the conclusion that there was no point in using old theories about smoking causing cancer; the industry's highly successful arguments of no scientific "proof" and of personal choice and assumption of risk would always win. A new theory was needed. "It was like choosing the right weapon in war," said Scruggs. "If you use the wrong weapon against a tank you're not going to blow it up."

Scruggs, Barrett, and Moore were to make a formidable legal team. Over the next year, they would push Mississippi into the forefront of the battle against the tobacco industry. Thanks to them, Mississippi became the first state in the union to sue the tobacco companies using an entirely new cause of action: recovery of monies the state had spent looking after the victims of smoking-related diseases. It was an entirely new challenge to the industry and would eventually become a more effective weapon than that of Gauthier's group in New Orleans.

THERE ARE SEVERAL VERSIONS of who first came up with the idea of suing for reimbursement of Medicaid expenses, but they rarely give credit to a 1977 article by Donald Garner, a liberal law professor at the University of Southern Illinois. Long convinced that the tobacco companies should be made to pay for the public health havoc they wreak, Professor Garner was always on the lookout for new legal theories to bring the industry into court. In an article entitled "Cigarettes and Welfare Reform" published in the spring 1977 issue of the *Emory Law Journal,* he noted increasing economic waste caused by cigarette smoking, especially when it came to health costs.

Back in 1969, in testimony before the House of Representatives on proposed legislation to require a stronger warning on cigarette packages and to prohibit television advertising, Arthur Ross, then chairman of the Franklin National Bank, estimated that various identifiable costs related to smoking, including fire insurance, life insurance, and costs of forest fires, came to about $12 billion. "Fairness dictates that we must not allow cigarette smokers to impose a heavy financial inequity on nonsmokers," he said.

The cost of public health care was going up. In 1928–29, the public paid 13.3 percent of the $3.6 billion health bill. By 1959–60, it was 24.7 percent of $25.9 billion; by 1972–73, it was 39.9 percent of $94 billion. Medicare, the all-federal program for the elderly, was the largest government health-care program; for Medicaid, the program for the poor, the states and Washington share the costs. Together Medicare and Medicaid paid 54 percent of the 1973 public medical-care bill. Noteworthy as well was that the number of deaths from cigarette smoking was rising, as was the cost of attending to smoking victims. (Later, one study from the Center on Addiction and Substance Abuse run by Joe Califano, former Secretary of Health, Education, and Welfare under Jimmy Carter, estimated that tobacco-caused illness accounted for $1.7 billion in 1991.)

In his 1977 article, Professor Garner suggested that the states get the appropriate cigarette manufacturer to pay the direct medical cost "of looking after patients with smoking diseases." He did not claim to fully understand how this cause of action would work in the courts and he acknowledged that there might be a problem proving that the illnesses were caused by smoking. But that issue could be overcome, he suggested, by using a method similar to that used to assess the eligibility of coal miners for black-lung disease benefits. Under the Coal Mine Health and Safety Act of 1969, when a coal miner develops the lung disease known as pneumoconiosis, the mine operator is required to pay certain disability benefits. Proof that the individual coal miner's pneumoconiosis was caused by working in a coal mine is accomplished by employing a legal tool called "rebuttal presumption": after ten years in the mines, the miner's black lung, or his death from a respiratory disease, is presumed to be caused by his employment and the burden of proof shifts to the operator to rebut the presumption.

IN THE SPRING of 1993, the Mississippi Medicaid case was born. One of Mike Moore's Ole Miss classmates, a lawyer named Mike Lewis, who ran a small-town practice with his wife, Pauline, in Clarksdale, Mississippi, called Moore to tell him how angry he was about the death of his bookkeeper's mother. After a lifetime of smoking and a long struggle with lung cancer, the woman had died, having exhausted her personal assets and, in her last days, had her care paid for with state Medicaid funds. The cost of her illness eventually exceeded one million dollars. Lewis was vengeful. He told Moore, "I'm on a crusade. I want to go after these bastards. I want to sue the tobacco industry to recoup that money."

Lewis's idea was that he should personally sue the tobacco companies on behalf of the state. Such an action was unusual, but it could be done through federal law using the provision in the federal False Claims Act that allows a private citizen to bring a suit in the name of the government if he or she considers the government has been wronged and has not moved to protect itself. The provision was basically designed to stop fraud on government contracts, when a private citizen might have inside information and be in a better position to sue than the government itself. (Sometimes, if the case gets too big for the private citizen to handle, the Justice Department will either provide legal aid or take over the case entirely.) Scruggs had once thought of using the False Claims Act himself in preparing a suit against the tobacco companies and he had mentioned his tentative plan to Moore. So when Lewis came up with a similar idea, Moore put him and Scruggs together. As Scruggs would later say, "The idea blossomed into a very elegant legal concept."

In Mississippi, half a million people—out of a total population of two and a half million—rely on Medicaid. Not all of them have tobacco-related illnesses, of course, but Moore estimated that the state spends between $70 and $100 million dollars a year as its share of the Medicaid funds expended on smokers. In addition, about $8 million of the state's health insurance plan goes toward tobacco-related diseases. Once Scruggs and Lewis had realized how much the state was spending, they started putting together some legal theories they could use to recover these funds.

The traditional legal theories for an injured person did not apply because the state was, in effect, a third party paying the bill for the injured party. The state doesn't smoke. People do. Two legal doctrines could be used. One was the doctrine of "subrogation," which gives someone other than the victim the task of recovering damages. For example, if someone runs a red light and hits your car, your insurance will pay for the repair of the car and pay your medical expenses. The insurance company then engages in subrogation. It will sue the other driver on your behalf and try to recover the money.

The second possible route used theories of recovery based on equity—such as the doctrine of restitution, or "unjust enrichment." The first maxim of equity is that no one "will suffer a wrong without a remedy." In the case of a state obligated as a matter of law to pay medical bills of the poor, the state can recoup costs from the person who caused the injury.

Throughout the summer of 1993, Scruggs, Lewis, Moore, and Barrett talked over the theories with several law professors, among them David Owens at the University of South Carolina and, later, Laurence Tribe at Harvard Law School. And they spent a weekend at the seaside home of Ron Motley, in Charleston, South Carolina.

They quickly ruled out the theory of subrogation—or being a "surrogate"—for the tens of thousands of individual smokers whose health bills the state had to pay. It was not feasible for the state to file thousands of suits to recover monies for individual smoking victims, nor was it feasible to recover medical costs for each health-care recipient. It would be an overwhelming task beyond the capacity of the state, or the judiciary.

Instead, Moore chose equitable theories of recovery. The claims were not in tort. The premise was that unlike the smoker who supposedly had a "choice" to smoke, the state had no choice in providing health care to its citizens. In legal parlance Mississippi's claims would be based on restitution, or unjust enrichment, indemnity, common law public nuisance, and injunctive relief to protect the interests of minors. Mississippi claimed the tobacco companies had been "unjustly enriched" because the state paid bills that were the consequence of them selling cigarettes to Mississippi citizens. The industry, the state claimed, should have paid the bills "of the economic by-products of its enterprise."

The concept of "indemnity" called for shifting the loss incurred by the state onto the companies, again because the state was an innocent third party and had no choice but to pay the medical bills. Under "public nuisance," courts have allowed governments to take action to recover expenditures on such things as cleaning up water pollution and fighting fires. Moore would argue that the state acted to abate a public nuisance created by the tobacco industry by providing health care to keep Mississippians from getting sicker, or dying sooner, from smoking-related illnesses.

Moore also wanted to stop the industry from targeting children with advertising and promotions, such as T-shirts and other trinkets. As Scruggs put it, "A major reason for the equity court's existence is the protection of children; they can provide such relief."

By confining Mississippi's suit to these claims, Moore aimed to have the case heard before a single judge in the state's Chancery Court. After Barrett's experience with the Horton trial, he thought they stood a better chance with a judge than a jury. Also, a recent study had challenged the widely held assumption that juries were more sympathetic than judges in cases involving personal injury. In one of the biggest tort areas—defective products—plaintiffs who opted for a jury trial won only 28 percent of their cases, whereas those who went before a judge won 48 percent.

The tobacco companies would object and try to move the case to federal court and a jury trial. There would be big battles over discovery and prolonged wrangles over depositions, but Moore and his team were ready. Initial estimates suggested the case would cost about $5 million to bring to court, and Moore deputized Scruggs, as he had done in the asbestos cases. Together they assembled a team that purposely included both Republican and Democratic law firms; Moore was a Democrat and Scruggs a Republican and the two men did not want this to be a partisan attack. Scruggs, Barrett, and the other firms also took the case without a contingency fee contract with the state. This was to fend off attacks from the state legislators that the plaintiffs' firms were getting too much money. If they won, the plan was that Moore would apply to the court for attorney's fees—but they were to be paid by the defendants, not by the state.

AT THE BEGINNING of 1994, Moore was starting to prepare his charges against a dozen of the major tobacco companies and a handful of associated organizations (such as the industry's public relations concerns) when the attention of all plaintiffs' lawyers was suddenly focused on a surprise announcement from the Food and Drug Administration in Washington.

On February 25, FDA Commissioner David Kessler charged there was "mounting evidence" that the tobacco companies controled the levels of nicotine in cigarettes in order to satisfy the smoker's addiction. This was an astonishing departure from previous FDA policy toward the tobacco industry. For decades, the nation's regulator of consumer products had never pressed to oversee the production of cigarettes, taking the position that tobacco was neither a food, nor a drug. The antitobacco forces had been vainly pushing the FDA for decades to impose stricter controls on tobacco and, since 1988, a petition had been sitting on the commissioner's desk from the Coalition on Smoking or Health, which included the American Cancer Society and the American Heart Association and American Lung Association, asking the FDA to regulate cigarettes as a drug.

Now, in a letter to the Coalition's chairman, Scott Ballin, Kessler said evidence suggested that the manufacturers intended their products to contain enough nicotine to satisfy "an addiction," and therefore should be regulated as a drug. "In fact, it is our understanding that manufacturers commonly add nicotine to cigarettes to deliver specific amounts of nicotine." If the agency were able to prove these facts in court, Kessler went on, "it would have the legal basis on which to regulate these products."

Kessler gave no reason for the sudden change in FDA policy, but it was partly an outgrowth of a secret investigation made by the agency and partly the result of an inquiry by the staff of an ABC muckraking news program called *Day One*. Two years earlier, Kessler had directed his staff to take the agency's first serious look at tobacco, and by coincidence ABC's inquiry had been in parallel. Kessler scooped the TV network by three days.

On the night of February 28, ABC aired the *Day One* program. This program had been fifteen months in the making. It originated from a conversation between Clifford Douglas, a lawyer and antitobacco activist, and Walt Bogdanich, an ABC television producer who had won a Pulitzer prize while on *The Wall Street Journal*. Bogdanich was intrigued by the idea that cigarette companies could artificially control the level of nicotine in cigarettes, not simply by blending different varieties of tobacco, but also, possibly, by adding nicotine from other sources. In the program, there was no equivocation about "mounting evidence," no legalese such as "our understanding is . . . " The report directly accused the tobacco industry of "artificially spiking" cigarettes with nicotine to keep smokers hooked. Under the alluring title, "Smokescreen," ABC charged that the tobacco companies used a secret process that included adding a "nicotine rich" tobacco extract from outside suppliers. The revelations, the program declared immodestly, "could change the tobacco industry forever."

The industry immediately denied the allegations, saying it never added any nicotine that wasn't in the original leaf. Philip Morris, the largest of the U.S. companies, went on to sue ABC for $10 billion, the biggest libel claim on record. Their complaint focused on the word "spike." ABC would eventually settle the case and apologize for mistakenly reporting that companies "add significant amounts of nicotine from outside sources." The case would end up costing the TV company $15 million in the out-of-court settlement, but the publicity given to the case added to the changing public perception of what exactly does go into a cigarette, and it raised the question of whether the companies could control nicotine levels to keep smokers hooked. The program would also push Wendell Gauthier into action in New Orleans and trigger the world's largest class-action suit. Don Barrett would get a call from Gauthier, whom he had never met, asking if he would like to join the Castano group. For a while, the Mississippi suit was to be overshadowed.

2

A DEATH

IN THE FAMILY

Cry "Havoc!" and let slip the dogs of war.

—*Shakespeare*, Julius Caesar

THE METAIRIE CEMETERY is a splendid New Orleans landmark. Built six years after the Civil War on the former site of a race track, it has four thousand vaults and tombs, all above ground to protect them from the times when the flooding Mississippi rolls over its levees. Greek Revival marble crypts stand among lavish and ornate temples. Rotundas compete with soaring Egyptian obelisks. Metairie is the most elaborate burial ground in a city renowned for overdoing every aspect of life—and death.

Josie Arlington, who ran a brothel on Basin Street, was buried in a grand mausoleum of her own design made of pink granite imported all the way from distant Maine. Today, not even madams from the French Quarter can afford such elaborate memorials. The city's recently dead rest mostly beneath bronze plaques like the ones in Plot No. 149. There, fixed in the coarse Southern grass beside a man-made lagoon, a plaque and a small metal vase of dried flowers mark the final resting place of Peter Castano, a local lawyer who died in 1993 at the age of forty-seven. Castano's death certificate says he died from lung cancer due to smoking. He was a heavy smoker who started in his teens and even though constantly counseled by doctors and friends to give up the habit, he simply could not do it. His wife, Dianne, had agreed to marry him on condition that he stop smoking and, though he promised that he would and even swore on the Bible several times that he had done so, the truth, which was common knowledge to his wife and to his friends, was that he never gave it up. The best he could do for Dianne was not to smoke in front of her. She knew, of course. The evidence was the acrid smell of nicotine on his clothes. But Dianne was so fond of him that as the years went by she reprimanded him less and less. They had two children and lived in the pleasant middle-class section of Old Metairie at the back of the cemetery, on a street lined with oak trees laden with Spanish moss. He was a good provider who made a reasonable living from his criminal-law practice, but he had never expected to make legal history.

In the normal course of events, Castano's untimely death would have been the tragic story of a smoker who had died prematurely from his daily pleasure. He would have become a mere government statistic, one of 425,000 smoking-related deaths recorded annually by public health officials at the Centers for Disease Control in Atlanta and at the National Center for Health Statistics in Maryland.

Like many tobacco widows, his wife, Dianne, was angry and wanted to sue the tobacco companies, even though she had been warned against such action by Peter's lawyer friends. The tobacco companies, they told her, were too rich and powerful and had never lost a lawsuit. They were well known for bullying their opponents into submission with endless pretrial motions, armies of highly paid lawyers, and limitless funds. Don't sue, they advised. You can't win. For Castano's widow it would be different.

Castano's closest companion since law school at Loyola had been Wendell Gauthier. A venturer, Gauthier had shunned the orthodox legal career of his friend in favor of the riskier plaintiffs' bar, with its potential for rapid fame and riches. For several years Gauthier had represented the victims of man-made disasters—hotel fires, airplane crashes, railroad accidents—and by the time of his friend's death, he had amassed a small fortune.

The son of a Cajun construction foreman, Gauthier grew up in Iota, which is literally a dot on the map of the rice-growing region of southern Louisiana. His father served as a city councilman and his mother was a schoolteacher, but Gauthier was the first member of his family to attend college. To do so, he had to find his own funds. He sold cow manure and scrap iron and then taught high school and gave private driving lessons. Embarked on a law career, Gauthier used a formidable combination of diplomacy, cunning, and showmanship to become one of the leading members of the plaintiffs' bar. His first break, a $1 million verdict against Louisiana Gas, came from representing a family whose home exploded due to faulty gas lines. Six more exploding homes gave Gauthier six more cases and eventually put him on a panel of experts to study the problem. They solved it. "They also put me out of the gas pipe business, but I was glad to be a part of the panel," said Gauthier.

He went through what he called his "ego trip" of owning a Rolls-Royce and a Jaguar and developed a liking for sharply tailored double-breasted suits. Unlike his flashier colleagues, however, he had no yacht, no private plane, no vacation home in Florida. Instead, he lived in a large but modestly decorated house in Old Metairie, just around the corner from his friend Castano. And rather than have an office like other successful New Orleans lawyers in one of the skyscrapers erected by the oil companies downtown, Gauthier ran his law practice from a utilitarian two-story building in Metairie's sprawling business district. His one indulgence was a small back room attached to his main office where he would play cards with friends on Saturday afternoons.

His business was mostly local, or mostly Louisiana. He became a confidant of the state's governor, Edwin Edwards, part owner of the New Orleans Saints football team, and the head of a group of investors building a casino on the banks of the Mississippi. Although friendly and full of mischief, Gauthier was always working on a new case and rarely seen in public except when negotiating his Rolls-Royce around the narrow streets of the French Quarter where his wife, Anne, had an antique shop. Close friends shortened his surname and called him "the Goat."

In court, Gauthier was known for unconventional tactics that would keep opponents off balance. He loved to play practical jokes, like the baked Alaska he sent to the tobacco lawyers. One day, after the Castano case was launched, an ABC News television crew came to interview him. He was late. The crew was waiting with John "Bhopal" Coale, who was acting as the Castano suit's publicity director. Gauthier called from an outside pay phone pretending to be the sheriff. He told the crew there'd been a bank robbery and the robber had entered the office building. "Stay on the floor by a window, and put something over your face. We may have to use gas," Gauthier told the crew. They believed him—until he called back to say the robber was on his way to their floor and Coale recognized his voice. "He had us all on the floor with jackets over our faces," said Coale.

"You tend to discount him as just a clown, it throws you off your game," said one past opponent. Another said, "What it takes to win within the system, he will do. Whether you call that fair, or unfair, I won't characterize." Among Gauthier's booty could be counted millions of dollars litigated from a fatal explosion at a grain elevator, an airplane crash, the 1980 MGM Grand Hotel fire that killed eighty-five people in Las Vegas (settled for $208 million), and the Dupont Plaza fire in San Juan, Puerto Rico ($230 million). In a class action involving 200,000 women who had received breast implants, Gauthier was among seventeen liability lawyers who would be awarded a settlement of $4.2 billion, the largest single civil damages award in history.

Gauthier had never smoked and had been impressed as a youth by the work of Dr. Alton Ochsner, the New Orleans surgeon who was an early proponent of the idea that smoking was linked to lung cancer. Gauthier had pleaded with his own children not to take up the habit. That was one case he lost. He had often been tempted, in the years before Castano's death, to enter the minefield of tobacco litigation, but rich and adventurous as he was, the odds of a courtroom victory against the tobacco industry were too great, even for him.

When Dianne Castano asked him after the funeral to file a claim on her husband's behalf, he refused. In any event, Gauthier feared that Castano's smoking history would not stand up to the tobacco industry's standard defense that smokers choose to smoke, even though they know it could kill them. Intelligent people like Castano know the risks. Since 1966, when the government warning labels went on cigarette packs, juries had bought the "personal choice" argument. Frustrating though it was for Gauthier to lose his best friend, he thought it was just a waste of his time and money to pursue a claim. But he assured Dianne Castano that he would keep looking for a way. Almost a year would go by before Gauthier found it.

The night ABC aired the *Day One* program on "spiking" cigarettes with nicotine, Gauthier was at home in Metairie. From what little he knew of the tobacco plant and the manufacturing process, Gauthier was struck by the tobacco companies' response. They said they never added nicotine that wasn't in the leaf, but that still left open the possibility that they manipulated the levels of nicotine by varying the kinds of leaves in the tobacco "blend" to keep a smoker hooked. For years, the companies had openly blended cigarettes, and different brands had different levels of nicotine that were advertised on the pack in milligrams, alongside the level of so-called tar. The companies had long had the expertise to extract nicotine from tobacco; they could put it back in, or keep it out, whenever they chose. In its report, ABC had interviewed an industry official whose identity was not revealed and who appeared only in silhouette but who had said, "They put nicotine in the form of tobacco extract into a product to keep the consumer happy." The official was said to have worked as a manager for R. J. Reynolds, the second-largest tobacco company and the maker of Camel cigarettes.

Gauthier saw a new way to sue the tobacco companies. Kessler's letter and the ABC program were an invitation to file a lawsuit based on nicotine addiction. If only part of what the program had alleged was true—that companies manipulate the nicotine content of cigarettes to keep smokers hooked—then how could the tobacco companies claim smokers choose to smoke? At least some, if not all, are addicted to nicotine. In Gauthier's experience, Peter Castano was one of them.

Over the next few days, Gauthier ran and reran the thirteen-minute ABC tape in his office. The more he saw, the more he was tempted. But if he brought a liability suit based on addiction, he would have to prove something that the tobacco companies had always denied, namely that nicotine was an addictive substance. And he would have to prove that they knew it. The question was, How much of their private research on nicotine had the tobacco companies managed to conceal over the years? One of the most recent of the tobacco cases suggested the companies still had a lot of dirty secrets to tell.

AT THE END of the 1980s, the tobacco companies came as close as they had ever been to losing a lawsuit. A New Jersey woman named Rose

Cipollone, who had had begun smoking at sixteen during the Depression, had developed a three-centimeter lesion at the rear of the upper lobe of her right lung by 1981. Operations and chemotherapy followed, but nothing could stop the onward march of cancer cells, which eventually invaded her liver and then her brain. In 1983, she sued the tobacco companies, seeking unspecified damages from three of them, Philip Morris, Lorillard, and Liggett & Myers, all makers of the brands she had smoked: Virginia Slims, True, and Chesterfield.

Her complaint was that all three companies had failed to warn her properly of the health risks of smoking. The companies' defense was, as usual, based on the idea that Rose, who was a regular reader of the newspapers and a viewer of television, would have known about the dangers of smoking for decades—at least since the 1950s. If smoking had caused her cancer, which the companies did not accept, then it was her fault for smoking. She died in 1984 before the case came to trial, but her husband, Antonio, carried on the suit.

Rose's lawyer, Marc Edell, had defended asbestos companies in their fight with plaintiffs' lawyers in the 1970s and 1980s. Now he saw an opportunity to make a name for himself as the one who ended the tobacco companies' winning streak. For almost a decade, he fought the companies on Rose's behalf. He went further than any lawyer before him in forcing the companies to delve into their archives to produce internal memos and research papers on smoking and health. In all, Edell made the tobacco industry spend an estimated $50 million in legal fees.

But in the end, he, too, was beaten. The jury agreed that Rose's cancer had been caused by smoking and that one company, Liggett & Myers, whose Chesterfields Rose had smoked more than any other, had failed to warn her of the harmful effects of tobacco prior to the 1966 government warning labels on cigarette packs. But the jury awarded Rose's estate no damages because they found the company only 20 percent responsible for her death and New Jersey law requires a finding of at least 50 percent responsibility. Philip Morris and Lorillard were let off because Rose had smoked their brands after 1966. The jury, however, took pity on Tony Cipollone, awarding him $400,000 as a sort of consolation prize for being a dutiful and concerned husband. It was the first time a jury had awarded any damages in a tobacco lawsuit, but it was an odd, unconventional gesture from the jury with no legal basis, and the award was overturned on appeal.

That was not the end of the case, however. Various court irregularities gave an opportunity to each side to appeal and the case went to the Supreme Court. The justices eventually agreed that Edell had been prevented from trying a big part of his case because the industry, post-1966, had concealed or misrepresented the truth on the smoking and health issue. The Court allowed a retrial on that issue, but by then Edell's law firm had had enough. They had been representing Rose on a contingency fee basis and they had spent nearly $3 million. They pulled out of the case, and the tobacco industry declared victory.

For Gauthier, the important lesson was in Edell's unfinished business. In the course of pretrial discovery—when each side can delve into the history and document archives of their opponent and question its research scientists, engineers, and managers—Edell had tried to force the companies to surrender 1,500 documents. They had refused on the grounds that these were communications between client and counsel, and therefore privileged. The judge in the case, H. Lee Sarokin, a liberal-minded jurist given to moral indignation about corporate wrongdoing, had ordered a private review by the court to see if the companies' claim of privilege was justified. In his ruling, Sarokin issued one of the sternest judgments ever made from the bench against the industry. It included the following two paragraphs:

> All too often in the choice between the physical health of consumers and the financial well-being of business, concealment is chosen over disclosure, sales over safety, and money over morality. Who are these persons who knowingly and secretly decide to put the buying public at risk solely for the purpose of making profits and who believe that illness and death of consumers is an appropriate cost of their own prosperity?
>
> As [the facts of the case] disclose, despite some rising pretenders, the tobacco industry may be the king of concealment and disinformation.

To Gauthier, Sarokin's allusion to hidden documents was like a croupier spinning the wheel for the start of play. Forcing companies to reveal incriminating internal papers is a key element of the liability lawyer's art. Gauthier would later recall, "That comment alone made me take another look at the case." And the handful of documents actually released during the trial bolstered Gauthier's theory that addiction—not failure to warn of the health dangers of smoking—was the new legal issue.

Those internal memos and research reports from the Cipollone trial records showed how tobacco industry scientists, contrary to company statements, believed that most people smoked to get a shot of nicotine, not for the pleasure of the act of smoking nor for the taste of the tobacco smoke, as the companies had asserted for so long. One of the more explicit memos, dated 1972, came from Philip Morris psychologist William Dunn. In it, he concluded, "The cigarette should be conceived not as a product, but as a package. Think of the cigarette pack as the storage container for a day's supply of nicotine. Think of the cigarette as a dispenser for a dose unit of nicotine."

Given such memos, Gauthier decided to go ahead and put together a suit on behalf of Castano. But though it would carry his friend's name, it would be a massive class action on behalf of all nicotine-addicted smokers, potentially tens of millions of Americans. The case had an attractive simplicity about it: the injury was addiction and the cause was nicotine. Gauthier would ask for two kinds of damages. The first was the establishment of a medical monitoring fund—to pay for checkups of addicted smokers for lung and heart disease and help them to quit the habit. The second would be punitive damages. Gauthier had in mind asking the courts to force the companies to pay fines from the sale of cigarettes. With 45 million smokers, an estimated half or more able to qualify as addicted to nicotine, the total amount the industry would be asked to pay, Gauthier figured, would come out to hundreds of billions of dollars.

While the addiction theory seemed a viable means to legal action, Gauthier knew it was foolish to think of taking on the tobacco companies by himself. He had made a fortune, but it was still a small one by the standards of the tobacco companies. They could outspend and outlast him in any legal battle. He had to build up a team of plaintiffs' lawyers, the more the better. He had no idea how they would react to his plan, but when he started talking to them he found many were thinking of suing. Kessler's letter and the ABC program had demonstrated a possible weakness in the tobacco camp. Gauthier found himself listening to stories of a colleague's relative or close friend who suffered from illness or death because of tobacco.

Gauthier would always be the first to admit that the prime motive for the plaintiffs' bar to take on cases was money and the rich tobacco companies promised the greatest booty of all, but the tobacco case had another layer: revenge. These plaintiffs' lawyers were personally involved. John Coale's father was ill with emphysema; so was the father of Atlanta lawyer Ralph Knowles. Danny Becnel, of New Orleans, had lost his father to lung cancer. Both parents of the lawyer Leslie Bryan had suffered smoking-related heart attacks. Russ Herman's mother, a lifelong smoker, was staying alive by breathing from a portable oxygen tank. Motley's mother had died of emphysema. Gauthier was careful to keep emphasizing the risks, but some lawyers were so fired up they didn't want to hear him. Calvin Fayard, a member of the Castano committee from Baton Rouge, told Gauthier, "Don't tell me how we can lose, tell me how we can win." It was during a dinner in New Orleans with Danny Becnel and Ralph Knowles that the three came up with the idea of each putting up $100,000. The collection box filled more quickly than Gauthier had imagined. It was "almost like spontaneous combustion," said Richard Heimann, of San Francisco's Lieff, Cabraser & Heimann.

IN HIS RECRUITING, Gauthier turned first to his Louisiana colleagues, many of them friends of Castano. But he knew he also needed some of the better-known members of the plaintiffs' bar, the celebrity lawyers. As always in liability cases, propaganda would be a key weapon. Gauthier's friend and grand old tort campaigner Melvin Belli, then eighty-seven years old, was an obvious choice. Belli was the living symbol of the flamboyant trial lawyer, with his yacht and his cowboy boots and his pen with gold ink and the sign outside his San Francisco office that proclaimed the title of his single-partner law firm as "Belli, Belli and Belli." And he was no novice to tobacco litigation. He had brought his first tobacco case to trial in Louisiana in 1958 during the First Wave of cases. He lost. But he tried again in 1985. Again he lost.

But over five decades Belli had left his mark on the profession. He had pioneered a powerful weapon in the liability lawyer's arsenal with the introduction of demonstrative evidence—the graphic and gory pictures of personal injuries—and these had doubtless influenced jurors. It was his prompt arrival at the sites of air crashes and hotel fires that had given rise to the universal nickname for his colleagues—ambulance chasers. "I'm not an ambulance chaser," Belli once complained, "I always get there before the ambulance arrives."

Among Gauthier's other important recruits was Elizabeth Cabraser of the San Francisco firm of Lieff, Cabraser & Heimann. The firm had started in 1972 with three attorneys; by the beginning of 1994, it had emerged as a national player in lucrative class-action cases. Robert Lieff, the managing partner, acquired his taste for big-case hunting when he worked with Belli in the 1960s handling securities class actions and commercial litigation. Cabraser had joined the firm in 1977 as a summer law clerk. She was of a different generation than Belli but had instantly won the admiration of her colleagues for her prodigious memory of case history and class-action procedures.

Despite her fragile appearance—she's so tiny she looks as though she might be blown over in a gust of wind—Cabraser was as robust and competitive as any of the trial lawyers. She had even adopted some of the trappings of her trade—including a purple Mercedes-Benz 300E whose license plates read FRCP 23—the federal rules of procedure governing class actions. She was known for working through the night and sleeping on a couch in her office on the top floor of a thirty-story high-rise overlooking Alcatraz and the Bay. Robert Lieff, her admiring managing partner, installed a shower especially for Cabraser's nocturnal bouts.

Cabraser had also been on the short list for a judgeship on California's northern bench, and her colleagues thought she was more than qualified. She wasn't chosen—she thinks because of philosophical differences with Senator Dianne Feinstein, especially over the death penalty. Cabraser opposes it, Feinstein is for it. Cabraser has also said one reason she was turned down was because she is openly gay.

Pragmatic and serious, she has a strong social conscience. To any liability class action, Cabraser would bring a well-defined concept of her role. "I don't think that corporations are the guardians and insurers of American health, welfare, and safety," she has said, "but they do have a responsibility not to hurt people if they can help it. And they can actually help it."

Gauthier's next call was to Stanley Chesley of Cincinnati, who is one of the least liked of the leading members of the plaintiffs' inner circle, mainly because of his seemingly uncontrolled vanity and relentless name-dropping. Chesley is a big contributor to local charities as well as to the Democratic Party, which has earned him invitations to the White House. His vast office is fitted out to look like an old-fashioned Manhattan ballroom, with leather upholstery and horse paintings. Among his victories, Chesley lists the 1977 Beverly Hills Supper Club fire that killed 165 people in Southgate, Kentucky, across the river from Cincinnati. There, he put all the plaintiffs together in one class action, which was a novel approach to personal-injury cases at the time, and then he went after every manufacturer and contractor he could find with any liability. He won an out-of-court settlement of $49 million when most people thought he would be lucky to get $2 million because the club itself carried so little insurance. Chesley charged about $3 million—or about $875 an hour for his services. Chesley also has a reputation for rushing his clients into out-of-court deals. One colleague described his deals as "the ultimate grotesque, exaggerated perversion of what it means to be a lawyer." Chesley shrugs off the criticism. "I've learned to understand that goes with the territory."

Gauthier pulled in other famous trial lawyers, including Peter Angelos, owner of the Baltimore Orioles, and John O'Quinn of Houston, who is worth half a billion dollars, according to *Fortune* magazine. But one of the most important calls Gauthier made was to John Coale in Washington, D.C. If Gauthier's grand national strategy was to come to anything, he needed a person he could trust in Washington. Though younger than many of the Castano lawyers—Coale was then forty-two—his exploits as a liability lawyer had already landed him in enough controversy to be profiled on CBS's *60 Minutes*. The accounts were not flattering. CBS correspondent Ed Bradley suggested that at the Bhopal chemical disaster in India, Coale was really no more than a vulture who circled in on his victims to pick the bones. "No," replied Coale, "I pick the bones of the corporation bastards who did it to these people. That's the bones I'm picking."

Born of a large and wealthy Baltimore family—his grandfather was one of the founders of the Baltimore Orioles—Coale had been an errant youth. He was kicked out of private school in the eleventh grade for general misbehavior. After graduating from Baltimore Law School, he made a living as a courthouse hustler representing drunk drivers in Washington. A profile of him in the *National Law Journal* was head-lined "Red Hot Coale" over a front-page picture of his portly frame in rumpled shirt, loose tie, and suspenders. Some of his colleagues de-spised him so much that they routinely mumbled derogatory remarks at the mention of his name, but Coale shrugged them off. "They're too self-important and they're way too complex."

Coale's career was launched with the release of toxic gases in 1984 at the Union Carbide chemical plant in Bhopal, India. A total of 1,861 people died and another 27,000 were injured. Coale was in a Washing-ton, D.C., taxi when he heard the news on the cab radio. He decided to fly immediately to India, a country he had never visited, and search for clients. He called up the one Indian he knew well, his tailor, the man who provided him with his outsize suits. After Coale offered an all-expenses-paid trip to his homeland, the tailor agreed to help. He fixed the visas at the Indian embassy, and four days after the accident, Coale, his tailor, and two assistants were on a flight to Bombay.

Coale expected the competition to be fierce, and it was. On the day Coale flew to Bombay, Belli filed a $15 billion class-action suit in San Francisco claiming, falsely, that he already had two Bhopal survivors as clients. In the high-stakes game these liability lawyers play, it is crucial to be the first to file because then you get to manage the lawsuit, oversee the pretrial discovery process, and decide when, and if, to enter into settlement talks. The all-important instrument is the steering committee, and to get on it, you must be a decorated veteran of the bar or have clients. The more you have, the more clout you can command on the committee.

Belli arrived in Bhopal declaring, "I am here to bring justice and money to these poor little people who have suffered at the hands of those rich sons of bitches," but by then Coale had "fixed" the local mayor and had the names of 30,000 local people who had retained him as their lawyer. His story was that they had implored him to take their case as he walked around the devastated villages before the other Amer-ican lawyers got there. He even claimed that "through an intermediary" he had been contacted in Washington by the mayor of Bhopal. What actually happened was that Coale, on arrival, had arranged to have an invitation typed up from the mayor's office asking him to come to Bhopal "because of our business relationships and common problems." It was backdated to the day after the accident.

Coale returned to the U.S. to face the wrath of the more senior members of the bar, who considered him an irritating upstart. Chief among them were Stanley Chesley and Wendell Gauthier, neither of whom had been to India or, in fact, done anything more than attach themselves to Belli's lawsuit. Chesley was co-counsel on Belli's $15 billion suit and wanted Coale to hand over the names of his clients. Coale would receive a fee but not the riches he might earn if he got onto the committee. Once they had his names, Chesley and Gauthier were planning to settle out of court and walk away with a large percentage of the $350 million offered by the company.

Sensing that Coale would not be a pushover, Gauthier, the consummate manager, asked him and a few other lawyers to lunch in New Orleans. Coale recalled, "Wendell sent his Rolls-Royce and an attractive legal assistant to meet me at the airport. I wasn't impressed. I knew you could pick up an old Rolls for next to nothing." Over lunch, Coale was noncommittal. He knew that if he simply handed over his client list he would be in on any deal, but he would be way down the line for a decent payoff.

After lunch Gauthier took Coale aside and asked what he was going to do. Coale replied that he had had a lot of fun with the case, that it had been interesting for him watching how it all worked—the formation of the committee and so forth—but he was upset he wasn't on the committee. Waiting outside the room, Coale told Gauthier, was a reporter from *Playboy* to whom he intended to give the whole story of the American lawyers seeking to settle the cases of the unfortunate Bhopal victims and make a bundle of money doing it. That was also a lie, but Gauthier and Chesley weren't sure. They agreed to let Coale onto the committee. Coale struck his own deal for his clients names: 45 percent of the lawyers' award money, when it came, and all his expenses— amounting to $80,000—for his trip to India. Coale was now a member of the club.

As it turned out, none of the American lawyers made a cent. One of those who worked with Chesley and Gauthier was Mike Ciresi, then thirty-eight and a member of the big Minneapolis firm of Robins, Kaplan, Miller & Ciresi. Ciresi had earned his spurs in several landmark liability cases, including the 1985 Dalkon Shield contraceptive litigation that resulted in a settlement award of $38 million against the manufacturer, A. H. Robins Co. Unlike Chesley and Belli, Ciresi's instincts were to spend a lot less time with the leaders of the committee and a lot more time checking out other opportunities. He got himself hired to represent the government of India in its own suit against Union Carbide. While the others were trying desperately to arrange a quick settlement in the United States, Ciresi was biding his time waiting for the case to be transferred back to India. He was sure that was what the New York judge would eventually do, given the potential for endless squabbles among the American lawyers. And that's what happened. Ciresi was the only one who got paid. Union Carbide eventually paid $470 million to victims and their survivors. Coale got nothing—except a lot of experience and publicity, which, of course, he could take straight to the bank. Publicity is everything for lawyers starting out in the personal-injury business.

Ciresi ended up despising Chesley and Gauthier for being prepared to accept Union Carbide's earlier settlement offer. And Ciresi was full of scorn for the shabby way Coale had collected his clients. "I'm the bad boy, I'm a known sleazebag," Coale would chuckle later. But the truth was he didn't care what they thought of him. He was at the table with the big boys now. Because of the Bhopal experience, Gauthier was never going to invite Ciresi to join the Castano case. But Ciresi had another surprise. He was already putting together his own case—a Medicaid reimbursement lawsuit for the state of Minnesota. The next time they would all meet would be in the biggest contest of all for the riches of the tobacco industry.

In the meantime, the liability lawyers went back to plane crashes and hotel fires. The next big disaster—the fire in the Dupont Plaza Hotel in San Juan, Puerto Rico—put Coale even more squarely in front of the cameras. He worked on the case with Gauthier and took a one-third cut of the lawyers' fees from the $235 million settlement. Having at first circled each other like wary predators, Gauthier and Coale would now hunt as a pair.

THERE WAS ONE other notable exception to Gauthier's first list of recruits—Ron Motley, of Charleston, South Carolina, the ostentatious, self-appointed heir to the throne of Melvin Belli. His colleagues looked on him as a not entirely benign dictator who inhabited a strange Southern retreat of gated compounds, beach houses, garish motor yachts, and private jet planes, all funded through Motley's gains from ingenious and highly successful litigation in asbestos cases. The son of a used car salesman, Motley's meteoric rise to riches had shown flashes of brilliance in the courtroom as well as the back room where the deals are made. Most members of the plaintiffs' bar would regard him and his strategist, Joe Rice, an expert in out-of-court class-action settlements, as a necessary addition to any large class-action suit, especially of the kind Gauthier was putting together. But one of those deals had also put his colleagues on guard, creating a deep division at the bar over Motley's trustworthiness.

At the beginning of 1993, a full year before the launch of the Third Wave, Motley, Joe Rice, and a Philadelphia personal-injury lawyer named Gene Locks attempted a new type of $1.3 billion backroom settlement of thousands of asbestos cases with a consortium of twenty companies. The deal sought to settle the claims of the millions of victims exposed to asbestos at work who had yet to show any sign of disease—and, therefore, had not even made a claim. The idea was to take the companies out of asbestos litigation altogether; provide an annual fund to settle claims, and give Motley and Locks attorneys' fees for victims they had never met—a novel approach to class-action lawsuits.

Fred Baron, a Dallas lawyer who had been an ally of Locks, charged that the deal was a corrupt, unconstitutional sellout that benefited the companies and greedy lawyers. Other critics accused Motley of engaging in a collusive attempt to use the court system to resolve future claims of third parties who were not yet in the court system.

Motley retorted that it was a "creative alternative" to dealing with the tens of thousands of asbestos cases that were clogging the courts and forcing asbestos victims to wait years for compensation. Legal ethics experts were divided on the deal. Those in opposition were branded by Motley as "ivory tower academics" unfamiliar with the real world of trial law.

The problem of asbestos cases swamping the courts was a real one. In 1990, the Supreme Court warned of a "major disaster to both victims and the producers of asbestos products." In a special report, Chief Justice William Rehnquist suggested Congress should pass legislation similar to the black lung program, which had given compensation to coal miners in the 1970s. But Congress did nothing—even though more than 27 million people had been exposed to asbestos on the job, 350,000 of them would develop fatal cancer, and more than a million would suffer from nonmalignant asbestos-related diseases.

In an effort to expedite the cases, eight federal judges experienced in asbestos litigation had urged the consolidation of all complaints then pending in federal courts. Officials transferred a large chunk of the cases—26,000 of them—to the district court in Philadelphia, but they bogged down there as well.

The response to this was the Motley-Locks side deal. A consortium of twenty companies—half the nation's asbestos enterprises—proposed the $1.3 billion deal to Motley and Locks. The deal, which became known as Georgine after one of the class-action representatives, Robert Georgine, president of the Building and Construction Trades department of the AFL-CIO, envisioned that 100,000 claims would be paid out over ten years. Under the settlement, Motley claimed, victims would be paid in six months and more of the award money would actually reach the victims. About 65 percent of it had been going to lawyers, so far.

The labor movement was split on the deal. Critics charged that the money was less than plaintiffs could get if they filed individually; there was no adjustment for inflation, and many victims would not be compensated rapidly because there was a cap on the yearly award fund. Moreover, the settlement unfairly barred people who may have been unaware that they had been exposed to asbestos—it takes fifteen to thirty-five years after initial exposure for related diseases to appear.

The Philadelphia district court approved the deal, but it was appealed by several of Motley's colleagues. Eventually, it landed in the Supreme Court where it was rejected in 1997. But in 1994, Gauthier knew that inviting Motley would be raising the expertise and noise level of the Castano action, which he wanted to do. It would also be inviting trouble. Caught in this bind, he decided against asking Motley to join. Instead, he let Motley make the request, which was, of course, accepted. It was the beginning of a turbulent relationship, as Gauthier had feared. But for Motley, the Castano case, prominent as it was, would be merely a stepping stone to his larger involvement with the attorneys general and their key state Medicaid cases, especially in Mississippi: cases that had not yet even been filed.

WHILE GAUTHIER ASSEMBLED his team from the comfort of his Metairie office, another front of the Third Wave was being opened up in Washington. On March 25, Congressman Henry Waxman, a Democrat from California and a veteran antitobacco campaigner, began hearings on Capitol Hill under the uncompromising banner, "Regulation of Tobacco Products." Of all the congressional investigations into the industry over the years, and there had been many, these were to be the most hostile. The star witness against the industry was Dr. David Kessler, commissioner of the FDA. He would be building on the themes introduced in his February letter a month before—that nicotine is an addictive drug and that the industry manipulates nicotine levels. His staff had found several tobacco company patents that mentioned ways of "adding nicotine" or "maintaining or increasing nicotine content," and of substances that might allow "the release of nicotine in controlled amounts." Kessler admitted that none of his evidence meant the patents had been used, and the companies protested vigorously that they had not been. But Kessler's point was that the industry had at least experimented with the idea. The technology was available.

The tobacco industry's traditional congressional allies counterattacked. They complained of Kessler's "precipitous and reckless conduct" in charging the companies with trying to hook customers. They said his goal was the prohibition of tobacco. His agency did not even have jurisdiction over the industry. That was Congress's job, they said, and always had been. They also attacked Kessler for suggesting there was something new in saying nicotine was addictive. But Kessler's point was that the companies knew this and appeared, from the patents, to be ready to manipulate the levels of nicotine in cigarettes to keep smokers hooked. But he had not yet demonstrated manipulation; that was to come. The FDA's work would grow in intensity, bolstering Gauthier's offensive.

On March 29, 1994, in the U.S. District Court on Poydras Street in downtown New Orleans, Gauthier and twenty-five plaintiffs' law firms, only a handful of which had ever been involved in tobacco litigation, filed *Castano* v. *American Tobacco Company,* Civil Action No. 94-1044.

Besides Peter Castano, the names of four other local plaintiffs who had tried to give up cigarettes and failed were on the papers. Ernest Perry had tried hypnotic therapy, acupuncture, injections in the ear, an ear-clip device, and a variety of nicotine patches. George Solomon, one of Gauthier's partners in the casino venture, had also used a hypnotist, injections, and other methods in unsuccessful attempts to shake off his desire for nicotine. Gloria Scott had started smoking Camels in 1958 and complained of headaches and stomach problems when she tried to give up. And Deania Jackson, a New Orleans attorney who had started smoking in junior high school in 1973, had quit for six years, but couldn't keep off cigarettes and had taken up the habit again in 1992.

There were eight named defendants: the American Tobacco Company; the Philip Morris Companies Inc., the nation's largest tobacco company and maker of the most successful brand, Marlboro; the R. J. Reynolds Company, which makes Camels and is the second-largest manufacturer; Brown & Williamson; Lorillard Inc.; the Liggett Group; and the United States Tobacco Company, the biggest maker of snuff. BATUS Inc., onetime owner of the Kentucky-based Brown & Williamson, was also named. (It is now owned by BAT Industries.)

The complaint charged that the companies engaged in fraud and deceit by misrepresenting that nicotine is nonaddictive; were negligent in not accurately describing their products; violated consumer protection statutes; breached an express warranty that their products were not addictive and an implied warranty that their products were fit for consumption; and caused intentional, emotional distress on those who smoked their cigarettes. The suit sought compensatory and punitive damages, plus funds to treat smoking-related diseases. The total amount was impossible to calculate; if each addicted smoker received only $5,000 for medical monitoring, it could run to $100 billion, or more than twice the annual revenues of the industry.

Paragraph 32 of the fourteen-page Castano lawsuit listed the reasons why the lawyers believed it should be clear to anyone that nicotine is an addictive drug: at least two-thirds of adults who smoke say they wish they could quit; 17 million Americans try to quit each year, but fewer than one out of ten succeed; eight out of ten smokers say they wish they had never started smoking; after surgery for lung cancer, almost half of the smokers resume smoking; among smokers who suffer heart attacks, 38 percent resume smoking while they are still in the hospital; even when a smoker has his or her larynx removed, 40 percent try smoking again; 70 percent of young people between the ages of twelve and eighteen who smoke say they believe they are already dependent on cigarettes; and 40 percent of high school seniors who smoke regularly have tried to quit and have failed.

Although Gauthier was the unchallenged leader of the group, he deferred to his old friend Melvin Belli when the moment came for a press statement. "Thirty years ago," Belli bellowed, "I filed the first suit against these same tobacco companies in the same city, New Orleans. We lost because we couldn't prove the addiction of nicotine then, but now we will prove that the tobacco industry has conspired to catch you, hold and kill you . . . all without a moment of self-examination."

The tobacco companies, defiant and confident as ever, predicted the suit would fail. It was being brought by a band of money-grabbing plaintiffs' lawyers, they said, and was no different from previous attempts. Gary Long, a Kansas City attorney and spokesman for Philip Morris, said the company was "not surprised that a group of plaintiffs' lawyers had quickly jumped on the bandwagon created by ABC's television program and the comments of David Kessler. Addiction claims have been made previously in many cases against cigarette companies, and the companies have prevailed," he said. Peggy Carter, manager of media relations for R. J. Reynolds in Winston-Salem, North Carolina, also rejected the claims in the suit. She said government and industry research showed the amount of nicotine in cigarettes had dropped by 60 percent over the last forty years as consumers had demanded lower levels. What she failed to explain was that this process is automatic; when tar levels are reduced with filters, nicotine levels drop, too. The companies, long concerned that the nicotine would fall below a level that kept the smoker "satisfied," as they put it in the internal reports, had made the necessary adjustments.

The launching of Gauthier's suit, then the biggest legal challenge the industry had ever faced, was greeted with jubilation among the antismoking groups. "I think the moment has come," forecast Professor Richard Daynard. A more sober view was that Gauthier's group, with all its celebrities in the plaintiffs' bar, would get a lot of publicity, but that the issue was still one of smokers and choice. Gauthier's group would indeed make a lot of noise, and its contribution would be invaluable to the antitobacco forces trying to soften up the enemy, a process that continued throughout the spring of 1994.

Two weeks before the Castano case was filed, the Florida District Court of Appeal had given the green light for the first class-action suit on so-called secondhand smoke. A flight attendant named Norman Broin, who was battling cancer, represented the suit brought by 60,000 flight attendants and filed originally in 1991 by a Miami lawyer, Stanley Rosenblatt, at the end of the Second Wave of tobacco litigation.

Then, on May 7, 1994, *The New York Times* ran the first of a series of articles based on thousands of pages of internal company documents that had been stolen from Brown & Williamson, the nation's third-largest tobacco company. B&W, which makes Viceroy and Kools, is a wholly owned subsidiary of the British tobacco company BAT Industries. The story, headlined "Tobacco Company Was Silent on Hazards," focused on a 1963 memo from B&W's general counsel, Addison Yeaman. In an admission that was contrary to all public statements ever made by tobacco industry officials and was to become the most oft-quoted sentences from the whole collection of documents, Yeaman wrote, "Moreover nicotine is addictive. We are then in the business of selling nicotine, an addictive drug effective in the release of stress mechanisms."

That was only the beginning. Yeaman had made another observation that was very important for the antitobacco forces. He suggested that B&W own up to the fact that cigarettes cause cancer, remove the offending substances through a filter or by other means, and sell a safer cigarette. This was exactly the kind of evidence Gauthier was looking for.

IN MISSISSIPPI, on May 23, Mike Moore filed his four-count charge against the industry in Pascagoula. In the complaint, Moore contended the "tobacco cartel" had been reaping billions of dollars from Mississippi's citizens by selling them cigarettes without informing them of the "true carcinogenic, pathologic and addictive qualities" of those cigarettes. "Instead of honestly disclosing the genuine risks of smoking cigarettes, the tobacco companies have spent billions in slick, sophisticated marketing techniques designed to make smoking appear to be glamorous to our youngsters. In equity and in fairness, it is the defendants, not the taxpayers of Mississippi, who should pay the costs of tobacco-related diseases."

Moore went on to warn that the lawsuit would cause a "public relations and legal onslaught by the tobacco companies the likes of which Mississippi has never seen. These people wrote the book on dirty tricks . . . watch out for lies and slander. The tobacco companies will try to hide their fingerprints by creating front groups with innocuous-sounding names like 'Mississippians For Truth and Justice,' or 'Mississippians for Fair Public Health.' Don't take a name at face value. Follow the money trail. Look at the background and business interests of the people doing the attacking."

Moore was right. The industry would oppose him with all the forces they could muster. Moore's own governor, Kirk Fordice, whose political campaigns had been supported by the industry, would become Moore's main opponent. But the new front had been opened up. Florida would be next, with a special state law authorizing the state to recoup Medicaid costs from the industry. Massachusetts would pass a similar law. West Virginia, Louisiana, and Texas would follow with Medicaid suits within a year. With the Castano case now leading the charge, the Third Wave was rolling across the continent.

3

THE DRAMA TEACHER

A man may see how this world goes with no eyes. Look with
thine ears. See how yond justice rails upon yond simple
thief. Hark in thine ear. Change places and, handy-dandy,
which is justice, which is the thief?

—*Shakespeare,* King Lear

THE OLD MUSTANG CONVERTIBLE looked a little seedy. Its
driver appeared to be in his fifties, plump with unkempt sandy
hair and a boozer's ruddy complexion, the description I had
been given, more or less. But the car did not stop at the French café
where I had been told to wait for him. It kept going down the street.

A few minutes later, the car passed by again and I got a better look
at the driver. I was now convinced he was the man I had come to meet.
This time the car stopped. The man got out and walked toward the
café, wearily. He looked like someone who'd been up all night.

"I'm Merrell Williams," he said as we shook hands. "Sorry I'm late,
but I had to see if anyone was following me."

"They're still following you?" I asked, surprised.

"Oh yeah," he said, "they're there. They'll probably always be there.
They like to know everywhere I go and everyone I meet; essentially
everything I do."

TWO YEARS after he had been hailed as America's most famous secret
"leaker" since Daniel Ellsberg released the Pentagon Papers, Merrell
Williams was still on the run. He believed that the tobacco company

Brown & Williamson of Louisville, Kentucky, from whom he stole thousands of confidential memos and research papers, would never leave him alone. And he had good reason to be concerned. Since 1993, when he gave the papers to the Pascagoula plaintiffs' lawyer Dick Scruggs and they had ended up on the World Wide Web, the company had chased him out of Kentucky with a court order so strict that he couldn't even talk about the documents to his legal counsel. The tobacco lawyers had deposed him eight times to try and find out exactly what documents he had taken and what he had done with them. The more Williams refused to answer the company's questions, using his Fifth Amendment right against self-incrimination, the more the company pursued him. He was convinced they tapped his phone, followed him, watched him come and go through binoculars from secret hiding places. He was sure they would find a way to put him in jail one day, if he didn't meet with an "accident" before somebody nabbed him.

He was famous in this little seaside town of Ocean Springs on Mississippi's Gulf Coast, far from the commercial and political centers of the United States where he had caused such a stir. Before I met him, I had been round the corner from the French café to a little shop called Favorites: Books, Art, Etc. and had bought *Smokescreen,* a new book by *The New York Times* reporter Phil Hilts, who was the first to track Williams down and to write about the documents he had stolen. "Williams was in here yesterday and bought a copy of the book," said the nice woman who owned the store. "He lives here, you know," she added quietly as though this was privileged gossip. "Won't say a word," I felt like replying, marveling at how the exploits of Merrell Williams were still fostering an air of mystery and intrigue.

Like most corporate whistle-blowers, Williams was viewed as part hero, part fool, and always regarded with suspicion. Is he mad, or does he really have a social conscience? Is he out for personal gain? Or does he simply crave attention? In the 1960s and 1970s the first American whistle-blowers exposed toxic chemical dumping, unsafe drugs, and asbestos diseases and were often branded as leftist troublemakers: Karen Silkwood and her documentation of unsafe practices at the Kerr-McGee nuclear power plant in Oklahoma is one case.

Merrell Williams's stolen documents were certainly in this category. What he extracted from Brown & Williamson's confidential files had never been unearthed in forty years of litigation against the tobacco industry. The papers would be vitally important to those seeking to change the way the industry does business and especially to the anti-tobacco lawyers in the Third Wave. But tobacco was not nuclear power; Williams was a dissident in an industry that most people readily accepted as an essential, even desirable part of human culture, a big taxpayer and a key prop of American agriculture.

By liberating evidence of wrongdoing from the files of the tobacco industry, Williams was not destined for instant social sainthood. There was no guarantee that he would even become a national hero; just the grim prospect of prolonged litigation as the industry tried to make him the issue, not the documents. His decision to steal them in the first place was filled with conflicting motives, and then his second decision to hand them over to plaintiffs' attorneys suing the tobacco industry was complicated and probably will always be somewhat unclear.

IT WOULD BE FAIR to say that prior to 1993, little in Merrell Williams's half century of existence gave any hint that he would one day be famous. He was born in Louisiana into a middle-class family. After leaving high school, he had drifted in and out of colleges, jobs, and marriages. At one point, he was enrolled in drama classes at Baylor University, Waco, Texas, and dedicated himself to acting. Although he was, and clearly still is, rather accomplished at theatricals, he has not been on stage since his college days. Then, his appearances were interspersed with bouts of drinking and carousing as a member of a group of campus rebels who had united under the banner of the Brazos River Society, named after the river that flows through Waco. Among other pleasures, Williams smoked cigarettes—one of his favorites was Kools, a Brown & Williamson brand. He had a brief spell in the army, where military discipline and his own freewheeling lifestyle clashed in a terminal fashion one day only four months after he had joined up. Williams wanted to help a fellow private whose thumb had got stuck in the trigger mechanism of his M-1 rifle. The drill sergeant thought the unfortunate soldier should bear the pain without aid. Williams thought otherwise. The sergeant won, of course. Williams showed his disgust by rushing the sergeant and beating him on the head with his helmet, an act of foolishness that was put down to the excessive heat that day. He was honorably discharged shortly afterward.

Out of the service he went to Ole Miss (a decade before Scruggs and Moore). He showed promise in the liberal arts, earning a bachelor's and a master's degree in the same year, 1966. He met Noni, a law student, on a Tuesday and married her the following Saturday. The marriage was to last for nine years while he went on to the University of Denver and earned a Ph.D. in drama. He returned to Mississippi and taught at small colleges but was bored and unmotivated—by the subject and the students and by the meager financial rewards. He soon gained a reputation for being late for class and leaving early. In the late '70s he lost his job and moved to Oxford, an elegant university town. An old-car enthusiast, he tried importing classic cars from England and for a brief period ran an Irish-style pub. There he met his second wife, Mollie, a singer twelve years his junior. That marriage was to last ten years, and there were two daughters. The pub went bust, and Williams moved down to the Gulf Coast, where he then dreamed of becoming a shrimper.

Mollie soon tired of his lack of ambition and money. She persuaded him to move to Louisville, her home town, where Williams took a couple of menial jobs, raking leaves, house painting, and cleaning up at a car dealership. His health deteriorated, as did his relationship with Mollie. By the end of 1987, he was in the middle of his second divorce when a new opportunity suddenly arose. He had been taking prelaw courses at the University of Louisville and his name was on the list at the local bar association for students needing jobs. Toward the end of November 1987, he was called by the association and asked if he would be interested in a paralegal job—starting at $9 an hour—sorting documents for Wyatt, Tarrant & Combs, the largest law firm in Kentucky. His assignment, according to court files, would be "to analyze and classify documents in connection with the defense of smoking and health lawsuits."

Williams was put to work with paralegals from two other law firms, Vinson & Elkins of Houston and Atlanta's King & Spalding, both long-term tobacco industry counsel. The task went by the noncommittal title of "Subjective Coding Project," which meant sorting archive documents on product promotion and smoking and health going back to the

'50s. The paralegals worked in an old warehouse in Louisville's East End, once the center of Kentucky's tobacco industry but now a run-down neighborhood of abandoned buildings. The room where they worked was filled with boxes of documents and a sign over the doorway read, "No One Permitted in the Room Without Authorization." The clerks were required to sign a confidentiality agreement. They were given photo-ID badges and required to keep time sheets. There was a permanent guard on the building.

The company documents were not confined to Brown & William-son, but often included exchanges of memos and letters with other tobacco companies. B&W was a wholly owned subsidiary of the British tobacco giant BAT Industries, and many of the documents concerned contacts with its London-based parent. Williams quickly learned that the tobacco companies had done extensive research about the effects of nicotine and the cancerous agents in tobacco smoke, but had not made that research public. He began to realize that he was looking at a widespread cover-up of the harmful effects of smoking. The company lawyers had actively participated in this cover-up, using lawyers' de-vices, such as attorney-client privilege, to keep internal memos confi-dential. The lawyers had even set up a secret fund enabling them to sponsor, and monitor, tobacco research that would be especially useful in defending liability suits. They had also suggested ways that scientific reports could be censored to remove facts embarrassing to the industry. Some of the documents were so startling that Williams started to make notes on scraps of paper, taking them to the bathroom and stuffing them into his socks.

Over time, Williams grew bolder. He took whole documents out of the building and copied them during his lunch hour. He would care-fully fold the documents into envelopes so they wouldn't get dirty and then put them inside his shirt, or sometimes he would wear an old exercise back brace and stuff them into that. The problem was they made a crinkling noise as he walked. So Williams carried an open bag of potato chips and munched as he passed the guard. Occasionally, he would offer the guard a chip. He was never stopped.

Stealing the documents became an obsession for Williams, but as the collection grew, he wondered what to do with it. Should he make the papers public and, if so, how? Williams says the resolution to his problem came one cold day in February 1990, when he went for a walk in the hills outside Louisville. A lapsed Catholic, he started to pray, "God, just tell me what I've got to do, just help me, send me a message. Send somebody to help me." He says that quite suddenly he lost his fear and decided he must make the papers public. "I'm not saying that God told me to do this, but after that, I did."

In the Louisville library a few days later, Williams came across reports on the Nathan Horton trial in Mississippi and on the appeals in the Rose Cipollone trial in New Jersey. Often quoted in these accounts was Professor Dick Daynard of Northeastern University in Boston, who ran the Tobacco Products Liability Project. Williams persuaded a friend in Louisville who was training to be a lawyer to call Daynard and say he knew of a woman who had some confidential tobacco documents. (He thought the pretense that he was a woman would give his identity added protection.) Daynard agreed to talk to "the woman" and gave a number to call. Williams called back, admitting his true identity, and they set up a meeting at the home of an old undergraduate friend of Williams's in Orlando, Florida. Williams brought a box of the documents to the meeting. Daynard was stunned at what he saw and immediately warned Williams that if he passed on the documents and was discovered, he could be in very serious trouble. At best, given the power of the Wyatt, Tarrant law firm, he would certainly never find another job in Louisville; and, at worst, B&W would sue him for stealing the documents and he would end up in jail. As to publishing the documents, Daynard said it was possible Northeastern might do it, but his own organization—the Tobacco Products Liability Project—had no money, and even the university would be extremely wary of the legal risks. Daynard had one further suggestion—a meeting with Morton Mintz, a retired investigative reporter with *The Washington Post* who, as a freelancer, was still writing articles about corporate wrongdoing, including the tobacco companies. A second meeting was arranged to which Mintz came. He, too, was astonished by the documents. He suggested to Williams that the two might collaborate on a book, but Mintz abandoned the idea after a few months. As a freelancer, he had no financial backing and he was also concerned about the wrath of Brown & Williamson's legal department. Once the company discovered he had the documents, as it would as soon as he started checking them out, they would sue him even before he could publish anything. Mintz said later, "I thought about it and decided it's one thing to be a martyr for some productive reason, but there's no sense in being a martyr for no productive reason."

During the next two years, Williams continued to collect documents from the law firm. In the meantime, he married his third wife, Sherry Gibson, a nurse who lived in his apartment building. He was granted custody of his two daughters from the previous marriage and the restructured Williams family lived a relatively normal life—until February 1992, when Williams was told the project at Wyatt, Tarrant was being cut back and his job had ended. The role of Williams the mole, the undercover agent, was at an end. It had been the most exciting period in his life and merited a grand finale. On his last day at work, he brazenly took out his final, and biggest, batch of documents in a banker's box. Neither his supervisor in the documents room nor the guard on the door asked to look inside.

He sat at home for a year without a job, except for a short stint trying to sell cars. He was not feeling well. In March 1993, Williams felt "a curious little hum" in his chest, went to the emergency room of the local hospital, and minutes later was on the operating table having a quintuple bypass operation. Considering how he had maltreated his body over the years, Williams made a good recovery. By fall, he was fit enough to return to the question of what to do with his documents, but he was no longer feeling so sanguine about his role as courageous dissenter. Instead, he decided to turn his bypass operation into a personal-injury case, with Brown & Williamson as the defendants. In his collection of stolen papers he had internal company documents discussing how cigarette smoking caused heart disease. He needed a lawyer.

For his divorce from Mollie he had hired a well-known local lawyer from an old Kentucky family with the grand Southern name of Fox DeMoisey. During the divorce proceedings, Williams kept mumbling to DeMoisey about a highly sensitive project that he was working on and how it was bothering him but he couldn't talk about it—not yet anyway. DeMoisey was a busy man who ran his office single-handed, with his wife as the office manager, and he had simply ignored Williams's mystery project. A few weeks after Williams's operation, DeMoisey got a call from his strange client asking to come and see him

THE DRAMA TEACHER   63

in DeMoisey's office in downtown Louisville, a skyscraper building right next door to Brown & Williamson's headquarters.

"He looked terrible, like ten miles of bad road," DeMoisey recalls. Williams launched into a rambling, incoherent account of the giant fraud that he believed he had uncovered. Toward the end of the conversation, Williams told DeMoisey that he had copied thousands of documents, many of them communications between lawyers. DeMoisey told him to stop the story right there. He didn't want to hear any more. Those documents were, in theory at least, covered by attorney-client privilege. In stealing them Williams could go to jail, and he, DeMoisey, could lose his license if he received them, or any information about them. Wyatt, Tarrant was the largest law firm in Kentucky, with 175 lawyers, a top-drawer client list, and an office building shared with one of the state's biggest banks. It also dominated the local bar association. One procedural slip and they could make a lot of trouble for a lawyer acting on his own, even if he was part of the Louisville establishment.

But DeMoisey, a man of six feet, six inches with a bushy mustache and the military bearing of a Civil War general, had never shirked a legal challenge, especially one that tweaked his own social class. He pondered the case over the weekend and met Williams the following week. Williams had three choices, he said: dump the documents in the Ohio River, try to go public, or settle the matter with a private claim against the company for damages to his health, implying that he would be using the documents as evidence. DeMoisey recommended that Williams file a private claim and, at the same time, give the documents back. That way, the documents would be authenticated, at least. In his job at Wyatt, Tarrant, Williams had access to company letterheads. For all DeMoisey knew, he could have forged the whole set of papers, and that was almost certainly what the company was going to charge, whatever the truth. B&W would simply brand Williams as a fraud. If Williams returned the documents and then demanded them back in litigation, as in the normal pretrial discovery, there was only one way B&W could prevent those documents from being produced and that was if they insisted that the documents were subject to attorney-client privilege, or work product—that is, work done by lawyers in anticipation of a lawsuit. In order to do that, B&W would be admitting that the documents were real. Another reason to return the documents was that B&W was bound to accuse Williams of being a thief. The legal definition of thievery is taking property with intent to permanently deprive. By giving the documents back, Williams would be confusing the charge. Whether Williams had actually stolen anything was questionable. There were laws about copyright and trademarks, but was it possible to steal information? He didn't think so.

DeMoisey warned Williams that he was dealing with people who, for whatever reason, believed passionately in tobacco, from tobacco farmers, to the cigarette salesmen, to the company lawyers and executives. Accidents could happen. Not that either of the two men thought the law firm, or B&W, would be involved in harming them physically, but they were concerned about fringe elements. DeMoisey asked Williams to write up a summary of the documents in the form of an affidavit in expectation of death. It sounded dramatic, said DeMoisey, but the reason was that "either because of your own heart condition, or because some bubba from Shelby County could blow your shit away. Once they know that there is this document floating around, it will come to their attention that the last thing they want to happen is for you to die," said DeMoisey. Williams agreed to the plan after secretly making a copy for himself. DeMoisey sent the documents back in a sealed box with a covering letter saying he had a client, whom he did not name, who had these documents and had become ill as a result of smoking and wanted to file a lawsuit. The law firm replied that they knew perfectly well that DeMoisey's client was Williams and that Williams was unhinged and the documents were meaningless. In fact, they had already probably been made public in previous lawsuits.

It was the bluff DeMoisey had expected. DeMoisey replied that if the documents were indeed meaningless, then Wyatt, Tarrant should give them to him for examination, and if they were right, he'd drop Williams and the case; otherwise his client would go ahead with a lawsuit. He wanted a reply within a week. Before the deadline, Wyatt, Tarrant went into local court in Louisville claiming that Williams had violated his confidentiality agreement and that if he was not restrained from disclosing the contents of the documents, the company would "suffer immediate and irreparable injury, loss, and damage." Without even looking at the documents and taking Wyatt, Tarrant's view on faith, Judge Thomas Wine, of Kentucky's Jefferson Circuit Court, issued an order that was so severe it even prevented Williams from talking to his own lawyer, DeMoisey.

Actually, DeMoisey was quite happy with the outcome, though it was absurd. By their actions, Wyatt, Tarrant had confirmed that the documents were real, and it was going to be a long, drawn-out affair. For the moment, DeMoisey couldn't move on the case because he couldn't talk to Williams about the case. "In some twenty years of law practice, I had never experienced such a thing and nor had any of the lawyers with whom I discussed the case," he said.

B&W was apparently worried that Williams had more documents than he had included in the sealed box. In fact, he had no more documents. The company made several unsuccessful attempts to depose him, but he always invoked his Fifth Amendment protection against self-incrimination. In October 1993, the frustrated Wyatt, Tarrant lawyers asked DeMoisey whether he would consider some kind of settlement if Williams would drop his claim and agree to a permanent injunction similar to the restraining order then in effect. DeMoisey insists no money was discussed. "How could we demand money for documents they already had?" he protested. The talks went nowhere. In the end, as far as Brown & Williamson was concerned, Merrell Williams was a thief and an extortionist, and they would continue to pursue him through the courts to ensure his silence. But Williams was no ordinary document thief: greater forces were at work.

THOUGH BROWN & WILLIAMSON made no further legal moves against him, Williams felt the noose of the tobacco company tightening. Brown & Williamson was calling him a thief on the front page of the Louisville *Courier-Journal,* and he lived in an increasingly insecure world of his own, imagining his movements were traced and his phone calls monitored—by whom he did not know. There was no evidence of such things. But he was isolated and afraid. He couldn't talk to anyone about the documents, not his lawyer and not even his current wife, Sherry. By his own admission, he was driving Sherry crazy and he felt that if he stayed in Kentucky under such pressure, sooner or later something really bad was going to happen. In early February 1994, he decided to return to Mississippi. He had no job and had still not decided what to do with the documents.

Williams remembered the Nathan Horton case and the country lawyer, Don Barrett, whose spirited but ultimately unsuccessful challenge to the American Tobacco Company Williams had admired from afar. His mother, who lived in Jackson, had once met Barrett's father, Pat, and Williams decided to play his Mississippi connection to see if he could get a job with the Lexington law firm. He sent a fax to Barrett, who called him back and agreed to meet him at the Olde Tyme Delicatessen in Jackson.

When Williams arrived at the delicatessen, he found that Barrett had brought along Dick Scruggs, who was then unknown to Williams. They chatted for an hour and a half, mainly about social things and his need for a job. He says he never discussed Mississippi's suit against the tobacco companies. He thought that the smooth talking, neatly turned out Scruggs was an FBI agent, or something like that, such was his paranoia about the stolen documents. For their part, the two lawyers say Williams was nervous—"like a scared little deer"—and started an incoherent monologue about the tobacco companies hiding their knowledge of the hazards of smoking. He hinted that he had some incriminating documents, but never actually produced any. In fact, his conversation was so muddled that after the meeting, Scruggs and Barrett looked at each other and asked, "What exactly did he say?" Only one thing had been clear—Williams wanted a job. Scruggs gave him his phone number in Pascagoula, telling him to call if he needed help looking for work.

A few weeks later, Williams called from a pay phone outside Popeye's restaurant in Pascagoula. Scruggs was vactioning in Bermuda, but his secretary got him right away and he phoned Williams back at Popeye's. Scruggs arranged for Williams to take a paralegal job at a Pascagoula law firm. Although Williams never had a formal interview, he says that he never traded the documents for a job, or anything else. In one of the later depositions, B&W lawyers asked Williams, "They were prepared to hire you as a favor to Mr. Scruggs?" But Williams would say only, "They were prepared to hire me. They did hire me."

They paid him $36,000 a year—more than he had ever earned in his life.

When Scruggs returned from vacation, the two met again in Scruggs's offices in Pascagoula. B&W has charged that there was a conspiracy of plaintiffs' lawyers—including Barrett and Ron Motley—to buy the documents from Williams. Each time he was asked about this in a deposition, Williams took the Fifth—in violation of the court's order. Despite persistent questioning from B&W, he has refused to say who was at that Pascagoula meeting, whether he discussed the fact he had the documents, whether he produced any documents, or even whether he agreed to produce any at a later date. DeMoisey, his lawyer at these depositions, complained that B&W was trying to turn a civil-discovery deposition into a criminal-discovery case. At one point, DeMoisey told the judge he was having a problem trying to advise his client about how to answer "this nebulous potpourri of possibilities that they pick and choose from whenever it suits their fancy."

Whatever was discussed, and whoever was present, the facts are that on April 15, Williams and Scruggs flew in Scruggs's private Learjet to Orlando, where Williams had deposited a copy of his documents with a friend for safekeeping. Williams arranged for the friend to bring the three boxes of documents from her house to the airport and have them transferred to the hold of Scruggs's plane. That way, technically, Williams did not personally hand over the documents and, therefore, technically was not in violation of the Louisville court order. Scruggs also found his own reason for not returning copies of the papers to B&W—which would have been the proper legal thing to do. Instead, he relied on an important exception in the law. If private company documents show evidence of fraud, then legal niceties covering their return to company headquarters, including the sanction of attorney-client privilege, go by the board. Scruggs asked Mike Moore and Don Barrett down to Pascagoula to join him when he opened the boxes and, in their minds at least, there was evidence of possible criminal wrongdoing.

Williams was later hired by Scruggs's own law firm. Scruggs also arranged for Williams to have a car and a small sailing boat. "I wanted to make sure Merrell was protected," Scruggs would say. "Merrell was penniless and very ill from his surgery. He was frightened. I wanted to make him secure in Mississippi from the retribution and the revenge of the tobacco industry, so I'm glad I have been able to play a role in that."

ON APRIL 14, the day before the document exchange in Orlando, seven CEOs of tobacco companies testified before the Waxman committee in Congress. One by one they took an oath and swore their belief that nicotine was not addictive. Now, with Williams's documents in hand, Scruggs told his colleagues, "These guys are toast." The official version of what happened next is that Scruggs showed the papers to Moore, who quickly understood that the documents suggested a massive fraud against the public health. The two men then hopped into Scuggs's Learjet and flew a copy of the documents to the Waxman committee in Washington. They actually flew to Washington with the papers on May 6, but a copy of the documents was with Waxman by the time they got there—courtesy of John Coale and Wendell Gauthier.

Uncertain how to handle the documents initially—after all, they were under a gag order—Scruggs and Barrett called Gauthier in New Orleans. Gauthier suggested Barrett bring the documents to the next Castano executive committee meeting and read out some of the better ones. There would be nothing wrong in that because the meeting included only lawyers and everything was privileged. They would then decide what could be done with them. Scruggs was not a member of the Castano group, but Barrett was. At the second meeting of the Castano executive committee in Coconut Grove in Miami on April 21, Barrett got up and started reading from the more sensitive documents. There was silence in the room. Barrett said he planned to give the documents to a state official (actually Mike Moore, although he didn't say so) and perhaps a newspaper in Biloxi. Coale, hearing the documents for the first time, grabbed Wendell and took him out into the hall. "You've got to get me a copy," he told him. "I can make hay with these in Washington. Taking them to a state official is crazy. This is information, and in D.C., information is currency." At the time, neither Coale nor anyone else outside the tightly knit Mississippi group of Scruggs, Moore, Barrett, and Motley knew that Moore was getting ready to file the first Medicaid lawsuit.

Gauthier and Coale copied a set of Barrett's documents. Neither Gauthier nor Coale knew at the time where they had come from, and the first time they heard the name Merrell Williams was several weeks later from another Phil Hilts story in *The New York Times.* Coale thought the documents had probably come from another case, maybe Cipollone in New Jersey. Coale had a contact in the office of Congressman Ron Wyden, Waxman's deputy on the committee. Coale called the contact and said, "These are the smoking guns you guys want." In return, Coale said he wanted a line to the committee hearings to know what was going on. The next day, Coale FedExed a copy of the documents to Wyden's office. Back in Washington, Coale then ran off several more copies and started sending them to the media. This was not yet the full set, only a few hundred pages of the best documents Barrett had pulled from the three boxes of material.

The first member of the media to get the documents was Phil Hilts, who reports on medical and science matters for *The New York Times.* In late April, he received a call in the *Times*'s Washington bureau from a government official who said he had internal documents about the tobacco industry. He asked Hilts to his house that evening; he didn't want to come to the *Times.* When Hilts arrived, the documents, about a hundred of them, were laid out on the official's dining-room table. They appeared genuine, and Hilts set about checking names, dates, and events. In fact, they were copies of the ones Coale had given to Wyden. On May 7, Hilts wrote what was to be the first of several newspaper stories about Williams's documents. This one was headlined, "Tobacco Company Was Silent of Hazards," and was based on the Addison Yeaman memo that had so shocked Scruggs, among others. Hilts's story said only that the documents had been stolen by a former employee of a law firm doing work for Brown & Williamson. Regional papers—including the Louisville *Courier-Journal*—picked up the story. It was Kentucky Derby day, and Williams got a call from his estranged wife, Sherry. "You're all over the papers where the horses normally are," she told him.

BROWN & WILLIAMSON tried desperately to plug the leak. At the company's request, the Superior Court of the District of Columbia issued subpoenas to Congressmen Waxman and Wyden to appear before B&W's attorneys "for the purpose of inspection and copying of all alleged B&W and affiliated companies' documents" in their possession. Members of the media who had written stories about the documents also received subpoenas, including *The New York Times, The Washington Post,* National Public Radio, CBS, and the *National Law Journal.* Waxman was stunned. "It was quite remarkable, not only had I never received such a summons, I had never heard of a committee chairman being subpoenaed by the target of its own investigation."

The congressmen protested to the D.C. court and Judge Harold Greene ruled that B&W could not order members of Congress to appear anywhere, and certainly not before the attorneys of a corporation under investigation by Congress. Judge Greene noted that the Constitution gave immunity to members of Congress "for any speech or debate in either House" and that the so-called speech or debate clause had been broadly read to include everything "generally done in a session of the House by one of its members in relation to the business before it" as well as "those matters that are an integral part of the deliberative and communicative processes." That included material gathered for the investigation, said Judge Greene, and he agreed with Waxman and Wyden that forcing them to release the documents could reveal the identity of their source to whom they had promised confidentiality. Breaking this promise would deter other sources from coming forward.

B&W had argued that it was only trying to recover stolen documents, but Judge Greene wasn't buying that explanation. As no one had been found guilty of any criminal activity and the congressmen had not been involved in the acquisition of the documents, Greene focused instead on Williams, the whistle-blower. Here was a man trying to make public documents that were a matter of concern for the public health. That's what the case was about, he said. B&W's "simple yet ingenious strategy" of concentrating on the theft of the documents could have been obscuring a public health threat. He concluded, "One may well doubt, to put it charitably, that B&W would be mounting a tremendous and costly effort in Kentucky and in the District of Columbia, in proceedings against members of a Congressional committee and against the mass of the media, if the documents at issue did not represent the proverbial 'smoking gun' evidencing the company's long-held and long-suppressed knowledge that its product constitutes a serious health hazard." It was apparent, he said, that B&W was using the subpoenas "to intimidate and, in a sense, to punish" both Williams and the congressmen for their efforts to reveal the truth. The D.C. court should have no part in "so high-handed a course of conduct, and one so patently crafted to harass those who would reveal facts concerning B&W's knowledge of the health hazards inherent in tobacco." For its part, the media claimed First Amendment privileges and the subpoenas against them were not pursued, but the threat of legal action remained against anyone who revealed the contents of the documents.

MEANWHILE, Gauthier, Scruggs, and the fast-growing band of plaintiffs' lawyers joining the antitobacco bandwagon were thinking of ways in which the Merrell Williams documents could be cleared for use as evidence in court. In January 1995, Ron Motley, the most persistent and energetic document hunter of the plaintiffs' bar, was the first to refer to them in a court motion. Motley was representing Burl Butler, a nonsmoking, clean-living, God-fearing barber from the small town of Laurel, Mississippi (population 9,000). In 1992, Butler had been diagnosed with lung cancer, which he claimed he had contracted from the cigarette smoke of his clients in the barber shop. He sued R. J. Reynolds, Philip Morris, Brown & Williamson, and ten other companies, claiming personal injury, fraud, and negligence.

As in the Horton case, industry lawyers and private investigators descended on Laurel. Before they had finished, everyone who had ever known Burl, or been into his barber's shop, his church, or his home, had been interviewed, and in the midst of chemotherapy, even Butler himself had undergone four days of depositions—the whole operation designed to find out if there was anything in his life that might have caused his lung cancer other than the smoke from his clients' cigarettes. The company sought information about everything from his wife Ava's recipe for gravy to the types of chemical fertilizers Butler might have been exposed to while plowing his father's farm with mules as a child. One of the defenses used by the tobacco companies is that cancer is a "lifestyle" disease—people who are "risk-taking personalities" tend to develop cancers more easily than the shy and retiring types. The companies noted that Butler liked to hunt and, as if these might be factors, worked with power tools and had been known to eat red meat. The tobacco lawyers found that cancer ran in Butler's family and they also discovered traces of cancer-forming fibers of talc in Butler's lungs. In the past, Butler's lawyers would probably have ended the suit right there; to pursue a case where talc, not tobacco, might be the cancer-forming agent looked even harder to win than many of the cases that had been lost. But the Merrell Williams papers had given the lawyers new confidence. Instead of dropping the tobacco companies, Motley added the talc companies to the suit.

Whatever had caused his cancer, Butler was dying from it, and tobacco lawyers wanted to be as close as they could to that event. On the day Butler died, a helicopter hovered over his house for no apparent reason and the unconfirmed story is that it was flown by agents for the tobacco company who were waiting for the ambulance to arrive to take away the body so that the company could be present at the autopsy. The company did ask to be present at Butler's autopsy but later withdrew the request, apparently deciding that it wouldn't look so good from the public relations viewpoint. Coincidentally, Butler died on May 7, 1994, the same day *The New York Times* published the first report on the Merrell Williams documents. His claim was continued by his wife.

Motley wanted to use several of the Williams documents in his case and argued in the brief that he should be able to because they had already been widely distributed by the media and also by the University of California at San Francisco, which had placed a full set of the documents in its library. Until Motley mentioned the university library, it was not generally known there was a copy in the archives. Certainly, Brown & Williamson had not known copies of the documents were there, and they lost no time in trying to get them back—and trying to discover how they had got there in the first place.

Within days of Motley's brief being filed with the Mississippi court, the prevailing air of calm and scholarship at the university library was suddenly disrupted by the presence of two strange men seen hanging around outside the library's special collections department, where the documents were stored. They were recording researchers coming and going. One of the men accompanied a woman colleague into the read-

THE DRAMA TEACHER 73

ing room to look at the papers. It turned out she was a paralegal from the local law firm representing Brown & Williamson. The men were private detectives. As the archivist, Florie Berger, came to work one morning, one of them said to the other, "That's her." Berger was so upset she called the university lawyer's office, claiming the men, whoever they were, were intimidating her. University officials threatened to have campus police remove the detectives. They were withdrawn that day, but reappeared a few days later.

B&W filed a claim in San Francisco Superior Court to have the documents returned on the grounds that they had been stolen. The company sent Ernie Clements, who had been Williams's supervisor at the document room at Wyatt, Tarrant in Louisville, to review the archive collection. He claimed all of them were confidential. The university refused to give them back, citing the company's "cloak and dagger" operation as well as the academic and public interest value of the documents. Arguing that the documents had already been well aired in the media, the university lawyers said that to take them away from public view would be like "using a tin cup to bail water on the *Titanic*." Eventually, the two sides reached an agreement that the documents would not be available to the public until the claim could be resolved. The university added that the documents had been sent anonymously to a member of the faculty.

That faculty member was Stan Glantz, a longtime antitobacco professor of medicine. Glantz is the very model of a sixties campus professor—witty, slightly rumpled, somewhat mischievous, and unashamedly political. He still drives the Dodge Dart convertible he bought in 1969. He trained as an engineer, actually a rocket scientist, and he had helped put men on the moon as a member of the space agency. He earned his doctorate at Stanford in engineering and economics, studying the heart muscle and other pump mechanisms. He is an editor of the *Journal of the American College of Cardiology,* one of the world's leading heart journals, and he cares deeply about the public health, particularly that part of it which has been so consistently damaged by tobacco. At some point in his heart research, he looked at drugs that affect the pump rate, including nicotine. That's how he came across the tobacco companies, and the more he learned about how they had concealed their own research and what they knew about nicotine's effects on the heart, the more he began to despise them. Like other academics of his generation, he decided to step beyond the laboratory and the classroom and, in his case, devote his life to exposing the way the tobacco companies have consistently lied about their product.

For their part, the tobacco companies call him a zealot, a derogatory term for any scientist because it suggests a biased and messianic approach. On the other hand, it does describes the gusto with which Glantz goes about his work. He is a crusader, a progressive academic who believes fervently that big corporations must be made to act in the best interests of the public, and not simply of their shareholders. In the case of tobacco, this means stricter government regulation of the industry. To this end, Glantz has lectured, written papers, and attended conferences all over the world. In recent years, he had been interested in the effects of secondhand smoke—whether nonsmokers can be seriously harmed by being in the presence of others who smoke. He has also exposed the industry's support of so-called grassroots smokers' campaigns, and their funding and lobbying efforts in local state legislatures.

To Glantz, May 12, 1994, was a turning point in his mission. A Federal Express box containing four thousand pages of Merrell Williams's stolen documents arrived at his office on the San Francisco campus at eleven o'clock in the morning. He had no idea where the box had come from. The sender's name was "Mr. Butts," the cartoon character in "Doonesbury." No return address was given but, although Glantz didn't bother to investigate who Mr. Butts was, he thought it was probably Dick Daynard, from Northeastern University. So did B&W. The company tried to depose Daynard to find out if he had copies of the documents and whether Williams had violated his gag order in giving the professor another set. But the redoubtable Daynard was not to be intimidated and refused to comply with the court order. He argued that copies of the documents had been in circulation for almost a year and he could supply no material evidence. Moreover, he ran an information collection center for lawyers and public health officials and whatever information he obtained was private and of vital concern to government and congressional inquiries and, therefore, should be accorded First Amendment protection. B&W wanted the Massachusetts court to hold Daynard in contempt and compel him to appear, but the court declined. In fact, Mr. Butts was not Daynard; it was Don Barrett. He had sent a copy of the documents to Glantz after Scruggs had delivered them to the Waxman committee on Capitol Hill.

Glantz immediately saw how embarrassing the documents were to the industry, and to B&W especially. Many of them were about nicotine addiction. Others detailed a sophisticated legal and public relations strategy to ensure that the tobacco companies kept chalking up victories in court. His first thought was to send them to colleagues working in these areas, but word soon got out through the antitobacco grapevine that Glantz, as well as Waxman's committee and the media, had copies of the documents. Because there was no single source of the documents, no one was quite sure—especially Brown & Williamson—whether anyone had a full set. Academics and reporters began arriving at the university to see if Glantz's box of documents contained papers or memos that they hadn't seen before, or read about in the media. His tiny office was hopelessly inadequate as a viewing room, so he decided to put them in the archives of the university library and there they stayed, available to anyone who cared to take a look, until Brown & Williamson discovered them.

B&W's attempt to block publication of the documents faced the same heavy burden imposed on all suits involving prior restraint; unless publication can be shown to directly endanger the lives of citizens or national security, courts have been reluctant to grant such requests. The university thought it was on solid legal ground despite the fact that academic institutions had rarely gone to court over the right to publish sensitive material. On June 29, the California Supreme Court rejected the request by B&W to stop the university library from making the documents available to the public. By coincidence, it was the twenty-fourth anniversary of the Supreme Court's decision allowing publication of the Pentagon Papers. It was quite a coup for the library and for the university legal department, whose chief counsel, Christopher Patti, said, "The university felt that it shouldn't bend to that kind of pressure. The feeling was that this is an issue that was central to the university's purpose and charter." The library put them on the World Wide Web portion of the Internet on a page located at http://www.library.ucsf.edu/tobacco and also made the collection available on CD-ROM. Within a year, half a million people had visited the web page. Floyd Abrams, the New York First Amendment lawyer who specializes in the media, observed, "If Daniel Ellsberg were to have come into possession of the Pentagon Papers today, he would not need to find a newspaper to publish them." Of the library affair, Stan Glantz observed scornfully, "We basically told them that book burning went out in the thirties."

After a second failed effort to plug the leak, B&W issued a statement charging the court's decision was an invitation to employees to steal company documents and that it allowed plaintiffs' lawyers to sidestep the normal process of pretrial discovery. "This decision invites any person to steal documents and launder them" through a library so that "plaintiffs' lawyers can then argue that the documents are public," the company said. Indeed, that was exactly the core of Ron Motley's brief to the Mississippi court in the Butler case. Merrell Williams's documents were now available to be used in evidence against the tobacco industry.

4

THE PERFECT PLEASURE

A cigarette is the perfect type of a perfect pleasure. It is
exquisite, and it leaves one unsatisfied. What more can one
want?

—*Oscar Wilde,* The Picture of Dorian Gray

All we would want then is a larger bag to carry the money to
the bank.

—*from BAT,* "Structured Creativity Group" (undated)

I F A SINGLE IMAGE symbolizes the Third Wave of the tobacco wars,
it is surely the chief executive officers of America's seven largest
tobacco companies standing side by side, with their right hands
raised, swearing to tell the truth about smoking to a committee of the
U.S. Congress.

On the morning of April 14, 1994, having turned down many
invitations over the years to appear before Congress, the seven CEOs
lined up before Henry Waxman's Health and Environment Subcommittee and were asked to state their opinion for the record. "Yes or no, do
you believe nicotine is addictive?"

William Campbell of Philip Morris was first. "I believe nicotine is
not addictive," he stated loud and clear.

Then came James Johnston of R. J. Reynolds. "Mr. Congressman,
cigarettes and nicotine clearly do not meet the classic definition of
addiction. There is no intoxication."

He was followed by Joseph Taddeo, of U.S. Tobacco, the leading
manufacturer of chewing tobacco. "I don't believe that nicotine or our
products are addictive," he said.

Three more executives, Andrew Tisch of the Lorillard Tobacco Company, Edward Horrigan of the Liggett Group, and Thomas Sandefur of Brown & Williamson, each repeated the sentence, "I believe that nicotine is not addictive."

The last was Donald Johnston, of the American Tobacco Company. "And I, too, believe that nicotine is not addictive," he said.

No one had expected them to say anything else, of course. After a century of claiming they sold cigarettes containing nicotine "for taste and pleasure," and after at least thirty years of denying what everyone who had ever worked in the tobacco industry knew well, namely that most people continue to smoke cigarettes because of a sometimes uncontrollable desire for a shot of nicotine, the CEOs were not about to change their story. Moreover, corporate custom demands not that a company spokesmen tell the whole truth about the product, but only that they tell a corporate version of the truth cleared by the board of directors and legal counsel. For some listeners there were echoes of Alice's encounter with Humpty Dumpty: "When *I* use a word it means just what I chose it to mean—neither more nor less."

Mr. Campbell of Philip Morris was personally affronted at even being asked to consider the question. "Smokers are not drug users or drug addicts, and we do not appreciate or accept being characterized as such," he complained. He wanted Congress to know that he was one of 50 million smokers in America and, as far as he was concerned, nicotine was no more addictive than coffee. "Mr. Chairman, coffee contains caffeine and few people seem to enjoy coffee that does not. Does that make coffee a drug? Are coffee drinkers drug addicts? I think not."

Mr. Johnston of R. J. Reynolds spoke eloquently about nicotine playing "an essential role in the overall smoking experience." Nicotine, in his view, had many pleasing properties, none of which should be regarded in the same light as hard drugs. "It enhances the taste of the smoke and the way it feels on the smoker's palate and it contributes to the overall smoking enjoyment," he said. Nicotine could not be put into the same class as heroin and cocaine. "You don't need to be a trained scientist to see this. . . . All you need to do is to ask and honestly answer two simple questions. First, would you rather board a plane with a pilot who just smoked a cigarette, one with a pilot who had just had a couple of beers, or snorted cocaine, or shot heroin, or popped some pills? Second, if cigarettes were addictive could almost 43 million Americans have quit smoking, almost all of them on their own without any outside help? The answers are obvious, and that is precisely my point. Cigarettes are clearly not in the same class as addictive, mind-altering [drugs] like heroin and cocaine." The term "addictive" had been misused, he said. "The allegation that smoking cigarettes is addictive is part of a growing and disturbing trend that has destroyed the meaning of the term by characterizing [as such] virtually any enjoyable activity whether it is eating sweets, drinking coffee, playing video games or watching TV. This defies common sense." His written company statement to Congress added that smoking was no more addictive than Twinkies.

Thomas Sandefur of Brown & Williamson agreed. Use of the word "addiction" was far too loose, he said. It had been used to describe everything from an enslavement to hard drugs to an inability to lose weight or watch less television. The former Surgeon General C. Everett Koop, well known as being antitobacco, had himself proclaimed in 1982 that children were "addicted" to video games. As more than half of American smokers had quit—90 percent of them without help— Sandefur declared that "equating cigarettes and hard drugs is nothing more than rhetoric."

Waxman and his colleagues protested. To compare tobacco to common foods was "a calculated attempt to trivialize" the effects of smoking, objected Waxman. "You know and I know that Twinkies don't kill a single American a year. The difference between cigarettes and Twinkies . . . is death."

Ron Wyden from Oregon was struck by the obvious, "that people who have no vested financial interest in this particular subject say that nicotine is addictive" [he mentioned the National Institute on Drug Abuse, the Surgeon General, the American Medical Association, and the World Health Organization] "and the people who have a vested financial interest in saying otherwise argue that it's not."

But it was John Bryant, an old-fashioned Texas Democrat, a believer in strong government intervention as long as it doesn't affect the price of oil and natural gas, who struck at the heart of the matter. "It is the case, is it not," he said, adopting a prosecutorial tone, "that your usual defense is the smoker smoked voluntarily as a matter of free choice and, therefore, assumed the risk and you are not responsible? Is that not the case?"

"That's correct, sir," Mr. Johnston of R. J. Reynolds replied.

"It is also true that your argument that smokers continue to smoke as a matter of their own free choice is a key part of the defense. Is that not right?" asked Congressman Bryant.

"I wouldn't characterize it as essential," Mr. Johnston answered. "It is part of the defense, yes, part of the American record."

"Is it not the case that that defense would be wiped out if you conceded here today or [in] any forum that nicotine and your products are addictive?"

Johnston was caught off balance. "Mr. Congressman, I don't know. Addiction is a term that is—"

"We all know what it means," Bryant shot back. "Would it not be the case that if you conceded here today that nicotine was addictive and your products were addictive, that you would no longer be able to claim that the sick or dead individual smoked as a matter of free choice? Is that not the case?"

"I can tell you what juries believe," said Johnston. "Juries usually believe, because of the common definition of addiction, that the person was addicted but the person can quit."

"The fact of the matter is," retorted Bryant, "that you cannot sit here today and say to us that people made a free choice to smoke if you also concede that once a person starts, they are addicted. Now, you cannot do that. So, it is very clear that you all have an economic interest in telling the American people and in sustaining the idea and saying and not deviating from the assertion that your products are not addictive. I think that is a matter of logic."

"I respectfully disagree with you. . . . Mr. Congressman, I'm not a litigation lawyer or expert," pleaded Mr. Johnston.

"But I hope you are a logical thinker."

"I am, I hope."

Congressman Bryant then observed that when all the CEOs replied to the addiction question in virtually the same way it raised the question of whether their response had been rehearsed. He asked Horrigan, of Liggett, "Did your lawyer tell you that you needed to affirm that you did not believe nicotine is addictive?"

"No one had to tell me anything about my opinions about addiction, sir," replied Horrigan.

Bryant then asked, "Did this group [of CEOs] discuss the need to state clearly in the same words as you all did . . . that nicotine is not addictive?"

Campbell: "Absolutely not."

Horrigan: "That's absolutely outrageous."

But Bryant would not be stopped. "It is very difficult for me," he said, "to find you at this table characterizing anything as outrageous after seven apparently intelligent people have stood here and told the American people, 250 million of whom know better, that cigarettes are not addictive. What could be more ridiculous?"

IN NEW ORLEANS, Pascagoula, Minneapolis, and San Francisco, Wendell Gauthier, Dick Scruggs, Mike Ciresi, Elizabeth Cabraser, and their comrades of the plaintiffs' bar celebrated. In Washington, D.C., John Coale, who was fast becoming the man the media turned to for quick reactions to the growing litigation, joked, "We were concerned about statute of limitations—when did they last say nicotine was not addictive?" Of course, they had never said anything different. Gauthier himself would forecast, "With the documents we have, there's no way this industry can stand before a jury and say, 'We want you to return a verdict that says smoking isn't addictive.' It's just not going to happen."

The Merrell Williams papers demonstrated that the research Brown & Williamson and its British parent, BAT, had conducted into nicotine more than thirty years earlier gave them a sophisticated and scientifically accurate understanding of nicotine pharmacology, including an explicit recognition of nicotine's addictiveness. There was evidence from other companies, Philip Morris and R. J. Reynolds, showing they also fully recognized that the pharmacological action of nicotine was the main reason why many people continued to smoke cigarettes. There was nothing surprising about this in-house research. Indeed, it would have been surprising to find out that the companies had not carried out such basic work on their product. But the Williams papers provided ample evidence that the companies had covered up their understanding of nicotine's actions on the body, using euphemisms such as "taste" and "satisfaction" to explain nicotine's hold. There was evidence, too, that although the scientific community generally referred to nicotine as a drug, the tobacco companies had censored use of that word in their scientific papers, substituting "compound" instead. They had also suppressed publication of scientific papers that discussed aspects of nicotine's addictiveness, or "dependence" or "habituation."

Gauthier and his colleagues were now prepared to go into court and argue in front of a jury something that every medical scientist, every doctor, every lawyer, every public health official, every person who had ever smoked and most of those who had not, had known perfectly well for decades: nicotine is addictive. Billions of dollars, not to mention the health of smokers, were riding on the outcome of this debate. Once a jury had declared nicotine was addictive, the industry would lose their first line of defense: that smokers choose to smoke.

OVER THE YEARS, medical science has struggled with the definition of addiction. What should the criteria be? Does the drug have to be able to intoxicate the user to the point of impairment, like alcohol? Should it always exhibit unmistakable withdrawal symptoms, as heroin does? Does it have to show "tolerance"—which means the person who is taking the drug keeps wanting more? Should any drug that causes uncontrollable antisocial behavior be classified as addictive? This was a genuine and ongoing debate.

The tobacco companies could not participate in this scientific debate for fear that they would be stuck with a definition that risked their first line of defense. Instead, they chose "common sense": to any reasonable person, nicotine is not addictive because it does not possess the properties of illegal narcotics such as heroin and cocaine. As Campbell of Philip Morris put it in his testimony, "I have a commonsense definition of addiction which tells me . . . basically [as a smoker] I can function in quite a normal way, my judgment is not impaired." In essence, people who smoke cigarettes do not become intoxicated.

Common sense would also tell you, the industry said, that the withdrawal symptoms of nicotine are not the same as those of heroin. Smokers don't get convulsions if they are deprived of cigarettes. They don't steal or murder for a smoke. And look how many smokers actually do give up smoking without help—millions every year. As for the question of tolerance, addicts of hard drugs like heroin and cocaine can never have enough. They always crave more. Smokers of cigarettes reach a certain level of consumption—you hear them say "I'm a one-pack-a-day or a two-pack-a-day person"—and that's it. They never smoke more for the rest of their lives.

Finally, cigarettes are legal, sold without prescription, consumed by the hundreds of billions every year (485 billion at the last count), said the companies. Smoking is part of human culture, celebrated in literature, opera, film, and art. Jean Cocteau had written, "One must not forget that the pack of cigarettes, the ceremony that extracts them, lights the lighter, and that strange cloud which penetrates us and which our nostrils puff, have with powerful charms seduced and conquered the world." Smoking is associated with sex, pleasure, virility, women's liberation, Satan, death, and the gods. The desire to smoke did not begin with the cigarette companies, whose enterprise is barely a century old. It cannot be attributed to the $6 billion they currently spend on advertising and promoting cigarettes.

Concluding their case, the tobacco companies pointed to the words of Dr. Luther Terry who, as Surgeon General, was charged with the task of adjudicating on this issue by President Kennedy. In his 1964 report he concluded: "Smokers . . . usually develop some degree of dependence upon the practice, some to the point where significant emotional disturbances occur if they are deprived of its use. . . . In medical and scientific terminology the practice should be labeled *habituation* to distinguish it clearly from *addiction,* since the biological effects of tobacco, like coffee and other caffeine-containing beverages, betel morsel chewing and the like, are not comparable to those produced by morphine, alcohol, barbiturates and many other potent addicting drugs."

So who are the real addicts? According to the tobacco industry, as Dr. Terry said, "It is generally accepted among psychiatrists that addiction to potent drugs is based upon serious personality defects from underlying psychologic or psychiatric disorders which may become manifest in other ways if the drugs are removed." America's 50 million smokers surely could not be put into this category. The basic problem with these conclusions is that they are at least thirty years out of date. Medical science has moved on.

SECONDS AFTER a smoker inhales, the nicotine is absorbed into the bloodstream and sets up a biological chain reaction in the brain. Nicotine acts like a neurotransmitter, the natural chemical messengers in the brain that send information from one nerve cell to the next. Nerve signals travel electrically and at junctions between the nerve cells must cross gaps called synapses. The natural neurotransmitters are released by the nerve cell on one side of the gap and dock on the other side with a receptor protein. In the instant of pleasure, the signal from one of these messengers, acetylcholine, triggers the release of another messenger, dopamine, which stimulates nerve cells involved with pleasure. Nicotine mimics acetylcholine and grabs some of the nerve sites normally used by it. So a gulp of tobacco smoke containing nicotine triggers a rush of pleasurable dopamine.

The natural messenger, acetylcholine, is absorbed by its receptor protein and then promptly released and reabsorbed by the nerve cell that set it free. But nicotine gets stuck on the protein, preventing the receptor from working again for a while. Thus, nicotine gives a quick buzz, after which the stimulation declines gradually until the receptors are freed again.

The brain cells quickly adapt to having sites blocked by nicotine by generating more sites. When the nicotine eventually unblocks these sites, there are then more sites available than normal and the result is overstimulation, which causes a person to become irritable and cranky—a symptom of nicotine withdrawal. When smokers say smoking "relaxes" them, what they are actually saying is that the new nicotine "hit" from a fresh cigarette is treating their nicotine withdrawal symptoms.

The paradox of the nicotine "fix" is that it can be either a "high" or a "low": nicotine can act as a stimulant, increasing attentiveness, heart rate, and blood pressure, but it can also act as a depressant, inhibiting the flow of information between nerve cells.

As the nervous system adapts to nicotine, a smoker slowly increases the number of cigarettes smoked and hence the level of nicotine in the blood—until the number of sites stimulated and blocked by nicotine is balanced by the new sites made available by the neurotransmitters. The smoker has reached a "target level," which he then needs to maintain by keeping up his level of nicotine.

When the smoker goes to sleep, the nicotine level drops dramatically—about forty-five minutes after a cigarette is smoked the concentration of nicotine in the blood is half what it was—which is why smokers often talk about the first cigarette in the morning being the best. The length of time between a smoker waking up and his first cigarette is a measure of the severity of his dependence. More than one-third of smokers reach for their first cigarette within ten minutes of waking; nearly two-thirds within the first half hour. When a smoker stops smoking, it takes one or two weeks for his brain chemistry to return to normal. Some studies suggest long-term smoking can make near-permanent changes in the brain.

So, WHY DID the 1964 Surgeon General's report say smoking was a nicotine "habit," not an "addiction"? At the time, the two nongovernmental authorities then charged with classifying drugs—the World Health Organization and the American Psychiatric Association—used two categories, "habituating" and "addicting." Drug "addiction," said the WHO, was a state of periodic or chronic intoxication produced by the repeated consumption of a drug that creates an overpowering need, or compulsion, to increase the dose and a psychological dependence, with detrimental effect on the individual and society. Included in this group were the opiates and barbiturates. "Habituation," on the other hand, was a desire but not a compulsion, with little or no tendency to increase the dose, some degree of dependence but no withdrawal symptoms, and with possible detrimental effects on the individual but not on society. Cocaine, amphetamines, and nicotine were included in this group.

In the 1964 report, the section dealing with nicotine addictiveness was a mere five pages out of a 387-page review of the scientific literature on smoking and health. Dr. Terry had made a point of inviting the tobacco companies to submit names of experts so that the report should be seen to be fair. The addiction section was written by Maurice Seevers, chairman of the pharmacology department at the University of Michigan, whose name had been put forward to the Surgeon General by the tobacco companies.

Seevers was an expert on habit-forming drugs. From the start, he dismayed some of his colleagues on the committee writing the report by refusing to label nicotine an addictive substance, but they had to concede they did not have his expertise. As one of them acknowledged subsequently, he was "one tough hombre," who would not even concede that the issue of the effects of nicotine was controversial.

The key distinction, according to Seevers, was that hard-drug takers can harm society; nicotine only affects the individual. Seevers relied on the then generally accepted view of psychiatrists that addiction to potent drugs is based upon personality defects; true addicts are abnormal. A smoker in withdrawal from nicotine was not likely to become a burden on society. (Of course, he could find his fix at the local store. Seevers did not discuss the most obvious difference between hard drugs and tobacco—that the first are illegal, and tobacco is not.) Seevers's report did not explore another aspect of addiction: while some tobacco smokers were able to quit with seeming ease, others could not give up—much like any addict. Indeed, roughly two-thirds of current tobacco smokers have tried at least once, and one-third try in any given year. The relapse rate for tobacco use is remarkably similar to that of heroin. But apparently Seevers wanted a clear distinction between habit forming and addictiveness. The tobacco companies could not have wished for a better result.

The distinction was dropped shortly after Dr. Terry's report. To move the whole debate away from the moral and social issues associated with the term addiction, a new term, "dependence," was adopted. The key change for the American Psychiatric Association was the new medical description of nicotine-withdrawal syndrome, which included the craving for the drug, irritability, frustration or anger, anxiety, difficulty concentrating, restlessness, decreased heart rate, and increased appetite or weight gain.

Twenty-four years later, the report of the then Surgeon General of the United States, Dr. C. Everett Koop, stated boldly that nicotine was addictive and the "pharmacologic and behavioral processes that determine tobacco addiction are similar to those that determine addiction to drugs such as heroin and cocaine."

In the preface to his 639-page report, Dr. Koop wrote, "Some people may have difficulty in accepting the notion that tobacco is addicting because it is a legal product. The word 'addiction' is strongly associated with illegal drugs such as cocaine and heroin. However . . . the [biological] processes that determine tobacco addiction are similar to those that determine addiction to other drugs, including illegal drugs."

The central element of all forms of drug addiction, he said, was that the user's behavior is largely controlled by a psychoactive (mood changing) substance. Other criteria included compulsive use of the drug, repeated self-administration, "reinforcement" because of the drug's rewarding properties, and "tolerance," whereby a given dose of a drug produces less effect or increasing doses are required to achieve a specified intensity of response. Finally, absence of the drug produces withdrawal symptoms. Nicotine was such a drug, the report concluded.

The industry immediately claimed the change was motivated by politics, not science. Dr. Koop had "moved the goal posts," complained R. J. Reynolds. But the problem for the tobacco companies was that virtually the entire medical science and psychiatric community supported Koop's conclusions.

The tobacco companies were left with a handful of psychologists who had been promoting the idea that people smoked according to their personality or their genetic makeup and not because of a chemical addiction to nicotine. Extroverts smoke, introverts tend not to, was the message. To call nicotine addictive merely on medical science criteria of what happens to the brain was not a meaningful statement, merely a hypothesis, according to these researchers. In place of the "addiction hypothesis," a small group of psychologists proposed what they called the "resource hypothesis": that smokers use cigarettes primarily as a "tool" or "resource" that provides them with psychological benefits, such as increased mental alertness, reduced anxiety, and an ability to cope with stress.

The legal departments of the tobacco companies had often relied on the work of a British behavioral psychologist, Hans Eysenck, who argued that smoking and lung cancer were related to genetic makeup:

that people were cancer-prone because of their genes, and their genes also somehow caused them to smoke. The companies also relied on the provocative writings of another English psychologist, David Warburton of the University of Reading. Attacking Koop's 1988 report, Warburton argued that nicotine fit only a few of the new criteria agreed upon by the American Psychiatric Association and the WHO. Koop, he charged, was ignoring "the discrepancies in his enthusiasm to find criteria to compare nicotine with heroin and cocaine use."

Two R. J. Reynolds scientists, John Robinson and Walter Pritchard, working at the company's behavioral research and development center in Winston-Salem, North Carolina, joined the attack on Koop. They concentrated on the addiction criterion of intoxication—as their boss James Johnston would do at the Waxman hearings. If a drug did not result in intoxication, it could not be termed addictive, they said. Intoxication should be the key point in distinguishing between habituating and addicting drugs. They also argued that nicotine did not fit the "compulsive use" criterion since many smokers can do without a cigarette for long periods.

Most importantly, however, they said, "Common sense tells us that nicotine is *not* [their italics] like heroin, cocaine or any other 'classic' addicting drug. . . . One does not have to be a trained behavioral scientist to come to this conclusion. Simply ask, and honestly answer, the question as to how many people would board a plane piloted by someone who had just consumed an addicting drug (alcohol, cocaine, barbiturates) versus a plane piloted by someone who had just had a cup of coffee and smoked a cigarette." (Johnston would use the same words in his congressional testimony.)

Other behavioral psychologists, however, agreed with the new definition of nicotine as a dependence-producing, or addictive, drug. Intoxication was not central to dependence, they argued. In the end, it was a matter of the industry's out-of-date, scientifically frivolous, "common sense" public position against basic biology. The companies knew the difference, of course.

THE MERRELL WILLIAMS PAPERS told plaintiffs' lawyers like Gauthier that in private, three decades ago, the company scientists had never bothered with the semantic distinction between habituation and addiction. Sir Charles Ellis, the chief scientist at BAT, the Brown & Williamson parent company, had said in a 1962 in-house conference that smoking "is a habit of addiction . . ." A 1963 BAT research paper entitled "The Fate of Nicotine in the Body" begins, "[Nicotine] appears to be intimately involved with the phenomena of tobacco habituation (tolerance) and/or addiction." Brown & Williamson's own chief counsel, Addison Yeaman, wrote in a 1963 memo, "We are, then, in the business of selling nicotine, an addictive product."

But toward the end of the '60s there were hints that company legal departments were at work. In a draft report of a 1967 BAT research conference, company scientists listed some "main" assumptions—among them, "There is a minimum level of nicotine. Smoking is an addictive habit attributable to nicotine. . . ." The draft notes that these assumptions were made "without any attempt to justify them [or] to agree on their correctness at this time," and then a handwritten edit on the document changes the phrase "an addictive habit" to "a habit."

While the companies in public used the words "taste," "satisfaction," and "impact" to describe the effects of nicotine, in their private research papers they talked about the pharmacology of nicotine, its effects on the brain, and the "need" of the smoker for those effects. People smoked primarily for their dose of nicotine. "The cigarette should be conceived not as a product but as a package. The product is nicotine. . . . Think of the cigarette as a storage container for one day's supply of nicotine," wrote William Dunn, Philip Morris's research scientist, in 1972. "As with eating and copulating, so it is with smoking," Dunn wrote. "The physiological effect serves as the primary incentive; all other incentives are secondary." Another BAT study in 1976 referred to "Low Need" and "High Need" nicotine smokers. "The indications are that cigarettes delivering around 1.0 to 1.5 mg [of nicotine] are better suited to Low Need clusters, while cigarettes delivering 1.5 to 2.0 are better suited to High Need clusters."

In the early '70s, the tobacco companies explored the possibility of finding a replacement for nicotine that would not cause health problems. For example, the companies were aware of the harmful effects of nicotine on the cardiovascular system—it increases pulse rate and contracts blood vessels—and they would try to find a chemical substitute, a so-called analogue, that would mimic the effects of the drug on the brain without affecting the blood supply.

In 1980, a young behavioral psychologist named Victor DeNoble went to work for Philip Morris at the company's research labs in Richmond, Virginia. His job was to find that analogue, and he and his co-worker, Paul Mele, set up a series of experiments on rats. They linked the rats to a catheter so that if they pressed a lever they would get a shot of nicotine directly into the heart. The rats kept pressing the lever, showing that nicotine acted as a "reinforcer"; that one dose was pleasurable enough for them to want another. In fact, the rats would press the lever several times for one injection, showing how great was their need. The rats also developed the condition known as "tolerance" to the drug; as time went on, they needed more nicotine to achieve the same effect. The work was not duplicated in outside laboratories until 1989.

The implications of the study for Philip Morris were immense—even though, as DeNoble was the first to point out, it was a single observation in rats and it was not possible to project the results to humans with any scientific certainty. All one could say was that nicotine had what behaviorists like DeNoble call "an abuse liability." But Philip Morris didn't want to take any chances. Security at DeNoble's lab was tightened. Fresh supplies of animals would be brought in at night, or early in the morning, to minimize questions about the work from other technicians. DeNoble and Mele were not allowed to discuss their work at the company's research committee meetings. In the fall of 1982, DeNoble and Mele wanted to publish their results. They submitted a paper ("Nicotine as a Positive Reinforcer in Rats") to their superiors for permission to publish. Approval was given and they sent a draft to the journal *Psychopharmacology*. They also sent an abstract to a meeting of the American Psychological Association. At the time, Rose Cipollone had just filed her product liability suit against three cigarette makers, including Philip Morris, charging them with failing to warn her properly of the addictive nature of nicotine and other harmful effects of smoking.

Suddenly, DeNoble and Mele were summoned to Philip Morris corporate headquarters in New York to give a presentation of the results to their corporate bosses. They were met at the airport by one of the company's chauffeur-driven limousines and whisked to the Park Avenue headquarters; there they gave the presentation and had lunch in the executive dining room. It all seemed to go well and on the way back in the plane, DeNoble and Mele agreed they had done a good job. Only one of the questions asked by a senior executive had bothered them. He had asked something like, "Why should I risk a billion dollar industry on rats pressing a lever to get nicotine?"

The two researchers thought no more of the remark until a few weeks later when DeNoble was told by his superiors that his laboratory was generating information the company did not want: the results De-Noble and Mele were getting could be used against the company in lawsuits. DeNoble was told to withdraw his paper from publication, although it had already passed peer review and been accepted. He protested to no avail, and not wanting to lose his job, he complied with the company's request.

At the same time, three corporation lawyers moved into the room next door to DeNoble and Mele and started going through their files and photocopying their research papers. They also wanted certain words in the report changed. "I had said, you know, nicotine is a drug that is widely used . . . and they wanted the word drug changed to com-pound," DeNoble would say later. "We were not allowed to refer to nicotine or anything in tobacco as a drug."

Next, Shep Pollack, the president and chief operating officer of Philip Morris, flew down from New York with his attorney to see for himself what was going on at the lab. DeNoble set up the experiment, the rats pressed levers for nicotine, Pollack peered into the cages. So did his lawyer. The lawyer asked whether this test procedure was the same one that would be used by a government agency to demonstrate addiction, and DeNoble answered that it was. The lawyer shook his head and walked away.

A few months later, in April 1984, days before Rose Cipollone's lawyers filed a sweeping discovery request for Philip Morris research documents, DeNoble was called to the office of his superior and fired. He was told to shut down his experiments, kill the rats, and clear out his office. When he turned up at the research center the next day, he couldn't get into the building because his pass had been canceled. DeNoble and Mele were given new offices and provided with secretarial support to look for other jobs.

A week after he was fired, DeNoble returned to the lab and was astonished to find it had literally disappeared. "The equipment was gone, the cages were gone, all the data was gone. There were empty rooms."

Both DeNoble and Mele eventually found other jobs and still wanted to publish their work. The problem was that, like all other employees at Philip Morris, they had signed confidentiality agreements covering the work they had done for the company. At the end of 1985, they decided to take the risk and resubmit their paper to *Psychopharmacology*. They also delivered a paper on rat tolerance to nicotine to the Federation of American Societies for Experimental Biology. Philip Morris found out and sent the researchers a letter warning them that they had breached their confidentiality agreement. DeNoble was told that if anything about his work at the lab was published, Philip Morris would sue.

When DeNoble's troubles became known in the antismoking movement, he was contacted by the Food and Drug Administration and asked to help with the agency's own inquiries into the tobacco industry. A copy of his and Mele's paper also found its way to Henry Waxman's subcommittee in Washington. Waxman released the paper from his office in March 1994, in effect forcing Philip Morris to release DeNoble and Mele from the confidentiality agreements. The information about the rats was now public, and DeNoble would testify before Waxman's committee. It sounded like a triumph over censorship, but in fact Philip Morris had achieved its aim in hiding his results. In the interim decade, several independent papers mimicking DeNoble's experiments, and his results, had been published in medical journals. His work was now out of date.

5

A FOOL'S MISSION

He who lives without folly isn't as wise as he thinks.

—*François, Duc de la Rochefoucauld,* Sentences
et Maximes Morales, *no. 209*

LOYD VERNON JONES had tobacco farming in his blood. He
had lived all his life on an eighteen-acre plot of land in North
Carolina where he lovingly provided the care and attention
needed to nurture his delicate and unpredictable tobacco plants to maturity. He sowed the seeds in late winter and transplanted the little
shoots, six or so inches high, in the spring. All summer long he protected them from voracious pests and prevented them from growing too
high by topping the plants as soon as they flowered, thus assuring the
nutrients went into the sticky aromatic leaves. When the flowers were
picked, lateral buds of "suckers" grew on the leaf axils and these, too,
had to be removed.

In late summer, he picked the leaves, tied them together into
"hands," and hung them from tiered poles in the curing barn. There
they stayed, turning a pale, then a golden brown, and in the fall he
loaded them on his truck and drove them to the tobacco auction warehouse. Jones followed a ritual that had gone virtually unchanged for
three centuries, since the English settlers first started growing tobacco
in neighboring Virginia. It was time-consuming, back-breaking work
but it was a good little business, much more profitable on a small farm

than any other crop. He could average more than $3,000 gross income an acre, easily beating such staples as cotton and soybeans.

Local farmers acknowledged that Jones was one of the best small growers in the area, which is probably the reason he was selected in the late '70s by the tobacco giant Brown & Williamson to grow an experimental tobacco plant. The company never said why they had chosen him; their representative just turned up one day at his ranch house a few miles south of the small town of Wilson, and offered to rent his farm for several years and pay him for growing new plant varieties that had been crossbred to produce more nicotine. "His eyes were bugged out like a stomped-on toad," recalled his widow, Martha, in the fall of 1995. I laughed at her Southern aphorism and she smiled, but only briefly. Jones died in 1993 and it was difficult for her to remember the good times.

The money the company offered for Jones's land and his labor was more than he thought it was worth. It was steady money, too, at a time when the tobacco market was becoming as fragile as the plants Jones would be asked to grow. Consumption of cigarettes was falling each year—from 630 to 540 billion during the '80s—and tobacco farmers were fearful of the future. Some had already begun to diversify into other crops, cotton and even house plants. The backing of a big corporation was attractive, and Jones had eagerly signed up.

He never knew much about the exotic new plants, or what happened to the dried leaves and the seeds once they left his farm. He did know that whatever he was doing was important. The company sent tobacco experts from Europe—from England, France, and Germany—to watch the plants grow.

He planted five new varieties of *Nicotiana tabacum,* the common tobacco plant, but only two of them lived to maturity. The company codenamed them Y1 and Y2. Y1 turned out to be the sturdier and performed better during the curing process. Y2 turned black in the drying barn and smelled like old socks. The company was very pleased with Y1 and took it away—Jones didn't know where and didn't really care. It was none of his business, except that the plant had helped him through some hard times for small growers in the South.

The mystery of Y1 began to unravel in 1994, a few months after Lloyd Jones died. The new high-nicotine plant would become a key part of the Clinton administration's unprecedented effort to regulate nicotine and a vital piece of evidence for the liability lawyers in the Third Wave of litigation in the tobacco wars. Had he lived to hear the tale, the law-abiding, churchgoing farmer would have been amazed that he had been a part of such goings-on.

The story of Y1 begins far away from tobacco country—in the dreary offices of the Food and Drug Administration in Rockville, Maryland, a featureless overspill of Washington, D.C. The agency is responsible for the licensing, manufacturing, labeling, and advertising of thousands of everyday consumer goods—from foods to drugs and cosmetics. The exceptions are meat and poultry, which are controlled by the Department of Agriculture.

In 1990, President George Bush appointed a new commissioner of the FDA. He was David Kessler, a 39-year-old pediatrician. Dr. Kessler had worked on Capitol Hill for Republican Senator Orrin Hatch, a straight-laced Mormon who is as fiercely against government regulation as Ralph Nader is for it. Kessler's association with Hatch led some to wonder whether the new FDA chief would make much of an impact. His management experience was limited to a teaching hospital in the Bronx, which seemed poor preparation for running a 4,000-person government regulatory agency in an era of deregulation. Moreover, the FDA had become a stagnant, largely ineffective bureaucracy. During the Reaganite era of "get big government off our backs," the FDA's enforcement actions had declined sharply. Inspections of food and drug manufacturing plants had dropped by half and seizures of contaminated foods or adulterated pharmaceuticals had also fallen. The agency had been rocked by scandal: a number of drug companies had been selling adulterated and mislabeled products; others had falsified records and paid off inspectors. Four FDA employees were convicted of taking bribes to speed up drug approval. "We had become a paper tiger," Kessler would say later. "We would write a letter, and we would write another letter. And another letter. No one in industry took us seriously."

Certainly no one forecast that Kessler would be the first FDA commissioner to take the politically risky move of trying to regulate the big tobacco companies. Despite the harm cigarettes cause and the well-known pharmacological effects of nicotine, the industry had escaped being regulated either as a food or as a drug. The FDA had no control over the 4,000 compounds in tobacco smoke, nor any authority over how cigarettes were marketed.

In Congress, the persuasive power of the political campaign contribution had taken its toll. Tobacco industry funds had flowed into the coffers of Republicans and Democrats alike, and all but a few diehard antitobacco congressmen, like Henry Waxman of California, Ron Wyden of Oregon, and Mike Synar of Oklahoma, accepted the industry's propaganda that tobacco was an important cash crop that needed subsidizing and cigarettes should be left alone. Talk of regulation was almost un-American: the industry was older than the republic and tobacco leaves adorned the columns of the Capitol in Washington. As for nicotine, it was a mild, faintly pleasurable stimulant like the caffeine in tea and coffee.

Kessler's appearance, as it turned out—his youth, and his nerdish carrot-colored beard and spectacles—was deceptive. In fact, he was well suited to initiate a shake-up of the ailing agency and he would soon show that he had the guts and the stamina not only to reform the FDA but also to confront the tobacco companies. A Phi Beta Kappa student at Amherst, he was a graduate of Harvard Medical School and also of the University of Chicago Law School. Kessler had also received management training at New York University School of Business. He had always seemed to be juggling at least two jobs. While completing his residency in pediatrics at Johns Hopkins in Baltimore, he had combined exhausting work on the emergency ward with consulting at the U.S. Senate Health Subcommittee in Washington, an hour's drive away. By the time he took over the FDA, Kessler already knew a lot about how it worked because he had studied the agency for years. He saw reforming it as an intellectual challenge and he was quite confident he would accomplish many changes, even perhaps including the agency's relationship with the tobacco industry. His high school yearbook had said, "If you want something done, ask Kessler."

Although a registered Republican, he was not an ideological conservative. He considers himself basically apolitical. A student in the Vietnam War years, he was never a protester. When his fellow students took off for summer vacation, Kessler headed to New York for his summer job at the Memorial Sloan-Kettering Cancer Center. Before joining Hatch's staff, Kessler had volunteered to serve without pay as a consultant on FDA-related matters for Senator Edward Kennedy, then chairman of the Senate Labor and Human Resources Committee, but he had been turned down.

As a medical doctor, Kessler was concerned about the public health aspect of smoking, but when he first looked at the tobacco industry as FDA commissioner in 1991, he was warned off by agency veterans who told him it was a "fool's mission," a "crackpot crusade." The industry was too big, too crafty, and too powerful. Moreover, it had never been clear whether the FDA could prove that it had jurisdiction over tobacco.

Under the Food, Drug, and Cosmetic Act of 1938, the FDA has oversight over any substance for which the manufacturer has claimed a health benefit. In the 1950s, the FDA had challenged the outrageous promotional claims made for some cigarettes. Leaflets for one brand, Fairfax, claimed it prevented "the common cold, influenza, pneumonia . . . scarlet fever, whooping cough, measles, meningitis, tuberculosis . . . [and] parrot fever." The FDA's complaint was upheld but, as the tobacco industry pointed out, only because the promotional material made a therapeutic claim. In another case, Trim cigarettes were promoted as slimming aids or, as they put it, "reducing-aid cigarettes," and smokers were instructed: "Smoke one cigarette shortly before meals . . . and whenever you are tempted to reach for a late evening snack. Trim reducing-aid cigarettes contain a patented appetite satient that takes the edge off your appetite. Clinically tested . . ." The court agreed that Trim cigarettes should also be considered therapeutic under the law, and thus subject to FDA regulation.

Unless health claims were made, the FDA itself told Congress it did not have jurisdiction over cigarettes. Cigarettes were for "smoking pleasure, and not drugs within the meaning of the act unless a therapeutic purpose is claimed," as one former commissioner described it. When the act was amended to include oversight of "medical devices," such as syringes, as well as actual drugs, the FDA again said it did not interpret the law as covering cigarettes. They were not "medical devices," the agency decreed.

When, in 1966, Congress passed laws requiring that warning labels be put on cigarette packs, it stipulated that "any further regulation in this sensitive and complex area must be reserved for specific congressional action." In three successive years, 1977, 1978, and 1979, antitobacco congressmen pushed for FDA jurisdiction over cigarettes, but each time the bill failed to pass. Mike Synar, of Oklahoma, one of the most outspoken antitobacco congressmen, observed during a 1992 effort to obtain FDA regulation, "While the FDA has jurisdiction to protect consumers from unsafe foods, drugs, cosmetics and medical devices it is powerless to do anything about one of the deadliest consumer products—tobacco." Synar tried again in 1993, and again Congress said no.

The key clause that triggers FDA oversight is whether the manufacturer "intended" the drug, or substance, "to affect the structure or function of the body." Antismoking groups were constantly pressing the FDA to change its policy toward tobacco on the premise that nicotine was an addictive drug and there was evidence that the manufacturers "intended" the smoker's bodily function to be affected. The groups also argued that, despite what the FDA might say, the cigarette was indeed "an instrument, apparatus, or contrivance"—a delivery device in other words—designed to administer controlled amounts of nicotine.

The veteran antismoking activist John Banzhaf, of Action on Smoking and Health (ASH), had sought a judicial review from Kessler's predecessor, but the FDA successfully defended its position. The government's brief on behalf of the FDA stated, "In the seventy-three years since the enactment of the original Food and Drug Act, and in the forty-one years since the promulgation of the Food, Drug, and Cosmetics Act, the FDA has repeatedly informed Congress that cigarettes are beyond the scope of the statute absent health claims establishing a therapeutic intent on behalf of the manufacturer or vendor." The courts had agreed. Changing this tradition was obviously not going to be easy, and Kessler decided to put tobacco at a lower point on his agenda.

There were much easier targets. He started by strengthening the administration's corps of inspectors, hoping at the very least to restore respect. In his first year, he almost doubled the number of prosecutions and injunctions against companies that had failed to apply for licenses or were selling questionable products.

Kessler launched an offensive against food nutrition labels he considered hopelessly inadequate. One day, Kessler's raiders threatened to seize 2,000 cases of Procter & Gamble orange juice because the containers had a misleading label claiming the juice was freshly squeezed when it was actually made from concentrate. After weeks of refusing to answer Kessler's complaints, Procter & Gamble sent its lawyers to the FDA to straighten things out the way they always had done, by agreeing to consider the issue. But Kessler would not be intimidated. He told them he would seize the containers if the company refused to change the labels. The company lawyers, as companies had done for years, ignored the threat and walked out of the meeting. Kessler ordered his enforcers into action at dawn the next day.

Next, Kessler forced "fresh" labels off reconstituted spaghetti sauce and banned "fat free" claims from diet products. His idea was that the FDA should, as he put it, "drive the development of new products," not the other way around. What went into foods depended to a large extent on the type of claims allowed by the FDA. So a product labeled "low fat" was allowed only three grams of fat per serving. One labeled "light" would have to contain 33 percent fewer calories than the regular product.

No industry was spared, but Kessler's most controversial action was against the makers of silicone-gel breast implants. That also meant confronting the rich lobby of plastic surgeons. Breast implants made up a quarter of the work of America's four thousand plastic surgeons. As Kessler began to show an interest in the problem, the surgeons launched a $2 million campaign to stop him taking the implants off the market.

By 1990, implants had been on the market for nearly thirty years. But since the early '80s, several thousand women had complained that their implants had become hard and lumpy and sometimes painful. Some implants had shifted or leaked, causing pain and disfigurement. As "medical devices," they had come under the purview of the FDA, and manufacturers were required to submit applications for premarketing approval, including data on safety and effectiveness. When Kessler arrived at the FDA, he found that none of them had done so. Kessler told them there could be no more delay, but their response was still sluggish. At the end of 1991, a jury in San Francisco awarded $7.3 million to a woman who had complained her implant had caused a rare disorder known as mixed connective tissue disease. Evidence used in the case suggested the company, Dow Corning, had covered up possible dangers. Kessler came under pressure to ban implants.

The liability lawyers were on the case immediately. Their professional association, ATLA, joined forces with Ralph Nader's Public Citizen Health Research Group in urging Kessler to crack down on the devices. Kessler agreed. In April 1992, he restricted use of implants to those women who had undergone mastectomies as part of cancer treatment and who agreed to be part of a research program into silicone implants. The move effectively banned implants. Plastic surgeons called for his resignation, but Kessler defended his decision by saying that the burden of proof on implant safety rested squarely on the manufacturers. "Caveat emptor has never been—and never will be—the philosophy at the FDA."

The plaintiffs' attorneys rushed into court with breast implant victims. One law firm in Virginia opened new offices devoted entirely to breast implant cases. A Florida lawyer's toll-free number was 1-800-RUPTURE. Dow Corning, which was the biggest manufacturer, became the target of 30,000 lawsuits. Stanley Chesley of Cincinnati was the first to file a class action on behalf of women with implants, and he was joined on the all-important steering committee by his friend Wendell Gauthier. Two years later, the two sides reached an agreement. About 250,000 women claimed to have developed some illness connected to their implants and a record $4.25 billion was set aside for all women who had received breast implants of any type before the settlement date, June 1, 1993. The lawyers, in theory, were due their 25 percent, or roughly a billion dollars.

Kessler didn't stop to ponder the results. He had already moved to his next surprising target: the Red Cross. Kessler reproached them for not screening blood supplies more effectively for the AIDS virus. Then he attacked the American Heart Association for giving certain products a "red heart" symbol in return for a fee from the manufacturers. The opportunity for corruption was obvious, Kessler thought. The overall message from the new FDA was: the watchdog is back and it has teeth. Veteran inspectors at the agency said they hadn't seen so much activity in years. Industry dubbed him "Eliot Knessler," after the cop who pursued Al Capone. Newt Gingrich denounced the agency as the "leading job killer in America" and called Kessler "a bully and a thug."

Kessler was courting political disaster. The FDA depends on Congress for its budget, after all, and the Gingrich Republicans who came into power in 1994 talked of closing down the FDA altogether. But Kessler would not be cowed. He hadn't come to Washington to win a popularity contest, he told those concerned for his future.

While he was making headlines changing food labels and banning silicone implants, Kessler kept thinking about regulating cigarettes. On one of several TV appearances as the new FDA policeman, Kessler bumped into Dr. C. Everett Koop, whose bushy white beard and piercing eyes had become familiar to Americans during his term as Reagan's Surgeon General. He took Kessler aside before the show and told him to "do anything you can" to regulate tobacco. "The country is going to be behind you," he assured the young commissioner.

Meanwhile, smoking-related deaths increased each year. The Centers for Disease Control in Atlanta said the figure was now more than 420,000. That is more than the combined deaths from homicide, suicide, AIDS, automobile accidents, and alcohol and drug abuse. And it is more each year than U.S. military deaths during the entire Second World War, which numbered 292,131 from all services. Antitobacco forces liked to point out that the 420,000 figure was the equivalent of two-and-a-half jumbo jets crashing each day of the year.

STILL, REGULATION OF TOBACCO looked like a fool's mission, as the FDA veterans had warned the newcomer. Government efforts to control smoking had always been singularly unsuccessful. When the English monarch, James I, wrote "A Counterblaste of Tobacco," calling the custom "loathsome to the eye, hateful to the nose, harmful to the brain, dangerous to the lungs, and in the black stinking fume thereof, nearest resembling the horrible Stygian smoke of the pit that is bottomless," his diatribe had no effect whatever on his subjects. The bloodthirsty Turkish sultan, Murad the Cruel, tortured, multilated, and hanged smokers. Still his people smoked. The Russian Tsar Michael, grandfather to Peter the Great, slit the nostrils of any citizen found indulging in the novelty of smoking tobacco. Smoking continued. When the royal households of Europe discovered they could finance wars from tobacco taxes, they imposed such heavy burdens on tobacco merchants that for a while it seemed the industry might be taxed out of business. In the 1660s, tobacco duties from the Virginia colonies accounted for roughly one quarter of total English customs revenues, and as much as 5 percent of total government income. As for religious and temperance groups, tobacco has been under permanent attack from them and, since the end of World War II, their numbers have been joined by medical researchers. Over time no barbaric ruler, no tax burden, no medical statistics, no admonishments from doctors, schoolteachers, or parents, no government health warnings on cigarettes packs have been even remotely successful in parting people from their tobacco.

The original 1906 Food and Drugs Act was designed to put a stop to quackery and the sale of impure foods. The law set up the FDA and gave the agency powers to regulate any drug that appeared in the U.S. Pharmacopoeia, a national list of substances that affect the functioning of the human body in some fashion, the modern equivalent of the apothecaries' recipe books of the Middle Ages. Tobacco, under its Latin name, *tabacum,* had been widely used as a medicine during the colonial period in America because of the properties of nicotine. "Nicotian therapy" was used as an analgesic, an expectorant, a laxative, a salve, and it was also meant to help keep the body's "humors" in balance. During the nineteenth century its medical use declined, along with many other herbal remedies, but it remained in the edition of the Pharmacopoeia as late as 1905. In 1906, it was suddenly dropped from the eighth edition, the same year the Food and Drugs Act became law. Legend has it that the tobacco companies arranged for *tabacum* to be dropped from the national drug list, thus avoiding FDA regulation, in exchange for the votes of tobacco state congressmen for the 1906 act. There is no hint, however, of such a deal in the *Congressional Record,* nor in the papers of Dr. Harvey Washington Wiley, a physician and pharmacist who had been in charge of the precursor to the FDA, the Agriculture Department's Division of Chemistry. *Tabacum* was dropped, it seems, because its properties as a cure had been superceded by other substances.

To regulate the industry's activities, Kessler would have to show that nicotine was indeed a "drug" in the accepted medical definition of the term; that it affects the structure and function of the body, that it is addictive, and that, despite their denials, the manufacturers "intended it to affect the structure or function of the body." The key word was "intend."

The 1976 amendment to the federal Food, Drug, and Cosmetic Act gave the FDA the power to regulate medical devices and Kessler's agency now argued that cigarettes were "drug delivery systems." If the drug being delivered is deemed unsafe, it said, the agency can ban it. Since the FDA believed cigarettes were "plainly not safe," Kessler could have announced a ban. In fact, Kessler knew that was what the tobacco industry would accuse him of planning. And they did charge him with "backdoor prohibition." But it was, in fact, not Kessler's intention. As he said, to do that would present a public health problem; because since nicotine was an addictive substance, its sudden withdrawal would cause great discomfort to those so addicted. Prohibition of cigarettes was also a bad idea, he believed, just as silly as the efforts to ban alcohol had been at the beginning of the century; it would encourage a black market. In fact, in those early days, he was not clear exactly what restrictions he would impose.

BEFORE KESSLER ARRIVED at the FDA, a young political activist named Jeff Nesbitt, who had joined the FDA as spokesman, had been badgering the staff about regulating tobacco. Nesbitt, then thirty-one, had worked for the muckraking journalist Jack Anderson and for Ralph Nader. Soon after he arrived he began asking the simple question, "If you're going to regulate consumer products, why leave this big gap?" When Kessler arrived, eighteen months later, Nesbitt's father, a heavy smoker, was dying of lung cancer, and he was more agitated than ever about tobacco. He had some talks with Kessler about it, and the new commissioner said he wanted to do something, but it had to wait until after he had attended to more pressing issues. In the spring of 1991, Nesbitt, then chief of staff, called a brainstorming meeting at the Rockville headquarters of the FDA. The topic was tobacco regulation.

About thirty people attended, representing all the agency's power centers—general counsel, the drug group, the food group, the policy-making and regulatory apparatus, plus all the deputy commissioners. They met in Kessler's conference room and quickly divided into two camps. Essentially, the old guard was against regulation of tobacco. They had heard the arguments before. The younger staff members were for it; so was the FDA's legal counsel, who said regulation of the industry was within the FDA's power.

The naysayers had several compelling arguments. First, any such move would entail a long, drawn-out legal process, fought every inch of the way by the tobacco companies, and the FDA did not have the resources for such a campaign. Second, Congress by its inaction had effectively told the FDA that the tobacco industry was untouchable; there would be no support from the Hill, especially in this era of deregulation. Third, before any offensive could be launched, more inside information about the industry's products was needed to satisfy the key provision in the law: that the companies "intended" to hook people with nicotine. A cache of "smoking-gun" documents would have to be found to ensure victory, but the agency had no authority to compel the companies to produce such data. The conclusion: to challenge the tobacco companies would be tilting at windmills.

On the other side, the FDA's legal counsel argued that it had always been theoretically possible to regulate the industry under the "intent" clause; thus congressional approval was actually moot. Nesbitt emphasized that the political climate had changed. He recalls telling the meeting that two things had changed. Few members of Congress wanted to stand up anymore to support a product that puts children on a path to early death. Second, there weren't nearly as many tobacco states as there used to be—essentially Virginia, North Carolina, and Kentucky. Congress would be more receptive. The tobacco lobby, like the National Rifle Association, was operating under different rules than in past eras.

Nesbitt had a good argument. Ever since the ski resorts of Aspen and Vail pioneered smoking bans in restaurants in 1985, there had been a steady campaign to limit smoking in restaurants, offices, airplanes, and in public places. Hundreds of cities had smoking restrictions. The Environmental Protection Agency was working on studies that would declare secondhand smoke a carcinogen. Despite the arrival of the Gingrichites, support for the tobacco companies in Congress was eroding. Health-conscious Americans were turning away from cigarettes. Consumption had fallen 1 to 2 percent annually since 1982. But teenage smoking was on the rise. The latest drive of the antismoking forces had begun focusing on how the tobacco companies aimed their marketing strategies at youngsters. Members of Congress, Democrat and Republican, would support a move that cut back youth smoking. At the end of the meeting that day, Kessler was cautious, but he told the group it was a policy worth looking into. A task force, including his brightest lawyers, was formed. For a few months before he left to become former vice president Dan Quayle's communications director, Nesbitt was the team's agitator. Even after he left he continued to badger his former boss about tobacco.

Kessler likes to tell the story of how he led his troops into battle. "I walked into the Library of Congress, sat down at the computer and typed in the word 'nicotine,' " he told CBS's *60 Minutes* long after the event. Up came hundreds of studies funded by the tobacco companies, putting the lie to the industry's claim that nicotine plays an incidental role in smoking and is in cigarettes for "taste." "Why fund those studies if you're not interested in nicotine?" was the question Kessler asked CBS correspondent Lesley Stahl. Of course, a trip to the library was not necessary for the commissioner of the FDA; he could have called any number of nicotine experts in person. But the self-confessed "science jock" wanted to take command of the operation. It also made a good story to have the FDA commissioner doing his own research in the library. Kessler was "media savvy."

Kessler's team became interested in the way tobacco companies control the levels of nicotine in cigarettes. Between 1957 and 1987, the average tar and nicotine yield of American cigarettes had fallen dramatically from 34 mg to 13 mg for tar, and from 2 mg to 0.9 mg for nicotine. The lowest nicotine brands on the market contained 0.6 mg, but no one was selling a nicotine-free cigarette. Philip Morris had spent $300 million developing one and christened it "Next," but it was a flop in test marketing and only confirmed what they already suspected: people won't smoke cigarettes that don't contain nicotine.

The data showed, while tar levels in cigarettes had dropped over the last decade, nicotine levels had not fallen proportionately. This was odd because it was known that the chemical process of reducing tar also reduced nicotine. It appeared that the companies were boosting nicotine levels in some fashion. The FDA analyzed three varieties of one cigarette brand, high, medium, and low tar. The lowest tar had the highest concentration of nicotine. The question was, How does the industry do this?

In March 1994, Kessler provided some possible answers to the Waxman Subcommittee on Health and the Environment. The young commissioner put on quite a show. Using a series of charts, he described numerous patents the FDA had unearthed showing the ability of the industry to control nicotine levels in cigarettes. Eight patents described adding nicotine to the tobacco rod, five to the filters and wrappers. Kessler conceded that patents can only describe an invention and do not indicate it has been used, but the wording of the patents suggested there was "intent" to use nicotine to change bodily functions. One talked about "maintaining the nicotine content at a sufficiently high level to provide the desired physiological activity, taste and odor." Others spoke of "maintenance of the proper amount of nicotine," and "the release in controlled amounts of nicotine," and "manipulation of nicotine."

"The public may think of cigarettes as no more than blended tobacco rolled in a paper," Kessler said, "but they are more than that. Some of today's cigarettes may in fact qualify as high technology nicotine delivery systems." Kessler referred to a 1972 Philip Morris research memo that had been discovered during the Rose Cipollone case. The memo said, "Think of the cigarette pack as a storage container for a day's supply of nicotine. Think of the cigarette as a dispenser for a dose unit of nicotine. Think of a puff of smoke as the vehicle for nicotine. Smoke is beyond question the most optimized vehicle of nicotine and the cigarette the most optimized dispenser of smoke."

Showing how deeply the FDA had dug into the files and the cigarette manufacturing process, Kessler also demonstrated how the levels of tar and nicotine on the warning labels on a cigarette pack may be very different from what the smoker actually receives. The Federal Trade Commission tests cigarettes with a smoking machine that puffs at a level representing how a human would smoke, and the contents are measured when the cigarettes are finished. Kessler argued that the advertised "low-yield" cigarette was "in many ways a myth."

Cigarette manufacturers put tiny, microscopic air holes in a band around the filters so that when the machine smokes the cigarette, additional air is drawn into the smoke mixture and dilutes it. Smokers, however, learn to get a bigger nicotine content in a puff by covering up the holes, either with their lips or their fingers. Studies had shown between 30 and 60 percent of people who smoke low-yield cigarettes cover up the holes, and some don't even know they are doing it. The cigarette makers also allow the smoker to increase nicotine levels, above the FTC-tested level by extending the paper that covers the filter—the so-called overwrap—down the cigarette rod. The FTC smoking machine is programmed to stop smoking when the rod is burned down to three millimeters before the overwrap. But in some cigarettes there is still more tobacco covered by the overwrap. Waxman and Wyden were suitably impressed and thanked Kessler for his excellent job. Kessler promised to come back when he had found out more.

The puzzle his team now faced was to find out precisely how nicotine levels were being manipulated. The basic tool for controlling the level of nicotine is "blending" tobacco leaves of different nicotine content. The FDA team started looking at experimental tobacco plants that produce leaves with higher levels of nicotine. They searched libraries for company patents and found out about the "blending" techniques. Kessler was lucky to have two scientists who had worked for the industry to help him. One had worked for Philip Morris and knew about that company's research on the addictiveness of nicotine. The other had been research director for Brown & Williamson. Both men had signed confidentiality agreements with their respective companies, and had to be careful about what they said, but Kessler enjoyed this cloak and dagger aspect of his work. In the end, a little air of mystery could only add to the drama and publicity value of his crusade. But at that time it was necessary to keep security tight and he gave his industry sources codenames: "Cigarette" and "Research."

The next time he appeared before Congress, in July, Kessler knew he had at least one answer to how the companies manipulated the nicotine levels. It was Y1. His secret source was "Research."

In the spring of 1994, the FDA asked for a meeting with Brown & Williamson officials at the company's research offices in Macon, Georgia. During the meeting, FDA lawyers asked about plant breeding techniques to increase nicotine levels and, according to the FDA's version, B&W said it was just not an issue because there was an agreement among U.S. cigarette companies that set limits on the nicotine yield of tobacco plants grown in the United States.

Back at FDA headquarters a few days later, an anonymous caller advised Kessler's investigators to check American Tobacco Company patents worldwide. So far, they had only checked U.S. domestic patents in Washington. The reason was the FDA's tight budget; it cost more to look up international patents. Now they tapped into the international database. Four days later, FDA librarian Carol Knoth turned up a Brown & Williamson patent that looked interesting, but it was a Brazilian patent in Portuguese. The key phrase was *"Variedade de fumo geneticamente estavel e planta de fumo . . . nicotiana . . . 6% ou maior."*

Even to someone who didn't speak Portuguese, which Knoth did not, it seemed that this plant produced levels of nicotine at 6 percent or greater of the total weight—and that was twice the normal levels of 2.5 to 3.5 percent. In fact the translation read, "The nicotine content of the leaf of this variety is usually higher than approximately 6 percent by weight . . . which is significantly higher than any normal variety of tobacco grown commercially." Kessler's team went into high gear. Listed as the three inventors of the new variety were Phillip Fisher, Hubert Hardison, and Janis Bravo. The FDA found Hubert Hardison working for a Brown & Williamson affiliate company named Export Leaf in North Carolina. Hardison confirmed his role in the creation of Y1 and put the FDA in touch with a former Department of Agriculture research botanist, James Chaplin.

Chaplin had been the director of the department's experimental station in Oxford, North Carolina, only an hour by car from Lloyd Jones's farm. There was nothing secret about Chaplin's work. In 1977, he had written about the industry's possible need for a higher nicotine tobacco plant in a trade publication, *World Tobacco.* Among other things, he said, "Manufacturers have means of reducing tars, but most of the methods reduce nicotine and other constituents at the same time. Therefore, it may be desirable to develop levels [that are constant] or to develop levels higher in nicotine so that when the tar and nicotine are reduced there will still be enough nicotine left to satisfy the smoker." Chaplin talked about crossbreeding commercial varieties of the common tobacco plant—*Nicotiana tabacum*—with *Nicotiana rusticana,* a wild variety high in nicotine but not used commercially.

Chaplin's crossbreeding experiments showed that plants could be developed with a nicotine content varying from 0.2 percent to 4.0 percent by weight. He had produced plants with a nicotine content up to 6 percent, but they were weak and invariably blew over in a strong wind. Chaplin used to tell the story of his high-nicotine plants at tobacco conferences he attended and this was how Brown & Williamson learned of Y1. The company obtained sample seeds from Chaplin and rented Lloyd Jones's farm to grow them. Chaplin, who had just retired from the Agriculture Department, was taken on by B&W as a consultant.

He told the FDA what happened after Lloyd Vernon Jones had succeeded in growing the plant. In 1983, B&W took the plant to a genetic engineering lab, DNA Plant Technology, or DNAP, then based in New Jersey. B&W wanted a male sterile version of the plant, a procedure that effectively prevents commercial competitors from stealing and reproducing the new variety. In order to protect their precious Y1, Brown & Williamson eventually filed an application for a Plant Variety Protection Certificate in February 1991. In September of that year, the company filed U.S. patent application No. 761,312 in the Patent Office in Washington, D.C. A year later, they also filed a patent in Brazil, where the company intended to grow the first batch of Y1. Southern Brazil has excellent soil and growing conditions for tobacco, and the major tobacco companies grow substantial quantities of their product there.

Growing Y1 offshore—in Brazil—and then bringing it back into the country would also be a way of circumventing the gentlemen's agreement among the tobacco companies not to grow tobacco with more than agreed-upon levels of nicotine. The question the FDA wanted answered was, Had B&W used Y1 commercially? If they had, the FDA would have powerful evidence that the company was manipulating the level of nicotine in its cigarettes. Moreover, instead of putting it there for taste and flavor, as the companies asserted, they were including it at a certain level to assure the needed pharmacological action on the smoker's brain.

The FDA investigators found Janis Bravo, one of the names on the Brazilian patent. She worked for the genetic engineering company DNAP. Bravo cooperated with the FDA agents. She told them how she had worked on Y1 and was certain seeds had been shipped to Brazil on more than one occasion, but she did not know the quantity; nor did she know whether the seeds were intended for a commercial operation. She knew of one seed shipment that weighed ten pounds, or enough to grow 2 million pounds of tobacco. Both Chaplin and Bravo told the FDA they had actually seen Y1 growing in Brazil in the 1980s. The farms were under contract to Souza Cruz Overseas, another BAT subsidiary.

But had any Y1 been shipped back into the United States for commercial use? Kessler hired a former U.S. Customs official and sent him on a painstaking computer search of the U.S. Customs imports database. When that exercise turned up nothing, a separate manual search was made of customs receipts of shipments from Brazil. "It was really like looking for a needle in a haystack," Kessler would say later.

A week after the Brazilian search, the FDA investigators found what they were looking for: two invoices showing that more than half a million pounds of Y1 had been shipped from Souza Cruz Overseas to Brown & Williamson in Kentucky in September 1992. The shipments had come via the Souza Cruz offices in the Cayman Islands and did not mention Brazil. The order was entitled "Project Y1." Still, the FDA did not know if Y1 had been used commercially. DNAP should have known because they had an agreement with B&W whereby they would be paid a royalty if Y1 were used commercially. But the company did not know.

Kessler's inquiry had alerted B&W, of course. The company's attorneys, King & Spalding of Atlanta, sent Kessler an angry letter objecting to the FDA calling on B&W employees without the permission of the company. The letter said B&W "found these contacts extremely disturbing" and urged "that agency inquiries . . . be made through official channels in a businesslike manner." The FDA responded that the agency's efforts were justified because of the company's earlier reluctance to cooperate. He reminded B&W of the earlier Macon visit when B&W had not been as forthcoming as they might have been about growing tobacco plant varieties.

B&W requested another meeting. This time the company brought a team of lawyers and executives to FDA headquarters. One of them was Hugh Hardison, who had told the FDA about Chaplin. Now, he repeated his story of getting the seeds from Chaplin and contacting Lloyd Vernon Jones, but he said that his knowledge of the experimental plant ended in the early 1980s. Another B&W official, Drew McMurtry, took up the story, telling the FDA that B&W had four and a half million pounds of Y1 stored in tobacco warehouses in the U.S. He also volunteered that the company had used Y1 in its brands—Richland, Viceroy, and Raleigh—the last mentioned being the favorite, as it happened, of Martha Jones, Lloyd's widow. McMurtry said the company had experimented with Y1 as a "blending tool."

"What do you mean?" asked the FDA officials.

McMurtry replied that the company was trying to lower the tar and still maintain the nicotine level. The FDA's lead counsel on the Y1 case, Mitch Zeller, said later, "That flies in the face of the industry's assertion, under oath, that they don't design cigarettes for nicotine but only for tar." As far as the FDA was concerned, the Y1 story was prima facie evidence that Brown & Williamson had manipulated the nicotine content of their cigarettes to keep smokers hooked on the drug.

Kessler returned to the Waxman committee. At the end of June, he said that his earlier testimony had been "suggestive" of the industry's control and manipulation of nicotine. Now, he was ready to present "actual instances" and he told his detective story about Y1, adding the strange final action B&W had taken. He told about B&W's application for a patent for the Y1 plant and also for a Plant Variety Protection Certificate. The company had also deposited samples of Y1 seed with the National Seed Storage Laboratory in Fort Collins, Colorado. But the plant certificate application had been withdrawn on March 14, just eleven days before Kessler's first appearance before the Waxman committee. The company had also removed the Y1 seeds it had deposited in Colorado. The U.S. patent application had been rejected at first but the company had filed an appeal on February 25, 1994, the date of Kessler's original letter about nicotine manipulation. Two weeks later, before receiving a ruling on the patent application appeal, B&W abandoned the patent altogether, withdrawing their application. Although he had no hard evidence that the dates were anything more than coincidental, Kessler was hinting there was something fishy about the whole affair.

To reinforce his nicotine-manipulation charge, Kessler also introduced another piece of the puzzle. He had learned from his whistle-blowers how the tobacco companies "free up" more nicotine for the smoker by the addition of ammonia to the tobacco blend. In April, under pressure from antismoking forces, the cigarette companies had released a list of 599 ingredients added to tobacco. Among the chemicals were several ammonia compounds. Ammonia, Kessler had discovered, had multiple uses. It strengthens the adhesiveness of the tobacco on the production line before it is chopped up and made into cigarettes. It also reacts with sugars to produce different flavors. But most important to Kessler's inquiry was the fact that ammonia can affect the delivery of nicotine. When added to a tobacco blend, ammonia reacts with nicotine salts to free nicotine. Kessler read from a tobacco company blender's handbook, which said, "As we know, extractable nicotine contributes to impact [nicotine effect] in cigarette smoke and this is how ammonia can act as an impact booster . . . this means . . . a cigarette incorporating ammonia technology will deliver more flavor compounds, including nicotine, into smoke than one without it." He wouldn't name the company that had produced the handbook, but it was from Brown & Williamson, courtesy of "Research."

Kessler concluded, "Why spend a decade developing through genetic breeding high-nicotine tobacco and adding it to cigarettes if you are not interested in controlling and manipulating nicotine? Why focus on the enhanced delivery of nicotine to the smoker by chemical manipulation, if you are not interested in controlling and manipulating nicotine?"

B&W's chief executive, Thomas Sandefur, denied there had been anything sinister in the growing of Y1. There was never any secret about it, he claimed. The FDA's story about his company holding back information was "grossly misleading and unfair." He accused Kessler of "grandstanding" and also complained about Merrell Williams's theft of documents. It was like being back in the bad old days of McCarthyism, he said "when blacklisting and vilification of honest and reasonable people were sanctioned for the sake of advancing a political agenda."

But what had Kessler really achieved? Y1 was a great detective story and the way Kessler's team had pursued it, delving into libraries and patent records and toughing it out with tobacco company lawyers, was certainly the most strenuous effort ever made by the FDA to address the public health problem of smoking-related illnesses. The way Kessler himself had presented it to Congress, aided and abetted by Waxman, Wyden, and Synar, was masterful antitobacco agitprop. But there was a lot more work to be done. If the FDA was ever going to regulate tobacco, Kessler had to declare nicotine an addictive drug, which was something the FDA had never done. And he had to issue a set of rules to bring the industry under his jurisdiction. He could only do that with consent of the White House, and President Clinton was about to face a re-election campaign. The president's pollsters had told him he needed to win the tobacco states to be assured of victory. To get to the president, Kessler had to convince the pollsters that the issue could bring a bonanza of public support. There was a lot of work still to do.

6

THE SWEET SMELL

OF GAIN

. . . The sweet smell of gain makes the smell of tobacco less perceptible and less offensive. . . .

—B. Ramazzini, De Morbis Artificum

ANY LAWYER who challenges the big tobacco companies in court inevitably encounters the ghost of a domineering biologist named Clarence Cook Little. In a long scientific career in cancer research, mostly as an administrator, he became one of the world's most famous breeders of mice for laboratory experiments.

In his "mouse house," as the lab at Bar Harbor on the coast of Maine was affectionately known, some of Dr. Little's mice proved highly resistant to cancer and rarely developed the disease, while other groups were so prone that almost all the mice had cancer in one form or another. In the 1940s, when most scientists were looking for cancer-causing agents in the array of complex, man-made compounds then being dispersed into the environment, Little advocated what was known as a "constitutional hypothesis"; that is to say, it was a person's genetic makeup, perhaps even a distorted or damaged gene, that was probably the basic cause of cancer. The damaged gene allowed the abnormal and, in the end, unrestrained growth of cells.

This was not an original thought. From the earliest days of cancer research, scientists expected to find that some people were more prone than others to the disease simply because of their genes, and indeed this notion has been borne out in modern research. But there was one form of cancer that scientists were beginning to believe might have something to do with smoking tobacco, a particularly insidious type which attacked the bronchial passages and the lungs.

There was good evidence to support this notion. For example, the disease was extremely rare in Iceland, where smoking was not introduced until the '30s, and in Norway, where smoking had not been widespread. On the other hand, the disease was particularly common in Finland and Austria, two countries where people had smoked for years. In fact, researchers could not find any evidence of a population that did not smoke but had a high incidence of this type of lung cancer. Nor could they find a low incidence of lung cancer in populations that had smoked for a long time. In other words, there was no evidence to support the suggestion that one group of people could regard themselves as immune to developing lung cancer from smoking.

As the statistical evidence grew for the link between lung cancer and smoking, Dr. Little refused to believe in tobacco's causality and, instead, remained wedded to the "constitutional hypothesis." Some people get it and some don't, depending on their genetic makeup, he maintained. In the early 1950s, when researchers actually found a statistical link between smoking and lung cancer, Dr. Little sided with skeptics who argued that one factor, smoking, could not be a cause, and many factors probably should be considered, including heredity, sex, hormones, diet, and vitamins. Dr. Little's position called on the scientific community to unlock the secrets of the human cell before accepting any link between smoking and cancer. Needless to say, the tobacco companies became very interested in his opinions.

IN 1953, the tobacco companies faced the first real threat to their livelihood. A young epidemiologist, Ernst Wynder, the son of a German Jewish doctor who had fled the Nazis, had been testing so-called tars from cigarette smoke on mice at the Memorial Sloan-Kettering Cancer Center in New York. The mice he used in the experiments were selected at random from Little's "mouse house" in Maine. He shaved the hairs from the backs of eighty-six mice with an electric razor and painted the skin with the sticky brown substance he obtained by condensing the smoke from Lucky Strike cigarettes. At the end of a year, sixty-two of the painted mice had survived and 58 percent of them had developed cancerous tumors. Wynder concluded that "the suspected human carcinogen has thus been proven to be a carcinogen for a laboratory animal." The experiment had provided "a working tool which may enable us to identify and isolate the carcinogenic agent(s) within the tars." Skeptics remained, of course, some complaining Wynder's "tar" mix was too highly concentrated and therefore not comparable to the smoke inhaled by humans. Others said that cancer experiments on mice were irrelevant to humans. But for the first time doctors generally began to take the link between smoking and lung cancer seriously.

In his mouse house, Little had a marvelous opportunity to conduct similar experiments of his own, which in retrospect could have been of enormous value to society. Instead, short of funds and near retirement at the age of sixty-five, he was persuaded to take another route. He sold himself to the tobacco companies, as their chief scientific administrator and spokesman. Over the years he performed brilliantly for them. Whenever the question of the link between smoking and lung cancer arose, as it did more frequently and more persuasively year after year, Little would counter the statistical evidence with his "constitutional hypothesis," leaving the public, as the tobacco companies had planned, with a lingering doubt as to whether lung cancer had any direct link to smoking.

The problem in those days with the constitutional hypothesis is the same as today; it's partly right. Medical-science research indicates that the differences in vulnerability to cancer are partly genetic, appear to be partly nutritional, partly chemical, and partly psychological (stress causes breakdowns in the body's immune system, leaving it more vulnerable to cancer growths). In insisting, in his day, on a genetic solution to the exclusion of others, Little was perverting his own hypothesis and using it as a mantra to shield his tobacco-company paymasters from another more obvious scientific fact—that though there are genetic differences in vulnerability, cigarette smoking is dangerous and does cause lung cancer and heart disease in many, if not most, people.

But Litttle's simple and oft-repeated message was that some smokers, even the heavy ones, never got cancer at all even though they lived to a ripe old age when cancers were more prevalent. So, how could smoking be a factor? Confused by the conflicting advice, millions continued the habit, even as others took it up and the lung-cancer rate soared.

Little's dictum placed a formidable legal roadblock in the way of lawyers seeking damages for smokers with lung cancer. When the smoker and his lawyer blamed the cigarette, the tobacco companies would simply say, "Prove it." And the plaintiffs' lawyers couldn't. There was no scientific "proof" as such; no researcher had identified the chemical or biological agent in tobacco smoke that actually caused tumors to develop. The human medical evidence was only statistical: people who smoked were more likely to get cancer of the lung than people who did not. And the more they smoked the more likely they were to develop the disease.

Little would perform his mission with a zeal that matched the most ardent protesters of the antismoking movement. He even reversed a lifetime's belief in the significance to man of experiments on laboratory mice, agreeing with those who said that the data showing tobacco tars caused cancer in mice were not relevant to humans.

Faced with the conflicting and confusing evidence, jury after jury in tobacco-liability suits concluded that there was, indeed, a reasonable doubt that smoking could cause lung cancer, and the tobacco companies chalked up an unblemished record of courtroom victories. The so-called controversy became one of the most powerful weapons in the industry's legal arsenal and in its argument against government regulation of its business. For more than fifty years, into 1997, doubt about the causal link—Dr. Little's "controversy"—remained the cornerstone of the industry's defense against lawsuits.

From a public health point of view, Little's insistence on scientific proof was a travesty. Scientific proof of a link between a chemical or biological agent and a disease is not, never has been, and never should be required for a government to take action against a substance suspected of causing epidemics. Before the discovery of bacteria by Pasteur in 1860, the control of human plagues depended solely on medical statistics, primitive though they were. In 1796, Edward Jenner recommended vaccination with cowpox for protection against smallpox. He did not know the "cause" of smallpox; he only knew that milkmaids who previously had cowpox had immunity against smallpox. This was a purely statistical association. The virus of smallpox was not discovered until the early 1900s—over a century after the disease had been brought under control in developed countries. In 1854, during an epidemic of cholera in London, John Snow recognized the statistical association between cases of cholera and drinking water supplied by one of London's many water companies. Snow investigated the inner-city Soho area and hypothesized, based on statistical evidence, that a noxious substance was coming from one of the wells, and shut it down. The epidemic subsided, but it would be another forty years before health officials learned that cholera was caused by water polluted with sewage. Percivall Pott, a British doctor in the eighteenth century, suggested, by simple observation, a causal link between coal tar and scrotal cancer in chimney sweeps a hundred and forty years before its experimental confirmation. As public health officials have pointed out, cancer's long latency period, ten, twenty, or even thirty years, requires that the concept of cause be based on a statistical association. In the case of smoking and lung cancer, the early epidemiological studies provided grounds for assuming for all practical purposes that the observed relationship was causal. Little's demand for scientific, or experimental, proof in the presence of a persistent "causative factor" was merely a formula for inaction and delay.

As the liability lawyers fashioned their new legal weaponry, the life and times, not to mention the sayings, of Dr. Clarence Cook Little became a key part of their arsenal in the Third Wave of tobacco litigation. While the rest of the scientific world began to accept the link between smoking and disease, Little adhered absurdly to his "not proven" line. Some of his sayings were almost too good to be true for plaintiffs' counsel. By 1960 many government agencies, including the American College of Health Physicians, the U.S. [Government] Study Group on Smoking and Health, the British Medical Council, the British Ministry of Health, the Danish National Health Service, the National Cancer Institute of Canada, the Netherlands Ministry of Social Affairs and Public Health, the Royal College of Physicians, and the World Health Organization, had concluded that there was sufficient evidence to establish a cause-and-effect relationship between smoking and lung cancer. Little had rejected them all as "oversimplified and perhaps superficial conclusions . . . that concern themselves solely with suggestive or incomplete data." He claimed such surveys "stifle or delay needed research to find the basic origins of lung cancer and cardiovascular diseases, which are most powerful, diversified and deadly enemies to our well-being."

After his death in 1971, no one showed much interest in Dr. Little, but in the internal company documents unearthed during the Third Wave of litigation against the tobacco companies, his name popped up time and again. His papers, which had been stored largely untouched in the archives at the University of Maine, were suddenly in demand. In the spring of 1995, much to the astonishment of the archivists, lawyers arrived and burrowed into the files. Their aim was to create a portrait of the man who had taken tobacco's shilling. Little's story became an essential part of the plaintiffs' case: that the tobacco companies had engaged in a massive deception of the scientific evidence by intentionally promoting the "controversy" about smoking and cancer. The industry's choice of Dr. Little, a retired biologist not on the cutting edge of scientific research, demonstrated how the tobacco companies never had any intention of supporting the best research into the effects of their product.

For as long as biologists have studied cancer they have assumed that damaged cells can result in odd, cancerous growths. That these cells could be inherited was also accepted. The question was what "initiated" the abnormal growth. Was it the damaged cell itself, or was it an outside agent? One of the man-made chemicals then proliferating in industrial plants, perhaps? Was it the exhaust from automobiles? Was it agricultural pesticides and insecticides? Or could it be some of the thousands of chemicals formed when tobacco is burned in a cigarette? When it was found that condensed tobacco smoke did cause cancer on the shaved skin of laboratory mice, Dr. Little said it wasn't relevant to human beings. As the evidence of the link between smoking and lung cancer grew from medical statistics, Dr. Little told his audience not to worry, some smokers live to a ripe old age so smoking couldn't be a cause of cancer. For all his pledges to be concerned with "pure science," Dr. Little promoted "junk science." As the liability lawyers sought to paint the tobacco industry as the Evil Empire, they could not have wished for a better image than the socially privileged peddler of their junk science himself, Dr. Clarence Cook Little.

THE SON of Boston Brahmins—his mother a descendant of Paul Revere and his father the son of a textile and shipping merchant—Little grew up in luxury at the end of the last century on a huge estate in the suburb of Brookline. There the young Clarence was indulged, even encouraged in his youthful obsession with breeding pets. His father, who lived off a trust fund, bred dogs. At the age of three, Little was given some pigeons and by the time he was seven had bred a pair that won first prize in a local show. He became fascinated by the inheritance of color in his menagerie of mice, dogs, doves, and canaries. By the time he went to Harvard to study biology, he took with him a pair of mice inbred over several generations and he studied their descendants in the college genetics department.

His was the class of 1910 that included Walter Lippmann, John Reed, and T. S. Eliot, and although he was not a brilliant student, Little was an all-round success. Tall, square-shouldered, and athletic, with a closely clipped black mustache, he cut a dashing figure on the track team. He was articulate, witty, and charming. He had two nicknames, "Prexy" and "Pete," which endured for his lifetime.

After Harvard, he first attracted national attention as a college administrator. At thirty-four, he was made president of the University of Maine, then later of the University of Michigan. (He left Maine under the cloud of an extramarital affair, and he eventually divorced his first wife and married his assistant.) Like others of his generation, Little had great faith that science would improve the human race. He embraced the Eugenics Movement, a turn-of-the-century club of intellectuals who believed the human race could be improved by selective breeding. By the 1920s, they had picked up adherents among the members of America's Yankee ruling class, fearful of being overrun by the "lower elements," as they saw the Slavs, Latins, and Jews who made up the tide of immigrants. If something were not done to stem the tide, the Anglo-Saxon stock would be tainted beyond recognition. These fears, which led them to support restricted immigration laws, created a climate of approval for eugenic theories. The eugenicists advocated institutional isolation and sterilization of incorrigible criminals, the insane, and the mentally retarded. By the end of the 1920s, twenty-four states had laws permitting involuntary sterilization.

At the University of Michigan, where Little had landed after Maine, the college authorities were outraged by his advocacy of "selective birth control." The "uncontrolled and unintelligent addition of more people to the world by the production of undesired and neglected children is in my opinion as great a sin as the murder of these children by slow means," Little declared at his inaugural address on November 2, 1925. He advocated the sterilization of "criminals and mental defectives," and called state legislators who opposed such moves "nincompoops." His continuing speeches on this theme made headlines and horrified many of the God-fearing midwesterners who had hired him, especially the Catholics. The university forced him to resign. A former Michigan governor observed at the time, "Little is an ass."

He returned to the East Coast intending to devote his life to cancer research, using his fast-growing colonies of inbred mice. He said he frankly preferred mice to people, a statement that has the ring of truth in retrospect. Always short of funds, Little ran the "mouse house" like a summer camp, encouraging and comforting his staff with potluck dinners, holiday picnics, fishing expeditions, and campfire songs. In return, the staff worked hard and built up an international laboratory-mouse business.

In 1929, the year the lab opened, Little agreed to serve part-time as managing director of the fledgling American Society for the Control of Cancer, which later became the American Cancer Society. Run by medical doctors, it had been largely ineffective in its primary mission of public education about the disease. Little launched a nationwide program to teach local physicians better methods of examining patients in the early search for cancer and also persuaded the matrons of the American Federation of Women's Clubs to start a project to teach their members how to detect signs of unusual growths. The program was a big success and brought him considerable praise. It was only when a group of industrialists wanted to transform the society into a vast volunteer health organization, with a board made up of an equal number of doctors and laymen, that Little, voicing his disapproval, returned once again to Maine.

In those days, Little's view of the effects of smoking was no different from the one essentially shared by scientists, doctors, and most thinking people through the ages: that repeatedly filling one's lungs with the fine particles of tobacco smoke could not be good for you. "It is difficult to see how such particles can be prevented from becoming lodged in the walls of the lungs and when so located how they can avoid providing a certain amount of irritation," he wrote in 1944.

But that was before the tobacco companies offered to pay him to sing a very different song. Desperately short of funds for the lab, he began casting around for support from his friends and relatives. At the beginning of 1954, after a particularly lean year at the mouse house, he was advised by a relative to try R. J. Reynolds, the tobacco company with headquarters in Winston-Salem, North Carolina. "There is a tremendous amount of money in Winston-Salem," he was told. "Under the proper auspices you might get something out of it if you made a speech there." As it turned out, the tobacco companies needed him quite as much as he needed them.

BEFORE THE 1950s the tobacco companies had no serious predators, only moralizing tub-thumpers who repeated, to no enduring effect, that tobacco was inherently dirty and ungodly and encouraged crime. Some scientists and medical authorities had claimed for years that the use of tobacco could contribute to cancer-cell development in susceptible people, but so meager was the actual knowledge that the warnings were easily dismissed by the cigarette manufacturers. The companies concentrated on production efficiency, improvement of tobacco drying techniques, and stronger marketing methods. Sales boomed, especially in wartime.

Like the arms merchants, the tobacco companies came out of two world wars with remarkable prosperity: sales had shot up from 18 billion cigarettes in 1915 to more than 360 billion by the end of the 1940s. On the front lines, the generals respected nicotine's calming influence on troops before a battle as well as its ability to suppress the appetite and they demanded almost as many cigarettes as bullets. When the United States entered World War I in 1917, General John Pershing cabled Washington, "Tobacco is as indispensable as the daily ration; we must have thousands of tons of it without delay." Army doctors reported that "as soon as the lads take their first whiff they seem eased and relieved of their agony." The doughboys and the British Tommies came home singing one of the most famous songs of the war, "Pack up your troubles in your old kit bag and smile, smile, smile / While you've a Lucifer to light your fag, smile boys, that's the style."

Early rumblings about the harmful effects of tobacco among a handful of doctors were quickly subsumed by patriotic fervor. The *Lancet*, the oldest of the British medical journals, commented, "We may surely brush aside much prejudice against the use of tobacco when we consider what a source of comfort it is to the sailor and soldier engaged in a nerve-racking campaign. . . . Tobacco must be a real solace and joy when he can find time for this well-earned indulgence."

In World War II, President Roosevelt made tobacco a protected crop and draft boards gave deferments to tobacco growers. On the front lines in Europe, Africa, and the Pacific, tobacco was part of the daily ration. There was intense competition between the tobacco companies to produce the favorite smoke. It became a race between Camel, Chesterfield, and Lucky Strike. Reynolds claimed that "Camels are the Favorite! In the Army! . . . In the Navy . . . In the Marines . . . In the Coast Guard." Chesterfield recommended, "Keep 'em Smoking: Our Men Rate the Best."

In the postwar years, murmurs that cigarettes might be seriously harmful went unnoticed or were simply ignored by a confident and increasingly prosperous tobacco industry. It had understandably come to see its enterprise as one of the most commercially solid and legally untouchable in the world. Only the mint makes money more easily, was the saying. Seventy million Americans smoked, hundreds of millions more in Europe. The markets in Japan were opening, the Pacific rim presented a new opportunity, and Africa was untapped. Tobacco executives dreamed of the day when the communists would be thrown out of the Soviet bloc and those markets freed for the Marlboro stampede.

Why worry about a handful of isolated reports from a few young researchers who had found a statistical association between smoking and lung cancer and heart disease? Why be concerned that chewing tobacco had been blamed for the development of cancer of the mouth?

Public health officials in Britain and the United States were very worried, in fact, about the staggering increase in the number of deaths attributed to lung cancer. The disease had reached epidemic levels. In Britain, there had been a fifteen-fold increase since 1922. In America, the number of lung cancers per 100,000 males shot passed prostate, colon, and stomach cancers in the early 1950s, and kept on rising. Doctors thought the most likely cause would probably turn out to be industrial pollution, automobile exhausts, and possibly even the tarring of the roads. British researchers thought that arsenic might be the culprit because of its increased use in the treatment of syphilis.

There had been only hints about the link to smoking. At the turn of the century, tobacco workers in Leipzig had been observed to be especially prone to lung cancer. In the 1930s, an Argentinian researcher had produced cancers on a rabbit's skin with tobacco "tar." His study was largely discounted, though, because his "tar" was distilled at temperatures much higher than those found at the end of a burning cigarette. German and American studies at the beginning of World War II first suggested that smoking might cause an increase in human lung cancers, but the evidence was weak. Perhaps, some researchers thought, lung cancers were the result of a combination of atmospheric pollution and cigarette smoking.

In 1950, health officials were surprised by the results of two epidemiological studies of lung cancer patients, one in the United States and the other in Britain. In the American study, the New York researcher Ernst Wynder and his coworker Evarts Graham, a St. Louis surgeon, concluded that "successive and prolonged use of tobacco, especially cigarettes, seems to be an important factor in the induction of bronchiogenic carcinoma." Two months later, Richard Doll and Bradford Hill produced similar results from lung cancer patients in London. During the next few years there were more than a dozen studies, all supporting the first two. The medical profession was skeptical at first. Chest physicians had not concentrated on smoking as the cause of disease. They had not even attributed chronic bronchitis to cigarettes, though doctors acknowledged the existence of "smoker's cough."

Statisticians were also skeptical. In America, Joseph Berkson, the country's most eminent medical statistician, argued that the hospital patients used in the British and American studies did not represent a truly random population. In England, Sir Ronald Fisher, the leading theoretical statistician, attacked the epidemiological studies, suggesting that the supposed effect was really the cause: that people first developed cancer, then they smoked. The real causative factor was the individual genotype, he argued. Like Dr. Little, Fisher deplored the "excessive confidence" that the solution to the lung cancer problem had been found, because such a conclusion would be an obstacle to more penetrating research. And Fisher picked up on the one apparent flaw in the first British study: that those smokers who inhaled seemed less likely to get cancer. He also cited a study that showed monozygotic twins—from the same egg—tended to have similar smoking habits, and called this evidence that genetic factors were involved; genetic factors, he argued, caused a person to smoke and to be unusually susceptible to the disease. Fisher, like Little, had been a prominent member of the Eugenics Movement, and he believed in the "constitutional hypothesis" that relied on genotype. Like Little, Sir Ronald would also become a paid consultant for the tobacco companies. (In later British reports, which Fisher ignored, inhalers of tobacco smoke were found to have an increase of certain tumors. Fisher's "twins theory" was also later discounted by follow-up studies.)

Despite such attacks, word began to spread from the medical journals to the popular media. Coverage of the new studies had been minimal, largely because publishers were reluctant to print bad news about some of their best advertisers. The exception was *Reader's Digest,* which, as the magazine with the largest circulation in the nation, was not worried about losing tobacco advertising and had long taken a stand against smoking. *The New Yorker* would also stop cigarette ads.

In 1953, *The New York Times* published twelve health and cigarette articles, and twenty-one more in the first three months of 1954. The stories there and elsewhere had an impact on smokers. Cigarette sales started to decline for the first time. The years 1953–55 are key because it was at the end of 1953 that Ernst Wynder made public the results of his devastating "mouse-painting" study. There followed a distinct change in the disdainful attitude of the tobacco companies. "Even the old families have been shaken. Philip Morris has retreated from gloomy reality to find solace in its new snap-open pack," observed *The New Republic. Business Week* noted that "fast-paced events loosened up for the first time official tongues of the tobacco industry, which up until now has preserved a rigid silence on lung cancer." Paul Hahn, president of the American Tobacco Company (Lucky Strike, Pall Mall, and Tareyton), complained about the "loose talk" on the issue, and another tobacco executive promised, "If we are guilty and they find out what causes cancer, we'll remove it from the cigarettes." Even so, the industry leaders knew the crisis warranted more than reassuring statements. So they took their battered image to Madison Avenue.

EVEN AS LITTLE sought funds for his laboratory from tobacco giant R. J. Reynolds, the tobacco company mobilized to lead an industry-wide effort to stave off potential disaster from the lung cancer scare. Tobacco stocks had fallen sharply in the wake of Wynder's study, and Reynolds and the other big companies—Philip Morris, Lorillard, and Brown & Williamson—joined in the search for a public relations firm "to get the industry out of this hole." They chose Hill & Knowlton, of New York.

Although most of Hill & Knowlton's experience was in heavy industry—it had big accounts in steel and aviation—the company had worked for the distillers and so already had some experience with a potentially harmful product. Its founder and chairman, John Hill, was a strong believer in free enterprise. Leaders of industry tended to trust Hill instinctively, and he had worked hard for this reputation, deliberately creating a somewhat conservative operation in contrast to the razzamatazz often found in the rest of Madison Avenue. Hill resisted anything fast and flashy. The tobacco companies liked his subdued approach, but they were in need of a quick fix. Hill obliged by working unusually fast.

A week after he took on the job, Hill produced his "preliminary recommendations." Wynder's and Doll's research could cause great panic among smokers, Hill said; the industry's situation was such that "there is no public relations nostrum, known to us at least, which will cure the ills of the industry with one swallow. . . . There is nothing the manufacturers can say or refrain from saying that can stop people from being interested in their health, nor allay their fear of cancer. So long as the causes and cure of this dread disease remain unknown people will be subject to waves of fear regarding it."

As a matter of priority, he advised, the industry should reassure the public that it would get to the bottom of the cancer scare. Part of his strategy was to create one of the most notorious documents in tobacco industry history. It was to become the basis for all later plaintiffs' lawyers' fraud charges. Entitled "A Frank Statement to Cigarette Smokers," it included two key points: one was that the industry "accepted an interest in the people's health as a basic responsibility, paramount to every other consideration in our business." The second point was that there was no "proof" that smoking caused cancer.

To create and sustain the attack on the link between smoking and cancer, Hill launched the Tobacco Industry Research Committee (TIRC), a research and public relations arm that, he insisted, must have a scientific director. The tobacco executives agreed to appoint a scientist of "unimpeachable integrity and national repute" to oversee the research program. The PR agency's grand strategy was not only to create a doubt about the validity of the evidence being produced, but to sustain it for as long as possible. The director had to be a credible spokesman for the group and one who would continue to point up the controversy, whatever independent research was produced. Little was such a man, but neither Hill nor the tobacco executives could have foreseen how quickly the mouse-house director would rise to the occasion.

IN FEBRUARY 1954, Little accepted an invitation to become one of the scientific members of the newly formed TIRC, but he was really hoping to be made scientific director. To bolster his candidacy, he prepared several statements saying he did not feel that "the definite cause-and-effect relationship between smoking and lung cancer has been established," and that "further and more accurate factors involved should be devised and utilized." Even more disdainfully, he said, "If smoke in the lungs was a surefire cause of cancer, we'd all have had it long ago." And, almost offhandedly: "I doubt very much you get tar out of the end of a cigarette."

Hill's well-oiled publicity machine channeled Little's pronouncements directly into the newspapers, bringing him a barrage of criticism from colleagues as well as strangers. Several of these attacks are to be found in his archives at the University of Maine. A real estate agent in Manhattan wrote him, "Don't you think that in your position as a doctor, and hence what would be considered one of the great leaders of the community, that you should be more careful in intimating that cigarettes are all right?"

Those same archives show that Little was prepared to be more than a mere spokesman. He campaigned actively behind the scenes, as well. For example, in the spring of 1954, the Boston publishing house of Little, Brown & Company, interested in producing a book for doctors about the new debate on smoking and lung cancer, contacted him. They had in mind a book in which chapters would be written "by top authorities in various fields." Would he be interested in contributing? The last thing the tobacco industry needed was an intelligent debate on the lung cancer "scare"; any discussion was bound to be negative because each new study was more definitive in its support of a link between cancer and smoking. Little decided to crush the proposal and ingratiate himself with the tobacco companies, at the same time.

"My own feeling," he wrote the Boston publisher,

> is that at the present time (and possibly for a considerable period in the future) there is not, and will not be, a sufficient body of accurate and pertinent experimental and statistical data to prevent such a book from being superficial and controversial.
>
> I realize that in some cases a controversial topic is a good way of selling books. . . . But when the general practitioner is likely to form immature and erroneous conclusions, and to obtain an incomplete or warped picture of cancer risk from any substance or substances, I think that the situation is a serious one. . . .
>
> Please understand that I have no desire to smother any freedom of expression, but that because you mentioned the topic to me I am honestly and directly giving my opinion and personal reactions. In other words, I am not making an "official" statement, but am simply writing as one who for a great many years has watched the various books on different phases of cancer, the majority of which, unfortunately, have delayed progress, rather than accelerating it.

Little sent a copy of the letter to Hill & Knowlton, hoping it might help his chances of becoming scientific director. It was unnecessary. The tobacco companies had already decided he was their man. A letter of appointment was in the mail. He was to be paid $20,000 a year plus reasonable traveling expenses and a further $10,000 for an assistant "who would do the necessary legwork around the country, giving you time for more important work."

Little, without question, performed his duties as though his life depended on it—and to a large extent it did. Undoubtedly, the life he sought—of a high-profile cancer researcher with trips to New York and beyond—could not have been financed by the Bar Harbor mouse house alone. For almost two decades, until his death in 1971, Little dismissed the concern of friends and colleagues that he had "sold out" to a callous industrial enterprise that cared not at all for the health of its captive clientele. He wrote in glowing terms of the benevolent intentions of the industry. He was convinced, he told a colleague at the University of Chicago, of the industry's desire for an "unprejudiced investigation, regardless of whether evidence of harmful effects of tobacco is forthcoming." The companies realize, he said, that "they cannot maintain their industry without facing any and all problems of health, whether these are welcome or not." Whether he suspected it or not, the industry would do its best to curb unprejudiced investigation, especially its own.

In June 1954, the American Cancer Society published a landmark study by two researchers, Cuyler Hammond and Daniel Horn, showing that death from lung cancer was up to nine times more common among one-pack-a-day cigarette smokers than among nonsmokers, and up to sixteen times more among those who smoked over a pack a day. Heavy smokers also showed twice the death rate from heart disease. Tobacco stock prices fell. Hammond, who was a four-pack-a-day smoker, and Horn, who smoked one pack a day, switched to pipes, which had shown lower disease and death rates. (Dr. Little smoked a pipe, too. But he joked about it. "My nose is so long that when I smoke a cigarette down it's rather unpleasantly warm.")

In their report, Hammond and Horn concluded that the association between smokers and lung cancer and heart disease was simply no coincidence. "We know of no alternative hypothesis," they said. Within days the British epidemiologists Doll and Hill produced another new study showing mild smokers were seven times more likely to die of lung cancer than nonsmokers, moderate smokers twelve times, and

heavy smokers twenty-four times. Dr. Little downplayed the results as
"preliminary," called for more research, and emphasized the possibility
of a "more fundamental cause of a constitutional or hormonal nature."
No cause and effect relationship had been proved, he said, adding that
the result might have been obtained because the "type of person who is
an excessive smoker is a poor health risk—he has more accidents, more
ailments."

Throughout the late 1950s, Dr. Little continued to proclaim that
his TIRC had but one purpose, namely "to find the truth, the whole
truth and see that it is made known as quickly and effectively as possible." Yet the annual reports of the TIRC's scientific board might as well
have been written by a PR consultant. Perhaps they were; he was certainly required to submit drafts that were then vetted by the TIRC's
office in New York.

By the late 1950s, Dr. Little had moved beyond the talk of a debate
between two scientific hypotheses and was making misleading statements and stating downright falsehoods, ignoring work that was being
produced in the research departments of the tobacco companies. For
example, Little maintained that there were no known carcinogenic substances in tobacco "tar." And even if cancers were found, there were
many substances that caused tumors on the skin of mice and yet had
been used by man without harmful effect for years—sugar, albumen,
and even tomato juice.

Yet in February 1953, a year before Dr. Little signed up with the
industry, R. J. Reynolds researcher Claude Teague wrote a report titled
"Survey of Cancer Research with Emphasis upon Possible Carcinogens
from Tobacco," in which he said, "Studies of clinical data tend to
confirm the relationship between heavy and prolonged tobacco smoking
and incidence of cancer of the lung. Extensive though inconclusive
testing of tobacco substances on animals indicates the probable presence
of carcinogenic agents in those substances."

In 1956, a chemist for R. J. Reynolds, Alan Rodgman, wrote a
paper entitled "The Analysis of Cigarette Smoking Condensate. 1: The
Isolation and/or Identification of Polycyclic Hydrocarbons in Camel
Cigarette Smoke Condensate." Rodgman wrote, "Since it is now well-
established that cigarette smoke does contain several polycyclic aromatic hydrocarbons, and considering the potential and actual carcino-

genic activity of a number of these compounds, a method of either complete removal or almost complete removal of these compounds from smoke is required." A year later, five such compounds had been isolated.

In 1957, Paul Kotin, a young pathologist working at the University of California, who was on Little's scientific advisory board, said, "The statement . . . to the effect that 'the sum total of scientific evidence establishes beyond reasonable doubt that cigarette smoke is a causal factor in the rapidly increasing incidence of human epidermoid cancer of the lung,' represents a view with which we concur."

In March 1961, Liggett & Myers received a report the company had commissioned from the Boston laboratories of Arthur D. Little on the constituents of tobacco smoke. The report began, "There are biologically active materials in cigarette tobacco. These are: a) cancer causing; b) cancer promoting; c) poisonous; d) stimulating and pleasurable.

If Clarence Little ever saw these reports, or even heard about them, his knowledge was never reflected in his public statements, some of which even mocked the growing concern. "About fifteen years ago there were headlines and a propaganda flurry based on statistical evidence that direct exposure to sunlight was a causative factor in skin cancer. This point of view, which was widely accepted, received support from experiments showing skin cancer on the ears of rodents following exposure to ultraviolet light, a component of sunlight. In spite of this, no one asked for legislation to bring back the bathing regalia of the gay nineties, and no one attempted to educate children not to visit the beaches or wear swimsuits, nor were farmers and sailors urged to carry umbrellas."

As the evidence against smoking grew, Little's position became more isolated. By 1957, the British government had accepted the link between smoking and cancer and in that year, too, the U.S. Surgeon General's report showed movement toward an acceptance of such a connection. His report said it was "clear that there is an increasing and consistent body of evidence that excessive cigarette smoking is one of the causative factors in lung cancer." Echoing his old refrain, Little responded that the evidence was not yet sufficient, more research was needed. And he suggested that the alarming increase in lung cancer mortality rates might be the result of improved diagnostic techniques, greater attention being paid to the disease, the aging of the population to a point where cancers were likely to occur, and better methods of reporting and classifying causes of death. But while techniques for detecting lung cancer had improved, Little ignored factors that indicated the increase was real: it had been adjusted for aging, and it was faster in men than in women, and men smoked more than women.

By 1961, more than twenty-five retrospective studies in nine countries demonstrated the link to lung cancer. As doctors and scientists continued to attack him, Little's responses became more and more inadequate. When the companies launched their own in-house research programs to block out some of the harmful substances in tobacco smoke with filter tips, Little never bothered to follow the research. During one of several congressional hearings into smoking and health, Little was asked what he knew about the new devices. Remarkably, he said he knew nothing. He had never received any reports on filters from the industry and had never been shown filter experiments on his trips to cigarette factories. "I have no opinion about the filter at all. I don't know why it was done and I frankly care—if you don't think I am in contempt—care very little. I care less, really."

In his private papers, Little wrote grandly of the "pure science" and "pure research" he was funding. But despite his million dollar budgets, the TIRC never performed such basic research. Through December 1961, the TIRC had spent five million dollars and its grantees had published 197 papers of great diversity, from the chemistry of tobacco smoke to cancer research to human lung, heart, and circulation studies. But many were only remotely connected with the smoking debate and there was no overall plan, no central focus. The TIRC never set up a study to answer the crucial question, Would a decrease in cigarette smoking result in a drop in deaths from lung cancer? Those researchers who produced results the industry did not want to hear—such as a Rand study that found burned cigarette paper to contain a carcinogen—were not funded again. Instead, through his many public appearances in the media, Little distorted, misconstrued, and misrepresented the original efforts of others who were finding a credible link between smoking and cancer.

The tobacco companies could not have been more pleased by his performance, of course. A TIRC executive memorandum in 1962 congratulated Little: the 1954 emergency had been "handled effectively"; the operating principles of TIRC had been outlined with "humble but magnificent judgment." TIRC had "carried its fair share of the public relations load to stamp out brush fires as they arose."

Perhaps the most shocking aspect of Little's service to the tobacco companies was his failure to reflect in his public pronouncements the work being done outside the TIRC—and outside the U.S.—that was important to the debate on smoking and health.

In 1962, Britain's Royal College of Physicians released a report entitled "Smoking and Health" that concluded "cigarette smoking is a cause of lung cancer and bronchitis, and probably contributes to the development of coronary heart disease and various other less common diseases." The report suggested five immediate steps to curb cigarette use: substituting pipe and cigar smoking for cigarettes; discouraging smoking by adolescents; restricting the advertising of cigarettes; restricting smoking in public places; and increasing taxes on tobacco. The Royal College is the preeminent association of the British medical profession and could not be lightly dismissed as a campaigning body; the last time it had made representations to the House of Commons was in 1725, when it expressed concern over the rising consumption of cheap gin and had succeeded in bringing about legislation to control that epidemic.

Sir Charles Ellis, the chief scientific adviser to British American Tobacco (BAT) downplayed the Royal College conclusion, calling it "emotional," the work of doctors who were overcome with anxiety about the spread of lung cancer. They had hastened to find a culprit, Ellis said, though he agreed there were some facts about tobacco use that could not be disregarded. For example, smoker's cough, the lower airway irritation caused by smoking, was a "real phenomenon and obvious to everyone." If further research showed there "really was a chemical culprit somewhere in smoke," then it should be brought out into the open. Sir Charles was quite confident that once identified it could be eliminated.

One of the more enlightened officials to join BAT during this troubled period was Jim Green, an industrial chemist who was taken on as director of research immediately after the publication of the Royal College report. Considering his position, Green made some bold, even

radical suggestions. The best protection for the "serious" situation facing the company was candor, he suggested; the company should "adopt
the attitude that the causal link between smoking and lung cancer was
proven—because we could not be any worse off [in denial of the link]."
Heresy though this was at the time, it became an increasingly widespread view among the industry scientists in Britain.

In America, the industry issued its own pamphlet, "Cigarette Smoking and Health: What Are the Facts?" There was no proof smoking
caused any disease, it declared yet again; the Royal College report was
incomplete. Other factors—viruses, pollutants, heredity, stress—should
be considered. Dr. Little's annual TIRC report for 1962 said, "The
unquestioning, unreserved endorsement [of a report like that of the
Royal College] . . . which contains no new or original data but
amounts to a statement of opinion, is a disservice to scientific research."
The real disservice, of course, was being committed by the TIRC and
by Little himself.

He also ignored new work in America—key studies that took the
causation issue beyond the soft science of epidemiology and the uncertain relevance of mouse studies right into a laboratory where human
tissue was examined under the microscope.

A New Jersey pathologist named Oscar Auerbach, working with
war veterans under a grant from the American Cancer Society, had
spent eight years examining more than 100,000 slides containing cells
from the bronchi, the two main lower branches of the windpipe, of
more than 1,500 corpses, men and women. He found abnormal and
precancerous cells in smokers that did not show up in nonsmokers'
lungs. The heavier the smoker, the more frequent the cell changes. In
reaction to the irritation caused by the smoke, the lining of the bronchi
had grown an extra two layers, trying to protect itself from the smoke,
and in the process narrowing the air passage to the lungs. In a number
of cases this thickening had turned into so-called metaplasia, an abnormal proliferation of cells that can become cancerous if unchecked.
Auerbach called it "carcinoma in situ," cancerous growths that had not
yet burst through the bronchi and infected other sites in the body.

Dr. Little also ignored the growing dissent among some of the
researchers within the U.S. tobacco industry itself. Plaintiffs' lawyers
were to find plenty of evidence for it later in the Merrell Williams

papers, and also in documents they would unearth separately in pre-trial discovery.

Third Wave lawyers in a 1996 Florida case dug out another report, this time from 1962, by Alan Rodgman, the research chemist with R. J. Reynolds. He had been with the company since 1954 and this was his sixth report on the smoking and health problem. As BAT's Jim Green had done in the wake of the Royal College report, Rodgman made some remarkably frank judgments. "The majority of scientists accept these [statistical] data as indicative of either a high degree of association or a cause-and-effect relationship between lung cancer and smoking," he wrote. And yet, he said, after a decade of publicly faulting the studies for methodology, the (U.S.) industry had ended up with nothing more than the dictum that "you can't prove it" and that "mice are not men." Rodgman complained about Little's simplistic rebuttals of the epidemiological evidence, and pointed out that fewer than a dozen scientists and statisticians actually opposed the conventional wisdom that there is a direct cause and effect. He wondered why R. J. Reynolds was not doing more in-house research to tackle the problem and why the data concerned with "carcinogenic compounds" available from his department had not been published. How could a company continue to repeat Dr. Little's maxim of "not proven" when they had research of their own showing there was a link between smoking and cancer? he asked. The commercial risks of being found out to have hidden such research were obvious.

Rodgman said it was "not his intention to suggest that the company accept the cigarette smoke–health data at face value," but the company should be more active in such studies. And he concluded with this prescient warning: "What would be the effect on this company of not publishing these data now, but being required at some future date to disclose such data, possibly in the unfavorable atmosphere of a lawsuit?"

A much more threatening attack on the industry came in January 1964: the U.S. Surgeon General would issue a report that, for the first time, declared smoking to be a cause of lung cancer. It concluded, "Cigarette smoking is causally related to lung cancer in men; the magnitude and effect of cigarette smoking far outweighs all other factors. The data for women, though less extensive, point in the same direction." Smoking was also said to be the most important cause of chronic bronchitis and it increased the risk of dying from emphysema, although that link had not been established as causal. Male smokers were also found to have a higher death rate from coronary heart disease, although no causative role was proven.

Now it was official: smoking caused lung cancer. But, once again, Dr. Little dismissed the findings. The link had not been proven, he said in his annual report. One member of his scientific advisory board, Dr. Paul Kotin, spoke privately of resigning if Little continued to ignore the results emerging all around him. In reality, his TIRC had never been anything more than a collection agency for information on smoking and health for the private use of the industry; it had never been aimed at solving the problem of smoking and health.

Two British tobacco industry researchers, Philip Rogers and Geoffrey Todd, both with the U.K. industry's Tobacco Research Council (the equivalent to the TIRC in the U.S.), spent a month in the U.S. in the fall of 1964, interviewing tobacco company presidents and officials, industry scientists, publicists, lobbyists, and congressmen. At the end of their stay, they wrote a report blandly entitled "Policy Aspects of the Smoking and Health Situation in the U.S.A." A broad overview of the American tobacco industry, it is one of the most insightful documents to be unearthed by the Third Wave lawsuits whose lawyers refer to it as the "de Tocqueville report." It has two devastating passages; one on the lawyers' takeover of scientific research, and another on Dr. Little's research group, the TIRC.

The two British researchers concluded that Little's group was a sham as a scientific organization. Its research was confined "to the diseases with which smoking is statistically associated," but it did not research the actual contents of the cigarette. Pharmacological research into the effects of nicotine was "about as close as the research comes to a cigarette."

As for Little's scientific advisory board, the British report said the members "continue to meet and decide on applications for grants to carry out research on what appeared to us to be projects of no more than remote relevance to current problems." There was "either no interest in or indeed no mention of [Little's research program] amongst the companies."

Although spurned, and sometimes abused, by his colleagues, Little never once wavered in his industry cheerleading. He made only a feeble complaint a few months before he died in 1971, when he acknowledged that the "team spirit" of his scientific advisory board was under threat. More funds for basic research had to be found, he said in his annual report, for those who had "lived the faith for over fourteen years." But the funds never came. By then, it was too late. The tobacco companies had established a pattern of concealment of the harmful effects of tobacco. There was no question of modifying those policies, no going back—until Merrell Williams stole his cache of papers from Brown & Williamson, industry whistle-blowers began telling their own stories, the Waxman hearings turned the spotlight on David Kessler's FDA inquiries, and the buccaneer lawyers of the plaintiffs' bar launched their final assault.

7

KINGS OF CONCEALMENT

Who are these persons who knowingly and secretly decide to put the buying public at risk solely for the purpose of making profits and who believe that illness and death of consumers is an appropriate cost of their own prosperity? . . . Despite some rising pretenders, the tobacco industry may be the king of concealment and disinformation.

—*Judge H. Lee Sarokin*

N HIS GRAY double-breasted suit and snakeskin cowboy boots, Ron Motley was pacing the anteroom of a West Palm Beach hotel and fidgeting; a slender, neatly wrapped package of nervous energy. It was late afternoon and he was waiting to address a conference of lawyers suing the tobacco industry. A colleague greeted him, asking about the delay. "They're pushing me back a damn hour," Motley complained, flicking his floppy black hair off his face and looking hurt. "They're breaking into my beer time, I'm getting thirsty." In a burst of frustration aimed nowhere and at no one, he added, "Y'all fuckin' me up here." Nobody took any notice. They'd heard it before and they didn't mind.

A star trial lawyer of the plaintiffs' bar, Motley's the best there is, or so many would say; sharp, witty, passionate. So what if he likes a drink? The son of a gas station owner from the poor neighborhood of North Charleston, South Carolina, Motley jokes that he "grew up as a grease monkey," quickly adding that he was the first in his family of distant Irish immigrants to go to college, at the University of South Carolina. A courtroom orator in the populist mode, he once dressed up in a doctor's white coat to cross-examine a pretentious expert witness, and during one of his asbestos trials he spun "the asbestos wheel of fortune," with panels showing each of the industry's excuses for the diseases its product caused. A veteran of plaintiffs' victories over such consumer hazards as silicon breast implants and the Dalkon Shield contraceptive device, as well as asbestos, Motley is a self-styled junkyard dog. Once he clamps his jaws on a corporation suspected of knowingly injuring people, he never lets go. When he's not in court nipping at a witness or playing to a jury, Motley is ill at ease. Given a delay in one of his public performances, he's out of sorts, desperate to be back on stage. In 1993, with Dick Scruggs, at the end of one asbestos settlement, the two agreed they were bored with chasing companies whose wrongdoing was, by that time, well known and admitted, and they asked each other, "What's next?" Since 1984, when his mother, a longtime smoker, lay dying of emphysema, Motley had vowed to avenge her death. It was natural that Motley joined forces with Scruggs and Moore in Mississippi, and with Gauthier in New Orleans, and he could not wait for the chance to meet the tobacco industry in court.

On this day in the summer of 1996, he entered the conference room before the other speaker had finished and deliberately distracted the audience by walking up and down, looking at his watch, and shuffling the handful of file folders containing his speech.

Dick Scruggs, the Mississippi lawyer and Motley's partner in several Third Wave suits against the tobacco companies, was running the conference and he began to take the hint. He called an end to the dreary session on tobacco company liability insurance—nobody seemed to know whether the companies were insured and no one seemed concerned about it. There were more important things to worry about, like upcoming trials. And they were waiting for Motley.

Although Motley was well known among this group, Scruggs introduced him. "He is a senior partner in Ness, Motley, Loadholt, Richardson & Poole of Charleston, South Carolina. He gained a nationwide reputation as one of the leading litigators of asbestos-related personal-injury claims and has served as lead trial counsel in a number of consolidated asbestos cases. He currently serves on the board of governors of the American Trial Lawyers Association and is a member of the Inner Circle of Advocates." The audience applauded respectfully.

In silence, Motley set himself up at the podium, arranged his folders as he would for an opening address to the jury, sorted notes, and made sure the tabs were in the right place. He cleared his throat. It was a performance, after all.

He asked for the lights to be dimmed so he could show slides of tobacco industry internal documents; secret files that, he said, just keep pouring into his office from anonymous sources—the media, government agencies, and even from Europe. "We receive documents from 'Mr. Butts' (the Gary Trudeau cartoon character) and he seems to live all over the U.S. and never uses the same post office." It was an in-joke about the anonymous donor of the box of documents sent to Professor Stan Glantz at the University of California, the only one who had actually received a packet from "Mr. Butts." In all his long experience in running liability cases, Motley said, he'd never seen anything like the flow of documents on tobacco.

And so to the matter at hand, the tobacco conspiracy. "In 1954, the tobacco companies issued a 'Frank Statement To Cigarette Smokers' that accepted an interest in the people's health as a basic responsibility 'paramount to every other consideration in our business,' but all they created was an illusion . . . they practiced the Big Lie philosophy, like Joseph Goebbels. They told a lie over and over again on every occasion."

Motley assured his audience that the companies would pay for their misdeeds. No question about it. "This thing is not going to go away," he promised. "Trial dates are set: Mississippi, March '97; Florida, August '97." The evidence will all come out, he pledged—everything that the Evil Empire of tobacco did to the public health of America.

His speech was modestly entitled "The Conspiracy to End Conspiracy." And what a conspiracy it was, he said. This was not a cabal of high-flying businessmen involved in a big deal that made them rich; this was an orchestrated plot in which lawyers, not businessmen (pause for effect)—lawyers connived in a cover-up to suppress public access to information about tobacco and disease. The evidence will "startlingly belie the notion that the public was aware of the risks of smoking. . . . One of the most telling things we've learned in the last few months is the efforts of in-house lawyers and outside counsel to purposely and

fraudulently withhold information from the courts of our country. . . .
The evidence of wrongdoing here is so overwhelming."

From the stash of documents stolen by Merrell Williams, Motley
produced a 1957 paper showing how the British company BAT and its
American subsidiary, Brown & Williamson, were so concerned about
lawsuits that they began to use code for words like lung cancer and
suspected carcinogens in tobacco smoke. On the screen the document
read, "As a result of statistical surveys, the idea has arisen that there is a
causal relationship between ZEPHYR and tobacco smoking, particularly cigarette smoking . . . tobacco smoke contains a substance or
substances which may cause ZEPHYR."

"Now," said Motley adopting an advisory tone, "if you're in New
Orleans you'd say that ZEPHYR is a minor-league baseball club because that's what it is. If you were to look in the dictionary you would
find that 'zephyr' is a 'light breeze, a gentle wind, the West Wind, a
breath of air.' We know, however, that's not what they meant. . . .
ZEPHYR meant cancer of the lung. . . . We know that from the
Merrell Williams papers."

He paused. "Why do lawyers in a corporation and scientists in a
corporation speak in codewords if there's no conspiracy?" And he began
to cite the evidence.

Company lawyers interfered with industry research. They scruti-
nized and censored the work of a scientist who had demonstrated that
the inhalation of fresh cigarette smoke produced tumors in the bronchi
of mice. "Get that," said Motley, his voiced raised, "the attorneys decided that the 'quality of the work did not adequately support the
conclusion'—despite the fact the researchers had done ten years of research and had been receiving tobacco money time and time again."

Evidence: Lawyers tried to suppress the work of the pathologist
Freddie Homburger of Cambridge, Massachusetts. Dr. Homburger,
who had received nearly a million dollars of tobacco funding through
Dr. Little's industry research group over almost twenty years, had found
90 percent of his experimental hamsters exposed to tobacco smoke
showed severe cancers in the larynx. What happened to Homburger?
He was paid a visit by industry lawyers who made it clear they were
unhappy with his work and warned that if he didn't change the word

"cancer" in his research paper to "pseudoepitheliomatous hyperplasia," he would never get another industry grant. Homburger refused and published the study in 1974. That was the end of his funding.

Evidence: Industry lawyers warned that in-house company research could "turn sour" and, "if it goes wrong, it could become the 'smoking pistol' in a lawsuit. . . ." "That's their words, not mine," Motley assured his audience.

Evidence: "Dr. Little's Tobacco Industry Research Committee originally set out to do research *pro bono publico*. But in 1977, they admitted to themselves in this document" (pointing to the screen) "that they could no longer say that. Why's that? The reason was because the lawyers, not Dr. Little, not the scientists—the lawyers decided what was going to be funded and what was going to be published . . . the lawyers picked the research. Period."

Evidence: Tobacco company lawyers had lied under oath in past lawsuits about the scientific research being done by the companies themselves. "Lies like that," he said, "lies that any juror could understand, can win product liability cases."

He ended to prolonged applause from the audience.

THE MERRELL WILLIAMS DOCUMENTS had provided antitobacco attorneys like Motley with an unprecedented insider's view of the lawyers' takeover of the tobacco industry at the end of the '60s. Clarence Cook Little and the Hill & Knowlton public relations firm had been holding down the defenses until then, but the mounting medical evidence from epidemiological studies and the increasing threat of civil lawsuits and government regulation now presented the industry with a stark choice: either continue to lie about the health risks, or tell the truth about what they knew. The industry could abandon Dr. Little's "not proven" dictum and admit publicly what its in-house research showed (and what was now accepted by the British and U.S. government official medical bodies)—that smoking causes lung cancer and heart disease. Or, it could launch a much more sophisticated and systematic cover-up. In that case, the illusion of a controversy over smoking and health would have to be maintained and, at the same time, the industry's own research had to be protected from the prying eyes of resourceful and determined plaintiffs' lawyers like Ron Motley.

The Williams documents show that there was a debate—albeit a perfunctory one—on this issue inside the industry. Two lawyers, each with great influence in the industry, emerged on opposite sides. One was David Hardy, a conservative country lawyer from Missouri. The other was Addison Yeaman, the chief counsel of Brown & Williamson in Louisville, Kentucky. As a result of his contacts with B&W's British parent company, BAT, Yeaman had been exposed to a somewhat different viewpoint than Hardy. In Britain, where there was no contingency-fee system for lawyers, the threat of litigation against the tobacco companies was much reduced. In fact, there had been no lawsuits, so the companies were more open about the effects of smoking and had even entered into partnership research with the government. Tobacco company scientists in Britain discussed the link between smoking and lung cancer in their internal papers. Yeaman received their reports on a regular basis and began to believe that the best way, perhaps the only way to cope with the "crisis" over smoking and health, was to admit what the industry knew about the harm smoking caused and do something to clean up the offending chemicals in cigarettes.

Hardy, by contrast, had formed his opinions in the American heartland, in his hometown of Kansas City. He took up the challenge to defend the tobacco industry as though he were going to war, with plaintiffs' lawyers as "the enemy." His solutions were rigid and authoritarian: as far as he was concerned, the only way for the industry to survive legal challenges and governmental regulation was to put severe restrictions on the flow of company information. Company scientific research should be locked up, he believed. He saw no place for the radical solution offered by Yeaman.

The debate spread throughout the industry, and the result set the tobacco companies on a course that assured their legal superiority throughout the First and Second Waves of tobacco litigation.

IN EARLY 1963, the tobacco companies were in urgent discussions about how to deal with the upcoming report on smoking and cancer from President Kennedy's Surgeon General, Luther Terry. Several thousand studies had by now been published, and the word was that Dr. Terry's report would declare that smoking was not only bad for you but would declare officially for the first time in America that it was the cause of lung cancer. It was the most devastating attack on the industry since Ernst Wynder's mouse-painting study, a decade earlier.

At the same time, two of the latest BAT research reports on Yeaman's desk explored nicotine's strange dual action on the brain as a tranquilizer as well as a stimulating drug. This function was to become known as "Nesbitt's Paradox," named for the young Columbia University student, Paul Nesbitt, who first measured this phenomenon under laboratory conditions using a group of college students. The new British research, which had been carried out in private at the Battelle Memorial Institute in Geneva, Switzerland, was codenamed "Hippo."

The Hippo study involved animal experiments that observed the action of nicotine on the hypothalamus, a part of the brain then attracting much attention among medical researchers because of its apparent control over the pituitary gland, the body's so-called master gland. The body's normal defense against stress is to release hormones, known as corticosteroids, from the adrenal system through a complex joint action of the hypothalamus and the pituitary. Determining exactly how all this happens was then at the cutting edge of medical research. What concerned the tobacco industry was whether the adrenal corticosteroids, introduced as wonder drugs to cope with stress, might be better than nicotine, perhaps even replace it one day. The results of Hippo, however, showed nicotine was superior because it had fewer side effects, as long as it wasn't smoked, of course. As a bonus it also proved to be an appetite depressant, a property not exhibited by the other tranquilizers.

Although it had been known for years that smoking reduced the appetite—a fact army generals had observed since World War I—the complex chemical changes were not fully understood. It was now clear that nicotine degraded fatty acids. The Hippo experiments, which concluded that "nicotine is actually one of the most potent drugs against obesity," were well ahead of their time and preceded published accounts by two decades.

At the same time the Hippo results reached Yeaman, the research labs at Brown & Williamson produced a new filter that showed real promise in being able to keep out some of the more harmful constituents of tar. Straying well beyond his legal brief, Yeaman now seized on the seemingly beneficial effects of nicotine, plus the new filter, as a way to make a radical shift in the industry's defensive public relations strategy and create its "first effective instrument of propaganda."

In a two-thousand-word memo on company policy dealing with the upcoming Surgeon General's report, Yeaman made it clear that he had never been a fan of Dr. Little's approach because it seemed that sooner or later some combination of the constituents of tobacco smoke would be found to produce cancers. If the industry wanted to preserve its present "earnings position," it should either "disprove the theory of the causal relationship, or discover the carcinogen or carcinogens, co-carcinogens, or whatever, and demonstrate our ability to remove or neutralize them." If the industry admitted what had become clear to the rest of the medical and scientific community, it could then move on to the business of producing a cigarette with fewer harmful substances and begin to extol the virtues of nicotine as laid out in the Hippo reports. At that point, said Yeaman in the most oft-quoted sentence from the Merrell Williams collection, "We are, then, in the business of selling nicotine, an addictive drug effective in the release of stress mechanisms."

Yeaman suggested the industry should embark on "massive and impressively financed research into the etiology of cancer as it relates to the use of tobacco." This research should probably be a cooperative effort with the Surgeon General, the Public Health Service, the American Cancer Society, the American Heart and Lung Associations, the American Medical Association, and any and all other responsible health agencies or medical or scientific associations concerned with the question of tobacco and health. Once that was set up, the industry would be "free to take a much more aggressive posture to meet attack." It might, for example, stress the gaps in the scientific knowledge while showing it was doing all it could to close them—not just being party to a public relations front like Dr. Little's old TIRC. It could stress the "benefits" of nicotine over the new tranquilizers. B&W's new filter offered a "bridge," Yeaman argued, over which the industry might pass from its present defensive position to a counterattack.

There was a legal danger, of course. By admitting a health problem, the industry might worsen its chances in lawsuits. But Yeaman pointed out that with one exception the lawsuits against the tobacco companies had all been won relatively easily by the traditional defense of placing the assumption of risk on the smoker. The exception was *Green* v. *American Tobacco Company.*

Edwin Green had started smoking Lucky Strikes in the 1920s, when he was sixteen, and smoked up to three packs a day until 1956, when he was diagnosed with lung cancer. In 1957, Green filed a $1.5 million lawsuit in a Florida state court against Lucky Strikes's manufacturer, the American Tobacco Company, charging that by selling the product, the company had implied a warranty of fitness and should be held liable for any damages incurred. The jury concluded that Lucky Strikes had in fact caused Green's lung cancer, but awarded no damages because, they said, the company could not have known prior to the date Green's cancer was discovered that smoking Lucky Strikes would cause it.

The verdict was appealed on the grounds that Florida state law did not require the defendant to be aware of the dangers of its product in a suit involving implied warranty. A new trial was ordered. This time the judge ruled that the company could only be held responsible for breach of warranty if the cigarettes endangered an important number of smokers, not just one. In other words, Green's case was not enough to condemn an entire industry. Faced with finding whether cigarettes were dangerous to the general public, the jury found for the company, but it was a narrow escape for American Tobacco and the case caused great concern in industry boardrooms.

The question Yeaman had to address was how to ensure continued success in lawsuits after an admission that smoking caused disease. Not wanting to be, as he put it, "tarred and feathered" by his colleagues, Yeaman made what he called the "shocking" suggestion of putting a warning label on the cigarette pack. (As yet there were no labels; they were introduced in 1966 as a result of the Cigarette Labeling and Advertising Act, 1965.) Yeaman thought a suitable legend might be something along the lines of "excessive use of this product may be injurious to the health of susceptible persons." The companies could then point to the warning as evidence that the smoker had assumed a known risk.

People who smoked prior to the 1966 labeling date could and would continue to make claims, but the Green case suggested the companies could put up a viable defense that they could not have known of the dangers before the labels were put on cigarette packs. Yeaman recognized that there was another problem: although the buyer might be found negligent in smoking a product he knew was dangerous, he could still claim that the seller's negligence was the greater in failing to make his product safe. In that case, it was important to establish a new "massively financed" joint research organization with independent research groups to produce a "safe cigarette."

Yeaman had not suddenly turned into a public health advocate. As he had said, his plan was to find a way of keeping "earnings up." As the industry was in the "nicotine business," whatever kind of new, cleaner, and more acceptable type of cigarette was produced would, he suggested, be one that removes "whatever constituent of smoke is currently suspect while delivering full flavor—and incidentally a nice jolt of nicotine." This combination of admission plus commitment to new research would put B&W at a tremendous advantage over its competitors, said Yeaman. In case the marketing department of B&W had not got the message, Yeaman added, "And if we are the first to be able to make and sustain that claim, what price Kent?"

Such radical thoughts appalled B&W executives, not to mention BAT officials in London. None of them would admit to selling harmful products. Nor did they want their private research papers made public in any joint venture with a government or other research body. That much had already been made clear. All the tobacco companies had been invited by Dr. Terry to submit research papers to his review committees. There had been an anxious discussion inside BAT and B&W as to whether the Hippo reports and the B&W filter should be presented. In London, BAT executives had been impressed by their laboratory confirmation of the tranquilizing and antiobesity effects of nicotine but wanted to do more research before they told anyone. In Louisville, B&W's CEO, Ed Finch, worried about the Hippo report's mention of cardiovascular disorders. Researchers already knew that nicotine could increase heart rate and contribute to high blood pressure. The carbon monoxide in cigarette smoke was found to encourage the formation of atheromas, the fatty plaques found in the arterial walls that contribute to the blockage of blood supply to the heart. At this point, researchers didn't know how significant smoking was in the creation of heart disease. In the end, none of BAT's or B&W's expert knowledge was passed to the Surgeon General's committee.

Six months after Yeaman's memo, in January 1964, Surgeon General Luther Terry published his report declaring cigarette smoking was causally related to lung cancer in men and cigarette smokers had a higher rate of coronary heart disease. The in-house lawyers of the six biggest tobacco companies, R. J. Reynolds, the American Tobacco Company, Brown & Williamson, Philip Morris, Liggett & Myers, and Lorillard, began immediate action to counter what they expected would be a flood of new lawsuits. They formed a new policy body known as the Committee of Counsel to guide company policy on research into smoking and health. This body was supported by six lawyers from outside firms who formed what was known as the ad hoc group, which was chaired by David Hardy. These outside law firms began compiling lists of medical and scientific literature specifically for use in litigation. R. J. Reynolds, then the company with the biggest market share (36 percent, American was second with 23 percent, and B&W was third with 11 percent), had more than 20,000 scientific papers on record by the summer of 1964.

That fall, the two British tobacco-industry researchers, Philip Rogers and Geoffrey Todd, who had toured the companies and interviewed officials, wrote of the dilemma posed by the lawsuits in the United States. "The manufacturers have to choose," they said, "between (a) doing no smoking and health research and being represented in lawsuits as negligent . . . [and] (b) doing smoking and health research and being forced to admit in lawsuits that their experiments have caused cancer in animals and yet they have made no changes in tobacco smoke to eliminate the tumors. The manufacturers have chosen (a)."

Like Clarence Little, Hill & Knowlton would find themselves ignored in the aggressive lawyer takeover. The PR agency found it increasingly difficult to provide workable counterattacks to what was now the consensus of scientific thought: that smoking was a cause of lung cancer and probably also of heart disease. But the Hill & Knowlton executives also found the industry increasingly reluctant even to talk about their problem. "We had influence on policy at the beginning," recalled Loet Velmans, who had begun working at the agency during the health scare of the mid-1950s and later became H&K's chief executive officer. "We could consult with [the client], on what areas of research more specifically to look at, in terms of lung disease and, later, heart disease [but post-1964] the client shut us out after a couple of years, because he probably knew more than he would ever admit." The agency's original enthusiasm for defending the tobacco industry quickly faded. Velmans recalled, "Hill & Knowlton's position was, 'What are we doing in all this? We are only raking in money. But we are a privately owned company; we'll get another account or two, and we'll replace that.' " After a decade of promoting the U.S. tobacco industry as a caring concern that spent millions ensuring that smokers were not taking undue risks, the agency closed the account. Another Madison Avenue firm, Leonard Zahn, took over but they were never as important as H&K had been. The lawyers were now in charge.

The decade following the Surgeon General's report would see the rise to extraordinary prominence of a group of industry lawyers led by David Hardy. There would be no admission of the harmful effects of smoking, no acknowledgment that nicotine is addictive, no massive research to find the cancerous substances in tobacco smoke, and no policy to develop a "safe cigarette" as free as possible from carcinogenic compounds. Instead, in-house scientific reports would be monitored, censored, and hidden from public view in a scheme to keep the fabulously lucrative enterprise alive and free of government regulation.

HOW A SMALL LAW FIRM located hundreds of miles from the tobacco fields and cigarette factories of Virginia and the Carolinas became the industry's favorite defender was a chance affair.

In 1962, a Missouri man named John Ross, a heavy smoker of Philip Morris brands, lost his larynx to cancer and filed suit against the company in Kansas City. The first local lawyer chosen by Philip Morris as lead counsel for the defense was appointed a federal judge and had to withdraw. So their second choice, Dave Hardy, got the job. A native of rural Tipton, Missouri, Hardy was the epitome of a small-town American—wholesome, comfortable, confident, and driven. He worked such long hours that his nickname was "Fourteen-hour-a-day Dave." He had become a successful trial lawyer, and by the time Philip Morris came along, his firm had a score of partners.

For the Ross case, Hardy's long hours of homework paid off. By the time he had finished his defense, it took the jury of twelve smokers only an hour to conclude that Ross had not proven his cancer came from Philip Morris cigarettes.

From that moment, Philip Morris basically adopted the firm of Shook, Hardy & Bacon. With this lucrative tobacco business, the firm blossomed from a modest practice into an international enterprise with 175 lawyers and scores of specialist researchers, biochemists, statisticians, and veterinarians—the full arsenal of the tobacco defender—making it the largest law firm in Kansas City. Soon, there would be offices in London and Zurich. The firm would successfully represent five of the Big Six tobacco companies—American, Brown & Williamson, R. J. Reynolds, Philip Morris, and Lorillard, plus the Tobacco Institute, the industry's PR arm in Washington, D.C.

The firm's offices reflect its success, with tasteful furnishings in mahogany and marble. Security is tight, especially on the twenty-fourth floor, where the tobacco lawyers meet. The elevator leads to a long corridor with locked offices and a reception area with no receptionist.

Dave Hardy, who was a Marlboro smoker, died of a heart attack in 1976 at the age of fifty-nine. A portrait of him hangs in the attorneys' lounge. Hardy's son, another David, now leads the tobacco team. About one hundred of the firm's lawyers work in the tobacco division and over the years they have always commanded the respect of their colleagues. There was a time when even nonsmoking Shook, Hardy partners carried cigarette packs in their shirt pockets or briefcases out of solidarity. Even now antismoking gestures are frowned on. The story is told that when a Shook, Hardy lawyer showed his colleagues a Doonesbury antismoking strip of Mr. Butts, his superiors "looked at him like he'd brought out a dead animal." Moral pangs about the ethics of tobacco work, if indeed there are any, are not supposed to surface. "You don't buck tobacco," said one former partner.

Dave Hardy's service to the industry spanned the First Wave of tobacco litigation—from the mid-fifties into the seventies. It was a period that included the time when BAT's British laboratories were busy experimenting with the effects of tobacco tar on mice and also researching the effects of nicotine. The results were openly discussed at BAT research conferences and copies of the scientific papers were sent to B&W's Louisville headquarters for distribution among its research staff. These internal "leaks" of potentially damaging research caused concern on both sides of the Atlantic.

Changes in the Federal Rules of Civil Procedure governing pretrial discovery had made it easier for plaintiffs' to get copies of such documents. The tobacco company lawyers worried that a smart plaintiffs' counsel might uncover embarrassing reports by deposing a company employee, or by imaginative "interrogatories"—written questions that require answers under oath. These procedures could put BAT itself at risk. Even though the British company was in London, it was not free of the American states' "long-arm" statutes and could be brought into litigation if a plaintiff's lawyer had enough resources to try. BAT had already been named in one tobacco case in Chicago, but the anti-tobacco lawyer had made a mistake in the filing, alleging that BAT manufactured, marketed, and sold B&W brand cigarettes in the state of Illinois, which BAT did not. If the plaintiff's lawyer had used some other legal language, such as "by and through its agent and wholly owned subsidiary, B&W," then BAT might have remained a defendant in the case. In any event, B&W's legal department in Louisville had asked Dave Hardy, by now a veteran defender for the industry, to write a legal opinion on these tricky issues. Hardy was sent a number of BAT research reports to help him formulate the best approach. His reply not only advocated continuing the cover-up started by Dr. Little, but also suggested that research scientists who made "careless" comments about their work should be warned of the "consequences."

In a seven-page letter, dated August 20, 1970, Hardy advised that statements made by some employees in scientific reports and at research conferences "constitute a real threat" to the continued success of the industry's defense of tobacco litigation. "The effect of testimony by employees or documentary evidence from the files of either BAT or B&W which seems to acknowledge or tacitly admit that cigarettes cause cancer or other disease would likely be fatal to the defense of either or both companies in a smoking and health case," he wrote. Such an admission would give a plaintiff's case a "posture of strength and danger never before approached in cigarette litigation," he said. "It could even be the basis for an assessment of punitive damages if it were deemed to indicate a reckless disregard for the health of the smoker. Certainly, such evidence would make B&W the most vulnerable cigarette manufacturer in the United States to smoking and health suits."

Hardy was, in effect, impugning the integrity and company loyalty of the research scientists in BAT's labs in England who had become convinced that smoking did cause cancer and heart disease. He wrote, "We, of course, know that the position of BAT, as well as B&W, is that disease causation by smoking is still very much an open question. Cigarettes have not been proved to cause any human disease. Thus, any statement by responsible and informed employees subject to a contrary interpretation could only result from carelessness. Therefore, employees in both companies should be informed of the possible consequences of careless statements on this subject."

Of course, Hardy must have known from reading the reports that for a decade at least BAT's scientists had believed smoking causes cancer. But he wanted them to keep what they knew strictly to themselves. "Careless statements," in Hardy's view, included the mere mention of research into cancer or a "safer product," because they implied cigarettes then on sale were unsafe. For example, he complained about the following phrases and sentences from the minutes of a research conference held in Kronberg, Germany, in 1969: "a mouse-skin safer cigarette is a worthwhile objective"; "there is a possibility that the experiments taking place at [the BAT research facility at Southampton, England] with the membrane of the chicken embryo might be showing genuine carcinogenic effects in days"; "the conclusion of the conference was that at the present time the industry had to recognize the possibility of distinct adverse health reactions to smoke aerosol: (a) lung cancer (b) emphysema and bronchitis." Hardy also deleted any reference to the phrase "biologically active," which was used to mean cancer-forming.

Reviewing another BAT conference, this one held in St. Ives, in England, Hardy objected to statements referring to "the search for a safe cigarette" and a "healthy cigarette" that were, in Hardy's words, "most damaging." He wanted all such statements, opinions, and references deleted because they threatened his defense strategy in court. "Of course, we would make every effort to 'explain' such statements if we were confronted with them during a trial, but I seriously doubt that the average juror would follow or accept the subtle distinctions and explanations that we would be forced to urge."

To protect BAT and Brown & Williamson against such legal traps, Hardy even wanted to tear up the 1969 R&D agreement between BAT and B&W in which the two companies shared the costs of research being done in England by BAT. In the U.S. the tobacco companies had apparently been careful not to have any such formal agreements about potentially embarrassing research. In fact, there had been a "gentlemen's agreement" among the manufacturers to suppress independent research on the issue of smoking and health. This agreement was mentioned in a 1968 internal Philip Morris draft memo, which said, "We have reason to believe that in spite of the gentlemans [sic] agreement from the Tobacco Industry in previous years that at least some of the major companies have been increasing biological studies within their own facilities." BAT was one such company and that posed a problem, according to Hardy. A "carefully framed" pretrial discovery motion "might, in fact, be able to force production of certain documents from B&W which are presently in the custody of BAT only."

Hardy also advised B&W to protect itself from what he called "actual knowledge on the part of the defendant that smoking is generally dangerous to health, that certain ingredients are dangerous or should be removed, or that smoking causes a particular disease." In other words, the industry could not defend itself against antitobacco research if its own scientists had some of the same views on their product. For example, the industry could not maintain its position that mouse-skin painting was not valid for humans when a company report from Germany stated, as it did, that mouse-skin painting was the "ultimate court of appeal on carcinogenic effects."

HARDY'S ADVICE was not exclusive to B&W; he advised the industry as a whole and over the next two decades, company lawyers moved to monitor and censor internal scientific projects, eliminating those deemed unfavorable. The idea was to protect company files that could be used against the industry in court. Once they had chosen the approach suggested by Dave Hardy, there was no room for compromise.

As insurance against sensitive research documents slipping through and then being uncovered by plaintiffs, Brown & Williamson attorneys took two basic precautions. They labeled sensitive documents "privileged" or "work product" so they could be kept secret.

The attorney-client privilege rule is a mainstay of American jurisprudence. Essentially, it allows any communication between an attorney and his or her client to remain confidential and outside the scope of pretrial discovery. An attorney cannot be compelled to testify about communications with a client, unless the client consents. The work-product rule protects the work of an attorney in anticipation of litigation.

There was considerable discussion at B&W about which type of documents came clearly under the rules. For example, the B&W lawyers acknowledged that the 1969 research cost-sharing agreement between B&W and BAT probably "contradict the position that you were acquiring the reports for purposes of litigation." To clarify the situation in the company's favor, the B&W lawyers recommended that one company lawyer be assigned to monitor all scientific reports.

A decade later, by the mid-eighties, work at BAT's Harrogate labs in Britain had come to an end and BAT-sponsored research had stopped at other labs in Europe. But the lawyers were still worried about leaks.

Then, in 1984, Dr. L. C. F. Blackman, BAT's executive director for research and development, wrote a thirty-three-page booklet entitled, "The Controversy on Smoking and Health—Some Facts and Anomalies." It was intended to familarize company employees with reports that are "inconsistent with the view that smoking has been proven to be a cause of disease." Even though it only contained views favorable to the industry, B&W's corporate counsel, J. Kendrick Wells, considered it far too risky to disseminate and made forty-five line-by-line changes and deletions. He even objected to titles of sections. For example, "Background to Medical Dilemma" was changed to "Background to Medical Concern." Scientists who seemed to Blackman worthy of inclusion because they supported the industry's contention of a "controversy" in one paper were deleted by Wells because they had published work elsewhere that was not supportive.

Blackman had quoted British researchers Richard Doll and Richard

Peto as saying that epidemiological studies linking smoking to lung cancer and heart disease "does not necessarily imply that smoking caused them. The relation may have been secondary in that smoking was associated with some other factor, such as alcohol consumption or a feature of the personality. . . . " Although this was taken out of the context of the greater part of their work, it was certainly a good sound bite for the industry. Wells objected because Doll and Peto were the main British proponents of the causal link. "Any reference to Doll must be crafted carefully because he is a dedicated advocate of the causal hypothesis," wrote Wells.

Certain words were banned. Wells did not want tobacco referred to as a drug, nor would he allow mention of nicotine being "addictive," or even a reference to the pharmacological effects of nicotine. Donald Gould, writing in the *New Scientist* magazine in 1975, had said, "Cigarettes calm, they comfort, they give pleasure, they act as a kind of stockade, a visible barrier between the naked individual and a hostile world." It sounded good to Blackman, but Wells pointed out that elsewhere in the article Gould identifies cigarettes as a drug.

In another reference that Blackman thought would serve the industry well, Dr. W. S. Cain of the Yale University School of Medicine wrote in 1979 that smoking produces relaxation and reduces anxiety, enhancing the power to concentrate, self-confidence, and social facilitation. "Without the benefits of such features, most smokers would never establish the habit in the first place." Delete, demanded Wells. "The article identifies short-term and longer term pharmacological and physiological factors as important in the derivation of 'habitual cigarette smoking.' "

WELLS WAS CERTAINLY doing his best to protect the company's internal research papers from the prying eyes of plaintiffs' lawyers. The process generated much debate within the company. In a 1979 memo, Wells discussed how research material from BAT's laboratories in Southampton should be generally available to B&W's researchers but still be considered as "privileged" and therefore protected from discovery in a lawsuit. The law is quite clear: "work product" documents are only those prepared in anticipation of a lawsuit, not those prepared in the general course of scientific experiments and studies. This is how Mr. Wells suggested the company might overcome the problem:

"Continued Law Department control is essential for the best argument for privilege. At the same time, control should be exercised with flexibility to allow access of the R&D staff to the documents. The general policy should be clearly stated that access to the documents and storage of the documents is granted only upon approval of request." Wells suggested the documents should be categorized for their sensitivity and placed in a secure storage area. No more than abstracts of the less sensitive papers should be circulated—and then only to a list approved by the law department. In other words, the law department had total control over which documents scientists were allowed to see.

Evidently this procedure became too burdensome: most documents from Britain were not sensitive and clogged up the system in the law department, so Wells modified the plan. He suggested that all reports, instead of going to the law department, should be filtered through B&W's International and External Services Department. This office would, in effect, become B&W's "agent" for the acquisition of scientific material "in anticipation of litigation." The department would "separate the reports which were relevant to smoking and health, or otherwise sensitive, for special handling."

The issue of how to deal with sensitive research continued to be a problem. Of course, Wells realized that he could not shut down the flow of reports or plug all the leaks. It would help, he noted caustically, if BAT would stop producing research reports in Canada, Germany, and Brazil. A raft of studies on nicotine and "biological" (i.e., possibly carcinogenic) constituents of smoke were due to start in those countries. Whatever rules were put in place, preventing a plaintiff's access to in-house reports was bound to be a hit or miss affair. Even the lawyers acknowledged that a Merrell Williams was bound to emerge one day. A 1985 company memo entitled "B&W's Public Issue Environment," noted that the company "must assume that its documents, existing and created during the planning period, referring to marketing or smoking and health will be obtained by the plaintiffs' lawyers . . . and leaked to the press."

Wells also proposed in 1985 that certain medical research should be stored separately from other archives, and, perhaps, even shipped back to England. Included were the results of Project Janus, a series of experiments on the biological effects of cigarette smoke that had isolated some of the carcinogenic substances. Wells wrote, "I suggested . . . that this was part of an effort to remove deadwood from the files and that [no one] should make any notes, memos or lists." It is not known if any of the "deadwood" files were actually removed and sent to England.

Later, in a 1986 memo, Wells warned against B&W receiving reports in a form that "could serve as road maps for a plaintiff's lawyer." He wanted reports limited to "good science," that is, science that did not embarrass the industry, and to "information [that] is useful in the United States market." He wrote, "Our market is a 'tar' and nicotine market, and information pertaining to other constituent delivery levels and biological effects would not be helpful." In other words, Wells wanted to protect B&W against receiving "bad" reports about the "biological activity" or cancer-forming properties of other compounds in tobacco smoke.

PREVENTING THE DISSEMINATION of "careless" comments from British scientists who didn't have to worry about lawsuits was one thing: funding research projects in the United States that might come to the same unwanted and legally risky conclusions was quite another. After the 1964 Surgeon General's report, smoking and health research was still carried out in the United States by tobacco companies in their own laboratories and some research was conducted under contract with outside firms through the Council for Tobacco Research. But the research was very strictly controlled by lawyers. Topics were chosen specifically to perpetuate the controversy about health effects; biological experiments to test for potential carcinogens in smoke were avoided. The lawyers created a cadre of researchers who could be guaranteed to produce papers useful to a legal defense. These were called "Special Projects" and they were chosen and administered by the Committee of Counsel's ad hoc group of outside lawyers chaired by David Hardy. The group had six members, each representing a different tobacco company.

One of the lawyers was Ed Jacob of the New York law firm of Jacob, Medinger. Jacob, who represented R. J. Reynolds and Brown & Williamson, described how the system was set up. "When we started the CTR special projects [in the mid-sixties] the idea was that the scientific director of CTR [Dr. Little] would review the project. If he liked it, it was a CTR special project. If he did not like it then it became a lawyers' special project." But as time passed the lawyers took greater control, and initiated their own projects without consulting the CTR.

Several of the special projects were designed to bolster Dr. Little's "constitutional hypothesis." Others paid for researchers to go on trips or write papers supporting the industry's view. Individuals were paid from $2,500 to $4,000 to prepare these statements, which favored the tobacco industry's position. Some researchers were paid for "continuing consultancies," which averaged from $500 to $1,500 per month and ran as high as $62,400 for a two-year project.

Under this new regime, the lawyers ruled. In December 1976, the Addiction Research Foundation, directed by Stanford University pharmacologist Avram Goldstein, asked Dr. Little's CTR for $400,000 to construct a new research facility so that he could expand his work on opiate addiction to include nicotine addiction. The CTR replied that it was not in a position to provide funds for laboratory construction but would consider proposals "specifically directed to tobacco use and health." The foundation then applied directly to the individual companies, but they had been alerted by lawyers at Shook, Hardy, and Goldstein was again turned down. Finally, the foundation applied to Shook, Hardy, arguing that the tobacco industry should be interested because its work could lead to a "safe cigarette," one that "could create the nicotine effect that smokers enjoy without the toxicity of nicotine." The foundation even offered to delete the word "addiction" from their project, if that was what had "turned off" the tobacco companies. Still, the application was rejected; funds were not available for anyone who believed, as Goldstein's foundation clearly did, that nicotine was addictive. This policy was made clear in an internal Tobacco Institute memo that stated, "[The] foundation actually assumes tobacco (nicotine) is addictive and costs the US citizen $42 billion a year! [They] also believe tobacco causes 300,000 premature deaths each year. And [they] wonder if this is why we might not be interested."

Among the recipients of special account funds in the U.S. was Carl Seltzer, a professor of public health at Harvard University. He worked on Dr. Little's "constitutional hypothesis" and other topics countering the evidence that smoking causes heart disease. When Seltzer retired in 1976, he continued to work on "constitution and disease" at Harvard's Peabody Museum of natural history and was awarded grants of more than $750,000 until 1990. Seltzer went on lecture tours for the Tobacco Institute, the industry PR arm in Washington, D.C. One tour to Australia and New Zealand was rated a "great success." His lectures and radio interviews on that tour spawned headlines such as "Smokers—Take Heart," "Doctor Slams Link Between Smoking and Heart Disease," and "Smoking Does Not Cause Heart Disease."

Lawyers like Ed Jacob who ran the special accounts were always on the lookout for research to fund in other countries, particularly Britain. One recipient, Britain's most controversial psychologist, Hans Eysenck, was one of the founding members of the "constitutional hypothesis" so beloved by Dr. Little. At the end of the 1960s, Eysenck had published a book, *Smoking, Health and Personality,* in which he laid out his theory that smokers were essentially born, not made. There were smoking types, mostly extroverts, and nonsmoking types, mostly introverts. The tobacco industry loved this idea and heaped funds on Eysenck, who worked at London University's Institute of Psychiatry. According to the Merrell Williams documents, Eysenck received more than £70,000 from Special Account No. 4 and nearly £900,000 in research grants between 1977 and 1989. The institute itself received more than two million pounds sterling from tobacco industry sources over the same period.

Asked if he had ever heard of the special accounts, Eysenck said that Ed Jacob had called him one day after his book was published and suggested that he submit research proposals, which he did, and the money started to flow. So, did he have thoughts about tobacco industry lawyers being involved in selecting scientists for research projects? "Well, I really have no feelings. As long as somebody pays for the research I don't care who it is." Mr. Jacob did not respond to requests for an interview.

8

AN ORGY
OF BUNCOMBE

Not since the days when the vendor of harmful nostrums
was swept from our streets, has this country witnessed such
an orgy of buncombe, quackery and downright falsehood as
now marks the current campaign promoted by certain
cigarette manufacturers to create a vast woman and child
market.

—*U.S. Senator Reed Smoot of Utah, 1929*

EVEN WHEN he knew only a little about the marketing of cigarettes, David Kessler was a man obsessed. He could talk about
tobacco for hours. By the summer of 1995, when he knew a
great deal, he was almost uncontrollable. By then, this pediatrician-
turned-politician had focused his campaign on teenage smoking. In his
commissioner's office at the headquarters of the Food and Drug Administration, Kessler would take off his jacket, draw up his chair, and glare
at you through the thick lenses of his spectacles. It would not be an
interview so much as a lecture. In clear and measured sentences, as
though you might be encountering difficulty following what he had to
say, he would begin to expound the need for new rules to prevent the
youth of America from becoming addicted to nicotine. One hour would
quickly turn into two, then three.

"Nicotine addiction really begins as a pediatric disease," he would
begin, stretching out the syllables of *pe-di-at-ric,* for emphasis. "I mean
it's not only that eleven-, twelve-, and thirteen-year-olds begin to use
tobacco, it's that by the age of sixteen and seventeen they are addicted.
The tobacco industry would have you believe that smoking is a free

choice made by adults. They are wrong. Ask a smoker when he or she began, and you will hear"—pause—"the tale of a child."

In rapid succession he would cite evidence and produce exhibits. "Let me show you, in their own words, what they say about children and youth. Imperial Tobacco, the Canadian affiliate of BAT in the U.K., wrote this market report. 'If the last ten years has taught us anything it is that the industry is dominated by the companies that respond most effectively to the needs of young smokers.'

"Two documents, one called 'Project Sixteen' and the other called 'Project Plus, Minus,' really tell the story of who becomes a smoker. Let me read to you from Project Sixteen. Quote, 'However intriguing smoking was at eleven, twelve, or thirteen, by the age of sixteen or seventeen many regretted their use of cigarettes for health reasons and because they feel unable to stop smoking when they want to.' Listen to these words. They are not my words. They are from the tobacco industry. 'The fragile developing self-image of the young person needs all the support it can get . . . this self-image enhancement effect has traditionally been a strong theme for cigarette advertisements and should continue to be emphasized.'

"Therefore," he continued without a pause, "we believed at the Food and Drug Administration that the best public health strategy was to intervene before people became addicted. It's not about quitting; it's about starting. If you want adults not to smoke, the best way is to have a generation grow up tobacco-free."

Intense and animated, Kessler never stopped talking, but when he took a breath, I managed to insert a question. "Your critics in the public health community would say that by concentrating on children, you're making smoking an adult pleasure and therefore attracting children to the habit."

"Not at all," shot back Kessler. "What we're trying to do is reduce the positive imagery the industry has played up for so long. The tobacco industry spends $6 billion a year on advertising and promotion. They say it isn't aimed at children, but what are the three most heavily advertised brands in this country? They're Marlboro, Camel, and Newport. What are the brands that teenagers smoke the most? Marlboro, Camel, and Newport."

At this point Kessler holds up a glossy advertisement, a folded insert from a magazine for a rock concert sponsored by R. J. Reynolds, the makers of Camel cigarettes. As he opens it, Joe Camel pops up offering tickets to the concert. "This comes from magazines that my children have in their rooms at home. What we're trying to reduce is this positive imagery. . . . Once you look at the evidence, once you look at what's come to light over the last several years, you can never look at a cigarette in the same way. You can never say, 'This is just a usual commodity.' "

ONE YEAR AFTER Kessler's tobacco task force had solved the mystery of the high-nicotine plant, Y1, Kessler had found his real target, one that would eventually win over doubters in the White House and allow him to move forward with new rules to regulate the tobacco industry. The figures on youth smoking were alarming. Adult smoking had declined by 40 percent since 1965, but youth smoking had suddenly started to rise again, and no one was quite sure why. Teenagers had been using more drugs of all kinds since 1990, more marijuana, LSD and other hallucinogens, amphetamines, stimulants, and inhalants each year.

Three thousand teenagers start smoking every day and of those nearly one thousand will die prematurely, according to the Surgeon General. Among eighth-graders, the percentage of those who have smoked in the previous thirty days increased 30 percent between 1991 and 1994. Eight out of ten ninth-graders said they had no trouble buying cigarettes, even though the law says they have to be eighteen. Some estimates said as many as 255 million packs of cigarettes were sold illegally to minors each year.

Kessler blamed the industry's advertising and promotion. One study of cigarette use, commissioned by the U.S. Centers for Disease Control in Atlanta, has suggested teenage smoking is related to the amount the industry spends on promotion and advertising. The study showed that in 1980, when the tobacco companies spent $771 million on promotional giveaways, 5.4 percent of the fourteen-to-seventeen-year-olds started smoking. That figure had dropped to 4.7 percent by 1984, but then rebounded to 5.5 percent in 1989, the year the industry spent $3.2 billion on hats, T-shirts, outdoor adventure trips, coupons, and other promotional items. The highest increase in young smokers, 6.3 percent, was in 1988, the year R. J. Reynolds introduced Joe Camel.

When the anthropomorphic beast first appeared in 1988 to celebrate Camel's seventy-fifth birthday, Camels were being smoked primarily by adult men. But Joe spoke to youth. He gave dating advice called "smooth moves," and to show he knew what he was talking about, he was joined by a whole gang of hip camels at the watering hole.

In one R. J. Reynolds internal memo about a "Young Adult Smokers' " [YAS] campaign, a divisional manager in Florida issued instructions to his cigarette salesmen on ways to increase the exposure of the new Joe Camel campaign to the young adult market [YAM]. The memo asked sales reps to identify stores within their areas that were "heavily frequented by young adult shoppers. These stores can be in close proximity to colleges [and] high schools."Asked about the memo, the company said it was a mistake; the manager had violated company policy by targeting high school students.

Then, a second memo surfaced—this one from a divisional manager in Oklahoma. The memo advised, "The criteria for you to utilize in identifying these [YAS retail] accounts are as follows: (1) . . . located across from, adjacent to [or] in the general vicinity of high schools." Isolated memos by overzealous managers, perhaps, but in fact young people started to smoke Camels. By the end of the '80s, Camels' share of the underage market had risen from 3 to 13 percent.

As the 1996 election loomed, President Clinton had not yet made up his mind to support Kessler. He was being sent two different messages; one from Capitol Hill sought compromise; the other from the health groups called for FDA regulation.

Politicians from Southern tobacco states warned Clinton that any move to regulate tobacco would ensure his loss there in the elections. National polls showed Clinton slightly ahead of Dole, but one in North Carolina in the summer of '95 had shown him twenty points behind. Clinton carried Tennessee and Kentucky in 1992 and lost by only 10,000 votes in North Carolina.

The tobacco companies were also aggressively funneling money into Republican campaigns. And in an effort to head off White House action, Philip Morris, which sold about half of the 480 billion cigarettes smoked each year, and the United States Tobacco Company, the nation's largest seller of chewing tobacco and snuff, preempted part of Kessler's campaign. They jointly proposed a ban on vending machine sales, promotional giveaways, and transit advertising as well as restrictions on billboard ads. They were also willing to create a fund of $250 million over five years to help enforce restrictions on teenage purchases of cigarettes.

Some congressmen urged Clinton to accept the industry's voluntary restrictions. Democrat Ron Wyden, of Oregon, an antitobacco congressman on Waxman's committee, and Charlie Rose, Democrat of North Carolina and an old friend of Big Tobacco, favored a negotiated settlement that would avoid FDA regulation. Wyden's argument was that any FDA proposal would be tied up in a court battle for years. "Nearly everyone understands that tobacco kills," wrote Wyden in an Op-Ed article in *The Washington Post,* "but gridlock can kill too. . . . If the tobacco companies tie up FDA regulation for even three years, 3 million kids will start smoking and more than one million of them will die needlessly from tobacco." His plan called for a "binding agreement" between the tobacco companies and the federal government to take steps to curb youth smoking. The Wyden-Rose plan was backed by Missouri Democrat and House minority leader Richard Gephardt who, with twenty current Southern Democrats, had lobbied the White House to kill Kessler's plan. Gephardt, a big recipient of tobacco industry campaign funds, told the White House that the FDA proposals would become "a critical economic factor" in many of the Southern states.

In the end, however, White House private polls told Clinton the risk was worth taking. A tough stand against tobacco might lose him North Carolina and Kentucky, but an antitobacco image would help in other, bigger states—California, New York, New Jersey. Then Kessler's campaign got help from another, unexpected front outside the cauldron of Washington politics.

IN THE SUMMER of 1995, Brown & Williamson was still trying to stop publication of the Merrell Williams papers. The company had asked the

California Supreme Court to enter an emergency stay that would prevent the University of California at San Francisco from releasing the documents to the public. The court refused. On July 1, the university library put the entire set of 10,000 pages on the Internet. They could be called up on the following address:

http://www.library.ucsf.edu/tobacco

To coincide with this event, the *Journal of the American Medical Association, JAMA,* devoted its July issue to an analysis of the documents by Professor Stan Glantz and his colleagues. The analysis was accompanied by a hard-hitting editorial, which concluded that tobacco was a "drug delivery vehicle" and recommended that the industry be placed under FDA jurisdiction for "appropriate regulation as for other life-threatening drugs." It also suggested a ban on all tobacco advertising, plus a vigorous counteradvertising campaign.

To reduce teenage smoking *JAMA* recommended further steps: an education program for physicians, the public, and policy makers; medical schools and research institutions should refuse tobacco industry grants; politicians should refuse tobacco money for their campaigns; government agencies and local communities should continue to control smoking in public; state and federal taxes on tobacco should be dramatically increased; the federal government should stop the export of tobacco to other countries; and the public should continue to use the courts to sue the companies for damages.

President Clinton would later say that the *JAMA* articles, which he had read, swayed him toward a favorable decision on the FDA proposal. The same day the issue was published, Kessler sent his proposals to the White House.

On August 10, 1995, in a midday news conference at the White House, Clinton became the first president in U.S. history to stand up to the tobacco companies and order FDA regulation governing the sale of cigarettes. While Hillary Clinton ran a "smoke-free" White House (except for the president's occasional cigar), such a move had never been contemplated when the Clintons arrived in Washington in 1992.

In giving Kessler the go-ahead, Clinton said his goal was to cut teenage smoking in half by curbing the "deadly temptations of tobacco and its skillful marketing" by the industry. The government had a responsibility to save children from "the awful dangers of tobacco," he said. "The evidence is overwhelming and the threat is immediate. To those who produce cigarettes, I say today: Take responsibility for your actions, sell your products only to adults, draw the line on children, show by your deeds as well as your words that you recognize that it is wrong as well as illegal to hook one million children a year on tobacco."

The proposed rules were set out in a dense 324-page section in the Federal Register. The proposal detailed how the tobacco companies had long understood, and talked freely in private about, the addictive nature of nicotine, and how they intended, by manipulation of the nicotine levels in cigarettes, to keep their customers addicted. In theory, if the FDA rules survived tobacco-industry legal challenges and the agency maintained jurisdiction, Kessler could ban tobacco outright, or he could set maximum levels of tar and nicotine in cigarettes, but that was not his plan. His proposals were aimed at eradicating smoking as a "pediatric disease."

The proposals would prohibit sales to under-eighteen-year-olds and require photo ID for proof of age. They would ban sales through vending machines, prohibit free samples, and forbid brand-name tobacco advertising at sporting events and on products like T-shirts, tote bags, and cigarette lighters. Kessler also wanted to ban the sales of "kiddie" packs of less than twenty cigarettes and forbid billboard ads within 1,000 feet of schools. Tobacco advertising would be limited to black and white text only and manufacturers and distributors made responsible for illegal sales to those under eighteen. Finally, the proposal would require tobacco companies to create a fund of $150 million for anti-smoking campaigns directed at young people. The regulations would cover cigarettes and smokeless tobacco, but would not apply to pipe tobacco or cigars.

Among the studies cited in favor of the ad ban was one that found 30 percent of three-year-olds and 91 percent of six-year-olds can identify Joe Camel as a symbol of smoking. By comparison, 62 percent of six-year-olds can identify Ronald McDonald. It was a remarkable distinction, said the FDA proposal, because Ronald McDonald appears in TV commercials during children's viewing hours and there are no cigarette ads on TV. A number of industry memos included in the proposal showed how preoccupied the companies had been with youth smoking.

Clinton would turn the FDA proposals into a potent campaign theme. "When Joe Camel tells young children that smoking is cool, when billboards tell teens that smoking will lead to true romance, when Virginia Slims tells adolescents that cigarettes may make them thin and glamorous, then our children need our wisdom, our guidance, and our experience."

For Kessler, the proposed rules amounted to a first step only. They could be amended or blocked by congressional action, or rejected by the courts. Indeed, immediately after Clinton's August 10 news conference, congressmen from tobacco states voiced opposition. "My farmers lost out to the zealots. I am not only disappointed. I am hurt," said Senator Wendell Ford, a Democrat from Kentucky. North Carolina's Democratic governor, Jim Hunt, warned Clinton there would be a "big fight" over the rules. "Just getting into a fight that will get us into court is not the way to do it," he had told Clinton when the president visited Charlotte the day before the announcement.

Meanwhile, the industry pounded Kessler. He was "an unelected bureaucrat," part of an "antismoking cabal" on a "power grab." It should be obvious to everyone, they said, that he was using the youth-smoking issue as a "Trojan horse" with the ultimate aim of prohibition. Steve Parrish, the boyish-looking senior vice president of corporate affairs for Philip Morris, had emerged as the most frequently quoted industry spokesman. Parrish, who had started his tobacco career as a lawyer for Shook, Hardy & Bacon, claimed the youth market was really of no great consequence. "If there were no more kids in this country who were smoking," he said, "that would be great and it would not materially affect our business." Of course, studies of smoking suggested quite the opposite: that 90 percent of smokers start in their teens and that without the youth market, the industry would decline rapidly as old smokers died off.

After Clinton's news conference, it took only hours for the tobacco industry to respond with a lawsuit. Contending that the FDA had no jurisdiction over cigarettes, the five biggest companies—Philip Morris, R. J. Reynolds, Brown & Williamson, Lorillard, and Liggett—filed to

block the proposals in federal district court in Greensboro, North Carolina, the heart of tobacco country where the industry expected to get
the most favorable hearing. And it looked as though they would succeed. Out of seven possible judges who might examine the case, William Osteen was appointed. Osteen was a conservative who, since his
appointment to the federal bench in 1991, had made several rulings in
favor of the industry. Even before joining the bench he'd worked for the
industry. In 1974, he was hired by a group of North Carolina tobacco
growers to go to Washington, D.C., to lobby the then secretary of
Agriculture, Earl Butz, not to proceed with a plan to scrap the federal
tobacco production-quota program. (He had also successfully represented an R. J. Reynolds tobacco heir in a criminal matter in 1979.) As
a federal judge, Osteen had ruled that the tobacco companies had legal
standing to bring a lawsuit challenging the Environmental Protection
Agency's 1993 classification of secondhand smoke as a carcinogen.
Kessler and the antitobacco forces expected a rough ride in his courtroom.

Madison Avenue joined the tobacco industry in Judge Osteen's
courtroom. The new FDA would kill off Joe Camel and the Marlboro
Man by banning "romantic images" in ads. And the black and white
"tombstone" ads Kessler demanded would kill off most of the other
tobacco ads, as presently designed. Hal Shoup, the executive vice
president of the four A's, the American Association of Advertising
Agencies, showed an example of the "tombstone" format at a press
conference. An ad for Carolina cigarettes had been appearing against a
pine-covered hillside with the headline "Carolina on My Mind." Shoup
had made a mock-up of a Kessler-type ad with the letters in black
against a white background. "No advertiser in this category would pay
anything to run an advertisement such as this," said Shoup.

Hardest hit under the FDA plan would be the billboard advertisers.
In 1994, the tobacco industry spent $122 million on billboards—12
percent of the billboard business revenue. The industry spent $284
million on magazines, or 3.3 percent of that industry's revenue. The ad
and promotion agencies would also be affected because of the proposed
ban on brand-name promotional items, such as lighters, T-shirts, and
baseball caps.

But the billboard industry complained that they had already imposed voluntary restrictions and were not placing tobacco and liquor ads within 500 feet of schools and churches. If the limit was extended to 1,000 feet from schools, as Kessler proposed, that would eliminate billboard advertising in cities, the industry complained. "If tobacco is so bad, why not ban it entirely," said Kent Brownridge, senior vice president of Wenner Media and general manager of *Rolling Stone.* "How can you have something that is legal and yet can't be advertised?" He forecast that the government would go after ice cream next because it contains cholesterol.

The advertisers filed suit in the same North Carolina court, claiming Kessler's advertising ban would violate the "commercial free speech" interpretation of the First Amendment. Longtime tobacco foe John Banzhaf, the George Washington University law professor who had led the fight to get antismoking ads on TV free of charge, observed wryly, "The liquor industry doesn't protest its inability to sell spirits in vending machines. It's funny, things only become unconstitutional when it applies to the tobacco industry."

Under the federal regulatory process, the FDA was required to take public comment for ninety days—but the agency extended the period for two more months to January 1996. More than 700,000 comments came pouring into FDA headquarters, including 30,000 form letters provided by the tobacco companies. Philip Morris put its 300-page argument against the FDA rules on the Internet. Meanwhile, retailers and distributors joined in the lawsuit. The vending-machine owners were upset, as well. About $2 billion worth of tobacco products are sold through 400,000 vending machines each year. Sponsored events such as motor sports, stock-car and hot-rod racing, power-boat racing, and tennis tournaments would also have to find other backers.

Teenagers scoffed at the proposals, saying they thought it would always be possible to bypass any new laws on the sales of cigarettes, just as they had the old ones. Some suggested that the new enforcement effort would only lead to minors being more, rather than less, intrigued by cigarettes.

In the backlash, however, came a surprising and important voice in favor of Kessler's plan. In a letter to *The Wall Street Journal,* former Senator Barry Goldwater said he had devoted his life to fighting for limited government, but on this occasion there was a "social role" for government in protecting children from tobacco. "It is hard to think of a more compelling case for government action," he said. "Cigarette companies say such action is unnecessary because they will solve the problem of youth smoking on their own. Hogwash. I've watched the tobacco industry make promise after promise to avoid government oversight for the past forty years. With every promise they give an inch, grudgingly, and buy enough time to hook another generation. . . . It's time to stop kidding ourselves. Backroom deals and gentlemen's agreements never have worked with this industry and never will."

Goldwater said times had changed and it was time to move with them. North Carolina now produced more poultry and eggs than tobacco. Public opinion on tobacco had changed, too. You only had to look at his own home state of Arizona, which had raised cigarette taxes by forty cents a pack. "The tobacco industry used every trick in the book and spent millions to try and confuse the voters, but in the end they understood that the issue was protecting children," wrote Goldwater. It was a powerful statement from a once powerful and still respected figure, the kind of signal that was making the untouchable tobacco barons suddenly start to look vulnerable.

Wall Street analysts remained optimistic that the companies would evade regulation. Analysts did not believe the FDA's proposals would ever pass Congress and they forecast many years of legal challenges to the proposed rules. Still, investors were edgy.

WHILE THE TOBACCO INDUSTRY compiled their dossier on what they called Kessler's "reckless distortion" of FDA powers, the tobacco wars continued in the courts. In New Orleans, Gauthier's nationwide Castano class action had been certified by Judge Okla Jones two months after the dinner at Antoine's. Judge Jones ordered a two-step process where the plaintiffs would first determine if the tobacco companies had committed negligence and fraud in not revealing their knowledge of nicotine addiction, and then proceed to separate minitrials seeking damages for addicted smokers. The tobacco companies complained it was an attempt to extend the class-action rule beyond the limits authorized by law and appealed Judge Jones's ruling to the Fifth Circuit Court of Appeals. Meanwhile, the Medicaid cases in Mississippi,

Minnesota, and Florida were leading the pack of states now suing the industry.

Throughout the summer, rumors spread that ABC was going to settle the $10 billion libel suit brought against them by Philip Morris and R. J. Reynolds. They turned out to be true. On the August 24 evening news, eighteen months after the program in which they had accused the industry of "spiking" cigarettes with nicotine from outside sources, the network apologized. While conceding it should not have said the industry adds nicotine from outside sources, ABC's settlement agreement was quite narrow. The apology said, "ABC believes that the principal focus of the reports was whether cigarette companies use the reconstituted tobacco process to control levels of nicotine in cigarettes in order to keep people smoking. . . . ABC thinks the reports speak for themselves on this issue and is prepared to have the issue resolved elsewhere." In the end, it was an expensive adventure; the network paid $15 million in legal costs to Philip Morris and R. J. Reynolds, and there would be no reopening of the case.

During the fall of 1995, the tobacco companies launched a counter-offensive. In newspaper ads around the nation they asked, "Who should be responsible for your children, a bureaucrat, or you?" Under the picture of a grinning, tripled-jowled, snaggle-toothed, unidentified man, another ad asked, "Can We Really Make the Underage Smoking Problem Smaller by Making the Federal Bureaucracy Bigger?" And the ad declared piously, "We all agree we must do something to keep cigarettes out of the hands of children under the age of eighteen. A proven solution is to teach young people how to resist peer pressure and to enforce existing laws."

Meanwhile, the Third Wave lawsuits were uncovering a series of confidential documents showing how concerned the industry was, starting in the 1970s, about maintaining their youth sales. The documents put the lie to the notion, promoted by the companies, that they do not target youth. The simple reason was laid out in a 1974 RJR marketing interoffice memorandum: "Over 50 percent of main smokers start smoking fairly regularly before the age of 18 and virtually all start by the age of 25." A second 1974 RJR memo, from the company's marketing department, spoke of the high incidence—40 percent—of smoking in the sixteen-to-twenty-four age group, and why this should be so—adventure, peer pressure, providing confidence in stressful situations. "To some extent the young smokers 'wear' their cigarettes and it becomes an important part of the 'I' they wish to be, along with their clothing and the way they style their hair." RJR was particularly concerned about the success of Marlboro among teenagers.

In a 1973 memo entitled "Research Planning Memorandum on Some Thoughts About New Brands of Cigarettes for the Youth Market," Claude Teague, who was then R. J. Reynolds's assistant director of research and development, urged that more be done to attract the "twenty-one-year-old and under group." Teague wrote, "Realistically, if our company is to survive and prosper, over the long term, we must get our share of the youth market. In my opinion this will require new brands tailored to the youth market." New products should be marketed as a way to fight pressures of the teenage years, such as "stress . . . awkwardness, boredom," and as a way of achieving "membership in a group." Teague's view was that "there is certainly nothing immoral or unethical about our company attempting to attract these smokers to our products. We should not in any way influence nonsmokers to start smoking; rather we should simply recognize that many or most of the '21 and under' group will invariably become smokers, and offer them an opportunity to use our brands."

Teague recommended, in his convoluted way, that "now is the time to launch the next brand to become the 'in' cigarette with the next generation as Marlboro ages from 'in' to hopefully 'out' and over thirty status, [and] hence becomes something for youth to avoid." The next question, of course, was what to call this new youth cigarette. Teague had some ideas about that, as well.

"Ideally, the name should have a double meaning; that is, one desirable connotation in 'straight' language and another in the jargon of youth. A current example may be Kool. . . . A careful study of the current youth jargon, together with a review of currently used high school American history books and like sources for valued things might be a good start at finding a good brand name and image theme." This was really a matter for the marketing division, admitted Teague. He could supply expertise in scientific research, however.

The memo discussed the precise level of nicotine in a cigarette aimed at the youth market. As the beginning smoker had a low tolerance for "smoke irritation" (an industry phrase for nicotine level), the smoke in the cigarette aimed at such groups should be as "bland as possible." Teague suggested, "The rate of absorption [of nicotine] should be kept low by holding pH [acidity] down, probably below 6." On the pH scale anything below 7 is acid and anything above 7 is alkali. The more alkaline the tobacco mix, the greater the rate of absorption of nicotine. The implication of the memo was that the company manipulates the levels, something they still deny doing. John Schwartz, The *Washington Post* reporter who first wrote up the memo, called Teague at home to ask him about it. "I wouldn't care to talk to you, I don't talk to strangers," said Teague. "Why would I want to talk to you, what earthly gain would it be?" A Reynolds company spokesman called the memo a "draft document that reflects preliminary thoughts of one individual in research and development. We have seen nothing that indicates that it was ever reviewed or acted upon in any way." Shortly thereafter, the company made great inroads into the youth market with its reborn Camel brand, accompanied by the new cartoon character, Joe.

Lorillard, the fourth-largest cigarette company, also had concerns about the youth market, according to a 1970 letter that surfaced in one of the lawsuits. It was written by the then assistant creative director of Robert Brian Associates, a promotion agency working for the cigarette company. The letter is addressed to Charles Seide, then head of the art department at New York's Cooper Union college. The agency was preparing to market a cigarette, named "Kick," to youth and wanted a design from his students. "We're adults. You've got a group of talented kids," the letter began, then gave guidelines, including that the pack must contain the words, "Caution: Cigarette Smoking May Be Hazardous to Your Health." It cautioned the art director, "While this cigarette is geared to the youth market, no attempt obviously can be made to encourage persons under twenty-one to smoke. The package design should be geared to attract the youthful eye, not the ever-watchful eye of the Federal Government." Nothing came of the project.

Even though Philip Morris had Marlboro, the leading brand among youth in the early '70s, the company was always worried about losing its youth-market share. It hired pollsters and economists to keep a constant check on "college students living on campus, young people in the fourteen-to-seventeen age group, and men in the military services," as one pollster's memo put it. The company commissioned a study by the Roper Organization in 1974; this was not the "usual sample of 18–24; in this study no lower age limit was set." Other Philip Morris studies looked at the "higher Marlboro market penetration among 15–17-year-olds."

By the 1980s, Philip Morris was worried about the effect on the youth market of raising taxes. "Unfortunately," said a 1982 in-house report, "it is among the young that we have our greatest market penetration, and theoretically price increases should effect Philip Morris to a greater extent than the total industry." By the end of the 1980s, Philip Morris was sufficiently worried about this decline to launch a study on smoking among high school seniors. In 1988, an in-house report suggested that the decline was caused by the sharp increase in the price of gasoline between 1976 and 1979. High school senior males in 1976 smoked about the same as they did in 1979—up to the age of sixteen. Then they got their driving licences. Smoking among the class of '79, and later, started to drop; the inference made was that the school children could not afford gas and cigarettes. In 1978, it was possible to buy two gallons of gasoline and a pack of cigarettes for one dollar; by 1980 one dollar would not even buy two gallons of gas. The report concluded, "When it comes to a choice between smoking cigarettes or cruising around in his car, the average red-blooded American male would probably choose the latter." In other words, cut gas prices and youth will smoke more cigarettes. The company's "gasoline hypothesis" turned out to be credible. The end of the decline in smoking among high school males coincided with the stabilization of gasoline prices.

ON THE LAST DAY available to them, December 31, 1995, the tobacco companies sent in their comments on the FDA's proposed rules. Their response came in twelve volumes that stood more than a foot high. In it, they attacked the FDA on three fronts. First, they said that Congress had never intended the FDA to have authority over cigarettes, and it never would. Second, they said cigarettes could not be regulated as a "delivery device for nicotine" (although that's exactly how they were described in some company memos). Third, they said the FDA had no authority to restrict advertising. The companies were typically exhaustive in their arguments, covering any and all aspects of the law and delving deep into the congressional record.

The tobacco companies claimed Congress was the rightful body to deal with tobacco because it was necessary to balance three competing interests: maintaining the freedom of adults to smoke, informing the public of the risks associated with smoking, and preserving the significant economic interests involved in the manufacturing and marketing of cigarettes. Already, the companies noted, Congress delegates its authority over cigarettes to agencies other than the FDA. For example, Congress requires the department of Health and Human Services to review annual lists of cigarette ingredients and report back on any perceived health effects. The Department of Agriculture sets production quotas and price levels for tobacco leaf. The Bureau of Alcohol, Tobacco and Firearms regulates tobacco manufacturers. The Federal Trade Commission requires the tobacco companies to display government warning labels on their products.

But when Congress could have used other laws to move against the industry, it chose not to do so. In 1975, Congress had been asked to regulate cigarettes under the Federal Hazardous Substances Act, but had instead quickly amended the FHSA to exclude tobacco products. The 1976 Toxic Substances Control Act (TSCA) empowered the EPA to regulate chemical substances that might pose a threat to health. Congress included in TSCA's definition of "chemical substance" an exception for "tobacco or any tobacco product."

The industry's main argument was that it was "preposterous" to suggest that after Congress had excluded cigarettes from other laws it now meant them to be regulated under the Medical Device Amendments to the Food, Drug, and Cosmetics Act. The companies argued that the definition of a "device intended to affect the function of the body" was limited in the act to medical products for which the manufacturers made a health claim.

The FDA might as well regulate guns and bullets as "devices" because they were "intended to affect the structure or function of the body of man or animals," the industry claimed. In the same way, the FDA could regulate down jackets and flannel pajamas as "devices," since temperature regulation is a "function" of the body. The agency could regulate boots and raincoats because they keep the body warm and dry. Even beach umbrellas could come under the act because they shield people from the sun's rays and prevent them from developing skin cancer. You could also say bicycles and roller skates were "devices" under the meaning of the act because exercise is, or can affect, a function of the body. But the FDA didn't regulate these products because no medical claims are made for these "devices."

Finally, the companies claimed that the FDA could not treat nicotine as a drug at the same time that it regulated cigarettes as "devices." If nicotine is a "drug," a fact they disputed, then the rest of the cigarette is merely a "dosage form," not a "device." The FDA had long recognized the distinction, the industry argued. Nicotine patches and nicotine gum, for example, had been regulated as drugs, not as "nicotine delivery devices." Taking the FDA's new interpretation of drug delivery "devices" literally, then tablets, capsules, suppositories, creams, gels, powders, and aerosols were also drug delivery devices.

The "orgy of buncombe" of which Senator Smoot of Utah spoke so eloquently in 1929 when he rose in Congress to denounce the tobacco companies' "unconscionable, heartless and destructive attempts to exploit the women and youth of this country" was again in full swing. It would be left to Judge William Osteen to decide whether the tobacco companies had a case, or were engaged once more in a campaign, as Smoot put it, "whose only God is profit, whose only bible is the balance sheet, whose only principle is greed."

9

THE SCIENCE TEACHER

This guy is Jekyll and Hyde; he'll do whatever he needs to do for whoever is paying him.

—*Gordon Smith, a lawyer for Brown & Williamson*

MERRELL WILLIAMS CHANGED the balance of power in the tobacco wars. For a lowly paralegal, he had managed to select such explicit and damning confidential documents of such high quality that the antitobacco forces now possessed a potent arsenal of evidence. For all his cleverness, though, Williams was still only a clerk. He had no firsthand knowledge of how decisions were made in the company; no evidence that the proposals in the documents were actually carried out. He had not met anyone who made big decisions, only supervisors at the document center in Louisville. Brown & Williamson would make much of this distinction, claiming in many cases that the documents Williams had stolen were only the random thoughts of individual scientists or lawyers, not company policy. What the antitobacco forces needed desperately was a high-level executive who had knowledge of policy making, someone who could substantiate conversations at board level about nicotine addiction and cancer of the lung or heart disease. At trial, Williams would be useless as a witness. He was just a document thief, a $9-an-hour clerk who turned against the company. The lawyers needed a tobacco executive.

As it turned out, such a person had been found at the end of 1993 but his identity was being kept secret. His FDA code name was "Research." His real name was Jeffrey Wigand, a smart but somewhat erratic biochemist who once dreamed of being a doctor but had never made it to medical school. Instead, he worked as a scientific research manager in companies that produced health-care products. In 1989, he had just lost a job in New Jersey as a result of a company reorganization and had answered an ad in *The New York Times* for a company research director. A headhunting firm from Louisville, Kentucky, contacted him. They told him that Brown & Williamson was looking for someone to lead the company's research department.

Wigand had never thought of being employed by Big Tobacco, but he was interested in public health and knowing the problems of smoking and cancer, he thought he might be able to make a difference. In interviews he was told he would be working on the development of a "safe cigarette," one with much reduced harmful substances and tobacco additives. Wigand was intrigued. He embarked on a tortuous journey that would earn him lots of money for doing rather little and, in the end, give him a pile of trouble.

After four and a half years, Wigand was fired. But within months he was working as a consultant on the tobacco industry for the CBS program *60 Minutes,* and as a witness in the Justice Department's investigation into fire-safe cigarettes, and then as a consultant to the FDA on its inquiry. He would become the highest-ranking defector in the history of the tobacco industry. He would be hounded by hostile company lawyers and private investigators. He had little prospect of ever resuming a career in the pharmaceutical industry to which he had been attached for almost three decades. Eventually, he would teach high school for a tenth of the salary Brown & Williamson had been paying him. He would be divorced from his second wife; his personal life was in tatters. He was, however, not without friends and admirers, especially among the antitobacco forces. He was honored for what he had done—he blew the whistle on a powerful and secretive industry—and he became a national hero, of sorts. Most important, the tobacco industry would decide it could not afford to have Jeffrey Wigand on the witness stand. His defection was clearly one of the reasons why the industry would capitulate and go to the negotiating table in the spring of 1997.

Dick Scruggs, the Mississippi lawyer who was the prime mover behind the June 1997 tobacco industry settlement, drenched by a storm aboard his racing yacht *Gunsmoke*, at Chicago Yacht Club, September 1997. President Clinton had called for major revisions to the settlement proposal, delaying its passage through Congress. (PETER PRINGLE)

Mississippi attorney general Mike Moore jokes in his Jackson office in September 1996 about the bid by his governor, Kirk Fordice, to stop the state's lawsuit against Big Tobacco. "The governor has made a pact with the devil," said Moore. (JULIAN NORRIDGE)

Don Barrett at the Confederate war memorial outside the courthouse in Lexington, Mississippi. This is where Barrett developed his "tobacco habit" during the Nathan Horton trial in 1988.

Ella Horton, widow of Nathan, who claimed damages from the American Tobacco Company, recalls the company's paid "fan club" of local spectators. "Fifty dollars an hour. Nice pay. Just sittin' and listnin', that's all." (JULIAN NORRIDGE)

Peter Castano with his wife, Dianne, celebrating Christmas in New Orleans. He died of lung cancer in 1993.

(facing page, middle)
Brown & Williamson document collector, Merrell Williams, in the garden of his Mississippi house, which Dick Scruggs bought for him. "So, what did I steal? The truth?" (JULIAN NORRIDGE)

Wendell Gauthier appears on British television's Channel 4, October 1996. "When you think about it, if I had a product on the market that gave you a little dose of cyanide, and it killed 400,000 people a year, you'd lock me up. There's no difference. That's what we don't understand....Those rascals should be in jail." (JULIAN NORRIDGE)

Merrell Williams's first lawyer, Fox DeMoisey, in his Louisville office. "I thought it was a little odd for my client not to be able to talk to his own lawyer....I'd never really heard of that before."(JULIAN NORRIDGE)

(bottom) **T**he symbol of the Third Wave of tobacco litigation. The seven CEOs of the tobacco companies are sworn in before Henry Waxman's House of Representatives subcommittee, April 14, 1994. One by one they said that they believed nicotine was not addictive. *From right:* William Campbell, Philip Morris; James Johnston, R. J. Reynolds; Joseph Taddeo, U.S. Tobacco Co.; Andrew Tisch, Lorrillard Tobacco Co.; Edward Horrigan, Liggett Group; Thomas Sandefur, Brown & Williamson; Donald Johnston, American Tobacco.

(AP WORLDWIDE PHOTOS)

Congressman Henry Waxman in his office on Capitol Hill talking about the seven tobacco CEOs who denied nicotine is addictive at a 1994 hearing of his House of Representatives subcommittee on health and the environment. "They took an oath that they would tell the truth and then lied." (JULIAN NORRIDGE)

Victor DeNoble worked on a nicotine substitute for Philip Morris, and his laboratory was closed down overnight. "They wanted me to change certain words. I mean I basically said, you know, nicotine is a drug that is widely used, and they wanted me to change that to nicotine is a compound." (JULIAN NORRIDGE)

John Coale (left) and Wendell Gauthier after dinner at Antoine's. Coale, a founding member of the Castano group of sixty plantiffs' lawyers, said the lawyers "begrudgingly worked together and for the most part hated each other." (BLUE ANDRE)

Castano class action specialist Elizabeth Cabraser at the Harvard Law School conference on the tobacco settlement, July 1977. Of the industry, she said, "They can stop us this year. They can stop us next year. But they can't stop us forever, because we've now got the same perpetual existence that they have. There will always be a body of lawyers committed to this task." (PETER PRINGLE)

At the start of the Third Wave, Professor Dick Daynard, founder of the Tobacco Products Liability Project at Northeastern University, predicted that the spring of 1996 would see the first tobacco company pay damages for selling cigarettes. In an astonishing breach in the industry's united front, Liggett, maker of Chesterfields and the smallest player in the U.S. cigarette market, settled its lawsuits in March 1996. (PETER PRINGLE)

Bennett LeBow, the "Machiavelli of the foxy deal," CEO of the Brooke Group, which owns Liggett, turned "state's evidence" against the tobacco industry in the spring of 1997. (SHONNA VALESKA)

Mike Ciresi *(right)* poses in his law firm's Minneapolis skyscraper office with his tobacco team *(left to right)*: Susan Nelson, Roberta Walburn, Tom Hamlin, and Gary Wilson.
(*MINNEAPOLIS STAR TRIBUNE*)

Minnesota attorney general Hubert "Skip" Humphrey III, explaining to reporters on Capitol Hill why he refused to back the June 1997 settlement. He called it a "Trojan camel."
(PETER PRINGLE)

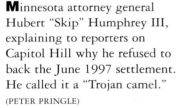

Woody Wilner *(left)*, the Florida lawyer who won the first individual lawsuit of the Third Wave, chatting to Sir Richard Doll, the British epidemiologist whose 1950s studies were among the first to show that smoking causes cancer.
(GINNY STEIGER)

June 20, 1997. Key negotiators of the $368 billion settlement face the media in Washington *(left to right)*: Dennis Vacco of New York; Bob Butterworth of Florida; Christine Gregoire of Washington; Mike Moore of Mississippi; Richard Blumenthal of Connecticut; Grant Woods of Arizona; Jeffrey Modisett of Indiana.
(AP WORLDWIDE PHOTOS)

Jeffrey Wigand, the Brown & Williamson whistleblower, being congratulated by Florida attorney general Bob Butterworth at the June 1977 settlement. The deal released Wigand from B&W's lawsuit charging him with breach of his confidentiality agreement. A grinning Ron Motley looks on.
(AP WORLDWIDE PHOTOS)

Former surgeon general C. Everett Koop *(left)* and former FDA commissioner David Kessler talk to reporters outside the White House about their opposition to the June 1997 settlement.
(AP WORLDWIDE PHOTOS)

Stanley Chesley, "the Master of Disaster," lobbying for the settlement in the U.S. Senate, July 1997. His Castano colleagues are *(left to right)* John Climaco, Hugh Rodham (brother of Hillary Clinton), and John Coale. (PETER PRINGLE)

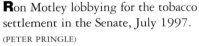

Ron Motley lobbying for the tobacco settlement in the Senate, July 1997. (PETER PRINGLE)

Professor Stan Glantz, hunted by the industry for placing the Merrell Williams papers in the University of California library and for his analysis of the effects of secondhand smoke.

WIGAND HAD JOINED Brown & Williamson in 1989 at their headquarters in Louisville. They made him head of R&D. His name was in a
box with all the other executives at the top of the company's organization chart. He had a budget of more than $20 million, a staff of 265,
and a salary of $300,000 a year—more than he had ever earned before.
For one who believed that his research skills were better, and certainly
more important to him, than his management expertise, this was indeed a challenge. Wigand accepted it with gusto. He became a willing,
even eager, participant in the strange, incestuous world of the tobacco
executive. He went to the parties they held for themselves and joined
the company's favored golf club. He even took up occasional smoking
"to understand the science of how it made you feel."

The big salary created a comfortable life at home, more comfortable
than it had been, perhaps ever. He had grown up the oldest of five
children in a strict Catholic household, first in the Bronx and then in
upstate New York, near Poughkeepsie. He dropped out of Dutchess
Community College to join the air force and to get away from a stifling
home life. He was sent to Japan, where he ran a hospital operating
room. He learned Japanese and the martial arts. He returned after one
tour and went back to school. He studied biochemistry at the University of Buffalo, where he earned a doctorate and wrote a master's thesis
on vitamin B_{12}. When his first wife developed multiple sclerosis, the
strain of caring for her began to take a toll. She left him after the birth
of a daughter. He met his second wife when he was director of marketing for Johnson & Johnson. They married in 1986 and had two daughters.

Why Brown & Williamson decided to hire Wigand is a mystery
because he was not their type. He cared too much about pure science to
sustain the untenable public position of the industry—that smoking
does not cause cancer and that nicotine is not addictive. And he grew to
despise their philosophy. For example, Wigand would find repulsive the
argument used by tobacco executives that an adult's right to smoke is as
important as a woman's right to an abortion.

Apparently, he had not revealed his true self at the interviews. He
was totally unsuited to life in the bunker of the tobacco industry where

being a team player is essential. That was never his strength. He couldn't keep his own counsel when silence was required for his survival. "I have a very bad problem—saying what's on my mind. I don't take too much crap from anybody."

On his first week at work, he was shocked to find the poor state of the company's research labs, which he said looked like "a high school chemistry lab from the '50s, filled with old-fashioned smoking machines. There was no fundamental science being done and no contemporary apparatus." (Indeed, testimony that first surfaced in 1997 from one of Wigand's predecessor's, Dr. Irwin Tucker, would suggest that the research department had long been the company's poor cousin. And the Merrell Williams papers would show that most of the group's research was done abroad by the British parent company, BAT Industries.)

Wigand hired a physicist, a toxicologist, and an analytical chemist and started work on two projects. One was a new low-tar cigarette and the other was fire safety—how to make a cigarette burn at lower temperatures to reduce the risk of fire. But it soon became apparent that the company had little interest in him completing what he was doing. A series of incidents occurred that would bring Wigand into confrontations with his superiors and eventually terminate his employment with the company.

The first was his indoctrination into the lawyer-run nature of the tobacco industry. As he tells the story, Wigand went out to Kansas City to meet the lawyers from Shook, Hardy & Bacon. They would explain how a tobacco company defends itself against lawsuits; how it would be necessary for the lawyers to know what the research scientists were doing to make sure no project endangered the well-being of the company. If there was any doubt about what this regime entailed, it was confirmed by a meeting in Vancouver of company researchers shortly after he joined. The meeting included scientists from BAT in England and its subsidiaries around the world and it left Wigand disturbed and concerned about his job.

The researchers had discussed the possibility of finding an artificial substitute for nicotine, an "analogue" in the chemist's lexicon. Other companies had been interested in nicotine analogues, which would have the same effect as nicotine on the central nervous system while avoiding the cardiovascular effects. At the meeting, Wigand would later testify, about fifteen pages of notes were taken by a British scientist. As head of R&D in Louisville, Wigand received a copy. A few weeks later, he was sent a truncated version of the notes, a mere three pages long, from the office of J. Kendrick Wells, B&W's corporate counsel. Wigand would say later that the deletions had been made to avoid "references that would be discoverable during any kind of liability action." Wells denied that the minutes had been improperly altered.

Such was his baptism into the world of censored scientific reports where potentially embarrassing material was excised by the legal department. Wigand would soon discover that despite his fancy title, head of R&D, there were other research reports from England that he was not privy to at all. Sent first to the legal department, there they stayed if they were considered too sensitive for circulation, even to the head of R&D. The scientists in England sometimes bypassed the system by sending documents to Wigand's home fax machine.

Wigand increasingly felt himself undermined by company lawyers. His answer was to immerse himself in strictly domestic projects. He started work on additives the company was putting into cigarette tobacco to improve taste. A large number of chemicals end up in cigarette tobacco besides the ones that come naturally in the tobacco plant. They include not only the residue of pesticides and insecticides, but also compounds added as flavorings in the factory. Still more are produced by the burning of the tobacco.

Unlike additives to foods, those in tobacco were not subject to government regulation in the United States. The tobacco companies had to submit a list of additives used to the Department of Health and Human Services, but under an agreement, the list was not published because the companies claimed it contained proprietary information. Under constant pressure from antismoking groups to reveal what was on the list, the companies, including B&W, debated the issue from time to time.

Like all tobacco companies, B&W had been concerned about an additive called coumarin, a vanilla-like flavor also used as a flavor fixative. It had been used as a food and tobacco additive for decades, but most commercial use was halted after it was found that coumarin caused liver damage in rats and dogs and was suspected of being carcinogenic. Coumarin was banned for use in foods in the United States. In the United Kingdom by the late '70s, levels of coumarin in tobacco were controlled by the government, but not in the United States where it continued to be used in cigarettes until 1984. B&W had stopped using coumarin in domestic cigarettes in 1982, but continued to use it in pipe tobacco. When Wigand found out, he said he suggested to Thomas Sandefur that the company should remove it from the remaining products and Sandefur was reluctant to do so because it would affect sales. (The company says coumarin is not used in any B&W company products today, and even when it had been used, the levels were entirely safe.)

The coumarin issue would turn out to be only one of several important differences Wigand had with Sandefur, a rough-hewn Georgian who had started at the company as a salesman. According to Wigand's testimony, he had two big fights with Sandefur. The first was about producing a low-tar cigarette.

FOR FIFTY YEARS the tobacco industry had plans to develop a safer cigarette, one that would contain less of the harmful substances in the "tar" of tobacco smoke. The companies had tried all kinds of modifications. First they added filters, which contained a wide variety of absorbent materials including cork, cotton wool, cellulose, charcoal, and even asbestos. Then they tried putting microscopic holes in the filters and the cigarette paper to increase the volume of air mixing with the smoke. They puffed up the tobacco like Rice Krispies in an effort to eliminate some of the harmful compounds. They even invented a new synthetic tobacco. They also invented a nonburning cigarette: a charcoal rod inside the cigarette heated up the tobacco so that it never actually caught fire. Out of all these, at least some of the harmful products of burning tobacco were eliminated.

Some of these experiments produced cigarettes that appeared to significantly reduce the carcinogenic effects of tobacco smoke, but none produced a cigarette that smokers wanted to smoke; they didn't taste as good and they didn't contain as much nicotine. And governments and antismoking groups were not enthusiastic about a product that could turn out to be a new version of the old.

The tobacco companies could never promote their experimental products as a "safer" cigarette because that meant admitting that the cigarettes they were already selling were harmful, or at least not as safe as the new ones. Producing a "safer cigarette" that was free, or freer, from the toxins of tobacco smoke was a legal trap. They would also be open to FDA control if they marketed a product that carried a health claim, as a so-called safer cigarette would. So, the attempts by the companies had always been half-hearted at best.

Brown & Williamson's parent, BAT, had tried to make a "safer" cigarette in the 1960s. Project Ariel produced a device that relied on burning tobacco to heat a central tube containing nicotine and an aerosol generator, such as water, which would then be inhaled. The tobacco provided a small amount of "taste" but many fewer toxins. Nothing came of Ariel. The companies concentrated on filters instead, which did cut down the tar levels considerably. But eliminating all the toxins was a problem the tobacco companies shelved. It was too complicated.

The problem was as bewildering in its way as the mix of thousands of compounds that make up tobacco smoke. Up to five billion particles are jammed into a cubic centimeter of smoke. Microscopic, oily droplets agitate and kick other particles around, coalesce with them, and grow bigger, turning into particulate matter known as "tar." In 1964, only 500 compounds had been isolated; by 1967, 1,300 were known. They included hydrocarbons of the polycyclic and heterocyclic types, phenols and polyphenols, trace metals, some of which are radioactive, toxic gases such as carbon monoxide, cyanide, and hydrogen sulphide. Many of these are not found in the tobacco leaf but are formed as the cigarette burns, and at least some of them produced or helped to produce cancers.

Painting the shaved skin of mice with the brownish-black gooey condensate of smoke produced tumors, but the question was, What in the tar does the damage? The polycyclic hydrocarbons are the product of the incomplete combustion of tobacco—chiefly benzpyrene. In its pure state it is a yellowish, crystalline material. In the smoke, it floats like microscopic blobs of asphalt. Benzpyrene can be produced by burning any vegetable matter and is found in minute quantities in roasted coffee beans and charcoal-broiled steak. It is a relatively weak initiator of tumors, but when it interlocks and combines with other substances, such as phenols, it is more potent. The phenols are tumor promoters, as are fatty acids.

But seemingly, B&W's leadership wasn't really interested in unraveling the problem. According to Wigand, Sandefur had told him, "I don't want to hear any more discussion about a safer cigarette. . . . Any research on a safer product would clearly expose every other product as unsafe and, therefore, present a liability issue in terms of any type of litigation."

In a deposition taken in 1995, Wigand was asked about the company's policy on such matters and whether, "If science affected sales, the science would take the back door?" And he answered, "Yes." Asked whether Sandefur expressed this policy, Wigand replied, "Several times." B&W says this is absolutely false; there never was such a policy.

Wigand's second important conversation with Sandefur was about nicotine addiction. Wigand would claim that BAT scientists had conducted studies on the levels of nicotine needed to keep smokers "using the product": "Below a certain level of 0.4 milligrams [the drug] does not sustain satisfaction . . . over 1.2 milligrams it becomes too harsh and has too much of an impact." Wigand claims that Sandefur understood perfectly well that nicotine was an addictive substance and had discussed it as such with him several times. The company denied the conversations ever took place.

Wigand admits he grew to dislike Sandefur intensely and couldn't help showing it. "Sandefur used to beat on me for using big words. I never found anyone as stupid as Sandefur in terms of his ability to read and communicate," says Wigand. "In terms of his understanding something and his intellectual capacity, Sandefur was just like a farm boy."

The dislike was mutual. When Sandefur was promoted to CEO of Brown & Williamson in January 1993, Wigand knew his days were numbered. He had been warned by a colleague that B&W management thought he was difficult and spoke out too much about company business.

On March 24, Sandefur fired Wigand. He was escorted from the building. He was not allowed to take any of his belongings, including his scientific diary. But he did leave with a two-year payoff and health insurance for his family, something that was becoming more important after he discovered that one of his daughters had spina bifida and required expensive treatment. The price of the severance package was Wigand's silence. He signed a lifelong agreement of confidentiality so severe that he would be in violation if he discussed anything at all that he had done for, or knew about, the corporation. And for Wigand this was a problem. The conflict between his eagerness to expose the wrong-doings of the tobacco industry and his need to keep his severance pay and medical benefits would land him in a lot of trouble.

AT ABOUT THE TIME Wigand was fired, a veteran CBS producer with *60 Minutes* named Lowell Bergman was looking for some expert advice on a story he was doing about fire-safe cigarettes. The tobacco companies had played with the idea, somewhat half-heartedly, of producing a cigarette that would burn at lower temperatures and extinguish itself if not puffed. If such a cigarette could be found, it could have a far-reaching effect in preventing the thousands of fires attributed each year to cigarettes. It could also be promoted as a socially responsible cigarette, and it might even be a commercial success. Philip Morris had started such a program, called Project Hamlet (to burn, or not to burn), but had abandoned it. *60 Minutes* was doing a segment, and Wigand knew about the issue. When he was at B&W he had been on a federal commission that included industry scientists looking into the possibility of developing such a cigarette.

Wigand agreed to help CBS and negotiated a fee of $12,000 for his services. He would help CBS decode the technical language and tell them what he knew of the federal commission on a fire-safe cigarette. He thought B&W would not consider that he was violating his agreement because his knowledge stemmed from a government commission, not from company work. In any case, the story was about a rival, Philip Morris, which had been far ahead with a fire-safe product in 1986–87 and had abandoned it.

Over time, however, Bergman and Wigand would discuss more than fire-safe cigarettes. Bergman saw there was another story entirely—about Wigand as a high-ranking tobacco research executive becoming frustrated about his work, the reluctance of the company to pursue the low-tar cigarette, his conversations with Sandefur about addiction, and the coumarin additive in pipe tobacco.

Wigand did not deflect Bergman's enthusiasm and his apparent willingness to cooperate was soon the talk of the antitobacco forces. In the spring of 1994, the FDA made contact and he started to tutor David Kessler about the way ammonia in cigarette tobacco can help boost the nicotine absorbed by the smoker. He was also approached by the Justice Department about fire-safe cigarettes and possible antitrust violations by the tobacco companies. He was contacted by Henry Waxman's congressional office. Would he appear before Waxman's committee on smoking and health? Then came the threatening phone calls.

Wigand says that in April 1994, he received two anonymous phone calls at his home in Louisville. "Don't mess with tobacco," warned a voice and hung up. The second call threatened his children unless he left town. A male voice said, "You have three children, how are they doing? Leave or else you'll find your kids hurt." A few days later he found a live bullet in his mail box. He called in the FBI and they traced the next two anonymous calls, one from a shopping mall and the other from a hospital. There was no suggestion that B&W was involved in these calls, but Wigand was frightened about what could happen if some thug were convinced that he was jeopardizing people's jobs or their welfare.

"From that moment the safety of our children became a cornerstone of our environment," he said when I interviewed him in the summer of 1996. "We changed the way we went to school. We followed them to school. I had a gun in my car. It was always legal." He was frightened, permanently on edge and sometimes erratic. Once a drinking man, who had given up alcohol when he joined B&W, now he started again. Two days after the threatening phone calls, he dropped into a liquor store while driving his two daughters home from school. He was in a hurry. He grabbed a bottle of Wild Turkey off the shelf and put it into one of the big pockets of his jacket, but when he got to the checkout he found he had left his money in the car. So he went out to get it. Thinking he had left without paying, the store owner called the police and held him until they arrived. Wigand showed the police he had $300 in cash in the car and paid for the bottle. No charges were pressed, and he thought the incident was closed. But it would come up again as a nasty surprise.

Meanwhile, he had given up hope of getting another management job. In January 1995, Wigand took a job at a high school in Louisville, teaching Japanese and chemistry at $30,000 a year, one-tenth of his tobacco company pay. Bergman was pressing him to be interviewed for a *60 Minutes* segment. Wigand agreed, but only if CBS would protect him if he were sued for breaking his confidentiality agreement. Bergman thought that was fine. As a TV producer for a muckraking program, he had often persuaded people to talk when their companies didn't want them to. The interview was taped, but as the program reached broadcast time in the fall of 1995, things went haywire.

Philip Morris had shown what could happen if you got part of a tobacco story wrong. ABC had just paid out $15 million in legal costs to settle their case. Also, CBS was about to be bought: Westinghouse was negotiating a $5.4 billion merger and there was a lot of money riding on the deal for current CBS shareholders. They would not appreciate a legal liability overshadowing the deal and possibly squelching it. Last but perhaps not least, Andrew Tisch, the chairman of Lorillard, was the son of the CBS chairman, Laurence Tisch. Might the CBS chairman not have strong opinions about Wigand's antitobacco stance?

In the end, after a lot of harumphing at CBS headquarters, the lawyers ruled the day. The *60 Minutes* interview with Wigand, who had not yet been publicly identified as the source of the segment, had been done and was due to run in early November, but CBS general counsel Ellen Kaden called the whole thing off. She said there was a problem of "tortious interference"—persuading someone to break a contract with a third party. CBS was "at grave risk," she said, and could face a multibillion dollar lawsuit.

CBS had to announce the segment had been pulled. The network was accused of wimping out. Mike Wallace claimed the ABC lawsuit had a chilling effect on CBS legal advisers. Media critics blamed lawyers for turning back the clock on real investigative reporting. First Amendment lawyers said CBS could have gotten away with it. But then CBS revealed that the decision had been somewhat more complicated than it had first appeared. They had a deal with Wigand to indemnify him in the event of a lawsuit on the *60 Minutes* segment. They had also hired him before as a consultant on their fire-safe cigarette story and given him a fee for that story of $12,000. That might look like financial inducement to a jury, if the network were sued. As for the merger with Westinghouse and its possible influence on the decision to drop the interview, chairman Tisch said he had not known anything about the *60 Minutes* program until he read about the affair in the newspapers. The merger went ahead.

But the story was far from over. Someone at CBS leaked a transcript of the Wigand interview to the *New York Daily News,* which identified Wigand for the first time as the CBS industry source. In the parts of the interview that the *Daily News* printed, Wigand claimed that Brown & Williamson lawyers had doctored documents and had been using coumarin as a flavoring in its pipe tobacco. B&W denied the charges and immediately sued Wigand for breach of his confidentiality agreement. In the first of a series of vicious personal attacks on Wigand, the company said he had "appalling disregard for the law. He attempts to portray himself as some kind of hero, when in reality he is simply out for personal gain. . . . He is a master of deceit."

Wigand himself, after searching for months for a lawyer willing to champion his cause as well as protect him, found Dick Scruggs, who agreed to take him on as a client pro bono. Scruggs quickly deposed Wigand for the Mississippi case. Scruggs also charged that B&W had "coerced" Wigand into signing a draconian confidentiality agreement. "They've put ten rolls of tape around his mouth," said Scruggs, adding, "I'm sure they're going to do everything they can to shut the guy up." But even he would be surprised at the lengths to which the company would go to silence their former employee.

To PUBLICIZE the darker sides of Wigand's private life, B&W hired John Scanlon, a sociable New Yorker of Irish descent who had a list of high-fee-paying clients. He was no stranger to tobacco companies, having worked for Philip Morris and Lorillard during the Rose Cipollone trial in 1989, briefing journalists with the company line at the end of each court session. Brown & Williamson wanted to portray Wigand as an unreliable witness. For Scanlon it was "business as usual," as he would say later. The company's investigators started digging—first into government files. The pickings were meager. They found Wigand's testimony about a fire-safe cigarette was somewhat inconsistent. He had talked to the Justice Department about the issue in January 1994, saying it was a "very, very complex" issue and one for which no reliable tests yet existed. However, a year and a half later, in July 1995, Wigand had given an affidavit in a Boston case against Philip Morris, saying that for a tobacco company to produce a cigarette with a "reduced ignition propensity . . . would be a simple matter." A B&W lawyer, Gordon Smith, concluded, "This guy is Jekyll and Hyde; he'll do whatever he needs to do for whoever is paying him." Scruggs came to the rescue. He pointed out that in the 1994 Justice Department testimony, Wigand was simply saying there was no reliable test to measure a fire-safe cigarette. At the time, he had also been accompanied by a B&W lawyer, a stipulation of his confidentiality agreement, and was "testifying with a gun to his head." By the time of the Boston case, said Scruggs, Wigand had learned more about the possibility of reducing a cigarette's potential for setting fires.

But the company's investigators kept digging. They eventually would accuse him of shoplifting, not paying child support, and spousal abuse. Each time, Scruggs rushed in to limit the damage. The shoplifting charges had been dropped, Scruggs protested. That was true. (The company investigators had unearthed the incident with the bottle of Wild Turkey.) The child-support charges had resulted from his divorce from his first wife and were eventually settled. The spousal-abuse charge was brought in October 1993, seven months after Wigand had been fired by B&W and was going through a "stressful time with his family." The charge was later withdrawn. Nevertheless, the company was relentless. The B&W lawyer Gordon Smith told *The Washington Post,* "Scruggs has been painting Wigand as a hero. These things suggest he's not credible. They suggest he can't be believed. Eventually he will be subjected to a thorough cross-examination and his Jekyll and Hyde personality will come out."

To which Scruggs replied, "If this is all they have on this guy after investigating him for several months, I'll sleep pretty well at night." But there was more.

Smear campaigns, however trivial, always work to a certain extent. The victim never fully clears himself. If B&W kept going the way they had started with Wigand, they could severely reduce his credibility as a witness. If CBS had run their *60 Minutes* program, Wigand would be looking much better. He would have told his side of the story, and with the backing of a big corporation. As it was, he was out there—alone.

One way to counter the smear was to leak the court-sealed deposition Wigand had given Scruggs and the Mississippi attorney general, Mike Moore, at the end of November. For two and a half hours in Pascagoula's tiny courthouse on November 29, Wigand had, almost uninterrupted, told his own story about his time with B&W. He was not cross-examined—that would come later—so his allegations went unchallenged. But leaking them would put B&W on the defensive.

Toward the end of January 1996, Alix Freedman of *The Wall Street Journal* received a copy of the transcript. It was a terrific scoop. Freedman, who would win a Pulitzer prize that spring for her reporting on the tobacco industry, turned in an article of more than 3,000 words. In it, she laid out Wigand's allegations one after the other. He accused his ex-boss Tommy Sandefur of lying under oath to Congress about his views on nicotine addiction. He charged that B&W in-house lawyers repeatedly hid potentially damaging scientific research, including altering the minutes of the Vancouver meeting. And he said that top company officials had insisted that coumarin remain in pipe tobacco, even though he had told them he was concerned about its safety.

Freedman included key sections of the transcript. One was Wigand's allegation that Sandefur had lied about nicotine addictiveness. The questions were asked by Ron Motley, the plaintiffs' trial lawyer from Charleston. By this time, Motley had maneuvered his way onto the plaintiffs' roster of several tobacco lawsuits. In the transcript, Motley had asked:

> Q: How many conversations would you say you had between 1989 and 1993, when you were dismissed by Mr. Sandefur, about cigarette smoking and the addictive nature of nicotine?
>
> A: There have been numerous statements made by a number of officers, particularly Mr. Sandefur, that we're in the nicotine delivery business.
>
> Q: The nicotine delivery business?
>
> A:—and that tar is nothing but negative baggage.
>
> Q: Tar is negative baggage? And so, were you in the presence of Mr. Sandefur, the president of the company, when he voiced the opinion and belief that nicotine was addictive?
>
> A: Yes.

Q: And did he express that view on numerous occasions?
A: Frequently.

Motley then asked about the addition of ammonia. Wigand answered that it is the "primary method of managing or manipulating the nicotine delivery." He said the company also used an additive called acetaldehyde as an "impact booster" to enhance nicotine's effects.

Finally, Wigand spoke for the first time about Y1, the high-nicotine crossbred tobacco plant publicized earlier by David Kessler at the Waxman hearings. Yes, Wigand said, he knew about it, and he also knew the company had sent seeds to Brazil for planting there. They had been taken by a company employee in a cigarette pack to hide them from customs officials.

"He hid them?" asked Motley, incredulously.

"He hid them," answered Wigand.

The company was furious and complained bitterly about unscrupulous plaintiffs' lawyers leaking documents at will to bolster their cause. Gordon Smith was again put up by B&W to defend the company. He denied the allegations, calling Wigand's account "absolute fabrication" in some instances and simply "not true" in others.

A week later, the company played the Scanlon card, but it backfired disastrously. Scanlon released a five-hundred-page dossier attacking Wigand. It was titled "The Misconduct of Jeffrey S. Wigand Available in the Public Record." Subheadings included, "Wigand Lies About His Residence," "Wigand Lies Under Oath," and "Other Lies by Wigand." The report portrayed Wigand as a liar, a petty thief, and a "wife beater," and generally a thoroughly dislikeable and dishonest person. As the media, led again by *The Wall Street Journal,* quickly discovered, however, many of the assertions in the report were petty and some of them simply were not true.

The list of Wigand's "misconduct" included that he once complained to an airline that they had somehow got his luggage wet and he wanted $95.20 in compensation for a cleaning bill. The item was apparently supposed to show Wigand as small-minded and capable of possibly fraudulent recriminations. Among other such charges, he was said to have complained about damaged or lost golf clubs, sunglasses, and a fountain pen—all listed under "Possible False or Fraudulent Claims" and all without substantiation.

Wigand was said to have "falsely claimed" he won a YMCA youth award in 1971. The tobacco investigators had interviewed a "Don Keiser" of the YMCA, who said he had never heard of the award. *The Wall Street Journal* found a Don Kyzer, who was head of the YMCA's Teen Leadership Program, who said he couldn't recall being asked about Wigand, and if he had been, he would have said he didn't have a clue because he only arrived at the Y in 1991.

The incident with his second wife was listed under the heading "Wigand Beats His Wife." The court docket said Wigand attended "weekly anger-control counseling and continued psychotherapy" before the charge was dismissed. Scruggs pointed out again that the story had been distorted. First of all he didn't beat his wife, that was not charged in the court files. She did call the police after an argument and afterward he volunteered to go into counseling. The counseling move was not related to the charge's dismissal.

The company looked sinister and ridiculous, both at the same time. (And Scanlon had shocked his fashionable friends in Manhattan and the Hamptons for having had anything to do with Brown & Williamson. In a sympathetic profile of Wigand in *Vanity Fair, 60 Minutes* producer Don Hewitt told Scanlon, "Next time you want to break somebody's legs, hire a capo." Scanlon was unrepentant. In a profile of him in *New York* magazine, prompted by the Wigand affair, Scanlon said, "It's embarrassing, but it was a one day story. The camel shits. The caravan moves on.")

Of course, true or false, the charges in the dossier were to leave a stain on Wigand's character. He was accused of making inflated, or false, claims about himself and his résumé in job hunting. And he had exaggerated his past in a mock job interview: when he left B&W, the company paid for an outplacement firm to help him find another job. In a videotape that Wigand made as a mock interview with a prospective employer, he had said he was a " '64 Olympian in judo" and "an alternate to the Munich games." Lies, said B&W. In fact, Wigand was at the Olympics in Tokyo in 1964, but only to spar with the U.S. team. And he did help train athletes for Munich in 1972. In any case, as

Scruggs said, it was a mock interview and not the real thing. It wasn't supposed to be seen by anyone. B&W had it because they paid for it.

The tobacco company investigators even hired a firm of scientific consultants in Chicago to look over Wigand's Ph.D. thesis. The firm reported back that it had had difficulty tracking down some of the publications Wigand had listed on his curriculum vitae. "There appear to be at least a couple of fraudulent entries," the firm noted, but went on to say it was hard to judge whether they were deliberate or "mistakes or typos." By then, the damage to Wigand's name had been done, of course.

Would any of this evidence be of use in trashing Wigand in court? One of B&W's attorneys contacted by the *Journal* said that was not the point. "All of it is admissible in the court of public opinion," he declared. "What it adds up to is that Jeffrey Wigand is a pathological liar. His entire life, as best we can tell, has been a tissue of lies."

IN THE TRANSCRIPT of the Mississippi deposition, Wigand actually had two things to say that were crucial to the tobacco lawsuits. One was that Sandefur was always talking about nicotine addiction. That was the basis of the Castano lawsuit. The second was about a safe cigarette. Wigand said Sandefur had told him that "there can be no research on a safer cigarette."

In the end, the value of Wigand's testimony depended to a large extent on Sandefur, but he would never reach the witness stand, or even be deposed. He died on July 15, 1996, of aplastic anemia, a rare blood disease. He was fifty-six. Coincidentally, another key company witness on the company's knowledge of nicotine addiction, Addison Yeaman, who had authored the famous memo—"We are then in the business of selling nicotine, an addictive drug"—also died that summer in Louisville. He was eighty-eight, and his personal story was sealed. He had refused to talk to reporters. Even so, Wigand was still the star witness for the plaintiffs.

1 0

VOYAGE OF DISCOVERY

Assuming it would take only five minutes to retrieve a document . . . it would take 750,000 minutes, or 12,500
hours, to review all the 150,000 privileged documents. This
is roughly 6.25 years of a lawyer's working career.

—*Judge Kenneth Fitzpatrick, Minnesota Medicaid case, 1997*

BY THE END of 1996, lawyers preparing Minnesota's Medicaid
suit had reviewed a stunning thirty million pages from tobacco
company internal files, more than that examined by any other
group of lawyers challenging the industry. Asked how it was done, one
of the leading Minnesota lawyers, Roberta Walburn, of the Minneapolis
firm of Robins, Kaplan, Miller & Ciresi, replied wearily, "One at a
time."

The tobacco companies were waging a war of attrition, as they had
always done; adopting the same strategy that had been so memorably
summed up after earlier court battles by an R. J. Reynolds legal counsel, Michael Jordan. "[The] aggressive posture we have regarding depositions and discovery in general continues to make these cases extremely
burdensome and expensive for plaintiffs' lawyers, particularly sole prac-
titioners. The way we won the cases, to paraphrase General Patton, is
not by spending all of Reynold's money, but by making the son-of-a-
bitch spend all of his."

In response to Minnesota's requests for internal company documents
on smoking and health, the companies had sent truckloads of reports on
such mind-numbing topics as the habits of the tobacco plant beetle,
wastewater treatment techniques, leaf storage, and soil erosion. Almost

none of it was of the remotest value in the Minnesota lawsuit brought by the state's attorney general, Hubert Humphrey III.

The industry's strategy was to make the process of pretrial document discovery—the lifeblood of liability lawsuits—as arduous, limited, slow, and expensive as possible. This was in direct contravention of the federal rules of civil procedure, which are designed to ensure the "just, speedy and inexpensive determination" of a civil claim and "to prevent use of discovery to wage a war of attrition or as a device to coerce a party, whether financially weak or affluent." Lawyers had protested. At one point in the Texas Medicaid case, the lead counsel for the state, John O'Quinn, complained to the judge in the court at Texarkana about what he considered to be the industry's rotten performance on discovery. O'Quinn noted that the state had come before the court naked, as the discovery process intended, but that the industry's counsel hadn't even got his socks off. In Mississippi, the state's legal team, frustrated by a particular industry motion to depose a former assistant to one of the state's proposed experts, had complained. "The defendants' strategy in this case, as well as other tobacco litigation, is to conduct extensive discovery on issues irrelevant to the subject litigation. These discovery tactics are a Trojan horse, used by the industry under the guise of being a 'legitimate' need for documents and depositions regardless of relevancy or admissibility of the requested information." The judge agreed and threw out the industry's request, saying it was not well taken.

Over the years of tobacco litigation, judges had also expressed shock at the abuse of the principles underlying discovery, but the companies ignored the complaints and continued to bluster and bully their way from one courtroom victory to another.

In the first case to be settled during the Third Wave—the $10 billion libel action against ABC News—Philip Morris, in reply to ABC's discovery requests, had sent boxes of documents on red paper that could not be copied. When ABC complained, the judge made the company switch to white paper. In the Minnesota Medicaid case, lawyers at the Minneapolis law firm of Robins, Kaplan, which represented the state, had looked for a shortcut through the blizzard of internal documents the industry was producing. The lawyers assumed that wealthy corporations with an extensive history of litigation, such as the tobacco companies, would have a computerized index of all documents that were relevant to lawsuits. The Merrell Williams papers had shown that Brown & Williamson lawyers had developed special procedures to shield sensitive documents from the discovery process by routing them through the company's legal department, thus creating a set of supposedly privileged documents.

The Williams papers also suggested that the companies may have sent sensitive documents abroad to foreign affiliates, or even had them destroyed to prevent them from being unearthed during discovery. In the infamous 1985 "deadwood" memo, J. Kendrick Wells, B&W's corporate counsel, had said sensitive documents should be thought of as "deadwood" and hinted that they might have been shipped to the parent company, BAT Industries, in England. The question was whether this suggestion of Wells's was ever implemented, and whether other companies had made similar provisions.

Believing that an index of these documents must exist, the Minnesota lawyers presented a motion to the court asking for it. The companies denied the existence of any such lists. "They kept saying they had no lists and we kept saying we know you do, and the letters and phone calls went back and forth," said Roberta Walburn. "They complained we were sounding like a broken record. But we knew they had to have them."

The determination of the Minnesota lawyers paid off. After six months of wrangling, the companies admitted there were indeed such lists. They could not be handed over, however, because they were all privileged; they had been produced by lawyers in anticipation of litigation.

In response, Robins, Kaplan asked the court to review the list—to see if the rules allowing such a privilege had been properly applied. Impossible task, said the companies. The indices were too varied and it would be difficult to compile them. So the judge asked for random samples. He quickly concluded that the claim of privilege did not apply. The indices merely gave the date, subject, author, and recipients of the documents. They contained neither attorney-client information nor attorney opinions—the two categories for which the companies could have rightfully claimed privilege. The judge ruled that the state must be provided with the lists. In fact, he added, there was no other sensible way to sift through tens of millions of documents.

The companies appealed the ruling to the Minnesota Supreme Court, which promptly sided with the judge. So the companies appealed to the U.S. Supreme Court, which, declining to hear the matter, left the lower courts' ruling intact.

Sixteen months after the state's first request, in February 1995, following eight orders from the judge and two appeals, the lists finally arrived. The Minneapolis lawyers were now in possession of a unique research tool that would put their discovery operation on a different footing from that of the other lawyers suing the industry. Not only could they skip over reports on beetle life cycles and soil science, but they could request the industry's most sensitive documents and, as Walburn said, read them one at a time. In the end, the Minnesota lawyers, using their special lists, needed to copy less than 2 percent of the material supplied by the industry.

In forcing the industry to produce the lists, Robins, Kaplan lawyers had won a key strategic battle in what became known as the "document wars." Their victory was part of the most widespread discovery hunt in the history of American civil litigation, taking their search beyond United States borders to tobacco companies and their affiliates in Britain and Europe. More than six million pages of internal files would be provided by the biggest U.S. company, Philip Morris. And in London, BAT would supply more than seven million pages. In Minnesota alone, the two sides would spend more than $100 million on the discovery phase of the lawsuit.

The document wars opened on several fronts—besides Minnesota, they were waged in Mississippi, Florida, Texas, and New Orleans. In Charleston, South Carolina, Ron Motley launched his own guerrilla operation. Besides the Castano case in New Orleans, Motley had attached himself as co-counsel to several other state lawsuits, which gave him the opportunity to file discovery requests in several different cases. He flew his team—his junkyard dogs, as he called them—around the country in one of the firm's two Citation jets. Each of the lawyers on the team was assigned a company. Andy Berly tracked down documents from Brown & Williamson and its Britsh parent, BAT. Susan Nial burrowed into the files of R. J. Reynolds. Ann Ritter pursued Philip Morris. They delved into court records of past tobacco cases, prised open sealed records, searched libraries, archives, and universities, building an arsenal of documents for what Motley called "the Conspiracy to End Conspiracy"; his personal script on the evils of the tobacco industry that he dearly hoped he would one day have a chance to use in court.

Motley would complain bitterly about the industry's "illicit efforts to cloak its most damning documents under unfounded claims of attorney-client privilege." One of the states he represented, Florida, filed scores of motions to compel the companies to produce documents they were reluctant to give up. But neither Motley's intensive discovery efforts, nor those of the other plaintiffs, would compare in size and scope to the encyclopedic operation in Minnesota, where the most thorough, dogged inquiry into the industry's past was launched from the twenty-seventh floor of the Minneapolis skyscraper offices of the law firm of Robins, Kaplan.

ONE OF the biggest law firms in the Midwest, Robins, Kaplan has 221 attorneys, maintains offices in every big American city, and has a reputation for taking on, and winning, complex civil litigation. The driving force in the Minneapolis headquarters was one of America's leading liability lawyers, Mike Ciresi, a fifty-one-year-old veteran of the plaintiffs' bar. A loner, Ciresi shunned the kind of group operation set up by Wendell Gauthier in New Orleans and disdained the theatrical performances favored by Ron Motley. Ciresi ran a no-frills operation and believed that this put him a cut above his flashier colleagues. In his last encounter with them—during the Bhopal tragedy—he had out maneuvered Belli, Gauthier, Chesley, and Coale to become the Indian government's legal representative in the United States—all the result of a chance introduction by a colleague to the Indian ambassador in Washington. The Bhopal incident had left Ciresi with some permanent enemies.

When Robins, Kaplan was appointed as the sole law firm representing the state of Minnesota in its Medicaid case, Ciresi's colleagues sniped at him from afar. "That little Napoleon," said Coale, whose dislike of Ciresi often seemed irrational. "I don't know what the hell they're doing up there," he would say when asked for a report on the

Minnesota case. "Anyone who lives in Minnesota has got to be slightly crazy." Ciresi and his team ignored the taunts and got on with their work.

Ciresi was raised in St. Paul. His father, who ran a grocery store and a liquor store, brought up the boy and his sister after their mother died of breast cancer when Ciresi was twelve. His father was tough and driven, strong on family values, self-responsibility, and accountability. Ciresi went to the local University of St. Thomas for his bachelor's degree and then graduated from the University of Minnesota Law School in 1971. He worked as a law clerk at Robins, Kaplan to help pay his way through college.

As a partner at Robins, Kaplan, Ciresi drove his lawyers hard, expecting the relentless pursuit of opponents. "It's not a country club," Ciresi once said about his law firm, pointing to the difference between his approach to practicing law and that of others in the profession. Some of his colleagues criticize what they call Ciresi's "scorched-earth, take-no-prisoners" style, but he has proven to be extraordinarily effective in complex patent and liability cases. He directed the firm's multimillion dollar victories against Minolta and other camera makers, for patent infringement ($497 million); against the A. H. Robins Co., maker of the Dalkon Shield intrauterine device ($38 million); and against G. D. Searle & Co, makers of the Copper-7 IUD ($8.75 million).

In the Third Wave of tobacco suits, Ciresi created a team of a dozen experienced attorneys who quickly developed a reputation as the armored division of the antitobacco forces: ponderous, but with the heaviest firepower. Ciresi's team, who would work long hours, rarely taking a weekend off, included Gary Wilson, a partner in the firm's mass tort department, and Roberta Walburn, a former reporter for the Minneapolis *Star Tribune* who, as a lawyer, had earned her partnership working with Ciresi on the Bhopal and Dalkon Shield cases. Walburn did most of the courtroom work, preparing motions and pounding the companies with questions about internal documents. The group also included Susan Richard Nelson, who had handled automotive and pharmaceutical product liability, and Thomas Hamlin, an expert in patent infringement.

While Gauthier was waging his propaganda war, and Motley was flying around in his private plane, picking up clients and holding high-profile depositions, and Dick Scruggs and Mike Moore were maneuvering Mississippi into being the first state to go to trial, the Minneapolis team was moving slowly and methodically toward its public confrontation with the industry. Motley and Coale mocked Ciresi's strategy of reviewing millions of documents, saying it was taking too much time and wasn't necessary to win the case. But that was how Robins, Kaplan worked. "Our view was not to be the first to go to trial, but to do it right," said Walburn.

Over time, the Minneapolis lawyers would become the industry's most implacable foes. Ciresi's team had always believed that the Merrell Williams documents were, as Walburn said, "just the tip of the iceberg," and they set out to prove it.

From their northern fastness, Ciresi's team kept up an unrelenting barrage of demands for documents, filing hundreds of separate motions to make the companies comply with a discovery request. They were the only ones to challenge the industry on the destruction or concealment of sensitive scientific reports from company files, and they launched the most comprehensive attack on the improper use by the industry of the attorney-privilege rules. Minnesota would force a judicial review of 250,000 documents—or more than a million pages—for which the industry had claimed privilege. They would uncover evidence that led them to charge Philip Morris with routinely destroying potentially damaging documents about smoking and health, a charge the company vigorously denied.

The Minnesota lawyers were also the first to include in their lawsuit the British tobacco giant, BAT Industries. BAT believed it had successfully "ring-fenced" its corporate structure so as to avoid the long arm of United States liability, but the Minnesota lawyers roped it anyway, forcing the company to set up a special document warehouse in England and fill it with seven million pages of the company's files. In a moment of reflection on the Minnesota offensive, Walker Merryman, vice president of the industry's Washington lobbying arm, the Tobacco Institute, would observe, "Minnesota is a state in which we always expect the worst."

THE MINNESOTA CASE was filed in August 1994 by attorney general Hubert Horatio "Skip" Humphrey III, the son of the former vice president. This was the second Medicaid suit to be filed—Mississippi had filed that May.

It was appropriate that wholesome, health-conscious Minnesota should be among the first to sue. Since the 1970s, it had been one of the country's leading antitobacco states, defeating persistent tobacco industry lobbying in its legislature to pass one of the nation's first anti-smoking bills in 1975. At the same time, the state had used an increased cigarette tax to fund medical insurance for the uninsured.

Ciresi and Walburn had first discussed suing in 1989 during the Rose Cipollone case in New Jersey, but no formal meetings were held with Humphrey's staff until early 1994 when, as in Mississippi, David Kessler's letter about nicotine manipulation, the ABC News *Day One* program, and the release of the Merrell Williams papers accelerated the process. Humphrey gave Ciresi an exclusive contract, making it the only one of the 39 states that would eventually sue to be represented by a single law firm. If Minnesota won, the state would ask the court to require the tobacco companies to pay all attorney fees. These would be capped at 25 percent of the damages, lower than the standard 33 percent retainer normally asked by law firms under contingency-fee arrangements, but enough to give Robins, Kaplan the promise of the biggest cut of the tobacco riches from a single case in the Third Wave.

In Skip Humphrey, who had just turned fifty, Ciresi and Walburn found a willing participant. Humphrey's father, who died in 1978, had smoked four packs of unfiltered Lucky Strikes a day through the 1950s and the young Skip had always hated the smell of cigarettes. He had inherited his father's liberal bent, particularly in matters of antitrust, health care, and consumer protection. He had an instinctive dislike of Big Tobacco, its political power and its riches, and he would become one of its harshest critics. He would use his political inheritance, his links to the White House forged when he ran Clinton's Minnesota campaign, plus his bid to be governor, to turn the state's lawsuit into the one most respected by the industry.

One reason for Big Tobacco's concern was Ciresi's terrier reputation for never letting go of a case, however complicated and drawn out it became. Another reason was Humphrey's use of Minnesota's tough consumer protection and antitrust laws. The Minnesota suit was never part of the bandwagon driven by Scruggs, Moore, and Motley. Like Mississippi, Minnesota was seeking recovery of Medicaid expenses, but in addition to demanding that the industry pay for the medical bills, Minnesota was charging it with consumer fraud in promoting and selling a product known to be harmful. The state alleged that the industry had engaged in a "decades-long combination of conspiracy and of willful and intentional wrongdoing."

The fraud began, said the state, with the infamous 1954 "Frank Statement" published by the tobacco companies in newspapers in virtually every city in the United States with a population of 50,000 or more. The industry statement declared, in part, "We accept an interest in people's health as a basic responsibility, paramount to every other consideration in our business." Minnesota alleged that the conspiracy continued when the companies learned of the addictive powers of nicotine but engaged in a "unified campaign of deceit and misrepresentation to hide this information." As a result, the companies had been unjustly enriched because they had not paid for the damage to people's health. Now, Minnesota declared, was payback time.

In a second departure from the Mississippi suit, Minnesota further charged violation of the state's antitrust law, which prohibited "unreasonable restraint of trade and commerce." It was the industry's suppression of research into smoking and health—in particular, its suppression of the development of a healthier cigarette—that, argued the state, "had the purpose and effect of restraining competition in the market for cigarettes."

Minnesota was also the only state to bring the suit jointly with its largest purchaser of health care, Blue Cross and Blue Shield. The state and Blue Cross were the two largest purchasers of health care in Minnesota. As an employer, the state provided health coverage to its 60,000 employees; Blue Cross had contracts with 12,000 doctors and clinics, 135 hospitals, and 6,000 allied health-care providers.

The state had estimated that cigarettes killed 6,000 Minnesotans each year—out of a population of 4.5 million—and caused thousands of others to develop smoking-related diseases. The total health bill paid by the state and Blue Cross and Blue Shield was estimated at $470 million a year. Total damages sought amounted to at least $5 billion. Any monies recovered could benefit all citizens of Minnesota in the form of lower taxes, and Blue Cross would give the damage award back to the consumer in the form of lower health insurance costs because it is a nonprofit enterprise.

In addition to reimbursement of tobacco-related health-care costs, the state also sought "an end to the forty-year conspiracy," including the dissolution of the industry's research and propaganda apparatus, the Council for Tobacco Research and the Tobacco Institute, and it demanded the industry open its files to the public, fund a corrective public education campaign, take steps to curb the sale of cigarettes to minors, and set up stop-smoking clinics. How long might this grand lawsuit last? "Our best guess," said Robins, Kaplan, "is two to five years. The tobacco companies may do everything possible to drag it out."

THE TOBACCO COMPANIES sent in their shock troops. At one early court hearing, no fewer than two dozen industry lawyers representing nine tobacco companies filed into the Ramsey County District Court, a splendid art deco building with a big onyx statue in the lobby of an American Indian smoking a peace pipe. The tiny courtroom of Judge Kenneth Fitzpatrick, the state judge assigned to the case, was too small to accommodate all the tobacco lawyers and they had to sit in the spectator seats. Ciresi's team was quite comfortable on their side of the court with only six lawyers.

Over the next few weeks, the industry sought to dismiss the suit using the same subrogation argument they had put forward in Mississippi: any claim for damages had to be brought on behalf of a smoker. By bringing the suit, the state was in effect stepping into the shoes of the smoker; the suit was really no different from a personal-injury claim and the traditional defenses of assumption of known risks should apply. The companies also claimed that Blue Cross and Blue Shield should be dismissed because they had suffered no damage: the extra costs of looking after smoking victims had been passed on to the insured in the form of higher premiums.

It took a year for the Minnesota lawyers to defeat these efforts to dismiss the case, but before Ciresi's team could begin the serious business of document discovery there was a small matter to clear up: BAT Industries of London claimed that it had been wrongfully named in the suit; that it was merely a holding company with only 164 employees and had no meaningful control over Brown & Williamson's activities in the United States. Minnesota countered that BAT not only had full control of B&W but had been selling more than four million cartons of cigarettes a year through its Kentucky subsidiary.

In the ensuing court battle, Ciresi had a special weapon—Minnesota's "long-arm statute." Most states have such laws to protect themselves against parent corporations that do business in their territory through wholly owned subsidiaries. If their products cause harm, the state has a chance to include the parent company in a claim.

BAT claimed it had never manufactured, tested, designed, marketed, packaged, sold, distributed, or advertised cigarettes anywhere in the United States. Neither had it conducted research with respect to tobacco products or any other goods or products sold or intended for sale in the United States, including Minnesota. It had no offices, or even a telephone number in the state. There were no direct contacts of any kind, the BAT lawyer argued.

Unhappily for BAT, Ciresi put Roberta Walburn on the case. The former newspaper reporter was expert at following corporate paper trails. Walburn unraveled what she would eventually describe to the court as BAT's "attempt to engage in a corporate shell game"; distancing itself from its American subsidiary, Brown & Williamson, through a complex succession of corporate intermediaries.

BAT Industries is a multinational corporation whose corporate pedigree goes back to James Buchanan "Buck" Duke, the founder of the modern cigarette industry. His family—the Dukes of Durham, North Carolina—had started selling snuff tobacco after the Civil War under the ingeniously misleading brand name of Pro Bono Publico. By the turn of the century, having created a cigarette monopoly in the United States with the American Tobacco Company, Duke went to England and joined forces with the Imperial Tobacco Company. In 1902, they created the British-American Tobacco Company Ltd., which became known as BATCo, or simply BAT.

Under the merger, the companies on each side of the Atlantic agreed not to compete for the other's domestic market and assigned brand rights to each other for home sales. Duke's operation in the

United States violated the Sherman Antitrust Act and, in 1911, the U.S. Supreme Court declared his American Tobacco Company to be an illegal monopoly. He was forced to sell his majority shareholding in BAT and cancel the trans-Atlantic covenants. BAT was thus free to conduct business all over the world and in 1927 the company bought Brown & Williamson of Louisville, Kentucky.

Today, BAT describes itself as "the world's most international cigarette manufacturer." The corporate pyramid has BAT Industries at the top, followed by South Western Nominees Ltd., BATUS Holdings, Inc., BATUS Tobacco Services Inc., and Brown & Williamson Tobacco Corp. At the time Walburn did her research, in 1994, BAT was trying to buy the American Tobacco Company, which it eventually did, a year later.

In 1993, BAT had revenues of $36 billion and sold tobacco products in more than forty-eight countries with profits of $2 billion from tobacco sales. As Walburn would observe sarcastically in court, "Not a bad feat for 164 employees." She was able to persuade Judge Fitzpatrick that BAT had created "a fact dispute." The Merrell Williams documents demonstrated that BAT was running tobacco and health research in England and that B&W was paying for it. Far from being a distant parent, BAT appeared to be "inextricably intertwined" with its Kentucky relative.

For example, in 1963, the chairman of the BAT group board had ordered B&W to withhold scientific research from the U.S. Surgeon General. Later, BAT's joint attempts with B&W to develop a "safe cigarette" had come to nothing after company lawyers had decided it would be an admission that other types of cigarettes "might be harmful." Walburn insisted that BAT employed a heavy "hands-on" approach, which was quite enough to satisfy the Minnesota "long-arm" statute, which merely required "minimum contacts." Such minimum contacts were said to exist wherever a nonresident defendant had "purposefully availed itself of the privilege of conducting activities within the jurisdiction." Actual physical presence—an office, a phone number—was not required under the law. Walburn argued that BAT sold cigarettes in Minnesota through its wholly owned subsidiary, B&W, knowing that they would cause adverse health effects in millions of smokers and would result in increased health costs. In the end, the only way to resolve the fact dispute was through discovery of BAT's internal files, she insisted.

Judge Fitzpatrick agreed; discovery was needed to resolve the issue. Now, the American companies were not the only target of Ciresi's widely cast discovery net. The second-largest international tobacco company in the world, BAT, was forced to open the special document warehouse in Guildford, south of London, and give Ciresi's team access.

They began their great voyage of discovery with a blanket request for all company records—the U.S. industry's and BAT's—on scientific research, safer cigarettes, nicotine addiction, and tests for tar and nicotine levels. For once, said Professor Daynard of Northeastern University Law School, there was a chance of finally "leveling the playing field with the companies."

MUCH DEPENDED ON the judge in the case. From the beginning, the Minnesota lawyers realized there would be no snap decisions, no judicial shortcuts to an early trial in the courtroom of Judge Kenneth Fitzpatrick.

A lifelong civil servant, he started his legal career as an assistant for then attorney general Walter Mondale, who later became a U.S. senator and then vice president under Jimmy Carter. When the Minnesota suit was filed, Fitzpatrick, who was nearing his sixtieth birthday, had been on the bench for twenty-two years. He was the state's chief judge.

In contrast to the spiraling demands of the lawyers on both sides, his courtroom style was conservative and cautious. As each discovery request was met with the obstructive maneuvers for which the industry had become well known, Fitzpatrick's patience was sorely tried. Five of Fitzpatrick's rulings were appealed, three of them on matters of discovery, and each time the arguments were more contentious than the last. All five appeals were upheld, but the pressure on the judge grew.

Fitzpatrick's answer was to allow the lawyers considerable latitude in making their arguments, chiding them only when absolutely necessary. "The court is not impressed with any chippy comments," he told the lawyers when a session threatened to get out of hand. And another time, rather than reprimanding the two contestants for their increasing hostility, he said, "I would hope . . . that all counsel will perform with dignity and respect for each other." He insisted that the tone of the courtroom remain serious at all times. "I assure you, throughout the entire proceeding I will not use or make any reference to the smoking gun," he said, adding, "I find it a very unappealing pun."

Minnesota was lucky in one key respect, however. Fitzpatrick was a computer buff and made notes on his laptop at the bench. Convinced that computers are an integral part of complex modern litigation, he came up with two key solutions to handling the mass of paper being produced. From the start, he ruled that all motions, briefs, and submissions should be filed electronically. Second, he ordered the creation of a single document depository in Minneapolis for all U.S. company documents. The industry had wanted to set up nine different document centers in nine different parts of the country to represent the nine tobacco company defendants—a solution that would have made it far more arduous and expensive for Ciresi's team.

In one of his early rulings, Fitzpatrick gave the nation's antitobacco forces what could have been a powerful weapon. He allowed other lawyers in the Third Wave access to the documents found by Minnesota—providing that the judges in their own lawsuits issued so-called protective orders similar to the one he had imposed on the Minnesota lawyers: Fitzpatrick had ruled that any document placed in the common depository was not a public document; it could not be released to the media until used as evidence in trial. The judge's order meant that the Castano lawyers or Motley's group or the lawyers from the other states could send their own teams to help Minnesota with the grueling task of sorting out the important documents from the mass of irrelevant paper.

But for many months none of them came and, in the end, out of the thirty-nine states that would eventually file suit, only Connecticut and Washington lent a hand. "The rest just sat back and waited and then copied the 1 or 2 percent that we had copied," said Roberta Walburn bitterly. Motley's view was that Fitzpatrick's protective order was too restrictive. In his guerrilla operation, the only good document was one you could give to the media and use to score a propaganda point. The other, perhaps overriding reason, was that none of the Southern lawyers wanted to be associated, in any way, with Ciresi's operation.

As it turned out, the method benefited the tobacco companies—as they had, of course, known it would. They provided the list of documents selected by Ciresi's team from the two depositories, and the other lawyers selected what they wanted from the Minnesota list. "The tobacco companies played people's laziness against themselves," was how Walburn put it. "In litigation like this it's beneficial to the plaintiffs to have different lawyers review the documents."

At the same time, the industry took every opportunity to make the discovery process as burdensome as possible for the plaintiffs. Documents were copied and sent out in unnumbered boxes, not in chronological order, and with the list of the documents that Ciresi's team had selected in every possible computer format, with each tobacco company using a different word processing system. In some cases, chunks of data were missing; the plaintiffs never knew whether this was intentional, or if there were viruses on the disks. In Minnesota, Ciresi had his computer staff working seven days a week for two years to keep up with unraveling the data so that it made sense.

Although Fitzpatrick's order meant that none of the documents could be made public before the Minnesota trial, there was one important exception. If a document was used as an exhibit in arguing a motion in court, it was automatically public unless sealed by the judge. In this way, Ciresi's team would make public several key documents, playing their own role in the barrage of propaganda against the industry.

IN MAY 1996, the Minnesota lawyers made headlines with one such document, an R. J. Reynolds research report from 1973. The memo was stamped "SECRET" and written by Claude Teague, assistant research chief at RJR. In those days, Reynolds had been wondering why Philip Morris's Marlboro cigarettes had become so successful, eclipsing Reynolds' most popular brand, Winston. Reynolds scientists had taken apart a Marlboro cigarette to see what it was made of. They found that while Marlboros delivered about the same amount of nicotine in the smoke as Winstons, more of the Marlboro's nicotine was "free," or volatile, which meant it was more easily assimilated into the bloodstream of the smoker. The reason, the RJR scientists found, was that Marlboro cigarette smoke was more alkaline than Winston's.

For some years (as Dr. Kessler at the FDA had discovered), the tobacco companies had known that as the pH, or acid-alkali value, of tobacco smoke increases and becomes more alkaline, an increasing proportion of the nicotine in the smoke occurs in the "free" or volatile form and is absorbed more quickly by the smoker. If the smoke is acid, the nicotine combines with acidic substances, becomes nonvolatile, and is absorbed relatively slowly by the smoker. Teague concluded in his memo that Marlboros could be "expected to show more instantaneous nicotine 'kick' " than Winstons.

The memo was important evidence in addiction cases, such as Castano, because it indicated manipulation of nicotine levels. Professor Daynard called the memo a "smoking gun," using Judge Fitzpatrick's least favorite pun. R. J. Reynolds dismissed it as preliminary research that proved to be incorrect, but it still left Philip Morris with some explaining to do.

Ciresi's team also focused on the possible destruction of internal files. As Roberta Walburn scanned the industry's lists of so-called privileged documents, she became increasingly aware that there was, as she would say, "point-blank evidence of document destruction." In a motion to Fitzpatrick, she complained, "In a typical lawsuit even one instance of intentional document destruction is cause for alarm. In the present case, however, initial discovery has revealed an extraordinary array of evidence of destruction. Much of [it] is remarkably explicit." Among the evidence, Walburn cited Philip Morris's use of third parties to maintain their documents "apparently to preclude discovery."

Walburn even argued that some of the companies seemed to have a "pervasive philosophy" of suppressing or destroying potentially damaging documents. As an example, she said, Philip Morris had apparently taken steps to destroy documents at its biological research lab in Cologne, Germany. This facility, known as INBIFO, was once a private laboratory but had been purchased by Philip Morris in the early 1970s. Over the years, Philip Morris had used INBIFO for extensive—and sensitive—scientific research. In fact, Philip Morris had regarded the German research center as a place where, as one internal company memo put it, "we might do some of the things we are reluctant to do in this country."

During her review of papers produced by Philip Morris, Walburn had discovered a handwritten note, with no author or date, in the files of Thomas Osdene, the company's director of research from 1969 to 1984, that discussed both the destruction and the unusual routing of INBIFO documents. It read:

> Ship all documents to Cologne . . .
> Keep in Cologne.
> Okay to phone & telex (these will be destroyed).
> We will monitor in person every 2–3 months.
> If important letters or documents have to be sent, please
> send to home—I will act on them & destroy.

Supporting evidence of document destruction appeared in a 1977 memo, also quoted by Walburn. In it, Robert Seligman, Philip Morris's then vice president for research and development, wrote, "We have gone to great pains to eliminate any written contact with INBIFO, and I would like to maintain this structure." He suggested sending research samples to a Philip Morris subsidiary in Switzerland "for transshipment to INBIFO," or creating a "dummy" mailing address from which the samples could be forwarded to INBIFO. He added that written analytical data would still have to be sent to the Swiss subsidiary "if we are to avoid direct contact with INBIFO and Philip Morris USA."

Still another Philip Morris memo produced in court by the Minnesota lawyers suggested efforts to suppress or destroy documents. It was written by William Dunn, a Duke-trained psychologist who joined the research staff of Philip Morris in 1961. In the memo he discussed what to do if a proposed scientific study into the addictive properties of nicotine produced results the company did not like:

"I have given Carolyn approval to proceed with this study. If she is able to demonstrate, as she anticipates, no withdrawal effects of nicotine, we will want to pursue this even with some vigor. If, however, the results with nicotine are similar to those gotten with morphine and caffeine, we will want to bury it. Accordingly, there are only two copies of this memo, the one attached and the original which I have."

Philip Morris vigorously denied the state's allegations, saying it would respond "in full, in detail, and in court." But Walburn would not be put off. She insisted that the companies list all instances of document destruction and identify each one by a search of all available indices, databases, and lists, whether maintained by the company, its in-house legal department, or outside counsel. The companies complained again that the request was "overly broad" and "burdensome," and that the documents concerned were privileged or the result of work-product. Nevertheless, Fitzpatrick ordered them to produce the lists. Whatever Walburn found was subject to Fitzpatrick's protection order, and would not be released until the trial.

To complete this phase of their document hunt, Minnesota needed to search the files of the international affiliates of Philip Morris. Walburn claimed that Philip Morris had failed to produce document lists belonging to Philip Morris International (PMI), the foreign sales affiliate of Philip Morris. The company lawyers protested. A search of PMI files would impose "extraordinary and unwarranted burdens," they said. Indeed, they claimed that PMI had been a separate corporate entity since 1987, with different directors and officers, and that Philip Morris USA had no control over the documents in PMI's files.

Philip Morris had previously told the state, Walburn countered, that, despite PMI's spin-off, no documents had been transferred to any corporate affiliate without Philip Morris retaining the original, or a copy. So she wanted the copies of PMI files now in Philip Morris's possession. She argued that the "separate entity" status of PMI was a recently created claim to avoid discovery. In response, the company called this "nonsensical," leaving Fitzpatrick to adjudicate.

For the first time, Fitzpatrick began to show his impatience. In March 1997, six months after the state had first raised the issue, Fitzpatrick issued an unusually stern rebuke to the company. Essentially agreeing with Minnesota that it had engaged "in an egregious attempt to hide information," he ordered the search of PMI files to proceed. The company's "attempts at hiding documents in the morass of interlocking related organizations shall not be tolerated by this court," Fitzpatrick concluded. "Nor will the court countenance Philip Morris's self-selected and voluntarily provided set of documents from selected sources. Philip Morris must respond to discovery requests properly."

The confrontation over PMI had put the document wars on a new, even more hostile footing, but the most heated battle was yet to come. It raged over the companies' claims of attorney-client and work-product privilege.

In April 1997, in a memorandum to Fitzpatrick, the state argued that the total number of documents for which the companies had claimed privilege had exceeded a "staggering" 130,000, or more than half a million pages. Included was scientific research into the health hazards of cigarettes that had simply been passed by the desks of company attorneys and could not, the state argued, properly be claimed as privileged. In some cases, the state added, documents were subject to the "crime-fraud" exception to the privilege rule. The "crime-fraud" exception prevents lawyers from using privilege as a shield behind which they take part in an ongoing crime or fraud. Minnesota asked for a private review of more than half a million pages by the court.

On May 9, 1997, in a great victory for Ciresi's team, Fitzpatrick ruled that the state had established a reasonable basis for believing that the crime-fraud exception should be invoked for thousands of documents. One of the documents on which he based his ruling was a 1979 memorandum from B&W's corporate counsel, J. Kendrick Wells, to Ernest Pepples, the company's vice president, which, as the judge noted, had been publicly available on the Internet "for months, if not years." In the memorandum, Wells had outlined a plan to wrap scientific information in attorney-client privilege in order to separate "sensitive" reports. Other documents demonstrated how the industry deliberately sought evidence that underplayed the health risks of smoking and made public statements denying those risks. A 1970 memo written by Helmut Wakeham, then head of research and development for Philip Morris, to the company's president, Joseph Cullman, discussed the raison d'être for the Council for Tobacco Research: "It has been stated that CTR is a program to find out the 'truth about smoking and health.' What is truth to one is false to another. CTR and the industry have publicly and frequently denied what others find as 'truth.' Let's face it. We are interested in evidence which we believe denies the allegations that cigarette smoking causes disease."

Given these and other examples of how the industry had tried to undermine public knowledge of the effects of smoking, the judge felt his own review was not broad enough and ordered that the documents for which privilege had been claimed be reviewed by a special master of the court. The problem was how to review so many pieces of paper—more than half a million. A full review was clearly an impossible task. It would last well into the next millennium, said Fitzpatrick. Supposing that it only took five minutes to retrieve a document and assess whether the companies had correctly classified it—as work-product or attorney-client communication—it would take 750,000 minutes, or 12,500 hours, or roughly 6.25 years of a lawyer's working career to complete the task.

To finish the job in the two months before the discovery period ended, it would take more than thirty people working two hundred hours a month. It just wasn't possible. Instead, Judge Fitzpatrick proposed that the documents be put into categories of the privilege claimed and the court's special master then do a random review or "spot check." In August, the special master declared that eight hundred of the privileged documents from the Liggett Group (the first to be examined) were, in his opinion, not subject to privilege and could be released. More documents were expected.

AS THE THIRD WAVE PROGRESSED, the Minnesota lawsuit would remain separate and apart. In the summer of 1996, as Scruggs and Moore started down the road to settlement, Minnesota refused to join in. "It's a combination of lawyers running scared and wanting to make a quick buck, and it's a very bad combination," said Walburn. As far as Skip Humphrey and the Ciresi law firm were concerned, they were going to trial on January 19, 1998, and there was still a lot of work to do. "Ten years from now," forecast Walburn, "people are going to look back and say Minnesota was the only state that stood up and didn't sell out."

11

THE FORDICE SAGA

You know what AG stands for, don't you? Aspiring
Governor.
                        —*Kirk Fordice, governor of Mississippi, 1996*

Our governor has made a deal with the devil.
                        —*Mike Moore, attorney general of Mississippi, 1996*

I N MISSISSIPPI, the state suit against the tobacco industry turned
into a personal tug-of-war between Mike Moore, the cocksure
Democratic attorney general, and his Republican governor, Kirk
Fordice. Before it was over, Fordice had joined forces with the tobacco
companies and together they had taken Moore to court in an unprecedented effort to stop the lawsuit.

When Moore filed the suit in May 1994, he knew that he could not
count on his governor's support. Fordice was the state's first Republican
governor since 1874, an old-style supporter of big business and the
beneficiary of generous campaign contributions from the tobacco industry. Moore was one of the state's new yuppie Democrats, a group of
moderate, reform-minded politicians who had swept into office in the
late 1980s under the banner of a progressive governor, Ray Mabus. At
thirty-nine, Mabus was the youngest governor in the nation. His secretary of state was thirty-eight. Moore was thirty-five. Camelot had finally made it to Mississippi, they said of the Mabus entourage. Their
goal was to "unravel the status quo," as one of them put it; to bring
"basic, drastic change" so that Mississippi would never again be at the
bottom of the national ladder in per capita income, employment, and
literacy.

The pace of change Mabus set was too breathless for the old Missississippi establishment and he lasted only one term. His political base was shaky. Blacks, who made up about 30 percent of the state's registered voters, supported him, but two out of three white voters had been against him.

In 1991, Maybus lost his bid for reelection to Kirk Fordice, a political throwback, an old-style bubba. Fordice, born in 1934, came from a generation dedicated to staunch resistance to social change. An engineer who started his own construction company, Fordice learned politics on the building site and later as head of the Associated General Contractors of America. His formula for Mississippi was traditional: a return to family values, tax breaks for the rich, and leftovers for the poor. Fordice campaigned against welfare abusers and racial quotas. The rest, he reckoned, following the blueprint of the new conservatism, would take care of itself—with little personal touches here and there; most of them embarrassing. He ordered signs placed on highways at the state line saying, "Only Positive Mississippi Spoken Here." A year into his first term, he called the United States "a Christian nation"; when people complained, he apologized, explaining that what he had meant to say was that "the overwhelming majority of Americans say they are Christians." He wanted convicts back in prison-striped clothing, called for a return of chain gangs, and declared Mississippi "the capital of capital punishment."

If people took offense, he reminded them that everything he said or did was all in the cause of turning Mississippi into one of the most attractive business opportunities in the New South. That is what he cared most about. And taking the tobacco companies to court—even if there was money to be had in it for the state's coffers—was not good for the image he was creating for Mississippi.

The tobacco companies showed their gratitude by pouring funds into the governor's 1995 reelection campaign. Rewarding friends around the country was part of the industry's agenda as it sought to fend off antitobacco attacks by the Clinton administration and David Kessler's FDA. In Mississippi, tobacco industry opponents, including the liability lawyer Dick Scruggs, responded by supporting Moore's bid for reelection to a third term, which he won with more than 70 percent of the vote in 1995. When Fordice also won reelection, a feud between the governor and his attorney general over tobacco was inevitable.

Moore, by then still only forty-two, was taking a big gamble; he rated the chances of success at about sixty to forty. If he lost the tobacco suit, it could end his political career. If he won, he would step out onto the national stage with new political possibilities—to be a U.S. senator, or governor. He and his old law school pal, Dick Scruggs, were moving far from the comfortable but limited horizons of their youth in Pascagoula and into a fast new world of high-flying financial deals in New York and backroom lobbying in Washington. Both were ready. Scruggs by this time was a liability lawyer of considerable personal wealth who was eager to spend his "war chest" on "what could be the trial lawyers' finest hour." He needed no encouragement and was not lacking in energy or resources. The two men complimented each other. Scruggs had done his time in the front lines and now was happy to be in the back room plotting strategy. Moore was to be the point man. He liked the limelight; some said he couldn't get enough of it.

Moore was ready for new adventures and when his other law school pal, Mike Lewis, urged him to take on the tobacco companies he needed to know only that Scruggs would come aboard before accepting the challenge. As fresh evidence of the industry's fraudulent enterprise turned up, Moore quickly learned how to translate it into sound bites. "I know that the tobacco companies have perpetrated the biggest fraud ever," he would say, "not only on the American public but probably on the public health in this whole world. . . . So I feel very, very good to have played a small part in exposing the truth about these companies. . . . We really are in Mississippi, this small southern state, kind of bringing them to justice for the first time." Within a year he was spending more than half his time on the lawsuit. Of course, it helped that everywhere he went, the Learjet of Dick Scruggs made the journey less arduous.

Scruggs's support bolstered Moore's self-confidence, already considerable for one so inexperienced and unknown in Washington and New York. As time passed and the Third Wave of tobacco litigation gained momentum, Moore would take on an arrogant air that irritated the state's old guard, especially Governor Fordice, who was being upstaged at every turn. Scruggs and Moore began to dominate the dispatches from the Third Wave. There were profiles in *The Wall Street Journal* and *The American Lawyer,* plus glossy pictures in *Vanity Fair.* Fordice could have sat back and quietly watched Moore take the heat from the industry. If he won, he could grab credit for having the bright attorney general on his team. If Moore lost, Fordice could have accepted credit for trying, without being seen as a loser. Instead, the excitable governor chose to join forces with the tobacco industry and take Moore to court. "What this is all about is money," said the governor, pushing the industry's line. "It's greed on the part of a few trial lawyers. It has nothing to do with the public health, or anything else. . . . It makes me want to throw up."

The first legal salvo came from the governor's office in February 1996, six months after Moore had filed the state's lawsuit for recovery of Medicaid expenses.

Fordice claimed that Moore did not have the authority to bring the suit in the first place. The state's Medicaid Division was part of the governor's office, Fordice maintained, and the attorney general was, in practice, the governor's lawyer. He could not bring a suit concerning any aspect of Medicaid without the governor's permission. This permission had not been sought and would not be given. Citing an obscure state law that allowed the Mississippi Supreme Court to order state officials to take certain actions, Fordice asked the court to order Moore to drop the suit.

As far as anyone could recall, it was the first time the governor of a state had tried to stop his attorney general from bringing a lawsuit that, if won, would clearly benefit the citizens of the state. Philip Morris, Brown & Williamson, and twenty-one other tobacco-related enterprises immediately filed the same request to the Mississippi Supreme Court. Moore commented, "Our governor has made a deal with the devil, and now the devil has joined him."

Fordice's excuse for opposing the suit was that it would send a message that Mississippi was antibusiness. "If this lawsuit is successful, I have little doubt that similar ones will follow against makers of other legally available products," said Fordice. "Who will be next? The proverbial floodgates will certainly open and a progressive, probusiness reputation that we have carefully nurtured will be ruined." Adding to the gloomy forecasts, an official in the governor's office suggested that the litigation would turn Mississippi into a "dumping ground" for other product-liability suits. Poultry and pizza parlors would be next— even red meat and motorcycles.

Mike Moore stood his ground. "When pepperoni kills 425,000 people a year, we'll go after the pepperoni business," he said. And then he added, "The tobacco companies were looking for a new Marlboro Man and they have found him . . . and his name is Daniel Kirkwood Fordice."

THE TOBACCO COMPANIES launched their offensive on the Mississippi lawsuit using all their old tricks. First, they sought summary dismissal of the suit in the chancery court, claiming that it was based on novel, and meritless, legal theories. They failed to convince the judge. What really upset the companies was that Moore had cleverly brought the case in the state's chancery court, meaning that it would be tried by a judge, not a jury. This was a big advantage. The case could be tried quickly because there was less demand on the chancery court's time, and the technical questions of state law on reimbursement of Medicaid funds could be argued more easily in front of a judge than a jury.

So the companies petitioned to move the case to federal court and a jury trial. Their argument, a flimsy one as it turned out, was that Moore had failed to comply with federal Medicaid regulations. Medicaid is paid partly by the state and partly by the federal government, depending on the state's wealth. In Mississippi, the federal share is 80 percent. Federal regulations required, among other things, that before the state could sue third parties for reimbursement of funds it must determine that the monies expected were more than the cost of recovering them. Moore had not made this calculation—mainly because he believed the cost to the state would be small. He had hired Dick Scruggs on a contingency-fee basis and most of the legal work would be done out of Scruggs's office in Pascagoula and around the corner from the Jackson County Chancery Court, where the case was filed. Moore had estimated that the cost of tobacco-related Medicaid services for the poor of Mississippi was about $100 million a year. Scruggs did not have a contract with the attorney general's office stipulating what percentage of any award his fee might be; he was prepared to take his chances with the judge at the end of the case. Moore could hardly be accused of taking the riverboat gamble the companies were implying, and that objection was also thrown out. (In fact, it would turn out to be the winning ticket in legal lotto.)

Tobacco's next challenge—and its central defense in the Medicaid suits—was to argue that the only way the state could pursue recovery of medical expenses was by stepping into the shoes of the smoker and asserting the smokers' rights of recovery. In other words, this was not the state seeking to recoup funds it believed had been wrongfully extracted from its coffers; this was really a personal-injury action by the state on behalf of smokers. As such, the industry would be able to rely on its traditional—and, in the past, always successful—legal defenses of "assumption of risk" and "contributory negligence." These said that the smoker, not the cigarette company, is to blame for the harm caused to him or her by smoking.

Moore, in his turn, argued that the state was not a surrogate or "subrogee" of the smoker. This was not a claim by individual smoking victims; the state was suing in its own right to protect its interests and to recoup funds that it had no choice but to provide under the federal Medicaid system. Mississippi was entitled to be repaid for Medicaid expenses because, as Scruggs put it, the state had conferred a "benefit" on the tobacco industry by paying the medical bills of injured smokers. The "injury," in other words, was to the Mississippi taxpayer, not to the smoker. In legal terms, the industry had been "unjustly enriched."

This would be the legal basis for all the Medicaid cases. In Florida in the summer of 1994, the state legislature had actually passed a law that recognized the financial injury sustained by the taxpayer in tobacco-related illnesses through the Medicaid system. The law, however, had been challenged by the industry. A similar law enacted in Massachusetts allowed the state's attorney general to bring a Medicaid reimbursement lawsuit against the tobacco companies. By the beginning of 1995, at least fifteen states were considering Medicaid reimbursement actions and they were all watching to see how the Mississippi judge would rule on Mike Moore's arguments.

On February 21, 1995, Judge William Myers of the Jackson County Chancery Court officially endorsed the logic of Moore's arguments against the state being regarded as a surrogate of the smoker, leaving the industry without its traditional defense of blaming the smoker. It was a tremendous breakthrough for Moore and Scruggs, and for the other states as well. It meant that Mississippi's case remained in the chancery court. The tobacco companies would continue to challenge the legal theory, but to no avail. On the same day as Judge Myers's opinion, Florida filed its Medicaid case. Others would follow.

The tobacco companies had been bloodied, but they still regarded Moore, Scruggs, and his entourage—Barrett and Motley—as minor irritants in a wider war they fully intended to win. If the state wanted to base its lawsuit on economics and fairness instead of personal injuries, the industry was ready. In fact, the economics of tobacco was one of their favored topics.

FOR DECADES, the $45 billion tobacco industry had promoted itself as an essential and indispensable part of the U.S. economy. It contributed billions of dollars in excise and income taxes and created thousands of jobs inside and outside tobacco production. Its advertising and promotion budget was $6 billion. In the early 1990s, for example, the industry claimed that 2.3 million Americans owed their jobs to tobacco, either directly as farmers, or in cigarette production or related industries. But this was the economic version of their claim that nicotine is not addictive, or that smoking does not cause cancer. The 2.3 million figure was grossly inflated, a concoction of the industry's lobbying arm, the Tobacco Institute, to oppose cigarette-tax increases in Congress.

The number of jobs in tobacco growing, manufacturing, auction warehousing, and wholesaling was around 260,000. There were 432,000 jobs in the retail and supply sectors, making a total of 692,000. To inflate that figure, the industry used a "multiplier" to show the "ripple effects" of tobacco-industry spending on other sectors of the economy. This, they said, added another 1.6 million, giving a total of 2.3 million. But those jobs were not in or related to the tobacco industry; this multiplier is used by economists to estimate economic activity that stimulates additional economic activity, not for estimating the actual number of jobs in a particular sector.

When faced with state or federal measures that could reduce smoking—such as excise-tax increases—the industry argued that the drop in tobacco consumption would result in a drop in employment not just in tobacco states, but nationally as well. They assumed that the resources spent on tobacco and its distribution would vanish if sales declined. Several economists challenged this picture, pointing to the flaw in the industry's argument. For example, a 1996 study done by Dr. Kenneth Warner of the Department of Health Management and Policy at the University of Michigan projected a decline in tobacco consumption and actually found a net increase in the number of jobs in nontobacco regions (which includes Mississippi), with a net loss only in the southeastern tobacco states. The overall national result, Warner found, was a small increase in total jobs.

The tobacco companies were equally inventive in their specific economic arguments against the Mississippi lawsuit. During the 1980s, a handful of economists had challenged the conventional wisdom among public health officials that argued that smoking costs the nation about $100 billion a year: $50 billion in smoking-related hospital charges, doctor fees, drugs, and nursing-home bills, and another $50 billion in lost working hours and income taxes from smokers who get ill and die early. Now leading the challenge to these figures was Kip Viscusi, a Harvard economist, who complained that the public health officials were ignoring the long-term, or "life-time," approach.

If you looked at smokers this way, you would find a set of savings; not costs. There would be savings from excise taxes paid by smokers, plus income taxes paid by doctors, pharmacies, and health-care providers involved in looking after smokers with tobacco-related diseases. Even in a nontobacco producing state, such as Mississippi, these taxes could be considerable.

But the Viscusi argument that drew the most attention was the one that said smokers produced extra savings in geriatric care, pensions, and social security payments by dying early—on average about eight years before nonsmokers. His detached analysis even suggested that the introduction of low-tar cigarettes might make them "perform less well from a societal standpoint, because you don't get the savings from the fatalities." In other words, smokers who smoke filter cigarettes with less tar don't die off early enough to produce meaningful gains.

The tobacco companies quickly adopted Viscusi's work, and his

claim became known among antitobacco forces as the "euthanasia defense." Put together, these "savings," or "offsets" as the economists call
them, had already compensated the states for any extra health costs, the
tobacco companies argued. According to one set of Viscusi's calculations, the total cost to society per pack of cigarettes sold, including
medical care, sick leave, group life insurance, fires, secondhand smoke,
and lost taxes on earnings of those who died early, was $1.37. The total
benefit to society, including excise taxes and savings on nursing homes
and pensions, was $1.95.

Moore had a list of responses. First, he argued, taxes are not debts
that can be offset against damages to property or health caused by
corporations. Second, the sales and income taxes claimed were not paid
by the companies. Third, the distribution of taxes is the sole domain of
the legislature: tobacco companies cannot direct them to health care or
anywhere else they find convenient for their business. As Scruggs put it,
"Taxes are not a damage deposit. They do not allow you to go out and
injure the public good to the extent of your tax payments. The guys
who blew up the federal building in Oklahoma City can't defend that
damage claim by saying, 'Well, we've paid more than that in taxes over
our lifetime.' "

Other economists also challenged Viscusi's analysis, arguing that
the model estimating a smoker's true medical costs is inherently unreliable. For example, they point out that the alternative to an early death
from smoking may be a long life under intense and expensive medical
care common to a tobacco-related illness.

Viscusi's calculations also fail to put a value on life itself, something
a court would have to consider. As one of the plaintiffs' lawyers observed, "I don't know that a court is going to agree with the tobacco
companies and say, 'Wow, you need an offset because you killed people.' " Jeffrey Harris, an MIT economist who is also a physician, argues
that government shouldn't weigh dollars saved from early deaths in
making public policy decisions; it's not the kind of argument that a
civilized society engages in. "Viscusi is not including a key benefit. We
value life."

The industry's argument gave politicians like Moore a chance to
take the moral high ground. "It is utterly repugnant to a civilized
society and must be rejected on the grounds of public policy," declared

Moore. His submission to the court on the matter called the argument "perverse and depraved," and he accused the tobacco companies of being merchants of death. "Seeking a credit for a purported economic benefit from early death is akin to robbing graves of Mississippi smokers who died from tobacco-related illness," he declared. "No court of law or equity should entertain such a defense or counterclaim. It is an offense to human decency, an affront to justice, uncharacteristic of civilized society, and unquestionably contrary to public policy."

The "euthanasia defense" had already been memorably rejected by the economist Thomas Schelling. In a 1986 article entitled "Economics and Cigarettes" in the journal *Preventive Medicine,* he wrote:

> The idea that people who smoke and die fifteen years early are net financial benefactors to the rest of society, by living most of a normal productive life and dying before they can claim their retirement benefits, is momentarily surprising and somewhat paradoxical. But, we must not reverse the conclusion. If we begin by thinking that smokers in the aggregate inflict costs on the rest of us, and that this is the reason we should encourage them to quit or penalize them financially, then discovering that those who die leave behind more than they take from us might seem to suggest that we should happily let them smoke and relieve us of supporting them in their old age. But that would be a perverse and unnatural conclusion.
>
> We do not hope that sixty-year-old fishermen die at sea, that sixty-year-olds neglect seat belts and die in their automobiles, or that sixty-year-old marital difficulties lead to suicide or homicide.

JUDGE MYERS would throw out these tobacco defenses, one by one, but Governor Fordice continued to brand Moore's lawsuit a "selfish attempt to gain publicity and enrich a few people"—by which he meant Dick Scruggs, Don Barrett, Ron Motley, Mike Lewis, and the other Southern attorneys who had signed up to help Moore. The tobacco companies joined in the mud slinging, accusing Moore, as Fordice had done, of politicking for governor.

In the spring of 1996, Judge Myers ruled that the attorney general is a constitutional officer with common-law powers to control and manage litigation on behalf of the state, and that included litigation against the tobacco companies to recover Medicaid expenses. "The Court is aware of no constitutional provision, statute or decision of the Mississippi Supreme Court, which gives the Governor of this State or the Division of Medicaid the power to bring or maintain an action on matters of statewide interest. Such authority is reserved to the Attorney General."

In most states, including Mississippi, the attorney general is elected by the people and entrusted by them with the common-law power—both legal and criminal—to represent them in all litigation that affects the public interest. Mike Moore believed that he did not have to ask the governor's permission to litigate the suit. Moreover, it was overwhelmingly clear to him that the citizens of Mississippi had a direct interest in whether their tax dollars were being used to pay for harm caused by the tobacco industry, or for roads or schools or some other worthwhile project. Following Judge Myers's ruling that Moore did have the authority to bring the lawsuit, Fordice and the tobacco companies appealed to the Mississippi Supreme Court.

Local Mississippi lawyers hired by the industry began to advise the companies that they had better start taking the case more seriously, but most of the national lawyers remained confident the case would be dismissed. Then, on March 13, 1997, the Mississippi Supreme Court rejected Fordice's petition. The court did not rule on the merits of whether Moore had the authority, but, in a 5 to 1 decision, said that the public interest would be better served by allowing the case to proceed in the chancery court. The issue of who had the authority and the right to file a Medicaid recovery action could still be decided by the court on appeal, if the industry wanted to pursue the matter. The mood of the tobacco lawyers changed overnight, recalled Charles Mikhail, one of Scruggs's leading lawyers who had argued many of the motions in front of Judge Myers. "It was almost like someone had slapped them in the face and told them to wake up and take the case seriously," said Mikhail. The Mississippi trial was due to start on July 7.

The tobacco companies complained, of course. R. J. Reynolds

charged that Moore had "carefully crafted a suit to avoid more than two hundred years of legal standards and to avoid allowing jurors in his state an opportunity to hear and decide the case." Philip Morris said only that it looked forward to raising the merits of the case again "at the appropriate time." But even as they spoke, the tobacco companies were about to enter secret negotiations that would stop the trial two weeks before it was set to begin.

1 2

THE IDES OF MARCH

CAESAR: The Ides of March are come.
SOOTHSAYER: Ay, Caesar, but not gone.

—*Shakespeare,* Julius Caesar

I T BEGAN with a drink in a Manhattan bar and ended, three months later, with the first breach in the tobacco industry's united front. At the end of November 1995, Don Barrett had left his rural redoubt in Lexington, Mississippi, to fight a liability case in New York about defective plastic-plumbing systems. Most of America's mobile homes had been fitted with plastic pipes that were corroded by chlorine. "It was the world's only biodegradable plumbing system," said Barrett. The case was settled for over a billion dollars and Barrett was on the winning team. He was celebrating by having a cocktail with a New York lawyer named Marc Kasowitz, who had represented the plastic pipe company.

"Here was a streetwise, fast-talking New York Jewish lawyer having a drink with a slow-talking, slow-thinking Mississippian," was how Barrett would begin the story. "He asked me what I was going to do next and I said that if and when I ever got paid for the plumbing case, I would use the money to feed my cigarette habit. And he just looked blank.

"I told him about the Nathan Horton case and the Wilks case in Greenville, and how I was involved with Gauthier's Castano group in New Orleans and the Mississippi Medicaid case. And he asked what was going to happen in those cases. I said the litigation is going to go on for a long time and eventually we're going to win.

"And he asked, 'Is there no way out?' And I said no, because the tobacco company executives are too stupid to understand that we are not trying to put them out of business. If they would be socially responsible and pay some measure of damages and quit marketing to children then we could make a deal. And I thought that was the end of the conversation. I went home to Lexington."

Barrett did not know that Kasowitz was the personal lawyer of Bennett LeBow, the financier who had a controlling interest in Liggett, the company that makes Chesterfield and L&M brands. As the smallest player, with just over 2 percent of the U.S. market, Liggett was barely staying alive. LeBow had sought a merger of his Brooke Group, which includes Liggett, with the tobacco unit of RJR Nabisco. The plan was to spin off RJR's food business as a separate company, but LeBow's offer had been rebuffed. Now, LeBow was waging a hostile proxy battle to take over the whole of the RJR Nabisco Holdings Corporation. His plan was to split off the food division to protect Nabisco's cookie profits from lawsuits and merge RJR tobacco with Liggett.

Kasowitz was intrigued by Barrett's mention of a possible deal. There was a clear opportunity for LeBow. If Liggett were to settle and in the deal the plaintiffs' lawyers agreed not to fight the spin-off of the food division, then LeBow would make his bid considerably more attractive. Moreover, if such a settlement also gave the same terms to any tobacco company that merged with Liggett, RJR's tobacco unit could be in an advantageous position compared with its big rival, Philip Morris.

Kasowitz thought the whole idea might appeal to LeBow, a one-time computer scientist who had a liking for complex, flashy financial deals. LeBow was a buccaneer, in much the same vein as the liability lawyers; he was both admired and despised for his adventurism and cunning, just as the lawyers were. But LeBow was an unlikely hero of the antitobacco forces. The fifty-seven-year-old scuba-diving leverage artist had been variously described as a "master finagler," a "weasely raider," and the "Machiavelli of the foxy deal." His ally in the raid on RJR was Carl Icahn. As *The New York Times* had put it, "LeBow is not a favorite of public shareholders, who have accused him of emptying companies he controls of their cash and assets. Brooke has poured millions of dollars into the LeBow family coffers through its purchase of assets controlled by LeBow."

As it turned out, LeBow did like the idea of trying to settle the lawsuits and authorized Kasowitz to go back to Barrett and start negotiations. But they had to be super-secret, LeBow insisted. If the other tobacco companies found out, they would try and scupper the deal. After all, this was breaking the gentlemen's agreement of no surrender that had been in place for half a century of litigation. He was most concerned about Philip Morris, whose attitude to the Castano class action and the state suits had been one of unrelenting hostility. Kasowitz said that LeBow told him, "I can't risk my company on your relationship with some redneck from Mississippi."

When Kasowitz called, Barrett was taken aback. He had not thought again about the conversation in the bar and was astonished to hear about the LeBow-Liggett connection. But he agreed to discuss the matter, agreeing also to total secrecy.

From Barrett's point of view, a Liggett deal looked good, too. It might even be key to the Castano suit's survival. The Fifth Circuit Court of Appeals was considering an appeal from the tobacco companies on the class action's certification by the District Court in New Orleans. The prognosis was grim. The Fifth Circuit was loaded with conservative judges who were expected to favor the tobacco industry's contention that Castano was a novel and invalid claim. Signing a deal with Liggett would show the court that Castano had clout. Before Barrett could make a move, however, he was supposed to clear it with Wendell Gauthier, the chairman of the Castano executive committee. But without telling Gauthier anything about Kasowitz, or LeBow, Barrett asked if there were any rules about committee members exploring settlements. Gauthier recalls, "I told him there were no rules. No one had the authority to bind the committee to a settlement, but anyone could talk. Don didn't show his cards."

Barrett was risking a lot. After his Horton and Wilks adventures and before the money from the New York plumbing cases arrived—if it ever did—he was underfunded, to put it mildly. He was also wary of dealing with Kasowitz on his own. He wanted another lawyer at his side, preferably someone who could also help with expenses. Bob Lieff and Richard Heimann from the San Francisco firm of Lieff, Cabraser, which was part of the Castano group, agreed to help.

Barrett also brought in Dr. David Burns, a professor of medicine on the San Diego campus of the University of California. Burns had testified on behalf of Nathan Horton and helped Barrett on the Wilks case. Now, Barrett asked him to draw up a set of public-health demands for LeBow. Burns was the author of the annual government reports for the Centers for Disease Control on the number of smoking-related deaths and had coauthored the 1975 Surgeon General's report on smoking and health. It was familiar ground to him. When the call from Barrett came, according to Burns, "Don began by saying he couldn't tell me anything about it, but he was involved in something that could lead to an extraordinary precedent for the tobacco companies. And then, of course, he told me what it was."

The two sides negotiated for two months in total secrecy. To avoid being discovered, the negotiating teams met in different places—Houston, New York, Memphis, and Miami, the city where LeBow spends most of his time. Barrett was so conscious of what the deal might accomplish that initially he didn't even tell his Mississippi buddies, Scruggs and Moore.

Three months later, LeBow would become the first tobacco company CEO to settle a lawsuit, admit his company was marketing to children, and take steps to curb youth sales of cigarettes. The truism of tobacco litigation in the First and Second Waves—that the companies had never paid a penny in damages—was now history. It was the first time a tobacco company had taken any responsibility for the tobacco-related diseases that Dr. Burns and his colleagues now estimated to be causing 440,000 premature deaths a year.

But LeBow did not stop there. Within a year, he had widened the scope of his settlement by finally putting an end to the carefully crafted scientific falsehood by which the tobacco industry had lived for so long. He would become the first CEO of a cigarette company to declare that nicotine was addictive and that smoking actually causes cancer. He would refer to himself as just another "whistle-blower," which, in effect, he was, except that he was the loudest of them all.

His break with the brethren at Philip Morris and R. J. Reynolds was viewed as nothing less than treachery. They accused him of engaging in a "reckless ploy" to take over RJR. Wall Street went into shock—but only for a moment. Investors soon realized that LeBow might actually have hit upon a great strategy in settling the industry's liability. They started bidding up the idea that the rest of the tobacco industry should also seek a permanent truce.

Keeping the plaintiffs' bar at bay had become a major investment, even for tobacco companies that turned an easy profit. The industry as a whole was now spending $600 million a year defending lawsuits. Five hundred and fifty law firms and thousands of high-priced attorneys were involved. More than half of the nation's largest law firms were working in some capacity for the industry. In a February federal securities filing, Philip Morris had listed ten pages of lawsuits. In Washington, the Justice Department was weighing perjury charges against the seven CEOs who had testified in April 1994 that nicotine was not addictive. Grand juries were probing whether the Council for Tobacco Research had been involved in criminal fraud. There were federal investigations into possible antitrust violations and cigarette smuggling. Each time a settlement was mentioned, it was not surprising that stocks surged.

The Liggett deal was essentially a self-interest gamble by LeBow, by the Castano group, and also by the attorneys general of the four states that would initially sign up.

The deal gave a much-needed legitimacy to the lawsuits—both the Castano case and the state Medicaid cases. They were not all novel and meritless claims, as the tobacco companies insisted, but they were untested departures in tobacco litigation. The deal demonstrated that one company, at least, took them seriously. The deal also made other attorneys general sit up and wonder if they, too, shouldn't be suing the industry. A year later the number involved in tobacco litigation had shot up to twenty-two. Finally, LeBow's gamble forced the companies themselves to publicly address the issue of settlement. The end game had begun.

BY LATE JANUARY 1996, Barrett and Kasowitz had a draft of the settlement. The money offered by Liggett—only a few million dollars a year—was bound to be small because Liggett was barely surviving as a cigarette company. It had a 2.3 percent share of the U.S. market and pretax profits of about $11 million. But the money was not the lure. Barrett and Heimann were insisting that there had to be some public-health concessions, especially on the issue of advertising aimed at children. Kasowitz was initially resistant. Dr. Burns had said they had to be the same concessions, or close to those in the FDA's proposed rule: no billboards within 1,000 feet of schools, no vending machines accessible to children, no promotional material such as T-shirts, sporting bags, and lighters, no shop-counter advertising, and all cigarette advertisements in black and white.

At first, LeBow took the position—the standard tobacco industry defense—that the company did not target children in its advertising. He also complained bitterly about the provision banning so-called point-of-sale advertising, or the rack of cigarette packs next to the cash register. If Liggett's Chesterfields were removed, Philip Morris would only grab the spot for Marlboro, LeBow said. He could not agree to such a condition. His company was in bad enough shape as it was without giving Philip Morris a further advantage.

In February, Barrett was ready to enlarge the team. But who should be next? Barrett was negotiating without any authority from the two clients he represented: the state of Mississippi and the Castano group. "It was like a little dog chasing a Porsche. You catch the son of a bitch. Now what are you going to do?" He brought in Scruggs, and then Moore. Moore would represent the other three state attorneys general who had filed suits. The unwieldy Castano group would only be brought in at the last moment to avoid leaks; once sixty law firms knew of the negotiations, it would be impossible to keep them secret.

Barrett's extended team continued to shuttle around the country meeting with Kasowitz and his law partner, Dan Benson. At one stop, in Houston, they panicked when they thought their plot had been discovered. Arriving in a limousine at the Four Seasons hotel, Scruggs and Barrett saw two well-known tobacco lawyers walking toward them, Robert McDermott of Jones, Day, who worked for R. J. Reynolds, and Philip Morris attorney James Scarboro of the Washington firm of Arnold & Porter. "Hell, do you know who they are?" Scruggs said as they passed. Barrett didn't know and when Scruggs told him, he feared the whole operation might be blown. But the tobacco lawyers were there on other business. They had no inkling of the talks with LeBow.

The negotiations resumed on the children's issue. As Burns explained how children get hooked at an early age and, in effect, replace those smokers who die off, LeBow started to shift his position. Barrett became convinced that he really was concerned about teenage smoking. "The refreshing thing about him, and the reason you can deal with him," said Barrett later, "is because he will tell you that he has selfish motives, that he wants to make a lot of money, but he also wants to do the right thing. He told us, 'Selling cigarettes is legal and I'll sell the hell out of them as long as they'll let me.' But I think he began to look at himself as a person who was doing something for America. I started to think he would be perfectly satisfied to see a smoke-free country in thirty years, providing he gets to make money in the meantime." Burns was impressed, too. "He's a businessman . . . but he was honest, direct, and concerned."

By the beginning of March, LeBow had agreed to many of the FDA proposals, and draft settlement papers were ready in Kasowitz's New York office. The negotiators were ready to bring in the Castano group, then still the most visible lawsuit against the industry.

"Scruggs, Kasowitz, and I were in a hotel in Miami and we invited Ron Motley to come over for a drink," said Barrett. "He walked in and saw us at the bar with LeBow and he was floored. He had known nothing about the negotiations. We then flew to New Orleans and told Russ Herman. (Gauthier was out of town.) But we're not giggling. These are sensitive people and they're prominent lawyers. We had to fall all over ourselves for not including them earlier. First, we had to tell why this had been secret, and then we had to tell them the secret. Everyone realized what a breakthrough it was." But under LeBow's rules, they couldn't talk about it until everyone involved—the four other states and the sixty members of the Castano group—had signed up.

THE FINAL HOURS of the three-month-long negotiations demonstrated what an unlikely conspiracy it had become. There was Barrett from Mississippi's hill country, Scruggs from the Gulf Coast, Mike Moore from the attorney general's office in Jackson, the theatrical Ron Motley and his numbers wizard Joe Rice from Charleston, Wendell Gauthier and his Louisiana legal team from New Orleans, and Bennett LeBow, the international financier from Miami, all packed into the conference room at Kasowitz, Benson, Torres & Friedman at 1301 Avenue of the Americas in Manhattan. Only a few blocks away in the Park Avenue headquarters of Philip Morris, with all its lawyers and its resources, there was no early warning of the bombshell that was about to burst.

For LeBow, security was now an even greater problem. Gauthier insisted that before the Castano group could sign off on any deal the entire membership of sixty law firms had to be notified. LeBow gave the Castano group the minimum time to okay the deal. He wanted a clear month between the announcement and the April 18 RJR Nabisco shareholders meeting that would decide his fate.

The Castano group flew to New York on Thursday, March 7. In addition to the Herman brothers and the Castano document keeper Suzy Foulds, Gauthier included another Louisiana lawyer, Calvin Fayard from Baton Rouge. Fayard was a veteran of state class-action suits. On the flight, they sat in the back of the plane and reviewed the draft of the settlement Kasowitz had sent by fax from New York. Several paragraphs bothered them. Gauthier thought the money Liggett proposed to pay Castano—5 percent of its pretax income, or about $50 million, over the next twenty-five years—was pitiful. He also objected to a "release clause" that gave Liggett immunity from all future claims, not only on addiction but also on lung cancer, emphysema, and heart disease. "They want total absolution," complained Gauthier.

Gauthier also wanted more concessions on promotions aimed at children, he would say later. He wanted specific agreements covering advertisements near schools, and promotions in shops, and he wanted an agreement not to use cartoon characters like Joe Camel, the R. J. Reynolds creation. To Gauthier, these items were all "deal breakers." If they weren't changed, he was not going to recommend the settlement to the Castano group.

At nine o'clock on the morning of March 8, about thirty of the players gathered at Kasowitz's law offices. LeBow had been in Russia and was flying in on the Concorde from London, so the morning was spent on minor issues—"dancing and wordsmithing," Fayard called it.

With LeBow's arrival progress was rapid. Gauthier complained about the release clause. It had to be changed, or there was no deal. LeBow backed down and they agreed that the immunity would cover claims for addiction only. Gauthier pushed for more money, even though he knew Liggett was short of funds. "We wanted to show the Fifth Circuit judges that we were in a good position to manage this claim—up to and including the point of reaching a settlement. The timing was as important for us as it was for LeBow."

It was Burns who persuaded Gauthier not to ask for more. He told Gauthier that he'd been in the tobacco wars for twenty-seven years and this was a gigantic step forward for the public health community. "Burns told me to forget the money, we were only talking two percent of the market," said Gauthier. "He also said there's probably not a single smoker out there who has only smoked Chesterfields so I was not giving anything up for our Castano clients by settling with Liggett. I agreed."

Next, Gauthier pushed for the FDA's "point of sale" provision, but LeBow stood his ground. The group broke up. In Barrett's view, Gauthier had almost "queered the deal."

But the talks reconvened, with LeBow and Gauthier chatting during coffee breaks and both sides leaving the room for consultations in the corridors. The "point of sale" issue was overcome with a "progressive settlement": the companies who settle first have to agree to any upgrading of the rules in later settlements. LeBow agreed.

The deal breakers had been eliminated. On Saturday, Gauthier flew back to New Orleans and arranged a series of conference calls to Castano members, preparing them for a meeting where he would present the final draft. To the few who complained that there was virtually no money in the deal, Gauthier repeated Dr. Burns's argument. A meeting of the full Castano group in New Orleans was scheduled for Tuesday, March 12, at 3 P.M. By then, the full text was to be ready. Russ Herman flew back to New York to be the Castano representative in the completion of the final document.

LeBow was now sure the deal would go ahead. On Monday night in New York, Kasowitz briefed *The Wall Street Journal,* knowing they could not publish the story until Wednesday. LeBow had taken the final step—without waiting for the approval of the Castano lawyers and thus putting pressure on Gauthier.

On Tuesday the rumors began. Reporters calling Castano headquarters in New Orleans were told no one was available to comment. In Washington, Scruggs and Moore were in a hotel rounding up support from the attorneys general of the four other litigating states—Florida, Massachusetts, West Virginia, and Louisiana—which had filed at the eleventh hour. Minnesota refused to enter the deal.

The talks at Kasowitz's law offices in New York dragged on; Russ Herman, Richard Heimann, and Don Barrett did not have time to fly to New Orleans in time on a commercial flight to brief the Castano group on the final draft, so LeBow lent them his private plane. They arrived at the Castano group's traditional meeting place—on the twenty-third floor of the Windsor Court hotel—with little more than an hour remaining before *The Wall Street Journal*'s 4:00 P.M. deadline. Gauthier phoned Kasowitz and told him it was impossible. "We have sixty lawyers here and they have to take our word for something. We can't do it."

But Russ Herman persuaded Gauthier to go ahead and try. Richard Heimann, who had been in the negotiations with Barrett from the beginning, reviewed the details of the settlement for the group. Essentially, Liggett had agreed to pay up to 5 percent of its pretax income, to a maximum of $50 million a year, for twenty-five years. The money would go toward smoking-cessation programs. Liggett had agreed to most of the FDA rules, including a ban on promotional T-shirts and other clothing, elimination of billboards within 1,000 feet of schools, black-and-white only ads in magazines, an end to free distribution of cigarettes at rock concerts and other youth events, plus a ban on all cartoon characters. Don Barrett then gave the history of the negotiations and why it had been necessary to keep them secret. Herman made an impassioned speech about the significance of the deal—the first concession with the industry curbing the sale of cigarettes to minors. Then he told the group why it was important to make a decision by 4:00 P.M.

Many said it was impossible, there was not even enough time to read through the document. But Gauthier reminded them that there would have to be a "fairness hearing" in which a judge would have to affirm the deal was fair to the Castano class-action members. If any Castano lawyer found anything they didn't like between now and the hearing, they could bring it to the attention of the court. At five minutes before four o'clock, Herman asked for a vote—with Kasowitz listening in on the phone line from New York. A roar of "ayes" filled the room.

Next day, March 13, the headline in *The Wall Street Journal* read, "Breaking Away: Liggett Group Offers First-Ever Settlement of Cigarette Lawsuits," with the subhead, "States' Health-Cost Claims and Smoker Class Action Are Included in the Deal—LeBow Gambit in RJR Fight." It was a "stunning break with the rest of the $45 billion tobacco industry," said the *Journal,* and was "likely to infuriate other cigarette makers, which have built their litigation and regulatory strategy on a united front against all attacks." This was an understatement. RJR called the deal "an irresponsible and reckless ploy in the proxy contest," and the tobacco companies vowed to fight on. Philip Morris "remained confident in the strength of our litigation position." Brown & Williamson said "a settlement is unlikely to ever become effective."

In fact, LeBow had a sweetheart deal: a small amount of money in return for settling his cases, partial immunity, and short-term glory. Castano agreed not to include the food section of RJR Nabisco in its lawsuit if LeBow were successful in his takeover bid. In that event, LeBow agreed that RJR tobacco would enter into a similar deal with Castano and RJR would cooperate with Castano litigation against the remaining tobacco companies. In other words, Castano would have access to Liggett and RJR documents to bolster their case. But the Brooke Group and Liggett also had the right to end the deal if the Castano class action was not upheld by the Fifth Circuit—and everyone, even the most optimistic Castano lawyer, thought the Fifth Circuit would reject the suit.

Each side pretended there was still a chance, however. If LeBow was successful with his RJR bid, Gauthier had thrown two personal touches into the settlement. RJR would pay the Castano group $25 million within sixty days of the approval of the settlement, the money going to establish an organization to provide notice of the deal to class-action members. They would also set up a Peter Castano Anti-Tobacco Research Committee, with $5 million in the first year and $10 million each in the second through the fifteenth years. The committee would be headed by Dr. Burns.

The deal was the high point of the Castano case. The day of the deal, Gauthier was besieged with phone calls from industry defense attorneys, and he was in a playful mood. "They were demanding copies of the agreement and I told them they had to be kidding," said Gauthier. "I said, 'What right do you have to have a copy. I can't get a document from you that you're supposed to produce when I want it.' They said I'd never get away with that kind of attitude. And I said, 'Y'all have for forty years.'"

The first to call was Scott Delacroix from the New Orleans firm of Adams and Reese. Gauthier knew him well. "Scott was real nice. He said, 'Man, you pulled one off, nobody suspected this. You blindsided us. Everybody is reeling over here. We don't know what to make of it. I know you can't tell me everything now, but after the litigation is over can we sit down and have a drink?'

"I said, 'Scott, that will never happen.' And he said, 'Why not?'

"And I said, 'Well, because you keep saying the litigation will never end.'"

In the rush to meet *The Wall Street Journal*'s copy deadline, the attorneys general had not, in fact, closed the deal. One reason was an unintentional mistake by Kasowitz's law firm. In their haste to get everyone the latest copies of the settlement, one page of an earlier draft had been mistakenly inserted into the copies faxed to the attorneys general. It was an earlier version of the money deal—considerably less than they were now being offered. "They went ballistic and thought they had been sandbagged," said Gauthier. "Their number crunchers were looking at that page and saying this deal is crazy, it isn't worth anything. Finally, Don Barrett realized the mistake. It was an honest mistake but it kept the states out of the deal on the first day."

Even during the negotiations, the states had almost pulled out because Liggett would not embrace the full FDA rules for limiting youth access. In the end, five states signed the deal, Mississippi, Florida, Louisiana, Massachusetts, and West Virginia. The only holdout was Minnesota. Mike Ciresi and Hubert Humphrey had never been a part of it. They were going to take the industry to court. Minnesota's partner, Blue Cross and Blue Shield, said the deal gave Liggett too many "outs" and provided "an unrealistic fraction of Liggett's potential liability." Scruggs would say later, "I think they think we're a bunch of yahoos down here." With a touch of bitterness from memories of the Bhopal affair, Gauthier said, "Minnesota stayed out and that's because of one person, Mike Ciresi, an excellent attorney. Mike is very thorough and very prodding and very detailed. He feels he can do better at some point."

The terms for the states were no better than for Castano. Liggett agreed to pay the states 2 to 7 percent of pretax income for the next twenty-five years. The total, including Castano, would cost Liggett less than $2 million a year. The company would also establish a $25 million fund for other states that had not yet filed lawsuits, plus a small $3 million fund for research on children's smoking issues. Mike Moore said the settlement was about children. "Thanks to this agreement, we will soon be able to bid a not-so-fond farewell to Joe Camel." But it was only a wish in those days.

WALL STREET GAVE a nod of approval to LeBow's strategy. His Brooke Group stock closed up $1.50 at $9.80. Of his success, LeBow issued the following statement: "The tobacco industry has lived for too long with the possibility of financial catastrophe from product-liability lawsuits that could destroy the industry. This settlement is a fresh and prudent approach to this problem. . . . Liggett's assets will no longer be held hostage by the tobacco litigation, and we will be free to run our business without this distraction."

The Castano group said it was "filled with pride and hope" over the settlement. "Exactly two years ago, attorneys from around the country launched and organized a crusade against the multibillion dollar tobacco industry. This [settlement] has now destroyed the tobacco industry's invincibility [but] the battle is far from over. The sixty crusading law firms which are dedicated to forcing the industry to live up to its pledge, that 'people's health is a basic responsibility,' will go forward with the lawsuit [against the other tobacco companies] that specifically addresses nicotine dependence and what that does to people's lives."

Others thought it would push the entire industry to settle with the plaintiffs. Professor Daynard, who in one of his many forecasts of when the tobacco industry would begin to pay out money for its past sins, had said the spring of 1996, now declared that since tobacco litigation had moved into "the settlement phase . . . all that remains to be worked out is exactly how and when and to what extent the industry will be found liable and what kind of deal the plaintiffs can get for themselves."

The shockwaves in the industry would rumble on, but the personal triumph of LeBow and the collective victory for the Castano group were short-lived. A month later, on April 17, LeBow lost his proxy battle for RJR Nabisco. (LeBow had actually conceded defeat on the eve of the vote.) And on May 23, the Fifth Circuit Court of Appeals would decertify the Castano class action, effectively canceling the settlement. LeBow had inserted a clause nullifying the deal if Castano lost the appeal. The bold venture had not produced the immediate gains the two parties had sought. And there was talk of industry retaliation against Liggett. "The industry's likely response might be to cut Liggett off at the knees," Gary Black, of the investment analysts Sanford Bernstein, had said on the day the deal was announced. But Liggett had its own problems. The agreement with the five states was still in effect, but each month another state would file a Medicaid suit, and none of them had joined the settlement. Within a few months, the company's exposure to lawsuits was potentially worse than it had been before the deal. Watching the battleground from his New York office, Kasowitz called Barrett and together they concocted another plan that would make the big tobacco companies even angrier.

SHORTLY AFTER the Castano decertification, Barrett received a call from Kasowitz. "He was fussin' at me," said Barrett. "He wanted to know why the new states that were filing Medicaid suits were not joining the settlement, and why I was not persuading them to do so, as I had said I would." Barrett had tried. He had been to Washington state and suggested they join, but they had not done so. "And I don't blame them," Barrett told Kasowitz, "because the antitobacco forces haven't got the kick out of the settlement that they need. You're not cooperating."

One of the provisions—Section 16.12—in the thirty-six-page settlement with the attorneys general required Liggett to disclose to an appropriate judicial body "any fraudulent or illegal conduct" by the tobacco companies that results in the unlawful suppression of evidence, or otherwise is "designed to frustrate or defeat" plaintiffs.

This pledge had special meaning for one plaintiff who was not connected to either the Castano group or the state suits. Janet Sackman had been a glamor model for Liggett's Chesterfield cigarettes in the 1950s, one of a line of celebrities that included Ronald Reagan, Peggy Lee, and Joan Crawford. When Sackman started appearing in the Chesterfield ads in magazines and on billboards, she was seventeen and didn't smoke. A tobacco company executive suggested she would be more authentic as a promoter if she started to smoke, so she did. Soon, she was smoking two packs a day and, in 1983, she was diagnosed with throat cancer, which eventually spread to her lungs. She had her voice box removed and learned to talk again by forcing air through her esophagus. At sixty-two, she decided to devote what was left of her life to helping others with her condition and to warning children not to be taken in by glamorous cigarette ads like the ones she had appeared in and which are still found today in magazines and on billboards.

In 1993, she filed a lawsuit against Liggett, charging the company had sold a defective and addictive product, failed to warn her of the health consequences, fraudulently and deliberately denied that smoking was a hazard, and conspired with other tobacco companies to conceal evidence of the health threat posed by smoking. An articulate and intelligent woman, she appeared in antismoking ads in the Massachusetts campaign to stop teenage smoking.

Her case moved slowly, with Liggett putting up all the usual roadblocks, including trying to prevent her access in the discovery process to documents from the Council for Tobacco Research about "special projects." Sackman's attorneys had asked for 123 documents relating to Liggett's participation in the CTR "Special Projects" program in the hope of showing that the company had used the documents to mount a public relations campaign designed to discredit the links they knew existed between smoking and disease. The thrust was to support Sackman's claims of fraud and conspiracy.

Liggett claimed, as other tobacco companies had done before them, that the documents were privileged under the attorney-client rule. Sackman counterclaimed that the documents fell within the crime-fraud exception to the rule. The court decided to hold a review of the documents in question and ruled, the same week of the Liggett deal, that they should be handed over. They were not privileged. Liggett and other tobacco company defendants appealed the ruling, delaying any resolution for another year.

The possibility of a raft of confidential industry documents being forced into the open spelled problems for the other tobacco companies, and they suffered stock losses. Tom Sobol, one of the attorneys representing Massachusetts, forecast that shareholders would now "seriously reassess whether it's in their short- or long-term interest to be fighting all these issues tooth and nail." One RJR shareholder asked, "Is Bennett LeBow on the same planet?"

Liggett, however, showed no signs of speeding the release of the disputed documents in the Sackman case. Neither was it offering any documents to help the attorneys general, despite the inclusion of Section 16.12. Barrett told Kasowitz, "You're not cooperating. You really didn't give up much." Kasowitz replied, "Bullshit, we can't cooperate because you're not giving us total peace. We cooperate and we cut our own throats in other cases." He meant the new state suits and others that might be filed from class actions other than Castano.

Again, Barrett went out on a limb. "Suppose I could put together a group that would give you total peace—all the AGs and a separate class-action settlement to cover everything," he asked. Kasowitz said it couldn't be done.

"We'll do it. But you're going to have to pay more money than you paid before, and the most important thing is that you're going to have to turn state's evidence." Barrett meant Liggett would have to hand over all the documents for which they had fraudulently claimed privilege. Kasowitz wanted time to think about it. Three weeks later he agreed.

Barrett went to see Mike Moore and outlined the plan. Mississippi already had its settlement with Liggett and Moore didn't think Barrett could put the new deal together. In any case he was already starting down another road with Dick Scruggs making overtures to R. J. Reynolds about a national settlement. So Barrett went to Grant Woods, the Republican attorney general of Arizona, who had just filed his state's Medicaid suit in which Barrett was co-counsel. Woods jumped at the idea. It would give him a high profile in the Third Wave even though he had not been among the first to file. He brought in Steve Berman from Washington state. Once Woods had agreed, Moore changed his mind and joined in. Then came Ron Motley and his settlement strategist, Joe Rice. Scruggs was always reluctant, in the beginning. He was playing the bigger game with R. J. Reynolds and, as RJR and Philip Morris regarded LeBow as a traitor, he didn't want to be seen playing both sides.

As the talks progressed into 1997, Woods and Berman kept up the pressure about releasing the documents. In January, *The Wall Street Journal* heard of the talks and announced that Liggett was proposing to turn over its files of the industry's little-known joint defense group known as the Committee of Counsel. Philip Morris protested. "If Liggett's notes reflect the legal discussions at a joint meeting, Liggett has no right to turn those over without the consent of everyone. If they do that we would take appropriate action." But LeBow went ahead anyway.

On March 20, 1997, a year and a week after the first Liggett settlement, LeBow delivered his second bombshell, agreeing to turn state's evidence. LeBow signed a new, broader settlement with the twenty-two states. In exchange for total immunity from the state Medicaid claims and from all current and future class actions and individual lawsuits, LeBow became the first tobacco chief to declare that nicotine is addictive and smoking causes cancer. He also agreed to turn over thousands of pages of documents the company had hitherto called privileged, including notes taken by Liggett lawyers at joint legal defense meetings with the other company lawyers in the so-called Committee of Counsel.

Announcing the deal in a Washington, D.C., hotel, Grant Woods said he believed this was "the beginning of the end for this conspiracy of lies and deception that has been perpetrated on the American public by the tobacco companies." Standing beside him, Mike Moore, who had called the original Liggett deal the first "crack in the wall," said this had "knocked that wall down." Woods said the documents to be released by Liggett were "extremely damaging," although he admitted that he had not actually seen any of them yet, and their privileged status still had to be cleared by the courts because of the challenge from the other companies. LeBow had promised full cooperation.

LeBow's tobacco colleagues were furious, accusing him of absurd double standards. Here was a man, they said, who three years ago in a deposition in the Florida secondhand smoke class-action suit by flight attendants had said nicotine was not addictive and he didn't know whether smoking caused lung cancer. Attempting to explain his sudden conversion, LeBow said, "I didn't really focus on it until about a year ago." Asked if he had changed his mind simply because it was good for business, LeBow said, "Let's say it was both. It was the right thing to do, and we made a settlement with the attorneys general which the company had to do."

This time, the settlement had been thoroughly covered in the media and the companies were ready. Hours before the formal announcement of the deal, the four biggest companies, Philip Morris, R. J. Reynolds, Brown & Williamson, and Lorillard, obtained a restraining order from a North Carolina state court judge barring Liggett from turning over the documents. The companies claimed that all proceedings of the Committee of Counsel were exempt from disclosure under what is known as "joint defense privilege," an extension of the lawyer-client privilege protecting communications that are part of an ongoing effort to set up a common defense strategy.

The other companies were confident that these documents would never be released, but the plaintiffs would pepper the courts with requests to unseal them. Judges in Illinois, Texas, Mississippi, and Minnesota subsequently ordered that at least some of the documents be turned over under seal for review, but only a handful would be released and they would not take the evidence of deceit much further. The documents on which the other companies claimed privilege would remain under court seal, at least for a while.

Wall Street analysts saw LeBow's move as the desperate maneuverings of the owner of a tobacco company that was about to go under. They said the company would probably have to file for bankruptcy in 1998, unless LeBow could find a buyer. LeBow, it seemed to them, would say anything to rid his company of litigation liability and make it a more attractive proposition.

The other companies remained defiant, continuing to say the states' Medicaid cases were meritless and would be defeated. The wall had not come down. But there was a chink in it. Philip Morris acknowledged, "As we have said in the past, we will explore and discuss all reasonable measures that may be in the best interests of our shareholders, including a comprehensive legislative solution to smoking and health claims." In fact, within a month of the signing of the second deal, the chief executives of both Philip Morris and R. J. Reynolds would sit down at the negotiating table with the antitobacco forces. LeBow may not have managed to sell his tiny, ailing company, but his deal helped push the bigger companies into a settlement of their own.

13

THE SORCERER'S APPRENTICE

They can stop us this year. They can stop us next year, but
they can't stop us forever because we've now got the same
perpetual existence that they have. There will always be a
body of lawyers committed to this task.

—Elizabeth Cabraser, Castano lead counsel

WHEN HATSY HEEP answered the lonely hearts ad from "professional engineer," she did it on a bet. Then she fell in love.
Two years later, at the beginning of 1996, Heep, a forty-
eight-year-old interior designer, was planning to marry Ron Tamol, the
sixty-two-year-old retired research engineer for Philip Morris who'd
placed the ad. Tamol moved into Heep's house in Richmond, Virginia,
and brought with him thousands of Philip Morris research documents
that he had collected during his thirty years with the company. Heep
was not entirely happy about the documents, but she indulged Tamol's
obsession with his past and allowed him to store them in her basement.
As it turned out, it was a bad mistake for Tamol.

In March, three other Philip Morris researchers who had worked in
the same Richmond laboratories as Tamol confessed publicly that they
had been secretly cooperating with the FDA's inquiry into the tobacco
industry. The FDA's David Kessler released their names and affidavits
about their work on the role of nicotine in cigarettes. One of the researchers, Ian Uydess, said that nicotine levels were routinely targeted
and adjusted by Philip Morris. Another, William Farone, had written a
research paper entitled "The Manipulation and Control of Nicotine and

Tar in the Design and Manufacture of Cigarettes." Philip Morris had always insisted that it did not manipulate nicotine levels in cigarettes and protested that the FDA's actions were all part of a "public relations gambit" to manipulate the media and "cloud rather than clarify the facts."

In the Heep household, the defections by the researchers caused quite a stir. According to Heep, Philip Morris knew Tamol had company files and the phone never stopped ringing as company lawyers demanded that Tamol either return or destroy all his documents—most of which were still stored in Heep's basement.

One day, two men came to the door and without identifying themselves demanded to see Tamol, who was not at home. Heep assumed they were from the company. "One of them tried to step right into my house, almost pushed past me," Heep said later. When she told the men that Tamol was not in, they said they would wait for him. "No, you won't," she said, "you'll leave and you'll leave right now. . . . You are standing on my porch with imported tiles from Padua, Italy. Get off them [and] don't ever come near my house again."

When Tamol returned, she told him about the two men. They then had a shouting match about the documents that ended when she told him to leave, and he did. A few days later, Tamol phoned wanting to come back to collect the documents. Never, she told him. Their affair was over and he could never return.

Heep was now convinced that she was holding documents vital to the future of the tobacco industry. As she recalled, she expected "Philip Morris people to come crashing through the doors at any moment." She decided to hand over the documents to the antitobacco forces, but she didn't know anyone on that side of the war.

Heep came from a famous ranching family in Texas and she did what any well-connected Texan would have done with a serious dilemma: she called the governor's office. They put her in touch with the office of the attorney general, Dan Morales, who had filed the Texas Medicaid recovery suit. But apparently Heep was not making herself clear. Morales's office put her through to the Texas public affairs office, where they suggested that if she needed information about cigarettes she should contact consumer affairs and get a pamphlet. Ms. Heep exploded. "I've been sleeping for the last two years with the man who developed these damned cigarettes," she said. "Now either you got somebody there that cares, or you don't. I'm not going to sit on hold anymore. I've had it," she said and hung up.

She knew from the newspapers and television that a Harvard law professor had been a consultant on the tobacco lawsuits. In fact, two Harvard professors had been advising the antitobacco forces. Laurence Tribe had been assisting Mississippi, Florida, and Texas, and Arthur Miller had been consulting with the Castano group. She called Professor Miller's office and was given the Castano number in New Orleans.

Delighted at the prospect of a document windfall resulting from a woman's scorn, Wendell Gauthier immediately dispatched a team of lawyers to Richmond. Within twenty-four hours, Tamol's documents and Ms. Heep were on their way to New Orleans. Heep stayed in a "safe house" while some Castano lawyers took her deposition. Meanwhile, other Castano lawyers found what they considered to be four sensational notes in the papers, all apparently written by Tamol. Each contained a reference to the amount of nicotine necessary to keep a smoker "hooked." One was stamped "R. A. Tamol," dated February 1, 1965, and read: "Determine minimum nicotine drip to keep normal smokers 'hooked.' " The handwriting appeared similar to Tamol's script on his country-club receipts and checks.

After taking Ms. Heep's deposition, Gauthier arranged for her to be interviewed on television and released her deposition to the media. The newspapers loved the story, of course. Contacted by reporters, Tamol said he had never written the notes in question, telling *The New York Times*, "Philip Morris is not manipulating nicotine." He said he had broken up with Ms. Heep because she was "basically unstable" and "a chronic liar." Philip Morris called the release of the documents a "bizarre stunt" that was "part of an all too familiar pattern of documents being leaked to the media." John Coale, the Castano lawyer in charge of publicity, countered that the documents were the "most devastating that have come to light." And Gauthier said he "couldn't wait to get before a jury" with the notes. "Those rascals should be in jail," he said.

Thus, Hatsy Heep and her spurned lover entered the annals of the Third Wave of tobacco litigation. Even though Tamol's documents yielded no more than a few pages of handwritten notes, it was a good media story; the last, as it turned out, of a series of great publicity stunts in the Castano group's highly successful propaganda war against the industry. Gauthier had masterminded an assault in the media that left the industry sputtering and defensive. As one Wall Street tobacco analyst, Roy Burry of Oppenheimer & Company, put it, Castano had created "90 percent of the noise factor surrounding the industry."

One of Gauthier's cheekiest propaganda moves had been directed at Wall Street analysts, including Mr. Burry. The Castano group had issued subpoenas to Burry and the other four leading tobacco analysts, Gary Black of Sanford Bernstein, Marc Cohen of Goldman Sachs, Diana Temple of Salomon Brothers, and Rebecca Barfield of CS First Boston. Casting his document-discovery net as wide as possible, Gauthier had demanded all reports, memoranda, notes, messages, calendar and diary entries, videotapes, disks, and electronic mail that would explain the "formulation of your opinions" on the purchase of tobacco stocks. "We're pulling them in [because] we wonder if they have information on the issues of addiction, manipulation and nicotine and because they write a lot about this," said John Coale. "We think analysts favor the tobacco companies and are consistently trumpeting the industry's position. We suspect that the companies have shared a lot of information with these analysts, and we want to know what it is." The analysts were outraged, declaring that the sources they used were all in the public record.

Gary Black complained directly to Gauthier. Ever since the dinner at Antoine's, Black had kept in touch with the Castano suit through Gauthier's associate, lawyer Danny Becnel, and he considered himself to be on friendly terms with the group. "How could you do this to us?" Black protested. Gauthier said they wanted to find out if the institutional investors knew they were financing a product that killed more than 400,000 people a year and if the tobacco companies had told investors that nicotine was addictive.

"Gary, it's this simple," said Gauthier, although Black doesn't remember this part of the conversation. "Suppose that I'm smuggling dope from Mexico and I call you and I say, 'Gary, I need a million dollars and I'll return you two million and you don't have to know anything about my smuggling operation.' Do you think you could be criminally charged?"

"Oh, that's different," said Black.

"Why?" asked Gauthier. "You know what the big difference is, Gary? The standard of proof is less in civil cases than it is in criminal cases. You're in more trouble than the example I just gave you."

"But I thought we were friends," Black said.

"It's got nothing to do with friendship, man," Gauthier answered. "These motherfuckers killed my best friend."

From Castano dinners at Antoine's and other famous New Orleans restaurants, "secret" meetings of the group's executive committee (to which at least one reporter was allowed, and of which TV cameras took before and after shots), to Gauthier's practical jokes and his highly printable bombast about tobacco, and, of course, to John Coale's release of the Merrell Williams documents to the media, the "Mother of All Lawsuits" had done more to focus public attention on the tobacco industry than anything else produced thus far by the Third Wave. Much to their own surprise, this group of legal warriors, who are constantly reviled by their colleagues for their boorish ways, unscrupulous courtroom tricks, and gigantic payoffs, suddenly found themselves being hailed as the "good guys," an image even they had never expected.

Perhaps more important, Gauthier created a phenomenon that the tobacco companies had long dreaded: a coalition of the nation's leading liability lawyers who had set aside primitive antagonisms and had come together as a cohesive fighting force under the banner of a public health cause everyone could identify with, even if they couldn't actually support it. This was an alarming prospect for any industrial enterprise, but for the big tobacco companies it was a sign that they had finally met their match. Gauthier's group entered the fray well funded, ready for the long haul. Even though they all suspected that the Fifth Circuit Court of Appeals would overturn the lower court's ruling and decertify the Castano class action, a cadre of antitobacco lawyers had been formed, well trained if undisciplined, battle scarred and determined to fight on. Rebuffed by the courts in New Orleans, the Castano lawyers would fan out across the land and challenge the industry in different cities. As Elizabeth Cabraser, Castano's lead counsel, said, "They can stop us this year. They can stop us next year, but they can't stop us forever because we've now got the same perpetual existence that they have. There will always be a body of lawyers committed to this task."

KEEPING THIS FORCE TOGETHER had been much more difficult than Gauthier's freewheeling style had suggested, however. A trademark of the plaintiffs' bar is independence. None of its members relishes being controlled, least of all by the collective will of a sixty-member committee. Behind the collegial niceties, old rivalries swirled. One member, in particular, could never fit. The capricious Ron Motley, the "Asbestos Avenger" from Charleston, started to nip at Gauthier's heels from the first. Motley was always complaining that the Castano group was not being run properly, not acting fast enough, and not fulfilling its potential in the pretrial investigations.

Some Castano lawyers became convinced that Motley was trying to organize a coup. He denied it of course, but he had his admirers; Richard Heimann of the San Francisco firm of Lieff, Cabraser was one, Don Barrett was another. So was Professor Daynard of Northeastern University. When Gauthier was not around, Motley quickly took over. "It didn't matter what it was; he just wanted to run the show," said a Castano lawyer. "My impression was that if he couldn't have Castano he was hell-bent on taking it out of the limelight completely."

Gauthier and Motley had clashed before, in Puerto Rico after the fire at the DuPont Plaza hotel. The smoke was still billowing out of the hotel when Gauthier sent John Coale to collect clients. Coale had done so well that Motley had been excluded and he went back to Charleston. "We had some run-ins with him," recalled Gauthier, who was quick to point out the irony in Motley's failure. "He came home and got into asbestos claims and made a fortune. We struggled on in Puerto Rico and we won but we made little money."

In Castano, Gauthier would shrug off the challenge people said Motley was making. "I heard things about Ron, but every time I asked him about them he denied it. It was my position that if anyone really worked themselves up to the point they wanted to take over, hell, I would just have become the number two, three, or five. That would have been great. To me it's about winning and if someone could carry the torch better than I to get us across the goal posts, I would defer to him in a New York second."

These two giants of the plaintiffs' bar, with their strikingly different personalities and methods, seemed bound for a confrontation. Gauthier liked to organize his lawyers, lead them into the courtroom, make the opening and closing arguments, but otherwise let them run the show. He always had several cases running at once. As he launched the unwieldy Castano group, Gauthier was involved in several other tort cases and was also leading a consortium of local investors in New Orleans's first land casino, a bold rival project to riverboat gambling. Throughout the turmoil in his office, however, he was almost always calm. Few things seemed to bother him. "He's the general," said a member of the Castano committee. "People take their orders and move forward."

As Gauthier invited respect and loyalty, Motley brought out uncertainty. "Motley is his own man," the same Castano lawyer continued. "We would vote in the committee and, if Motley lost, he would do whatever he wanted to do anyway."

Motley is known as a "showboater"; part Southern populist, part preacher, and part dictator. "It's either his way or no way," said another lawyer who knows Motley well. They used to say he ran "the Republic of Motley," right there in South Carolina. "The *Independent* Republic of Motley, please," added one of his lawyers, Andy Berly.

To say that Motley's staff worship him may be going too far, but he is the centerpiece of their life. He makes it so. Like any accomplished actor, he demands an audience, full-time. "In his own office, Ron is God," said a New Orleans lawyer. "They adore him. He built a kingdom and surrounded himself with courtiers who think he's the most brilliant man in the country. And as a team they think they're the best." And, in some respects, they are.

Motley is known for his elaborate and highly successful courtroom performances and his quick grasp of the essential evidence that will turn a jury. In these respects he has few rivals, his colleagues say. Motley's personal view of the plaintiffs' bar is that it's filled with junkyard dogs, always ready for a scrap. Once he picks up the scent of corporate wrongdoing—a company hiding evidence, an expert witness not declaring his interests, or a phony industry-funded front organization—he springs into action and relentlessly tracks down his quarry. He unearths documents, takes depositions, and unleashes his own shock troops on libraries, archives, company records, and expert witnesses. The tobacco companies had never encountered such zeal in their forty years of corporate litigation.

Motley's raiders became the SWAT team of the antitobacco forces. A third of the seventy lawyers in his Charleston firm of Ness, Motley, Loadholt, Richardson & Poole would eventually be assigned to the tobacco wars. No expense was spared. The team became known for their rough-hewn manners by day and the fine dinners they hosted by night in whichever town they were plundering for evidence. "It was always worth going just for the wine; it was invariably so fine that it had to be decanted," said one of the lawyers who attended such events.

Motley's arrival at a gathering of plaintiffs' lawyers, always by private jet and stretch limousine, was like the arrival of a pop star. People would ask, "Where's Ron?" And the answer would always be, "Ron's coming. Got delayed." But he would always turn up. Lawyers flocked around him as he entered the hotel foyer because he always had news of something important: a new document, a deposition, a whistle-blower. "Ron was constantly creating excitement and inviting people to his beach house, picking them up in the plane and getting them all worked up that he was on the cutting edge of the litigation and the rest of Castano was in the dark and clueless," recalled a Castano lawyer.

Motley loved to show off, perhaps more than any of his colleagues. Riches gleaned from asbestos cases gave him the opportunity to live like a star. Weekend work-and-play parties at his beach mansion on Kiawah Island became legendary. Shortly after he joined the Castano group in the summer of 1994, Motley asked some of the lawyers down for the weekend. They included the Southerners—Gauthier, Don Barrett, and Dick Scruggs. Dick Daynard had flown in from Boston. They spent the day talking about how to find more industry documents and, in the evening, Motley invited them out on his new yacht.

They boarded it around sundown, intending to sail a leisurely few miles along the coast to a restaurant. But it turned out to be more leisurely than planned. The boat wouldn't start at first and when it did, it would go only very slowly. By the time they reached the restaurant many cocktails had been served. Motley fell asleep at the table, and his girlfriend drove him home in his Ferrari. The boat and crew left without the guests, who were stranded—no boat, no car. The bartender took pity on the group and drove them home in his old Volkswagen van, with Don Barrett singing "Miss America" in the back. The next morning, Motley acted as if nothing had happened and immediately got down to business.

Motley's strategy was "slash and burn," said a Texas lawyer, who noted that the state had at first respectfully declined the offer Motley made to be the trial lawyer in the Texas Medicaid suit. "We thought his style was better suited to the Bible Belt." The Texas lawyers had not forgotten how Motley had moved into a hotel suite in Houston during an asbestos trial and lived high on the hog—even by the elevated standards set in those parts. They christened him "Hollywood." But they all respected the thoroughness of his investigation and his exhaustive depositions of high-placed officials from the enemy camp. Motley made it his business to be as expert on the subject as his witness. Quite how he managed it with his hectic after-hours life, no one could fathom, but Motley made himself indispensable. Every attorney general in charge of a state case, every lawyer in charge of a class action or an individual suit knew that without Motley on the payroll they would be missing something. So they hired him. In the Third Wave of tobacco litigation, Motley would represent thirty of the thirty-nine states that sued the industry. Even the fiercely independent Texas lawyers would change their minds and invite Motley to help try their case when it came up at the end of September 1997. "You have to admire the guy," said Coale after watching Motley closely for two years. "He's everywhere."

For all his dedication, his accomplished peformances, and his social energy, however, Motley failed to unseat Gauthier—if, indeed, that was his intention. In the end, it was not Motley but the Fifth Circuit Court of Appeals that pushed the Castano class action off center stage. But not before Motley had had a chance to skirmish with the enemy. Some wondered, after the event, whether the tobacco companies might settle the case right there. Their battle formation was at least temporarily in disarray.

IN OCTOBER 1994, seven months after the Castano suit was filed and during the early, unreal phase of the Third Wave, Motley was presented with a rare opportunity to skirmish with top tobacco lawyers. He had never faced them in court before, although his asbestos experience had given him a good grounding in the medical science of the lungs. He had learned about the synergistic effects of tobacco smoke and asbestos dust.

The industry had launched a counterattack on a broad front. They had poured money into the midterm congressional elections and into election campaigns in states making efforts to impose tobacco control, such as California and Colorado. Philip Morris was in an especially spiteful mood, threatening to move its Park Avenue headquarters out of New York and cut off the millions of dollars it gave yearly to the arts if the city council passed smoking controls in restaurants. In Washington, D.C., the companies had deployed their finest lawyers on a mission to oppose the federal government's plan to end smoking in the workplace. Despite hours of testimony from several hundred experts and witnesses on the effects of secondhand tobacco smoke, the plan by the Occupational Safety and Health Administration was being challenged on a daily basis by highly paid tobacco lawyers from the country's blue-chip law firms. Each day for several months, in the ground floor auditorium of the U.S. Labor Department building near the Capitol, a phalanx of industry lawyers, twenty to thirty strong, in their dark suits, white shirts, and scarlet suspenders, would sit on one side of the auditorium. They were led by John Rupp, a handsome, dark-haired, articulate lawyer who represented the Tobacco Institute. On the other side, pitifully outnumbered, would sit the three representatives of the antismoking health groups, the American Cancer Society, the American Lung Association, and the American Heart Association. They were led by Matt Myers, a sharp-witted, liberal-minded, public-interest lawyer for the Coalition on Smoking or Health, who was to rise to much greater things before the end of the Third Wave.

The atmosphere was oppressive and conspiratorial. The tobacco lawyers kept to themselves, refusing to speak to their opponents. Sherri Watson, a pleasant, caring woman, who was the public relations officer for the American Lung Association, sat through the entire performance and said at the time that she felt she was being followed wherever she went. "I would go to the telephone, so would someone else. I would come out of the ladies room, so would someone else. I'd go get some gum, so would someone else. It was the same person from the other side of the auditorium."

The health-group witnesses were subjected to withering cross-examination by Rupp and other industry lawyers, who knew as much if not more than the experts about the science of secondhand smoke. "We simply didn't have the resources to follow this," said Watson. "We knew we were going to have to find some other support." Myers said, "We were stretched so thin. The tobacco industry was gearing up to turn these hearings into their Armageddon on environmental tobacco smoke. I called Dick Daynard at Northeastern University and Ness, Motley and Ron Motley called back."

Within days, what became known as the "Torpedo Team" was flying into Washington. Jodi Flowers from Motley's office was first, then Hugh McNeely and Rhet Klok from the Castano group in New Orleans. They set up a field office in a hotel. Motley followed a few days later. "That was a glorious day when we heard Ron Motley and the others were coming," said Watson. "They were in another league. They came in with their little document carts and their black lawyer's cases. Motley looked so dapper with his cowboy boots. He was saying 'Hi' to everyone; a very confident gentleman."

Motley's strategy was to undermine the industry's witnesses and scientific experts by attacking their credibility. His first target was William Althaus, the former mayor of York, Pennsylvania, and now chairman of the National Smokers' Alliance, an industry-funded "grassroots" group. (The antitobacco forces called them AstroTurf organizations.) With a little bit of digging, Motley had discovered that Althaus, while mayor of York, had signed an executive order banning smoking in the city's offices. The order included the sentence, "The City should treat nicotine like any other addiction by providing financial assistance for a substance-abuse program."

"Have you ever declared smoking to be addictive?" Motley asked, out of the blue.

"I don't recall," replied Althaus.

"Have you ever declared environmental tobacco smoke to cause disease?"

"I don't recall," the mayor said again.

The next day, Motley was quoted in the mayor's hometown newspaper, the *York Daily Record,* as saying, "We ruined your mayor." Motley told the newspaper his aim had been to "reveal the NSA for what it is—a group of shills for the tobacco companies." Motley said he had been called in to stop the health groups being "beaten up by slick tobacco industry lawyers. They wanted some of our junkyard dogs, and we had a lot."

In the basement auditorium, the administrative judge running the hearing, a mild-mannered man named John Vittone, objected to Motley's characterization of the health groups as being "beaten up by slick tobacco industry lawyers."

> MOTLEY: Well, sir, I think my position simply stated is that the tobacco lawyers have a history of being well financed and well prepared to do a very effective job of pointing out deficiencies as they perceive them [and] the people who asked me to come here were not as well financed or prepared, or able to ask the same kinds of probing questions.
>
> JUDGE: I don't see that as beating up on witnesses.
>
> MOTLEY: Well, perhaps it's a matter of perception, your honor.

The judge then asked Motley if it were true, as the newspaper had said, that he had hired a private detective to get "dirt" on Althaus, because if it were true "it would indicate Motley had been beating up on a witness . . . . This is not a trial for damages." Motley said it wasn't true. He had only hired a detective to get a picture of York City Hall.

Motley had set a new tone for the entire hearings. A second lawyer on the Torpedo Team, Hugh McNeely, cross-examined Albert Nichols, an independent environmental economist with the National Economic Research Association of Cambridge, Massachusetts. He had been invited to give evidence by Philip Morris and had disputed the number, and therefore the cost to employers, of the nonsmoking lounges OSHA had proposed if their rule was enforced. OSHA estimated $68 million a year; Nichols said $7 billion. But McNeely was more interested in whether Philip Morris lawyers had vetted the draft of Nichols's paper before he presented it to OSHA.

> MCNEELY: Did the draft come back changed or altered in any way?

NICHOLS: It came back with some editorial suggestions.

MCNEELY: Did [they] suggest that you use such terms as "alleged risk" instead of terms suggesting a causal relationship between ETS [environmental tobacco smoke] exposure and cancer and other diseases?

NICHOLS: It's not really an issue in regard to my testimony since all of my testimony and information was on the costs of the rule and had nothing to do with the risk side of the rule.

MCNEELY: Well, you didn't answer my question.

NICHOLS: I guess I don't see the relevance.

MCNEELY: Judge, can I get him to answer my question, yes or no?

JUDGE: If you know the answer would you tell him yes or no, if you can?

NICHOLS: In a couple of cases they suggested that we use "alleged" before we used the word "risk."

MCNEELY: You did in fact alter the terms in accordance with the tobacco company's editorial comments, is that correct?

NICHOLS: Well, actually it was not the tobacco company, it was some of the attorneys. As I said, we did make some editorial changes, and some of them were of the nature of referring to modifying "risk" by "alleged" or "purported."

MCNEELY: Well, would you please identify each and every attorney that reviewed your original submission draft for editorial comment.

JUDGE: Why, Mr. McNeely?

MCNEELY: I'm trying to find out who wrote this report, your honor.

McNeely admitted later that asking about the word "alleged" had been a guess on his part. The tobacco company lawyers were not amused; they wouldn't even get into the same elevator with the Torpedo Team. But Motley had shown them something of what was to come. He was aching to have a chance to cross-examine the industry's officials, but by the end of November the tobacco companies had had enough of the Torpedo Team. They started to withdraw their witnesses—and then themselves. Philip Morris wrote a letter to the judge complaining about Motley and the efforts of plaintiffs' counsel "to misuse the hearing process for purposes of advancing their own personal and monetary interests." It was only the beginning of the chase.

WHEN JUDGE OKLA JONES of the New Orleans District Court certified the Castano case for trial in February 1995, he admitted he really didn't know how it would all turn out. "With this decision, the Court embarks on a road certainly less traveled, if ever taken at all," he said, referring to Robert Frost's poem. He was bound by Rule 23 of the Federal Rules of Civil Procedure: A class action must have too many plaintiffs to conduct individual trials; the claim must be typical of the class as a whole; and the representatives of the class must be able to safeguard adequately the interests of the class. Rule 23 adds two more conditions, which are known as "predominance" and "superiority." Under the first, questions of law common to members of the class must "predominate" over questions affecting individual members. In other words, if members of the class come from different states, which have different tort laws, the class action may not be an appropriate form of seeking justice. Under the second condition, the class approach must be "superior" to other methods available for the fair and efficient adjudication of the claims. It must be a better way for the courts to handle large numbers of claims.

The tobacco companies had argued that the number of smokers involved—tens of millions from all over the country—each needing individual medical diagnosis for alleged nicotine dependence, could not possibly fit the conditions of predominance and superiority. Differences in state laws apart, it should be clear that nicotine addiction, or habituation, or whatever you want to call it, varied greatly from one person to another. Even if a trial decided that nicotine was an addictive substance, each individual would have to prove nicotine addiction and that would clog up the courts for decades.

But Judge Jones decided to be creative and, as he put it, "look forward and invent" a way to process the claims as a class. Essentially, he split the lawsuit into two parts. The first would be a single trial of the claim that nicotine was addictive and that the tobacco companies had fraudulently failed to inform smokers of this fact, despite their possession of such knowledge. If the tobacco companies won that trial, the suit would be over. If they lost, Judge Jones envisioned a second series of trials to assess potential damages, but he took the option, which Rule 23 provides, of deciding how those second trials would be managed after the resolution of the first one. This was a progressive reading of the rules from a liberal judge, and the tobacco companies pounced on it and appealed immediately. A hearing on the appeal was set for April 2, 1996—a week after Texas became the seventh state to file a Medicaid case.

As the lawyers prepared their appeal arguments, Judge Jones died suddenly from leukemia. Although he would not have been involved in the appeal, his death seemed a bad omen for the Castano camp. The hearing was to be before three judges of the Fifth Circuit: Jerry Smith and John Duhe, both Reagan appointees, and Harold DeMoss, appointed by President Bush. Most legal experts, and the Castano lawyers themselves, assumed they would be bound by recent negative trends in class-action rulings.

One such class action in Chicago was particularly relevant. It involved 10,000 hemophiliacs who had been infected by the AIDS virus through blood transfusions. Nearly 2,000 had died of AIDS. The hemophiliacs formed a class action and sued the five national drug companies that had supplied blood-clotting additives. They claimed that the companies knew the product was contaminated with HIV. The lower court had suggested the same procedure that Judge Jones had recommended for Castano—a two-step trial. In the first, a jury would determine whether the drug companies had been negligent; if so, the class action would be allowed to pursue individual claims for damages in separate trials. The drug companies appealed.

The Seventh Circuit rejected the class action. In the decision, Judge Richard Posner said the issues of negligence could not be decided in a class action because the hemophiliacs came from all over the country and the fifty states have different laws governing negligence; as such, it would be impossible to adopt a single legal standard for the class. In other words, questions of law did not "predominate" throughout the class. The tobacco companies seized on Posner's argument and would use it against Castano in their appeal.

When the hearing opened, the federal courtroom on Poydras Street in downtown New Orleans was packed with more than a hundred and fifty lawyers, reporters, and Wall Street analysts. The media examination of the industry had been in full cry for months, and tobacco stocks had been reacting wildly to every tidbit of information—a new, embarrassing document, additional states suing for Medicaid costs, or rumors of more tobacco industry whistle-blowers. Roy Burry, an analyst for Oppenheimer & Company, observed, "There are billions of dollars at stake here. Everyone is reading the tea leaves." The tobacco stock analyst Gary Black could no longer contain his contempt for the Castano lawyers and declared, "It's a wonderful day. It's a very conservative panel. It dramatically increases the odds that Castano will go away."

The industry was defended by Kenneth Starr, a former U.S. solicitor general and the Whitewater independent counsel. Starr had been criticized for accepting the brief. How could he work for the tobacco industry and investigate alleged wrongdoings by an antitobacco president? asked his critics. Surely there was a conflict of interest? Not at all, said the confident Mr. Starr, who was an old tobacco industry campaigner. He had been counsel for Brown & Williamson in 1994 when they issued subpoenas against Congressmen Waxman and Wyden over the leak of the Merrell Williams documents. He had lost that battle in a Democratic Congress, but in New Orleans he was sure of victory. Gauthier was in the corridors, building up confidence among the Castano group. But even he looked nervous.

Starr walked into the court smiling, a noticeable spring in his step as he greeted the usual band of thirty or so industry lawyers. They looked less tense than the last time they had been in New Orleans for the certification hearing in December 1994. They seemed to smell a victory. Starr launched into a barrage against the Castano action. It was an "an extremely novel claim," he told the three-judge panel, a claim which had not been properly tested in the courts and was therefore unworthy of a class action. "This case is woefully premature," he argued, "and [the claims] so overwhelmingly individualized that it should collapse."

As to the matter of alleged nicotine addiction, Starr said, "The very concept of addiction is complex. It is elusive with definitions [of addiction] shifting over the decades covered by the complaint." Moreover, nicotine addiction was so overwhelmingly individualized that the whole idea of nicotine addiction as a cause of legal action should be tested in state courts before entertaining any thoughts of a national class action.

Elizabeth Cabraser, the petite San Francisco attorney with an encyclopedic command of class actions, argued the case for Castano. Cabraser's central point was disarmingly simple. This case was about "fraudulent statements" from the industry. Such a charge was amply supported by new evidence, she said. Taking Starr's objection that the claim of addiction was a "novel claim," she said, "Our claim is not a new claim in law. It's a fraud claim. What's novel about the claim is the facts that support it: facts that smokers in traditional trials have not had before, facts which were known to the defendants and were suppressed, and facts that have begun to emerge within the last two years."

Unwieldy though the class action was—tens of millions of addicted smokers, perhaps—Cabraser argued that Judge Jones had selected an appropriate two-step method of dealing with the cases. There was nothing in Judge Jones's certification that suggested there would have to be multiple trials in many jurisdictions. On the contrary, Judge Jones had deliberately deferred what happened "down the road not taken" until after the trial to establish whether nicotine was addictive and whether the companies had covered up that fact.

The Fifth Circuit judges were clearly not impressed by Cabraser's position. They were preoccupied with the problems posed by nicotine addiction and by the varying laws governing negligence in the fifty states. Was Castano not "so complex and individualized" as to be unworkable? they asked. Had Judge Jones not been "cavalier" in his treatment of its complexities down the road? Judge Duhe, himself a former smoker, thought that "considerably more analysis should have been presented" by Judge Jones on the issue of how to conduct the second trials.

The Fifth Circuit's ruling came sooner than expected, but the findings were not a surprise. On May 23, the panel reversed Judge Jones's certification. In a thirty-six-page opinion, the three judges agreed that variations in state law were too great—they adversely affected the conditions of "predominance" and "superiority." They agreed with Starr that nicotine addiction as a cause of action needed to be tested in state courts before creating a national class. The addiction theory was too novel, said Judge Smith, who then took one extra step. He called the nicotine addiction claim an "immature" tort, which he defined as one that lacks a "prior track record of trials from which the district court can draw the information necessary to make the predominance and superiority analysis of Rule 23."

This incensed Cabraser. In a paper for the American Bar Association, she would counterattack. In calling addiction an "immature tort" requiring experimentation in many trials, the judges, said Cabraser, had suited the tobacco companies' "interests and preferences admirably." It played directly into the industry's legal strategy of wearing down the opposition. A single plaintiff was likely to find the cost of litigating an addiction claim so much greater than the prospective award as to be of "negative value." It would cost much more than could possibly be gained in damages. Therefore, the plaintiff would be deterred from taking action. This had been the experience of the First and Second Waves of tobacco litigation. Cabraser concluded that scientific-sounding concepts such as that of "immature tort" were in fact attractive "catch phrases" that were "largely unsupported by any widely accepted body of evidence or jurisprudential consensus. In short, immature tort is an immature concept."

The *Harvard Law Review* agreed. Judge Smith's adoption of the maturity test was "decidedly premature," said the *Review*. "More importantly," it concluded, "Judge Smith's ability to subsume his distaste for novelty within the ostensibly objective maturity label raises the concern that judges may use the maturity test to implement their personal beliefs about the appropriateness of the class action." That was Cabraser's point, too.

Concluding her attack, she said that it appeared, "at least to the 'losing side,' as essentially a value judgment, in which one court's view of the merits of the case has become inextricably entangled with the neutral procedural principles of Rule 23."

The companies were jubilant and used the Fifth Circuit decision to castigate the liability lawyers. R. J. Reynolds said the rejection of Castano sent "a strong message that class actions created by entrepreneurial plaintiffs' lawyers will not be accepted by the courts"; Brown & Williamson said the signal was clear: "Stop the insanity in our nation's courts"; the ruling had declared "loud and clear to those who would twist the process to their own advantage that the line, indeed, had been drawn." Wall Street was happy, as well. "The class-action risk is gone," declared Gary Black.

AFTER THE FIFTH CIRCUIT DECISION, the tobacco companies no doubt hoped that Castano would die: that Gauthier's stunts would end and that the last had been heard from John Coale, Stanley Chesley, Ron Motley, and the others. But the Castano consortium had $2.2 million on hand and $1.5 million coming in every three months from the sixty law firms involved. Expecting to be turned down by the conservative Fifth Circuit, Gauthier and his colleagues had already prepared a contingency plan. They started to file "son of Castano" cases in every state in the nation. The Third Wave's oracle, Professor Daynard, forecast it would be like the Sorcerer's Apprentice—break one broom and two more appear, and then four and then sixteen and so on. Indeed, within five days, two such cases were filed—one in Louisiana and another in Maryland. Two months after the Fifth Circuit decision, there were seven such cases, including the District of Columbia, Indiana, Mississippi, New Mexico, and New York.

These cases would not recapture the media magic of the early Castano days; filing lawsuits in state courts is an uphill struggle, opposed at every turn by the industry. Gauthier held the line, even so. When the antitobacco forces massed in the spring of 1997 to negotiate a so-called global settlement with the industry, Gauthier, Stan Chesley, John Coale, and Russ Herman were all there, fighting for compensation for the nicotine addicted smokers of America—and, of course, for their attorneys' fees. Ron Motley, the wild card in the Third Wave, would leave the Castano camp and become a leader of the mass offensive of the thirty-nine states suing the industry for Medicaid costs. As such, he would play a key role in the end game the attorneys general played in the summer of 1997.

14

THE MAN ON
THE PINK BICYCLE

Somebody needed to take these people on. A lot of people
are dying of cancer.

—Grady Carter, August 9, 1996

It's hard for me to understand why this hasn't occurred
sooner.

*—Samuel Gaskins, retired postal-service supervisor and
foreman of the Florida jury that found Brown &
Williamson guilty of negligence*

THE PHONE CALL from the courthouse came in midafternoon.
The jury had reached a verdict. On any other such day, Woody
Wilner, a winsome, middle-aged lawyer in Jacksonville, Florida, might have mounted his shocking pink bicycle, stashed his court
papers in the front basket, and peddled the four blocks, mostly down-
hill, from his law office to the Duval County Circuit Court. He had
made this journey hundreds of times in the last twenty years. But
August 9, 1996, would be different. Wilner's career was at a turning
point; so was the Third Wave of tobacco litigation.

The jury had been deliberating for more than a day on a claim for
damages by Wilner's client, Grady Carter, against the tobacco company
Brown & Williamson. Carter, a retired air traffic controller, had lost the
upper lobe of his left lung to cancer after smoking for forty years. It was
the first tobacco case of the Third Wave to come to trial; the first time
the Merrell Williams documents had been used in evidence, and it was
Woody Wilner's first-ever cigarette lawsuit. Wilner thought he had

presented his case well. The jury seemed to have understood the issues and was not obviously inclined one way or the other. The judge had been fair, and Florida's consumer laws were on his side. Even so, Wilner remained deeply respectful, even fearful, of the unbeaten record of the tobacco industry. He rated his chances of winning at only a little higher than fifty-fifty. As befit the seriousness of the occasion, Wilner left his bicycle at the office and drove to the court with Carter and his wife, Mildred.

The tiny courthouse, old and worn from decades of use, was packed with journalists, television crews, stock analysts, and lawyers. The tobacco company's representatives looked confident, letting journalists know they would be available for comment when it was over.

Shortly after three o'clock, the six jurors, five men and one woman, ended nine-and-a-half hours of deliberation, and Judge Brian Davis asked the foreman, Samuel Gaskins, a retired postal-service supervisor, to read the verdict. The jury found the tobacco company negligent in selling Grady Carter an "unreasonably dangerous and defective product," and they awarded Carter and his wife $750,000 in damages. The courtroom murmured with disbelief. It was only the third time a tobacco company had been ordered to pay damages. The first award was for $400,000 to the family of Rose Cipollone, and that had been reversed on appeal. The second was a $2 million award to a California smoker who had developed mesothelioma, a fatal form of lung cancer, which the smoker had attributed to the asbestos fibers in the Micronite filters of Kent cigarettes. That award was on appeal.

A smiling Grady Carter leaned back from his chair at the plaintiff's table and squeezed Mildred's hand. "Somebody needed to take these people on," he said outside the court. "A lot of people are dying of lung cancer." Wilner congratulated his client and thanked him for being courageous under fire from the tobacco company's defense counsel. Wilner felt it was a close call, but he didn't show it. "We proved ninety-nine percent," he told reporters outside the courthouse. "I think you will hear carping about the one percent. Nobody's perfect. You can't prove everything." The tobacco representatives didn't stay to be interviewed, after all.

The shockwaves hit Wall Street immediately: Philip Morris stocks tumbled 14 percent, RJR Nabisco dropped 13 percent. American

Brands, which sold the Lucky Strikes brand to Brown & Williamson in 1995, and BAT, Brown & Williamson's British parent, were also down. Overall, tobacco stocks lost $14 billion in value in a few hours.

In official statements, the companies were defiant. The verdict would be appealed, promised Brown & Williamson. The company claimed the judge had allowed inadmissable evidence, such as permitting Carter to speculate about what he would have done if there had been a warning before 1966 on cigarette packs. They also complained about Wilner's insistence that the company should have marketed a "safer" cigarette. He had failed to offer any evidence of a design alternative, "much less one that would have avoided the plaintiff's injury," they said.

Philip Morris dismissed the verdict as an "aberration," implying that this small-time lawyer was merely lucky, and it wouldn't happen again. Stock analysts basically agreed. They thought that the Carter verdict would survive an appeal, but nothing in the Carter case necessarily meant Wilner could go on to win other individual cases. But questions remained: Had the antitobacco propaganda really changed the way juries viewed smokers? And what influence did the new evidence have on juries?

The only certain result was that if the verdict survived on appeal, Woody Wilner would receive his percentage of the award—he won't say exactly how much—and scoop up $1.8 million in fees that the judge ordered the tobacco company to pay separately. He had become a star of the plaintiffs' bar.

UNTIL THE CLOSING STAGES, the Carter trial had received little attention. It had seemed to most observers that Wilner was pursuing an old ritual that had been shown to be a failure too many times for any radical departures. For almost three weeks, Wilner, a partner in the small eight-lawyer firm of Spohrer, Wilner, Maciejewski, Stanford & Matthews, had stood alone against one of Big Tobacco's largest law firms, Chadbourne & Parke, of New York. This was not only Wilner's first time against the industry, it was his first time on the plaintiff's side of the court. For the last fifteen years he had made a good, but not spectacular living defending asbestos companies. Some members of the plaintiffs' bar scoffed at Wilner's switching to the plaintiffs' side just as the tide seemed to be turning against the tobacco industry. But Wilner could not be accused of hopping on someone else's bandwagon. He had created his own casebook.

Since 1995, Wilner had been advertising in Florida newspapers for smoking victims and had built up an inventory of more than two hundred individual cases, involving different tobacco companies. He planned to bring them to court one at a time, if possible once a month. "Every tobacco company will get their turn," he had said with a chuckle.

The Carter case received little attention until the final days. Grady Carter was anything but the perfect client. At seventeen he had started smoking unfiltered Lucky Strikes. They were made by the American Tobacco Company, which had been bought in 1995 by Brown & Williamson. Carter's family had pleaded with him for years to give up cigarettes. They had sent him newspaper and magazine articles on the dangers of smoking, but Carter kept smoking. He even declined an offer by his government employer, the Federal Aviation Administration, to send him to no-smoking classes. When his doctor advised him to give up, he switched to a doctor who smoked. Finally, he quit when he was told he had cancer and started coughing up blood. "I liked smoking," he admitted under oath. "I liked the taste, and I didn't like how I felt when I didn't smoke."

The telltale shadows had shown up on Carter's chest X ray in 1991. Doctors had removed part of the lung, and at the start of the trial the cancer was in remission and Carter himself was in reasonably good health. At sixty-six he was robust and had enough energy to ride a motorcycle for pleasure around the backstreets of Jacksonville on Sunday afternoons. He was not the most likely smoking victim to elicit much sympathy from a jury, and Wilner's lawyer colleagues had advised him against taking the case. It sounded like a typical one that the tobacco industry loves to fight: a smoker who knew all the risks and had made a personal choice to take them. In previous trials, jury after jury had balked at giving such smokers much sympathy, or any damages.

But the climate was changing and Wilner felt it was worth the test. The antitobacco propaganda of the Third Wave had been in full swing for more than two years. Liggett had defected and settled its case with the Castano group and five of the states that were suing the industry for Medicaid costs. Most importantly, Wilner had won the court's approval to use the Merrell Williams documents, stolen from Brown & Williamson's own confidential files in Louisville. Wilner said later that he thought they had made a big difference, reinforcing the claim that Carter was addicted to nicotine and that the company had been negligent in not telling their customers they were "dealing with a deadly product."

At the trial, Wilner had preempted the tobacco company's traditional "choice" defense by admitting early that the smoker shared responsibility. "Selling is a two-way street," he said, using the tactic adopted by Barrett in the Horton trial in Lexington, Mississippi. Wilner preferred to call it "breaking the ice" with the jury. Once that admission was out of the way, he focused on the company's liability.

Under Florida state law, it's the manufacturer, not the consumer, who is required to possess expert knowledge of their products, and to warn the consumer if the hazard is not obvious—or not as well known to the user as to the manufacturer. The consumer could be blamed if he misused a product, but Carter had not done that, argued Wilner. "Do they maintain that Mr. Carter smoked wrong? That he smoked too many cigarettes, that he smoked them too fast, that he smoked them too far down? No, Mr. Carter purchased the product, and used it as it was intended to be used," he told the court. It is the product, the cigarettes, that are "defective," argued Wilner. "Cigarettes are 'dangerous' to an extent beyond that which would be contemplated by an ordinary customer with the ordinary knowledge of the community."

Blaming the company for failing to warn Carter of the hazards of smoking before warning labels went on cigarette packs in 1966, Wilner accused the company of a dereliction of duty, a failure of civic responsibility. "Brown & Williamson has a debt to pay and it's time they paid it," said Wilner.

One of his exhibits was a videotaped deposition of Robert Heimann, former chief executive of the American Tobacco Company, which made the Lucky Strikes Carter had smoked. This was the same tape used by Barrett in the Nathan Horton trial.

In the tape, Heimann appeared arrogant and aloof, saying it had never occurred to him that one day researchers would establish that

THE MAN ON THE PINK BICYCLE 269

smoking causes cancer. Asked whether the Surgeon General was more qualified than he to determine if smoking is hazardous to health, Heimann replied, "No."

Shrewdly, Wilner did not ask for an outrageous sum. He wanted $1.5 million in compensatory damages and no punitive damages. In the Horton case, the jury had not responded well to Barrett's excessive recommendation that the jury award Horton's widow $17 million ($2 million in compensatory and $15 million in punitive damages) in one of the poorest counties in the nation. Wilner aimed at a more digestible level; he doesn't try his cases on sympathy. "My feeling has always been it's not the amount; it's establishing the process that the tobacco companies have been negligent that matters," he says. Wilner suggested $600,000 for Carter for past pain and suffering and another $400,000 for his future health problems, including the loss of six to seven years of life expectancy. Carter's wife, Mildred, should receive half her husband's award, or $500,000, he argued.

The company's defense was traditional. Even though the ground had shifted with the new evidence, the company's counsel, Bruce Sheffler, continued to claim that there was no scientific evidence that smoking *causes* cancer; Carter chose to smoke and assumed the risk. "This case is about Mr. Carter, his decisions, his choices, why he made them, why he didn't," said Sheffler. Had Carter quit when he was advised by his doctor and his family, he would have lowered his risk of developing lung cancer, but he chose to keep smoking. The company had a duty to warn only when the company knew more about the product than the medical community and the general public, and the company did not know the dangers in the 1950s when Carter started to smoke, claimed Sheffler. Later on, there were plenty of articles about the risks of smoking; Carter simply ignored them.

Importantly, Sheffler's defense provided no explanation of the Merrell Williams documents that clearly showed the company did know prior to 1966 that nicotine was addictive, and that tobacco smoke contained carcinogens. He presented no company witnesses to counter the damaging internal documents from the Merrell Williams collection. Instead, Sheffler described the key 1963 Addison Yeaman memo ("Moreover, nicotine is addictive. We are then in the business of selling nicotine, an addictive drug.") as the mere "musings" of a company lawyer. There was no scientific evidence to support such a claim, he said.

Finally, Sheffler urged the jury to dismiss the case because Carter had filed outside the four-year statute of limitations from the time that he knew, or thought he knew he had cancer. Carter was a few days late, said Sheffler. He had filed on February 11, 1995, and he had found out on February 5, 1991. "That's reason alone to return a verdict for the American Tobacco Company."

Wilner had reserved part of his summing-up time for rebuttal. "I've sat through two hours of nonsense, just now," he told the jury. This was 1996, he said, and yet the tobacco companies were still refusing to admit that smoking caused cancer. "Where is the accountability?" he asked. "When is it going to stop? It echoes in your brain, this scary refrain: More research. More research is needed."

The jury did not take instantly to Wilner's pleadings. At the start of the first day of deliberations, four of the six jurors had sided with the company. The four included a heavy smoker and the lone woman member, who had once worked on a tobacco farm. One of the two who favored Carter was Samuel Gaskins, the jury foreman. Gaskins could not get over what he called the "crass hypocrisy" of the company's argument that Carter was aware smoking was harmful, but they would not admit it themselves. "They can't have it both ways," he would later tell *The Wall Street Journal.* The second Carter supporter was Christopher Ray, a twenty-five-year-old marketing coordinator, who objected to the "almost abusive" cross-examining of Carter by Sheffler.

It was when the four jurors leaning to the company's side went back over the evidence that they began to change their minds. The 1963 Addison Yeaman memo, Heimann's arrogant deposition, and the lingering picture that Wilner had produced of the seven tobacco company CEOs—including B&W's Tommy Sandefur—declaring under oath before Congress in April 1994 that nicotine was not addictive, were key pieces of evidence that eventually would persuade the four to turn to Carter.

The question they had to answer was, Should Carter be held responsible for his smoking? They reread a key instruction from Judge Davis about Florida's consumer-friendly law, which says manufacturers have "the duty to possess expert knowledge" of the products they sell and to test them fully. By the afternoon of the second day, all six jurors had agreed that the company had failed its customers.

As an antidote to Wilner's case, the tobacco companies turned to another individual claim in Indiana, where a leftover from the Second Wave of litigation was coming to a close. On August 23, 1996, after sixteen hours of deliberation, a jury found four cigarette companies not responsible for the lung-cancer death of Richard Rogers, a fifty-two-year-old Indiana lawyer who had smoked two to three packs of cigarettes a day. The jury also rejected claims by his wife, Yvonne, that the four companies that had made the brands he smoked had sold a defective product. The companies hailed the verdict as confirmation that the Carter case was, in fact, an "aberration." Juries had not started to change their minds about the responsibilities of the smoker and the industry would continue to win in court.

But the two cases were strikingly different. Mrs. Rogers had claimed the companies had failed to warn of the health risks and addictive qualities of cigarettes. She sought $2 million in compensatory damages and an unspecified amount in punitive damages. There had been two Rogers trials. The first trial, in 1995, had ended in a hung jury.

Importantly, in the second trial, the judge limited the evidence to what had been admitted at the first; none of the new documents available in the Third Wave could be used. Indiana law was also less favorable to the consumer than Florida law. In Indiana, juries cannot rule for the plaintiff if they think the plaintiff bears more than 50 percent of the blame. Florida, as well as most other states, allows the victims damages even if they were 99 percent responsible for their own injuries. The jurors' comments after the trial suggested that Rogers would have won had it not been for the Indiana rule.

Even so, Chuck Wall, Philip Morris's senior vice president, claimed the verdict was the company's "most important victory to date dealing with the purported 'addictive' qualities of cigarettes." He added, "This unanimous verdict sends a clear signal that there is no legal groundswell in the American court system to reverse forty years of precedents that people are responsible for their own actions when it comes to tobacco use." RJR said the Rogers case showed that smokers could quit, if they wanted to. In its statement, Brown & Williamson declared, "The tide has not turned against the tobacco companies and common sense still prevails when it comes to these cases."

But evidence to the contrary was growing, and the skill and expertise of the antitobacco lawyers were expanding. In their statements, the tobacco companies had conveniently negelected to mention the Horowitz case in California. A year earlier, in August 1995, Milton Horowitz, a seventy-two-year-old university professor, clinical psychologist, and former smoker, had won $2 million in a California state court for his claim that his mesothelioma (a fatal form of lung cancer caused by crocidolite, or "blue" asbestos) had been the result of crocidolite in the Micronite filters of the Kent cigarettes he used to smoke. Lorillard, the makers of Kent, were held liable for $1.21 million and Hollingsworth & Vose, the makers of the filter, for the rest.

Woody Wilner was also the latest in a line of asbestos lawyers to join forces against tobacco. There was now a cadre of plaintiffs' lawyers across the nation armed with years of experience in lung medicine. They were well funded and knowledgeable. Among them were Dick Scruggs, Ron Motley, Walter Umphrey, John O'Quinn, and Madelyn Chaber (the plaintiff's lawyer in the Horowitz case).

If the juries hadn't changed, the caliber of the lawyers confronting tobacco certainly had; in the Carter case, Wilner had demonstrated that his courtroom style linked with his expert knowledge could give Big Tobacco a lot of trouble. He was able to talk to the jury in plain language about the often complicated science of the cigarette, tobacco smoke, and lung disease. Diana Temple, a stock analyst who had been following the tobacco industry for twenty years at Salomon Brothers, was at home ill during the trial and watched it on Court TV. She had thought the case would be another easy victory for the tobacco companies. But watching Wilner's irreverent style, she acknowledged, "I said to myself, 'My God, he makes the evidence more graphic. He could win eventually.' "

WILNER HAD TWO HUNDRED CASES to follow and if he had his way with the court, they would surface every other month, or so. The industry obviously had to be concerned about him, but there was not much they could do to stop the relentless march of Wilner's clients to the courthouse, and with them the possibility of more victories for the anti-tobacco forces. A large reason for Wilner's success is Wilner. He's a heavyset man with a high, domed forehead and receding bushy brown hair that hugs his ears. In the canine analogy favored by the plaintiffs' bar, Woody Wilner would be a St. Bernard; he appears solid and dependable. He also may be the only trial attorney who has an ounce of friendly humility, at least in public, and his outward appearance is anything but flashy. His partners joke about his suits, which they claim are off the peg and never cost more than $150 (he says they do cost more); his ties have a cheap, garish glare and they invariably clash with his socks. When *Esquire* magazine caught up with Wilner for a profile in the fall of '97, the joke was—his joke, actually—that in exchange for his time they had advised him where to buy clothes. The truth of the matter is that he has no interest in such things, which is certainly rare for his profession.

Until recently, he drove a battered '88 Ford van, but upgraded it to a newer model after his staff refused to ride with him anymore because the car had become so unreliable. His hobbies include in-line skating, rowing, and riding his pink bicycle. He is a licensed pilot, as was his mother back in the 1930s, but he does not own a plane, at least not yet. His mother lives down the street from him and at eighty-eight she sometimes flies with him. He is forty-eight, has never been in debt, even for a home mortgage, and perhaps because of it he radiates the confidence of the middle class, snug in an untouchable suburbia.

All this could suggest to someone who has not met him that Wilner is parochial; no match for the high-powered legal minds and maneuverings of the white-shoe law firms working for the tobacco companies. That image is not quite right.

Woody Wilner was born in Miami and went to Yale, where he received a degree in physics. He then worked for a year as a software programmer before deciding on law school at the University of Florida. When a reporter for *Barron's* asked why he didn't go to a better law school, Wilner replied, "My father had died by then. My mother didn't have a lot of money. It was cheap. And I guess it was also a combination of arrogance and naïveté. I figured if I became a lawyer, I'd be a very

good lawyer—and it wouldn't matter where I went to law school."
From his first, tedious paper-pushing job in a big Miami law firm,
Wilner was lured to Jacksonville by an older trial lawyer named Walter
"Bud" Robison, who had his own firm and one big case—representing
an asbestos company.

Robison died shortly after Wilner arrived and the young lawyer
took over the asbestos file. To make sure he was up to date on the
medical research into lung diseases, Wilner designed a computer program that contained all relevant scientific papers back to the turn of the
century. When he started with tobacco, he did the same thing with
nicotine and the carcinogens found in tobacco smoke.

Wilner may be the only trial lawyer involved in the tobacco cases
who can say polycyclic aromatic hydrocarbons or N-nitrosonornicotine
(a carcinogen found in smokeless tobacco) without a stumble. Even
though he had yet to try a case, he was soon in demand at trial lawyers'
conferences, giving his version of how to conduct an individual smoking case against Big Tobacco. His method is to divide the evidence into
palatable chunks, often opening like a college professor with the lines:
"We're going to spend a few minutes in the classroom looking at charts
and learning the meaning of some strange terms, and then we're going
to have some fun."

AFTER THE OPENING REMARK, Wilner invariably continues his case
with a grim-looking graph entitled "Cancer Death Rates: Males 1930–
1992." It plots rates of death per 100,000 people. Colon, prostate,
pancreas, esophagus, bladder, and liver cancers had remained roughly
the same, as had leukemia, which was somewhat lower than stomach
cancers, which had fallen gradually from 40 per 100,000 to under 10.
Lung cancers, by contrast, had shot up in a 45 degree line from under
10 to more than 70. "It's a serious matter," says Wilner. "It's not trivial
to say that people died to make this chart the way it is. It's catastrophic
and it belongs in your bedroom and your parlor. Meditate over it every
day; it's the only thing that looks like this in modern medicine. It's the
most extreme example of an epidemic unchecked, and further proof that
that [industry's] idea that we live in a cancer soup beneath a cancer

atmosphere and we eat cancer food is probably wrong. All other cancers maintain their balance, or are dropping, except lung cancer, which has gone out of control—for one reason."

Then the jurors see the document Wilner declares is the one that launched the conspiracy: "A Frank Statement to Smokers," the industry's famous 1954 promise—made after the crisis meeting of the tobacco chiefs at Manhattan's Plaza Hotel in December 1953—to find the truth about smoking and health and to always keep the health of the public in mind. But Wilner had a new angle. He had found a first draft of that report, which once included the sentence, "We will never produce and market a product shown to be the cause of any serious human ailment." *That* promise was left out of the final document—more evidence, says Wilner, of the industry's intention never to be concerned at any meaningful level with the public health.

To counter Wilner's focus during his trials on this pivotal period in tobacco history, when the industry could have taken a different course on so many key questions relating to smoking and health, Brown & Williamson produced what they hoped would be their secret weapon—a witness who would say there was no conspiracy and no deceit at the 1953 meeting. To his surprise, Wilner was put on notice by B&W to attend a deposition of a Dr. Irwin Tucker in the company's hometown of Louisville. In all his reading of tobacco industry history, Wilner had never heard of Dr. Tucker, who was eighty-two years old and, as it turned out, the last surviving senior member of the tobacco chiefs' 1953 meeting. At the time of the meeting, Dr. Tucker had just been appointed director of scientific research and made a member of the board.

Wilner objected to having to attend the deposition; he regarded it as a waste of time and money, as he complained to a local judge in Jacksonville. The judge said he had to go, but the company agreed that he could ask some questions of Dr. Tucker before the formal deposition. B&W were to wish they had never found Dr. Tucker.

ALTHOUGH THE DEPOSITION was organized by Brown & Williamson, attorneys for the other tobacco companies were in attendance—Philip Morris was represented by Shook, Hardy & Bacon, and R. J. Reynolds by Womble, Carlyle, Sandridge & Rice of their hometown, Winston-Salem.

First, Wilner established that Tucker's job as the company's director of research was to keep abreast of the scientific literature on cigarettes. He asked what kind of staff Dr. Tucker employed to help him evaluate the epidemiological evidence which was emerging at that time on smoking and cancer. Dr. Tucker, who was a chemist, replied that he had no medical doctor on his staff, no epidemiologist, and no statistician.

Q: So when papers on epidemiology and statistics were brought to your attention, what did you do?
A: Did the best I could.

Wilner asked if Tucker consulted the medical literature to establish whether B&W cigarettes were safe to smoke. Dr. Tucker replied, "Oh, seventy million people were using them."

Q: And how many were getting sick and dying?
A: A small fraction.
Q: Well, how many, sir?
A: I don't know specifically how many.
Q: No. All right, sir. How many people out of the seventy million would need to die before you would conclude that the product wasn't safe?
A: I would say better than 50 percent.

(Under cross-examination, Tucker later backed away, saying, "I think it would be very much less than 50 percent." But Wilner had already scored a bull's-eye.)

Asked what test B&W did to verify that its products were safe, Tucker said he consulted the historical records.

Q: Well, let's be a little more specific if we can. Do you— did you test, yourself, to determine whether the products were safe?
A: No, other than smoke them myself.

Q: So the scientific method that you were using was what? Would you describe for me the experiment?

A: We had a taste laboratory . . . in which people were put in a booth and given various samples to compare.

Q: So how would you determine whether that product was safe?

A: Well, if they were unsafe there might have been a reaction.

Apart from that, Tucker said, the company relied on consumers writing in to give their opinion of the cigarettes. There were no other tests.

The December crisis meeting had been called to consider the shocking results of Ernst Wynder's 1953 experiment that showed cigarette-smoke condensate caused tumors on the backs of mice. Dr. Tucker told Wilner that he had no scientific material that completely refuted the health charges being made—other than statistics showing the great many people who were long-term smokers who did not develop lung cancer.

Q: And did you regard that as proof that cigarettes did not cause lung cancer?

A: Yes.

The company made no effort, according to Tucker, to consult with medical doctors "as to whether that was a proper and valid scientific inference."

Asked whether he thought cigarettes caused cancer, Dr. Tucker said no. Asked what the causes of human lung cancer are, Dr. Tucker said, "I'd say the inhalation of very particular substances."

Q: Like what?
A: Like tar.
Q: Tar? What kind of tar?
A: From a bucket of boiling tar.
Q: Boiling tar?
A: Yeah. Being [the] kind that would be used on a roof.

Q: Okay. What do you base that on?

A: I believe there are incidences where industrial workers in the vicinity of asphalt and something like that have shown up with cancer.

At this point, Bill Hendricks, B&W's attorney from the Atlanta firm of King & Spalding, objected to what he called Wilner's "hectoring line of questions, where a question is asked, an answer is given, and then the answer is repeated back in an incredulous tone of voice." Hendricks said, "I think this has a harrassing effect on the client and should be discontinued, and I would move for the entire line of these questions and incredulous restatements of answers to be stricken."

The company's local attorney, Bob Parrish of Jacksonville, agreed. "It's also a violation of local rules in the Federal Court in the Middle District of Florida," he said. So Wilner asked the question again.

Q: You believe that boiling tar causes lung cancer in humans?

A: The vapors of boiling tar.

Finally, Wilner asked Tucker a trick question. Had he known, at the time of the December meeting, whether carcinogens had been identified in cigarette smoke? Tucker replied, "No, they had not been." Wilner then asked whether members of the R. J. Reynolds tobacco company had attended that meeting? Yes, they had, replied Tucker.

Wilner then produced the R. J. Reynolds scientific report entitled "Survey of Cancer Research with Emphasis Upon Possible Carcinogens from Tobacco," dated February 2, 1953, and written by Claude Teague, an RJR researcher. Wilner directed Tucker's attention to page 12 and a subtitle, "C. Carcinogens Identified in Tobacco Substances," and read the following sentence: "On the basis of the information at hand it would appear that polynuclear aromatic compounds occur in the pyrolytic [burned] products of tobacco. Benspyrene and 'N-benspyrene [sic],' both carcinogens, were identified in the distillates." Another sentence read, "On the basis of the information at hand it would appear that polynuclear aromatic compounds occur in the pyrolytic products of tobacco."

Q: Do you understand that sentence as a chemist?

A: Yes, go ahead.

Q: As of 1953, were you aware from any source [that] benzpyrene and N-benzpyrene had been identified in the distillate of tobacco smoke?

A: No.

Q: Did you know that [those compounds] were carcinogens?

A: Yes, I'd known them to be carcinogenic.

Q: And would it have been important for you to know in 1953, when the December meeting occurred at the Plaza Hotel, whether or not carcinogenic compounds had been identified in cigarette smoke?

A: Yes.

Q: And will you confirm for me, Dr. Tucker, that if such compounds had been identified in the laboratories of R. J. Reynolds Tobacco Company, that information was not shared with the personnel . . . in the meeting?

A: That's true.

Dr. Tucker was due to come back for more questions the next day, but B&W counsel announced that he would no longer be available. They said he was a sick man. Wilner was furious. He was having more fun than he had ever imagined possible with the witness—especially one supposed to be "friendly" to the enemy, and he wanted to continue.

Wilner considered Tucker's withdrawal outrageous and unethical. "You are not allowed to take a witness that has been subpoenaed, or appeared under agreement, and tell him he can leave," Wilner would say later. But he was not prepared for what happened next.

Through his office fax machine came doctors' letters from Louisville attesting that Dr. Tucker was indeed a sick man and should not complete the deposition. He had suffered a stroke in the early '80s, he was unsteady on his feet, there were disturbances in eye movements and muscle tone, and cognitive changes that "make his recollection of past events unreliable." One doctor wrote, "I think that any testimony that he might provide during a deposition or at the time of a trial would be suspect in reliability because of his advanced vascular disease secondary to, and including such factors as his underlying diabetes and hypertension." Another physician, in an affidavit prepared for the court, advised that Dr. Tucker's deposition should not be taken. If it was, then it should occur only under strict supervision. A medical "crash cart" with appropriate life-support equipment should be on hand at all times, with a certified "Advanced Cardiac Life Support" physician or technician in attendance. In any event, Dr. Tucker should be deposed for a maximum of two one-hour periods per day, with at least an hour and a half break between the two.

A weary Woody Wilner complained, "There are ways to terminate a deposition under the rules where you seek a protective order. None of that was done. The problem here is that the courts have to get over their feeling that just because these tobacco lawyers are highly paid doesn't mean to say that they're not unethical."

WILNER WOULD GO ON to lose his next trial in Jacksonville against R. J. Reynolds in the spring of 1997, but he had three others already lined up. By then, Wilner had become a phenomenon of the Third Wave, and his victory had given a big boost to secret negotiations for a truce opened up by Dick Scruggs and Mike Moore.

1 5

FIELD OF DREAMS

I believe in the field of dreams theory. If you build it, they
will come. Five billion dollars is an enormous amount of
money.

—Meyer Koplow, Philip Morris legal counsel on the
future of lawsuits after a settlement

OR ALL THEIR CRIES of betrayal over the Liggett deal, Philip
Morris and R. J. Reynolds were also anxious to settle their
lawsuits. Legal costs were skyrocketing. Shareholders were nervous and complaining. The army of corporate lawyers with expertise in
tobacco litigation was spread dangerously thin over the expanding bat-
tlefield. In the spring of 1996, R. J. Reynolds's CEO, Steven Goldstone,
gave an interview to *The Financial Times* of London that hinted at the
possibility of peace talks to reach a reasonable solution to the permanent lawsuits. "Why wouldn't the industry look at it?" he asked pro-
vocatively.

In Pascagoula, Mississippi, Goldstone's comment came just when
the antitobacco forces were beginning to strain their budgets. Dick
Scruggs had sunk more than $3 million of his small firm's money into
the Mississippi case and into lobbying other states to file Medicaid
suits. He was wondering how much this war would cost him. The joke
was that his Learjet was running on Southern mash. In Charleston, Ron
Motley and his document guerrillas were running up millions of dollars
in bills searching files from old court cases, and filing discovery motions
in states suing for Medicaid money. (In Texas, the private lawyers working for the state agreed to pay for the gas for Motley's plane.) In New

Orleans, the Castano group was facing nettlesome delays as they put "son of Castano" cases into the state courts. Both sides were looking for a deal.

In his war room in Pascagoula, Scruggs was working on a way to get the two sides together. He and Mike Moore discussed approaching Mississippi's Trent Lott to nudge the tobacco boys to the table. Lott was about to be elected Senate majority leader. He knew the tobacco industry and he had received a chunk of tobacco campaign money— $63,900 since arriving in Congress in 1973, even though Mississippi is not a tobacco-growing state. He also happened to be Dick Scruggs's brother-in-law. He could be the perfect link. On Capitol Hill, he was known as "Senator Smoothie," a deal maker rather than an ideologue. One of his favorite maxims was, "I'd rather have 80 percent of something than 100 percent of nothing."

Moore liked the idea and he gave Scruggs the go-ahead. He was still locked in combat with Governor Kirk Fordice over Mississippi's tobacco suit and, while he knew he would win out eventually since the law was on his side, Fordice (with the help of the industry) was dragging out the fight. Opening talks with the industry would be an insurance policy.

Scruggs made the call: "Do you think it's possible to pursue a resolution of the lawsuits through a national settlement sanctioned by Congress? And would you be interested?" Lott told Scruggs he would think about it.

Two days later he called back. He didn't want to be involved personally, he said, but he suggested that Scruggs should contact John Sears, a Republican lobbyist and international lawyer who had worked in the Nixon White House. Sears would be able to pass the idea on to the tobacco industry. Scruggs should also make use of Tommy Anderson, who had spent seventeen years working as Lott's chief of staff. He knew the industry well.

Scruggs immediately enlisted his chief legal theorists—Steve Bozeman, Charles Mikhail, and Lee Young, all veterans of the Mississippi Medicaid suit. This was not to become simply a settlement of the Mississippi lawsuit. Scruggs and Moore wanted nothing less than a blueprint for smoking and health for the next generation of Americans, a draft bill that could be sent up to Congress. It would be a new national tobacco-control policy that would completely change the way the tobacco companies did business.

The first draft was a two-page outline. No fancy legal language, just bullets. The Liggett settlement gave them a starting point. "We've got to cover kids, money, and immunity," Scruggs told his lawyers. "We knew the industry would not be interested in talking unless there was some kind of immunity from the lawsuits," said Mikhail, one of the drafters. Scruggs would take the drafts to Sears, who would pass them to Tommy Anderson, who in turn passed them to RJR's Goldstone. The message that came back was positive. "They made us think they were ready to talk," said Scruggs later.

The question was, Who were they? Was Goldstone speaking for the entire industry, or just RJR, or RJR and Philip Morris? That was never clear. Moore had settled Mississippi's case with Liggett; perhaps the next deal would be piecemeal as well. "We felt we were dealing with four different companies, Philip Morris, RJR, Brown & Williamson, and Lorillard," said Mikhail. "We thought that maybe we could do a deal with just two of them."

In July, a chance came to find out who really was on the other side of the table. Scruggs was invited to meet with the industry representatives. The idea was for them to explain their position. But he declined. "I thought we had a pretty good idea what the industry wanted. And I didn't think they would agree to our demands. I wanted them to acquiesce; I didn't want to be in a position of having to ask for their agreement."

While Scruggs was flying his Learjet between Pascagoula and Washington, Moore was putting together a committee of four attorneys general who would pursue the deal: Bob Butterworth of Florida, Scott Harshbarger of Massachusetts, Woods of Arizona, and himself. Moore, Butterworth, and Harshbarger had collaborated on the Medicaid suits from the beginning. They took part in what Harvard law professor Laurence Tribe called the "seminal" seminar on Medicaid suits that Tribe held in Cambridge in the summer of 1994. Mississippi had already filed. Florida had its special law. The discussion persuaded Massachusetts that the legal theory was viable. Woods came aboard later as the first Republican attorney general to file a Medicaid suit, in August 1996.

ON ONE of the trips to Washington, Scruggs and Moore went to see David Kessler at the FDA to try to discuss how the public health community would view such a deal. "We wanted to include everything Kessler wanted in the FDA ruling on tobacco," said Scruggs. Kessler suggested they get in touch with Matt Myers, who had been counsel to the Coalition on Smoking or Health but was then in a new job as vice president of Tobacco Free Kids, a group aimed at curbing underage smoking. Throughout the Third Wave, Myers, with his encyclopedic knowledge of the industry, had become the media spokesman for the public health community. Myers would often be at odds with those he was supposed to be representing and, in the end, would leave himself open to accusations of selling out to the industry.

By the beginning of August, the "term sheet," as Scruggs called his outline of a possible deal, was still "very rudimentary." Nonetheless, RJR and Philip Morris came back with an offer. Basically, they wanted full immunity from all future lawsuits for the next fifteen years and, although they would abide by most, if not all, of the FDA rules, they would *not* agree to its regulation of the industry. In return, they would pay out $150 billion over the next fifteen years to the states, the other class actions, and the individual lawsuits.

Scruggs's group was mulling over the offer at the beginning of August when Woody Wilner won his surprise victory in Jacksonville. Grady Carter's $750,000 award was another alarm bell for the industry, and Scruggs and Moore decided to act on it. They called a meeting in Chicago of the thirteen state attorneys general that had either filed or were about to file Medicaid lawsuits. The date set was for the weekend of the Democratic convention. But other forces were now at work.

On the eve of the meeting, *The Wall Street Journal* was leaked copies of the early drafts. "Someone in government did it," said Scruggs. "We had left a couple of drafts up there. It wasn't helpful." Scruggs was known for his Southern understatements, and this was one of them. The leak split the antitobacco forces down the middle—as Scruggs always knew it would. Most of the attorneys general were for the concept of the deal, but they wanted the rights of individuals to sue to be preserved. The plaintiffs' lawyers were in favor only if *their* ability to sue was preserved. Skip Humphrey, the attorney general of Minnesota, was an instant opponent. He had always been against any settlement (as had his legal team led by Mike Ciresi). Humphrey didn't see why the tobacco industry should be treated differently from any other business. He favored public trials over private deal making.

The health groups and the trial lawyers who were not involved in tobacco lawsuits were against the proposal. It sounded like tort reform to the lawyers. Key members of Congress also rejected it. For example, Henry Waxman called it a "sweetheart deal." Many were put off by the urgency of Scruggs and Moore, who mistakenly had begun to believe that there could be a deal before the November elections. "There's a tremendous amount of pressure for a quick fix," said Stan Glantz, an influential voice in the health community from his base at the University of San Francisco. (Glantz's book on the Merrell Williams documents, *The Cigarette Papers,* had just come out from his university's press.) As Glantz saw it, the only winners would be the trial lawyers. "These guys [the lawyers] will walk away from this just richer than God."

Officially, the tobacco companies claimed no knowledge of the proposal. RJR Nabisco said firmly, "Our tobacco subsidiary is not interested in—and has no intention of—settling cases against it and remains confident in the strength of its defenses." It was not true, of course. A spokesman for Goldstone admitted only to "the world's shortest conversation" with intermediary John Sears as a "favor to someone."

The August leak killed progress on the talks until after the elections. But the contacts had been made, and the two sides would continue to talk. Scruggs's phone call to Trent Lott had given rise to an idea that was to mature, slowly and often painfully, over the next year. By June 1997 there would be a proposal to restructure the commercial operations of the tobacco companies, end the culture of denial about the harmful effects of smoking, kill off Joe Camel and the Marlboro Man, and propose the costliest compensation and fines—$368.5 billion—in American business history.

THE WHITE HOUSE would play a pivotal role in the negotiations. Clinton had already been persuaded by Vice President Al Gore and then-presidential adviser Dick Morris to support the FDA's drive to curb teenage smoking. White House counsel Bruce Lindsey would co-ordinate the efforts. For its part, the industry longed for a change in the presidency, of course, and, for the first time, the Republicans were receiving by far the greatest share of tobacco money. In the past, the industry had been quite evenhanded with its funds, hedging bets be-tween the parties. In the 1988 congressional campaign, for example, it gave slightly more to Democratic political action committees and party organizations than to Republican coffers. But in 1990 the money began to shift. By the 1996 campaign, the Republicans received nearly $7.1 million, more than four times the Democrats' $1.6 million. In the Senate, the largest PAC contributions went to three Republicans, Jesse Helms of North Carolina ($57,250), John Warner of Virginia ($39,150), and Fred Thompson of Tennessee ($47,000). In the House, Thomas Bliley of Virginia received $34,675, Edward Whitfield of Ken-tucky $33,600, and Charlie Norwood of Georgia $33,500, all from tobacco-growing states. During nearly three decades in the U.S. Senate, Bob Dole had accepted more than $400,000 in tobacco-related cam-paign contributions. (At presidential campaign rallies, Democrat activ-ists plagued him with "Mr. Butts"—a supporter dressed up as a cigarette to look like the Gary Trudeau cartoon character.)

Al Gore, who had taken tobacco money when he was a senator from Tennessee and whose family had once grown tobacco, nevertheless be-came Clinton's point man against the industry, making an emotional speech at the Democratic convention in Chicago recalling his sister's death from lung cancer. On the campaign trail, he kept goading Dole to say whether nicotine was addictive. Dole ducked the issue—but then made one of the great bloopers of the campaign by suggesting that nicotine might be no worse for some people than milk.

In public, the industry would continue to deny any involvement in a deal for the next seven months, although Trent Lott's messengers, Sears and Anderson, were still busily acting as intermediaries between them and Scruggs. "This industry has no history of settling litigation," declared RJR's spokesperson, Peggy Carter. "We are certainly not go-ing to start with litigation that has no basis in fact," she added, repeat-ing the industry's view of the state Medicaid cases. Philip Morris was silent. Scruggs said, "The industry had to have deniability that we were talking. And I wanted it, too. We just did all our talking through John Sears."

Considering their unfamiliarity with the ways of Washington and Capitol Hill, the two Mississippi law-school buddies, Scruggs and Moore, would cut an extraordinary swath through the national political landscape. It did not turn out to be the instant "global settlement" the two bold architects of this grand compromise had once believed it could be, but from the days when the lonely plaintiff fought against impossible odds, it was a gigantic step forward. The "term sheet" would become a blueprint for a national policy to deal with the tobacco epidemic.

Scruggs and Moore would spend the next three months crisscrossing the country, drumming up support for the settlement among the other attorneys general, and picking up clients, at the same time. Wherever they went, Ron Motley would not be far behind (sometimes even in front) offering his services as co-counsel. He also went to state capitals that they didn't have time to visit. Scruggs would end up being co-counsel to twenty states besides Mississippi; Motley to thirty.

And the Castano lawyers would return to center stage. At first, Scruggs had purposely excluded the group; it was too unwieldy to have representatives in the initial discussions. But the wily Gauthier would make his own way to the negotiating table. The names on the guest list at the 1994 Antoine's Christmas dinner would reappear: Stan Chesley, Russ Herman, and John Coale. Elizabeth Cabraser, Professor Dick Daynard, and Dianne Castano, Peter's widow, would all surface in one way or another. And there would be yet another Gauthier surprise. Hugh Rodham, Hillary Clinton's brother and a Florida lawyer, would become the latest member of the Castano executive committee and provide the Castano group with special access to the White House.

DURING THE SUMMER, Tom Mellon, a personable young Castano attorney from Pennsylvania, had been working on a case in Florida with Hugh Rodham's law firm and had reported back to Gauthier that Rodham was interested in joining the Castano group. Gauthier was only too happy. "I felt that Dicky Scruggs had Trent Lott as his brother-in-law, so we one-upped him. I told him, 'Dicky, don't worry, we just out-brother-in-lawed you.' " Rodham, however, had a reputation for not making use of his family connections. He was in Florida and mostly stayed there. He had run for the state senate and lost. Rodham didn't know any of the Castano lawyers, so Gauthier gave Coale the job of introducing him. The two quickly became friends.

Coale recalls one September evening in New Orleans when the two of them were at the Bombay Club, waiting for Gauthier and some other Castano lawyers to turn up for dinner. "Wendell's never on time, so we were having fun," said Coale, "and we got to talking about what to do with all these lawsuits, and Hugh agreed he would talk to the president over Thanksgiving, the next time he was scheduled to see him for a family meal."

In the meantime, Coale concocted his own version of how to get negotiations moving—a plan that was bound to clash, sooner or later, with Scruggs's efforts. Coale put together a group of worthies—the "Three Wise Men," he would call them—to oversee the settlement proposals on behalf of the White House. He chose two former U.S. senators, Howard Baker, a Tennessee Republican whose first wife, Joy, died of lung cancer, and Howell Heflin of Alabama. Heflin had been a successful trial lawyer before being elected to the Senate in 1978 as a Democrat. He had a reputation as a details man on the Judiciary Committee. The third man was Leon Panetta, the departing White House chief of staff. Gauthier embraced the plan and made it part of the Castano group's approach, but before anything could come of the idea, word spread. Scruggs immediately called Gauthier, who was not in his office or at home.

Scruggs was told he was duck hunting on the Chesapeake Bay with his Louisiana buddies, Calvin Fayard and Mike St. Martin—*and* Tommy Boggs, a well-known Washington lobbyist for the tobacco industry. They were at a tobacco-industry playground called Tobacco Stick Lodge. Scruggs couldn't believe what he was hearing. What was Gauthier doing spending a weekend with Boggs?

According to Gauthier, Scruggs tracked them down at the lodge, finally getting through and announcing that he was flying in to join them. (According to Scruggs, he didn't "track down" Gauthier. "Wendell got word from the hunting lodge that I had been calling, and he called me back. I thought it was just typical Wendell.")

"But Dicky, you can't come down here, this is a social weekend," Gauthier told Scruggs. In fact, there were no "talks" with Boggs, but Gauthier mischievously left open the possibility there might have been.

Exasperated, Scruggs asked when Gauthier would be back in New Orleans. "Well, I'm getting home late on Sunday. How about Monday?" They agreed to meet.

The meeting was frosty. Scruggs asked Gauthier to drop Coale's "Three Wise Men" concept; the plan with Sears and Anderson had the cooperation of all the other parties and he didn't want to upset it. Gauthier held his ground; whatever Scruggs was doing would not interfere with what he was doing, and since he didn't know exactly what Scruggs was doing, he didn't see any point in stopping the Castano group's initiative. Scruggs quickly regrouped, suggesting that the two camps join forces. "It'll be fifty-fifty," Gauthier remembered him saying. "Dickie would swear to us a hundred times that it would be fifty-fifty and backed out of it every time," Gauthier said later.

Scruggs flew back to Pascagoula. Gauthier then set up a conference call that included John Coale. According to Coale, "The call got a little heated. Scruggs said the real problem he had with the Castano group was that the attorneys general didn't like the idea of joining forces with the Castano lawyers. They claimed their cases were stronger—and they had real, easily quantified Medicaid expenses to recoup. The Castano lawyers were only in it for the money. He mentioned Ciresi had said we were terrible people."

This time, it was Coale's turn to erupt. "That Ciresi. He's a good lawyer, but as a person he's a piece of shit," he recalled saying.

According to Coale, Scruggs also said he was under pressure from Trent Lott to come up with a deal. "The theory was that if they could come up with something that might be acceptable to the industry, they would ram it through Congress and it would be a done deal," said Coale. "I always thought that was extremely unrealistic because it doesn't happen like that in the real world, other agencies would have to be involved, the FDA, the health groups, and, of course, the White House."

NONETHELESS, from this point on the Castano team would be part of the secret talks. Relations between Scruggs, the attorneys general, and the Castano lawyers would always be tense, however. In one confrontation, the seemingly unflappable Scruggs would throw up his hands in despair and say, "We'll do this without you." But Coale claims he came to the rescue: "Don't walk, Dicky, we can sort it out. I'll deliver the boys." He talked Scruggs into keeping the team together, but to placate the Castano lawyers they had to stage a "reconciliation." Scruggs and Coale agreed that Moore would pretend to make a special trip to Florida to see Rodham and patch up the quarrel. They did meet but Moore was going anyway and the issue had been resolved beforehand. "The meeting was basically a showpiece," said Coale. But it worked. The team was back together again.

Over the next few weeks and into the new year of 1997, a small group—essentially Scruggs, Moore, Coale, Russ Herman (from New Orleans), and Rodham, and occasionally Matt Myers—met at the ANA hotel in Washington. Another draft was completed. The message via Sears was that the industry was now prepared to raise the ante—$250 billion over twenty-five years—plus make concessions on marketing and basically follow the FDA rules without FDA regulation. In return, they expected full immunity from lawsuits.

In February, Mike Moore went to the White House to meet Bruce Lindsey, who, as presidential counsel, had been assigned the role of presidential liaison. Coale and Rodham were there as well. Coale recalled that Moore was "very self-assured, like he is everywhere. He was shaking hands with everyone. He's a great politician."

Throughout the discussions there was no direct contact with the tobacco companies. Instead, R. J. Reynolds arranged for another message carrier: J. Philip Carlton, the son of a tobacco farmer, a country lawyer, and a close friend of the key tobacco state's governor, North Carolina's Jim Hunt. Carlton's appointment emphasized the increasing importance of contacts with the White House. He had helped run the gubernatorial campaign of Hargrove Bowles, father of President Clinton's chief of staff, Erskine Bowles. The dapper Carlton, with his natty suits and pocket handkerchief, would become a fixture in the negotiations and an important referee during the final stages of the talks. A further indication of the industry's increasing interest was the hiring of the influential Washington law firm of Liifert, Bernhard, McPherson and Hand to begin talking up the benefits of a settlement in Congress.

One of the firm's partners is George Mitchell, the former Maine senator and Democratic majority leader.

In March, the enterprise received an added boost from the second Liggett settlement. At first, Scruggs had doubts about making a second deal with LeBow. He simply didn't think that the "privileged documents" that LeBow was now offering in return for a broader settlement could be as important as LeBow, and others, said they were. Like Gauthier, Scruggs felt there was already enough evidence against the industry. As he had said when he first looked at the Merrell Williams documents, "These guys are toast." (As it turned out, Scruggs and Gauthier were right; the documents that were released, at least initially, did not add much to the weight of evidence.)

But Scruggs's real concern was that Philip Morris and RJR would hear about the new negotiations with LeBow and that would affect his settlement talks. "I thought it would crater my discussions," is how he would put it, using a bomber pilot's term for wrecking an airfield runway. But finally, Scruggs gave in: "We decided, in the end, it was a good insurance policy that really had no downside. LeBow was willing to produce these documents; so what if they're not great? He's not getting much out of it—except a promise for not being burned during a national settlement." That clause would come back to haunt LeBow and Scruggs. Essentially, LeBow wanted to make sure that in any national settlement, his tiny Liggett company would not have to pay more than he had agreed in his own settlement. Otherwise, his company would simply go bust. The clause in the second Liggett deal said the attorneys general would make their "best efforts" to ensure Liggett was not harmed. It didn't quite turn out that way—at least as far as LeBow was concerned. But far from hindering Scruggs's talks, the Liggett deal actually spurred them on. "It raised the level of the debate and energized Governor Hunt to get onto the White House and the president and get things moving," Scruggs said later.

THOSE BEHIND-THE-SCENES TALKS between Scruggs, Moore, and the Castano team were about to take a decisive turn. The Castano lawyers had always been edgy about Scruggs's control of contacts with the industry through Sears. They had suggested direct talks with the industry, but Scruggs would not hear of such a thing. All along he had insisted on no direct talks; he did not want to be in a position of asking the industry for its agreement. He preferred to keep sending them his "term sheets" and getting their reaction. His idea was that once the draft of the proposal was in good enough shape to become a bill, it should be sent directly to Congress.

But before anything went to Congress it had to be approved by the White House, and the president wanted the two sides to meet. Backed by the White House, the Castano group started to insist on meeting directly with the CEOs—to show good faith. Still, Scruggs wouldn't budge. "Scruggs always thought he could get this thing done next week—I suppose through his brother-in-law," said Coale, "but if Bruce Lindsey told me we had to have direct talks with the industry, then we had to have direct talks. There was no choice. We spent two weeks trying to convince Scruggs and Moore."

Phil Carlton also tried to persuade Moore to accept direct talks, but he said no as well. At one point, Carlton even suggested to Lindsey that if Moore couldn't accept the talks, then he should be bypassed and they should look for another leader of the attorneys general. "There are plenty of other AGs who will come if we arrange it," he said. Coale, who happened to be in Lindsey's office at the time of the call, objected. Moore was the obvious, and only real leader of the attorneys general group and should not be cast aside, under any circumstances.

Finally, at the end of March, Moore agreed—on two conditions. Goldstone of RJR and Geoffrey Bible of Philip Morris had to attend the first meeting. The meeting was set for April 3. George Mitchell personally called Matt Myers to invite him to attend; the White House said he was "an essential player." Myers agreed.

BY ACCEPTING THIS DANCE with the devil, Myers had put himself in a position of inevitable compromise. From that moment, Myers became the official negotiator for the health groups and would always claim that he had the "confidential" backing of the heart and lung associations. For a man who had once described industry leaders as lacking a "moral gyroscope," it was not an obvious transition—especially since he had also been one of the harshest critics of earlier efforts to produce a settlement. Myers had told friends in the antitobacco movement that he was worried a deal now would be selling out to the companies—and, worse still, he said, that Scruggs had no idea what he was giving away. "Why should the tobacco industry be immune, given the harm they've caused?" Myers had asked then. Through the end of 1996 and the beginning of 1997, Myers was telling the White House not to be involved in a settlement—and then boasting to his colleagues about it. Suddenly, there was a pirouette.

Myers's version is that the White House asked him to join the talks simply because he was the toughest critic. President Clinton's people said they would have nothing to do with the deal unless he was at the table. Some of his friends found this disingenuous. "So, why didn't he say no, not unless I have ten of my guys with me and there are free and open communications?" asked one of them. "What happened next was the original smoke-filled room and the negotiations proceeded on the understanding that Myers didn't get to talk to anyone, but the tobacco people got to talk to anyone they wanted to," said Dick Daynard.

"Anybody who had studied the public health agenda would have felt compelled to listen," Myers would say later, adding that not a day would go by when he didn't "reevaluate his position and swallow another dose of Maalox." Myers would have one important supporter among the antitobacco forces: Michael Pertschuk, who had worked with Myers at the FTC and had been an antitobacco activist ever since. Pertschuk thought the arrangement worked well. "It's the perfect inside-outside strategy," he said. "While Matt is at the table, the health community is free to say: 'We weren't at the table. Either you add these critical elements, or we walk.'" In effect, it gave them two chances to present their views.

If he was upset about what he was doing, Myers didn't show it. Quite the contrary, he seemed to relish his privileged access. Myers had always liked being a Washington insider—and he was good at it. "He was not a believer that there was wisdom in the grass roots, among the great unwashed outside the Beltway, and the industry played to that weakness," said one veteran antitobacco activist who had come reluctantly to the conclusion that Myers had eventually sold out.

ONCE THE PLAYERS had been identified, the question was where to hold the meeting.

Gauthier insisted it should be in New Orleans. This was where the first lawsuit of the Third Wave had been filed; this was where the sixty plaintiffs' lawyers had come together to launch a common attack on the industry. Phil Carlton, speaking for the industry, was ready to agree to New Orleans, but Scruggs and the other AGs wouldn't allow it. They wanted neutral territory, preferably Washington, a place known for its deals and historic compromises. In the end, they settled for a hotel in Crystal City, Virginia, a severe, unattractive pocket of concrete offices and hotels across the Potomac from Washington and a virtual append-age of the capital's National Airport. Goldstone and Bible liked the idea because they could fly in on corporate jets and out again as quickly as possible. This was, after all, only a ceremonial appearance.

The hotel room had a square table around which sat attorneys gen-eral from six states, including Mike Moore, Grant Woods of Arizona, Bob Butterworth of Florida, and a latecomer, Christine Gregoire of Washington state. Scruggs was with Moore, as always. Coale, Herman, Rodham, and Stan Chesley led the Castano group. Matt Myers sat on his own. On the industry side, Goldstone and Bible were accompanied by their lead lawyers: Herbert Wachtel, who represented Philip Morris and had led the company's $10 billion libel case against ABC News, and Arthur Golden, of the New York firm of Davis, Polk & Wardwell, represented RJR. "I had to pinch myself—twice," remembered Coale. "First because I was sitting down with the enemy, and second because this was a long way for me from drunk-driving cases in the D.C. courthouse. I think anyone who was honest with themselves had similar thoughts. It was bizarre."

George Mitchell opened the meeting, and short speeches by Gold-stone and Bible followed. They pledged to bring fundamental change to the industry's operations and promised to discuss advertising, FDA jurisdiction, financing for antismoking programs, and tight controls on youth access to tobacco. It was mostly ceremonial, according to those present, but Mike Moore warned them that he expected results. "Don't waste my time," he said defiantly.

After two hours, other sessions were arranged and the meeting broke up. The negotiations became a ten-week marathon of hectic shut-tling between Chicago, Dallas, New York, and Washington. They would be intense and exhausting, each side threatening on several occa-sions to walk out.

Even so, Bible and Goldstone would be hailed as the new breed of tobacco "deal makers," realists who were finally prepared to admit the dangerous nature of cigarettes and take action to stop them from ravag-ing the public health, especially the health of American youth. But what the industry sought was financial stability. During the company's annual meeting in Richmond, Virginia, Bible of Philip Morris had met with a group of investors and had confirmed what the companies al-ready knew: they were very upset about the fits and starts in tobacco stocks over the past two years. While increasing steadily, stock prices had reacted violently to each news item about Third Wave lawsuits. The shareholders were especially shocked at the $12 billion drop in value of the company's shares a few hours after the Grady Carter verdict in Jacksonville the previous August. More recently, each time word of a settlement leaked, cigarette stocks jumped. The industry could no longer ignore investor demand for the financial stability that a settle-ment would, in theory, bring—regardless of the price that had to be paid. Between August 1996 and May 1997, Philip Morris shares had increased over 60 percent. In the same period, BAT jumped 39 percent and RJR 43 percent. Even in a raging bull market, these figures were extraordinary. For the companies, there would be no turning back.

The talks were now on a more urgent footing—especially after some details of the April 3 meeting appeared in *The Wall Street Journal*. As the negotiators returned to the table, this time in Chicago, the pressure of the lawsuits was mounting on the industry. Courts were disallowing standard tobacco defenses and permitting the new legal theories behind the Medicaid suits to go ahead. In Pascagoula, the judge in Missis-sippi's suit rejected the industry's ghoulish "death benefits" defense, which claimed an "offset" for smokers dying early. Antitobacco forces continued to uncover embarrassing documents and were even begin-ning to break down the protective layers of legal privilege that had kept the truth about the tobacco enterprise from public view for so long.

By the end of April, the first Castano class action was certified in a state court in Louisiana. But the big shock for the companies was Judge

Osteen's ruling in North Carolina: the Food and Drug Administration, he found, did indeed have the power to regulate tobacco as a drug. Despite his tobacco connections, Judge Osteen rejected the industry's arguments opposing FDA jurisdiction. He did, however, rule that the agency could not impose controls on tobacco advertising. His decision was based solely on the scope of the Food, Drug, and Cosmetic Act, which does not mention advertising controls, and not on whether the First Amendment permitted such controls.

The ruling was an unexpected triumph for the antitobacco forces. There was "no need for deals" with the industry now, said David Kessler. The FDA could do it all—and the government would fight the advertising exception. For its part, the industry focused on the judge's denial of advertising controls, but tobacco stocks dropped sharply. Big Tobacco immediately filed an appeal.

Two weeks later, the industry had some good news. R. J. Reynolds won the second of the individual smoking cases being steered through the courts by Florida's Woody Wilner. After a month-long trial in the same courthouse in Jacksonville where Grady Carter had won $750,000 the previous August, Woody Wilner lost the Jean Connor case. The jury found R. J. Reynolds not responsible for the lung-cancer death of Ms. Connor, who had died at age forty-nine in 1995. Her claim had been continued by her sister, Dana Raulerson, and her three adult children. Although Ron Motley was co-counsel with Wilner, they couldn't pull off a second win—largely due, it emerged later, to the judge's severely restrictive instructions to the jury.

The jurors had been told to absolve Reynolds if they found the risks of smoking were "commonly known." In contrast to Brown & Williamson at the Grady trial, RJR produced an in-house scientist to show the company did its own safety research, and an historian to help persuade the jury that Ms. Connor had access to "common knowledge" of the risks of smoking. In a videotape deposition made before her death, Connor herself said that she generally understood the health risks of smoking, but smoked three packs a day of Winston and Salem brands for twenty years. Even worse, she admitted to the same camera that she had managed to stop only after her doctor insisted on it before she had a tummy tuck.

Woody Wilner vowed to keep going, predicting that he would win

50 percent of the other cases on his long list. The tobacco companies jeered: loss of the Connor case had shown the Grady case to be the "aberration" Philip Morris had said it was at the time.

THE NEGOTIATIONS RESUMED on May 6 at the law offices of Jones, Day in Dallas. Mike Moore reported that Matt Myers had been endorsed as the public-health group representative and would be working with Lonnie Bristow, ex-president of the American Medical Association. Meyer Koplow, a pudgy, amiable New Yorker from the law firm of Wachtel, Lipton, Rosen & Katz, led the discussions for the industry, in general, though he was retained by Philip Morris. He opened the session by saying the "ball is in our court" and restating the industry's goal—an end to the legal warfare. Big Tobacco wanted to settle all lawsuits. He reaffirmed that the industry had agreed on "fundamental changes" in the way it did business, particularly with regard to young smokers. Then he reviewed earlier preliminary agreements. It was an impressive-sounding list. It included proposed FDA rules, full disclosure of ingredients with food-type labeling, toxicology testing for non-tobacco and tobacco ingredients, stronger warning labels, elimination of all outdoor advertising, scrapping Joe Camel and the Marlboro Man, an end to brand sponsorship of events, and total elimination of vending machines. The industry was prepared to submit to manufacturing oversight with "real teeth," disclose smoking and health reports, move toward production of safer tobacco products, and accept penalties if youth smoking did not decline—the "look-back" provisions.

Essentially there were still four issues to discuss: the package of health-oriented reforms, the fund for compensating the states and Castano, the legal immunity, and the attorneys' fees. The talks had gotten off to a rocky start on the money package. At one point, the Castano group discovered that the attorneys general had been talking privately about money to the Wachtel lawyers. Coale boiled over at this side action. "I totally lost it," he said. "I said they were fucking rude, sneaking around like geeks in the night. Everyone had their eyes bulging out. They thought I had gone completely round the bend. Steve Berman [a lawyer from Seattle who represented several states] got up from the table and walked towards me. 'One more step and I'll fucking kill you,' I said. Then Moore said he had heard one 'fuck' too many and said he was not going to stand for such language in front of the women—there were one or two—and he walked out. Scruggs told me to get out with him. Stan Chesley loved it. Bob Redfearn [another Castano lawyer, this one from New Orleans] was mortified, and Hugh Rodham could see his life flashing by. They all came back in eventually and I apologized to Scruggs and Moore and then to the ladies, and it was over."

There were also some bright moments. Almost from the beginning, the companies had accepted all FDA controls, and they had agreed to controls on advertising. But they still insisted that the FDA should not *regulate* nicotine. Such a move would mean that the industry could be regulated out of existence if a future FDA decided to reduce nicotine content below the level at which smokers found satisfaction. Myers had proposed the ingenious "look-back" provision that would penalize the industry if it did not reduce smoking by young people—the next generation of smokers—by a progressive percentage each year. The fines were appealing, but not a substitute for FDA control.

The industry was now prepared to up its offer to $300 billion over twenty-five years. Gauthier recalled, "Russ [Herman] came back and said they had started at $250 billion, but I told him to go back and ask for more," said Gauthier. "I know $250 billion is more than I had ever imagined but if one day I found out that we had agreed to a $100 billion less than the companies had calculated they could spend it would make me sick, so I told Russ to keep pushing until they're about to walk away."

The money would go to the states for Medicaid expenses, to fund countermarketing measures and advertisements through the Department of Health and Human Services and the FDA, and to fund smoking "cessation" programs among the Castano class action. It would also provide money for damage claims from individuals.

The basic method of distribution of the money had been agreed upon earlier at a small meeting of industry lawyers and Scruggs, Moore, and two other attorneys general (Grant Woods and Richard Blumenthal), and Gauthier, who was the only representative from Castano. It was held in Pascagoula so that Gauthier could get there and back in a day from New Orleans because he was undergoing chemotherapy treatment for colon cancer. Settling the state cases was relatively simple; each was asking for a given amount to cover Medicaid expenses. The Castano class action covering all addicted smokers included tens of millions of smokers—at least 400,000 of whom die each year, according to government statistics. Gauthier recalled, "When we started calculating what it would take to compensate for the deaths alone, not to mention the injuries if we won, there wasn't enough money in the world. Just to cover the deaths at, say, $30,000 each would come to more than $12 billion a year. Everybody said, 'Jesus.' "

Woods and Blumenthal did not want any class-action settlements that would just hand over money to putative class members who had not litigated their claims. It was agreed that Castano class members would receive what they called "common benefits"—money to put them into smoking-cessation programs—which was Gauthier's original idea for the Castano suit. But Gauthier wasn't going to let the industry totally off the hook and demanded that future individual cases ought to be allowed. From there the group developed the concept of an annual fund, to come out of the $300 billion, to pay for individual lawsuits.

The industry's immunity was the most hotly disputed issue. Having conceded that individual claims would continue, they wanted no more class actions, or even "aggregation," a cluster of a small number of suits. They wanted a cap of $250,000 compensation on individual suits—and an end to punitive or exemplary damages. They insisted that all claims should be limited to fraud only—the most difficult case to prove. They wanted their old defense of assumption of risk preserved, especially since they were ready to admit in labels on cigarette packs that smoking *does* cause cancer and that nicotine *is* addictive. They wanted liability limited to manufacturers only, a demand that hit at the heart of the trial lawyers' strategy of pursuing all parties that had contributed, however distantly, to the injury caused, including retail distributors, insurance companies, tobacco-stock analysts, lawyers who had concealed evidence, and scientists who had skewed scientific reports. Specifically, the industry wanted to make certain the immunity extended to their food divisions and their many law firms.

Essentially, the industry wanted future cases to be too unattractive to bring into court for smokers and their lawyers. Neither the Castano group nor the AGs would agree to the terms. To the Castano trial lawyers it smelled of tort reform—something that threatened their entire livelihood. To the AGs it sounded like permanent political baggage, with the possibility that they would be branded forever as the ones who let a rogue industry off the hook. Scruggs, the top negotiator for the plaintiffs, and Moore, the leader of the AGs, said they would walk from the negotiations if there were caps on individual suits.

Later, in a private meeting with the tobacco lawyers, the Castano group suggested a compromise: raise the $250,000 cap to $1 million per case and they would agree to the industry's demand for no punitive damages. As the industry was providing a "fund" to pay for lawsuits (it would turn out to be $5 billion), it was a reasonable incentive to bring cases, and a ban on punitive damages would prevent one plaintiff from taking the entire purse, or a substantial part of it. As Gauthier said later, "I didn't want one guy hitting the whole fund for the entire $5 billion."

Moore asked for time to discuss the issue in a conference call with the other AGs. The next day, he reported that they were prepared to accept that no more than $1 million would be paid on an award in any one year, but, if the award was bigger it would be paid out of the next year's fund, at a million dollars a time. The industry agreed. The AGs also would accept a ban on class actions, but wanted the possibility of "aggregating" a small number of cases—up to fifteen. However, the ban on punitive damages, the kind of awards that often make the difference between a plaintiff's lawyer breaking even or making a profit, was a deal breaker. As elected officials, the AGs did not want to be party to curbing the rights of the tort lawyers. They saw it as unacceptable political baggage. There was "zero room to move," Moore reported.

At that point, Scruggs, who normally seemed so much under control, snapped. It wasn't that he was against lawyers suing big companies; he basically thought the legal system had been so unrewarding to smokers in the past that it was better to deal with the problem through a compensation board—like miners with black lung disease. "In that case the victims would get their money instead of having to hire a lawyer and roll the dice in court," he would say later. But if there was to be future litigation against the industry, he supported Gauthier; a ban on punitives would result in a more equitable distribution of the pot. The restrictions would insure the ability of all future victims to recover and not just the first in line.

Too few of the AGs could agree. Moore had insisted that they approve any deal with a 90 percent majority. The issue dragged on beyond Scruggs's patience. He shut himself in his hotel room and wouldn't come out. "He was in a rage," said Coale. "I tried to talk to him, saying that the world was looking at us now and they wanted the deal—we knew that from the polls—but he refused to come out of his room." "There are too many cooks in the kitchen," said Scruggs and he flew home. The talks were suspended for four days.

THE LOW POINT of the negotiations came, according to Scruggs, when the talks resumed in New York on May 12. This time it was Moore's turn to quit the talks. The industry wanted a two-tier system of liability: one for past misconduct and another for future claims. It was a complicated arrangement in which a person suing in the future would have to conform to certain restrictions. "We had fine-tuned it for weeks and then we had to tell the companies we couldn't sell it to the AGs; it's too complicated, we can't explain it," said Scruggs. Coale said, "I didn't know whether the tobacco lawyers could withstand the heat from their clients after the about-face." Moore left town, saying the public-health gains were now in jeopardy. But the talks resumed a few days later. The AGs dropped their demand on keeping punitive damages after an inventive compromise came from Bruce Lindsey at the White House. He suggested raising the $300 billion total payment by a "punitive sum" of a further $50 billion, which could be considered as a one-time punishment. It gave the AGs the political out they needed.

That settled, the last issue was the lawyers' fees. This matter had been deliberately left to the end because a struggle was inevitable—and none of the negotiators wanted the media to focus on it. The Castano group pushed for an equal division between themselves and the lawyers representing the states. The states felt that they had the stronger cases, with the prospect of bigger awards, and so they should command a larger percentage. Florida state attorneys insisted that their case was the most viable—because of the state law—and that fact should be recognized. Castano lawyers balked, insisting on the fifty-fifty split. If that was unacceptable they threatened to negotiate directly with the tobacco companies.

Some lawyers representing the states were retained on a fixed percentage, ranging from 13 to 25 percent of whatever the state was awarded. Others, like Scruggs in Mississippi, had deferred to whatever the judge in the case would allow. For Motley and Scruggs, who represented several states, the stakes were high. They stood to make fortunes.

The lawyers could only agree on one thing: keep the fees out of the public eye, or that would be all the media would talk about. Already, some journalists were speculating on 3 percent or a $3 billion total payout, or $360 million a year. The plan was to negotiate fees separately with the industry so that it was not part of the legislative package in Congress.

The industry wanted a cap on fees, but Castano and the AGs protested and that was quickly dropped. At a private session in New York on May 20, the Castano group met with Scruggs, who proposed a total pot of $6 to $8 billion with the creation of a fees "czar" to divide up the money. When the agreement was signed on June 20, the matter had still not been settled.

THROUGHOUT, the negotiators were under a time constraint. The talks had to end before June 20 or Mike Moore would have to go to trial in Mississippi. The state case opened on July 7. By the beginning of June, however, the tobacco companies themselves suddenly appeared to be in disarray. Martin Broughton, the chief executive of BAT in London, was apparently upset that the U.S. companies had not insisted on total immunity for the future and he was worried they might be pressured into allowing punitive damages. BAT's problem was that Brown & Williamson looked especially vulnerable if punitives were allowed because of the Merrell Williams papers and Jeffrey Wigand's testimony. For Broughton to participate at this late stage was somewhat odd given that BAT had been claiming in court that it was so far removed from its wholly owned Kentucky subsidiary, B&W, as to have no day-to-day control over operations. Clearly, this was an emergency; one that required a stern and steady hand. In a seven-hour meeting at Philip Morris's Park Avenue headquarters in New York, the fifty-year-old

Broughton, an accountant by training, voiced his strong views about America's "naive and parochial" attitude toward smoking and made his pitch for a tougher stance.

But the momentum was now too great; both sides wanted to bring the deal to a close. The negotiations were finally concluded in Washington after a hectic week in which the two sides shuttled back and forth between the Park Hyatt and the ANA hotels, working into the night and getting up before dawn. Last minute changes were overseen by the two referees sent by the tobacco industry, former Texas governor Ann Richards, in her silver beehive hairdo, and the courtly Phil Carlton, in pink striped shirt, electric-blue tie, and a handkerchief in his top pocket. Whenever called upon, they poured Southern charm over the troubled negotiators. As the participants emerged from their meetings ever more rumpled, it was clear the talks would continue right down to the June 20 deadline set by Mike Moore as the outside date when he had to leave the negotiations to prepare himself for his state's trial.

At 3:30 P.M. on Friday, June 20, a small group of AGs, led by Moore, filed into a ballroom at the ANA and announced the completion of "the most historic public health achievement in history." The emotional Mr. Moore said that every day he had worked on the proposal he had been thinking of what it would mean to his ten-year-old son, Kyle, and his generation of potential nicotine addicts. Moore was hailed as an American hero by his attorney general colleagues, several of whom flanked him on the podium. They included Dennis Vacco of New York, Bob Butterworth of Florida, Christine Gregoire of Washington state, Richard Blumenthal of Connecticut, Grant Woods of Arizona, and Jeffrey Modisett of Indiana.

Butterworth had the sound bite of the day. "The Marlboro Man will be riding into the sunset on Joe Camel," he said. The Massachusetts AG, Scott Harshbarger, suggested that "only the major discovery of vaccines could rival what this proposal promises to accomplish."

There was a feeling of unreality, as there had been throughout the talks. After four decades of denial about smoking and disease, would this industry really agree to take down their glamorous advertisements and stamp all future products with the label "Smoking Can Kill You," as the proposals demanded? And would child smoking be reduced by 60 percent in ten years? And would the industry pay out a staggering

$368 billion dollars to the states and to victims of tobacco? Perhaps Mike Moore and the tobacco industry CEOs would one day share the Nobel Prize for Health.

Connecticut's Richard Blumenthal brought the event closer to earth when he said, "We've left more undone than we accomplished. . . . We've shackled and caged a beast, but we haven't conquered it."

Steve Parrish of Philip Morris followed the AGs with a short statement in which he described the agreement as a "bitter pill." Accomplished as he was at presenting the company line, even Parrish stumbled. There were aspects of the agreement, he said, "with which we disagree," but then, quickly realizing the absurdity of such language, he corrected himself: "with which we do not necessarily agree." The industry looked forward to a "new era of tolerance with regard to tobacco," he said curtly and promptly left the podium.

And that was that. There was no ticker-tape parade. Only critics— by the score. They would pronounce that at various levels Scruggs and Co. had been hoodwinked, deceived, and outmaneuvered by a smarter enemy. Matt Myers would be branded by his own antismoking crusaders as a "sellout" and an appeaser.

Moore was shocked at the reception. Two months later he would say bitterly, "Probably, I didn't expect so much sniping. But others want to own a piece; the congressmen and the senators. As time goes by, they'll change a few things and call it their own."

BECAUSE THE DEAL had been negotiated behind closed doors and in a hurry, the actual piece of paper produced was a hastily typed draft lacking even the scantiest of peer reviews. The final clause slipped in at the last minute by Scruggs was an amnesty for Jeffrey Wigand and all other whistle-blowers, but even that was so ambiguously worded as to not be clear whether it included the first great whistle-blower, Merrell Williams. Scruggs assured Williams that it did. The sometimes confusing language caused everyone in authority, from President Clinton down, to greet the document with caution. David Kessler was the first to use the phrase, "The devil is in the details." He was followed by the former Surgeon General C. Everett Koop, who quickly branded its regulatory clauses as "woefully inadequate" and "deeply flawed." And the public health groups, which had supposedly been represented by the hapless Matt Myers, declared the provision that did not allow immediate regulation by the FDA as "absolutely unacceptable." Skip Humphrey, who had boycotted the talks all along, refused to sign the deal, calling it a "Trojan Camel." It was "inherently flawed" because it answered the wrong question. "The negotiators had asked, 'How much regulation will this industry accept?' But the real question was, Is this good for America?" he said.

EVEN SO, there had been remarkable gains for the public health, and it could certainly be argued that if implemented, the proposed agreement would do more for the nation's health than all of the lawsuits combined—as Mike Moore proclaimed. Under the deal, the industry would pay a total of $368.5 billion; $10 billion in the first year, of which $7 billion would go to the states and $3 billion to the federal Department of Health and Human Services to fund a smoking-cessation campaign, enforce a ban on sales to minors, and set up a compensation fund for smokers who win court cases. Thereafter, the industry would pay $8.5 billion rising to $15 billion annually in perpetuity. The figure of $368.5 billion covered the first twenty-five years.

This sounded like a tremendous amount of money—and it was the largest proposed industry payout in history. The annual payments were comparable with the gross domestic product of small- to medium-sized developing countries (Mozambique $10.6 billion, El Salvador $9.8 billion, Uganda $16.2 billion). But the stunning fact was that the industry could easily afford it, testimony to the "cash cow" that cigarettes had been for more than a century. A mere fifty cents on a pack of cigarettes, then at $1.80, would pay for roughly half the punishment, and the rest was tax deductible—a business expense. (By contrast, a punitive-damage award cannot be set against taxes.) According to market surveys, such a price hike would reduce consumption by only 10 percent. So the burden would fall mainly on the poor, addicted smoker.

Critics focused on two points. First, the industry escaped FDA regulation that would be available, in theory, now that Judge Osteen had found the agency did have authority over tobacco. Second was the question of whether the tort system had been violated by granting even partial immunity.

On the public health side, Matt Myers was quick to point to the extra advertising controls in the deal that would not be available under Judge Osteen's ruling. Among Myers's examples were a ban on all cigarette vending machines instead of only those to which children had access, putting cigarettes out of reach of buyers in retail stores, funds to enforce such measures, elimination of all billboard ads by consent decrees (to overcome First Amendment objections), an end to more "product placement" of cigarettes in movies and on TV, an end to calling some cigarettes "light" and suggesting they are healthier than other brands, and an end to the Marlboro Man, Joe Camel, and any other human and romantic images the advertisers might dream up. Health warnings would follow the Canadian government pattern, minus the ambiguities. They would say cigarettes "are addictive" and "cause cancer." The "look-back" provision would require the companies to reduce underage smoking by 30 percent in five years, 50 percent in seven years, and 60 percent in ten years. If they failed they would pay a fine—they preferred to call it a "surcharge"—of $80 million per percentage point, up to a maximum of $2 billion a year.

BUT DAVID KESSLER and C. Everett Koop refused to accept Myers's explanation. If Kessler thought anything positive had been achieved, he was very good at hiding it, and his disdain for Myers was made plain in several media confrontations immediately after the announcement. Kessler's anger was hardly surprising. The agreement had, in fact, whittled down FDA authority to regulate nicotine—which was his personal crusade of the past five years that had culminated with Judge Osteen's stunning decision in April.

The agreement prevented the FDA from regulating nicotine levels in cigarettes for at least twelve years. And it placed two extra burdens on the agency. First, the FDA would have to create a scientific advisory board to study nicotine and health issues. But the FDA has its own scientists, whose recommendations can always be challenged in court or rejected by Congress. The second provision was even more intrusive.

Before reducing nicotine levels, the FDA would have to show, with substantial evidence, that such a move would result in a significant reduction of the health risks associated with smoking, and would not create a black market for cigarettes with a higher nicotine level. "How could the FDA prove a negative?" asked Koop.

The proposal would reduce the burden of proof after twelve years to a "preponderance of evidence," but the tobacco industry would remain a privileged business, above the law. Normally, the FDA only has to show that it has not acted "arbitrarily or capriciously" in making a new rule. The prospect loomed of the tobacco industry's legal armies once again tying up FDA challenges in court.

At the request of a bipartisan group of congressmen led by Henry Waxman, Kessler and Koop formed a blue-ribbon advisory committee on tobacco policy and public health to study the proposals. In the wake of the agreement, they released their own report, recommending the restoration of the FDA's full authority and dropping the arbitrary twelve-year deferral and the industry-imposed standards of proof. The report had immediate support among health groups.

The American Lung Association attacked the advertising provisions of the agreement—the very section that Matt Myers had claimed as a substantial victory. But the lung association saw it otherwise. They complained that the restrictions as written were "a mere inconvenience" to the industry and still allowed powerful images in ads that could portray the romance of smoking. They pointed to the new ad for Camels, which used a motorcycle, the wings of an eagle, and a camel. They wanted all ads to be limited to black and white, showing only the product with no props or scenery, and only the warning labels as text.

Finally, the elimination of punitive damages and class actions came under fire from trial lawyers across the country. "Punitive damages are my sword," protested Woody Wilner. "My resources are already weak compared with the industry's and I need all the swords I can get." The restrictions on class actions seemed to some plaintiffs' lawyers effective immunity for the industry. But Meyer Koplow disagreed. Asked whether he thought there would by any future litigation against the tobacco industry if the proposal passed Congress and became law, he said, "I believe in the field of dreams theory. If you build it, they will come. Five billion dollars is an enormous amount of money."

EPILOGUE

AN ILLUSION
OF SURRENDER

A WEEK BEFORE the June 20 proposal, Professor Stan Glantz, his wife, and his daughter went out for a Father's Day dinner near his home in San Francisco. When they returned around midnight, a car followed them up the dirt lane to their garage. Glantz was alarmed to be followed this late at night. He zipped into the garage and quickly closed the automatic door. But as the door clattered to the ground, someone began to pound on it from the outside. Glantz hustled his family into the house, but the pounding moved to the front door. He ignored it and went to bed. He thought he knew what had happened. Earlier that day at Glantz's office at the university, a Brown & Williamson representative had attempted to serve a subpoena on the professor; the company wanted him to appear at a deposition for the Florida Medicaid case, but university rules say that court orders on faculty members can only be accepted by the college counsel. Glantz guessed that the company was trying to serve the subpoena again—at midnight.

The next day, a court processor acting for B&W called Glantz on the phone at home and, after apologizing for interrupting his Father's Day, said he had been instructed to harass Glantz until he accepted the summons. Glantz told the man about the university rules, and the subpoena was served the next day at the university legal counsel's office. It turned out that Brown & Williamson wanted to cross-examine Glantz about the book, *The Cigarette Papers*, Glantz and colleagues had written on the Merrell Williams documents.

The professor was no longer surprised at the antics of Big Tobacco. Ever since he had received copies of the Merrell Williams papers from his anonymous donor, "Mr. Butts," and had placed them in the university archives and then made them available on the Internet, he had been hunted by the protobacco forces. The industry's congressional lobbyists had tried, unsuccessfully as it turned out, to persuade congressmen to cancel the National Cancer Institute funding of Glantz's tobacco control studies. One of those had tracked the effects of tobacco money on state legislators' voting patterns. Another had looked at the industry's role in so-called grassroots smoker's rights campaigns.

Now, a new citizens' group with the high-sounding title of Californians for Scientific Integrity, which is partly funded by the industry, filed suit against the university, charging Glantz with skewing data in a 1994 study of the effect of smoking bans in restaurants. Glantz's study had concluded there was no economic impact, and antismoking forces had used the results to widen smoking bans in other states. In its law suit, the new group charged that Glanz had used state funds illegally to promote tobacco control.

They obtained a court order to "lock up" his computer and prevent him from destroying relevant materials. They also sponsored a critique of Glantz's report that charged the professor with manipulation of data. They demanded that the *American Journal of Public Health*, an ancient, prestigious journal where Glantz's 1994 article had been published, rereview it. The journal did so, but concluded that the article was sound and that the critique was, as one of the reviewers said, "much ado about nothing." The journal's editor, Dr. Mervyn Susser, wrote in the October 1997 issue that, "plainly, the aim is to destroy Glantz's career." Certainly, it appeared that the fine promises being made by the industry in Washington about new ways of doing business were as duplicitous as old pledges about safeguarding the public health. As Dr. Susser put it, the tobacco companies had once again created "only an illusion of surrender."

ON CAPITOL HILL, THERE was more evidence that the industry's old campaigners had not given up. In what was dubbed by *Time* magazine as "the biggest heist of the year," tobacco lobbyists led by Haley Barbour, the former Republican National Committee chairman, had quietly slipped a $50 billion tax credit for Big Tobacco, designed to offset the industry's settlement costs, into the new tax bill. The tax bill included a 15-cents-a-pack rise in Federal taxes (then at 24 cents, the lowest in the developed world). Over twenty-five years, this new tax would add up to $50 billion. In the last-minute rush to approve the bill, the provision was supported by the Republican leadership—Trent Lott and Newt Gingrich—and even given conditional approval at the White House. Clinton advisers, anxious to pass the tax bill, claimed that the credit was not meaningful until the terms of the June 20 proposal were fixed. But Senator Richard Durbin, a tobacco foe, spotted the ruse. Calling it "midnight madness that shines and stinks like a mackerel in the moonlight," Durbin, a Democrat from Illinois, proposed a motion to strike the provision, but he was resoundingly defeated 78 to 22. The $50 billion credit was such an obvious scam, however, that over the summer recess, members of Congress realized it couldn't survive.

When Congress returned in September, a new mood prevailed and the Senate reversed itself. A Durbin amendment to repeal the $50 billion credit was passed by a stunning 97 to 3 vote—the three being staunch industry supporters from tobacco states: North Carolina senators Jesse Helms and Lauch Faircloth and Kentucky senator Mitch McConnell. The result of the industry's self-inflicted wound was evidence of how volatile its congressional support had become.

BUT IT WAS the fine print of the June 20 proposal that began to turn it sour. The agreement had underscored what an incredible cash machine the industry really was. Even with the biggest dollar penalties in history, the industry would be comfortably secure. Wall Street said so. The projected figures were startling. An increase in the federal cigarette tax of 50 cents (on the 1997 average retail price of $1.88 a pack) could yield $10.8 billion annually in net revenues and still leave the industry with $5.4 billion in pretax profits. The industry could raise prices, make full use of tax deductions on the penalties—which are legitimate business expenses unless ruled otherwise by Congress—and easily cover the proposed maximum penalty of $15 billion a year.

As prices were raised, there was no danger of outside competition, in part because of the addictive property of nicotine. Unlike other products, which may suffer a rapid decline in sales when prices are raised, cigarettes have an "inelastic demand"; there are no substitutes that give equivalent satisfaction. And the industry is virtually unassailable because it's a classic oligopoly; that is, 90 percent of the market is shared by a handful of companies—in this case, actually only three: Philip Morris (48 percent), R. J. Reynolds (25 percent), and Brown & Williamson (17 percent). Being an oligopoly means that the tobacco companies can raise prices of cigarettes without fear of attracting new market competitors; the entry barriers are simply too high. Competition with the big three would not only require enormous capital outlay for production capacity, but also the establishment of new brands in an era that, under the terms of the proposal, would include severely restricted advertising.

The proposal contained several sweetheart clauses for the industry. One was an antitrust exemption that would allow the companies to "jointly confer, coordinate, or act in concert" to achieve the goals of the settlement. With this exemption, critics argued, the companies could raise prices far in excess of an amount needed to cover their annual payments under the settlement.

Another clause meant that the industry would end up paying significantly less than the $368 billion. The proposal pegged penalties to packs of cigarettes sold. As the companies raised prices to pay for the settlement, sales would decline but so would industry payments. Jeffrey Harris, the MIT economist, calculated that total U.S. cigarette consumption could fall from 24.2 billion packs in 1996 to 18.4 billion after twenty-five years. If that turned out to be true, the industry would pay $304 billion, not $368 billion. In addition, the $368 billion payment does not reflect the "present discounted value"—that is to say, the current market value of the payments, or the amount investors would be willing to pay today for a portfolio of twenty-five-year corporate bonds that promised to pay the settlement amount. Even when

Harris took into account the inflation-protection provision in the proposal, he found the present discounted value of volume-adjusted industry payments would be $194.5 billion over the twenty-five years. The Federal Trade Commission, doing their own separate calculations, estimated that the industry, by raising prices to the levels suggested to pay for the settlement, could reap a "windfall profit" of $123 billion.

The industry claimed that these figures were all highly speculative and assumed, wrongly, that a given price increase is all profit to the companies when, in fact, there may be changes in trade margins, sales taxes, and the inflation adjustment to the annual penalty payment. Even so, the prevailing impression was that the industry had gotten off lightly.

A PRICE INCREASE WAS, of course, central to the goal of reducing underage smokers (thirteen- to seventeen-year-olds), which were supposed to decline by 30 percent in five years, 50 percent by the seventh year, and 60 percent by the tenth year. The proposal prescribed a 62-cents-a-pack price increase, but the most recent economic research (a study by Frank Chaloupka of the University of Illinois at Chicago) suggested the 62-cents increase would cut teen smoking by only 18 percent in five years. The proposal's negotiators contended that the combined force of the price hike and the advertising and marketing restrictions would reach the 30 percent goal. But MIT's Harris calculated that that would take a price rise of $1.50.

If such an increase were mandated by Congress, and it was periodically revised to keep pace with inflation, then the face value of the payments to the Treasury would be $653.2 billion over twenty-five years, not the $368 billion under the proposal.

These disputed figures are merely one of many contested parts of the proposal that suggested months of debate in Congress. Others included restrictions on private civil litigation, especially the prohibition on class actions. Among these were the "forgotten plaintiffs": 2,000 labor-management medical-insurance trust funds that represented 30 million union workers throughout the country. Over the years, these funds had paid many millions of dollars in claims for tobacco-related illnesses (47 percent of all construction workers are smokers—double the national average). The funds had begun to file class-action lawsuits to recover those medical costs; sixteen had been filed by June 20. But the proposal terminated those actions without compensation and allowed them recovery only by filing individual lawsuits from the settlement fund. In any legislation, Congress would have to find a workable plan for compensating all the various governmental and private health-insurance programs, not simply Medicaid.

Also under fire were the provisions for disclosure of industry documents for which the companies claimed privilege. Under the proposal, a three-judge panel would review contested documents, but critics argued that this procedure would be slow—one document at a time—too expensive, and open to industry abuse. The industry's real history would remain under wraps for years to come.

Finally, there was the question of lawyers' fees. Because it was such a contentious issue, the June 20 proposal had deliberately left the matter to a separate agreement between the lawyers and the industry. But this was a partisan issue: Republicans were traditional seekers of tort reform and despised plaintiffs' lawyers, who, in their turn, tried to keep Republicans at bay by funding Democrats. Signaling a battle ahead, the congressional Republicans, led by Newt Gingrich, pledged that the lawyers would get not a penny more than they thought they deserved: fees at $150 an hour, considerably less than many had charged. "No matter how much it is it'll sound like a lot [and] be another black eye for all of us," said the Atlanta trial lawyer Ralph Knowles.

SHOWING HOW QUICKLY old enemies can become friends in this business, the key negotiators of the June 20 proposal—principally Mike Moore, Dick Scruggs, John Coale, and Stan Chesley—joined forces with the tobacco lobbyists to sell their extraordinary achievement on Capitol Hill. "I'm going up there arm-in-arm with Steve Parrish [of Philip Morris]," said Coale, "I actually like him."

Politicians of both parties found the process somewhat distasteful. "Who do these people think they are?" asked Arizona's Republican senator John McCain. The new partners encountered a stream of complaints. Senator Edward Kennedy, of Massachusetts, a longtime tobacco foe, complained that the proposals pandered too much to industry demands. "It is not for the tobacco industry to dictate what controls on tobacco are acceptable." He suggested that the industry's payment should be doubled to compensate federal taxpayers to Medicare (the federal health-care program for the elderly) that had also paid out for smoking-related diseases. "The concessions made so far by the industry should be regarded as the beginning, not the end," he said.

In response, Mike Moore admitted that the deal was "not perfect, but very good for the goals we have." He worried that the concessions gained could also be lost if the legislation took too long. "Move expeditiously," he urged the senators at one committee hearing. Referring to an industry lawyer, Scott Wise, who was sitting beside him, Moore said, "I've got my foot on his neck right now. Let's don't miss this opportunity." But Senator Tom Harkin, who grew up in rural Iowa, where his father was a coal miner, said, "Mr. Moore, I like how you say you have your foot on Mr. Wise's neck, but it's the first time this country boy has heard someone say he has his foot on someone's neck, and that guy says he likes it."

The congressional leadership of both parties looked at the lengthening list of disputed issues and forecast that there could not possibly be any legislation until the spring of 1998, or later—unless the president gave the proposal a strong endorsement.

The long-awaited White House response confirmed that the legislation would not be completed in short order. On September 17, in the Oval Office, President Clinton did not endorse the proposal. Instead, he outlined five broad principles: a combination of industry payments and penalties to reduce youth smoking by raising the price of cigarettes by up to $1.50 a pack; full authority for the FDA to regulate tobacco products; a voluntary ban on advertising to youth; legislation for broad disclosure of industry files; and moves to reduce secondhand smoke and to protect tobacco farmers and their communities. "We're not rejecting what the attorneys general have done, we're building on it," he said. The president praised David Kessler and the AGs and the "private lawsuits" for starting the movement to change the tobacco industry. "Look, if it hadn't been for what they did, we wouldn't be here," he said. Among the carefully chosen guest list in the Oval Office with Clinton were David Kessler, Matt Myers, Mike Moore, Stan Chesley, and Dianne Castano. There were no members of the tobacco industry. The president's message was clear: the legislation was too complex and the key issues far from resolved. It could not be done in a few weeks, or even a few months.

It was a great disappointment to Moore and Scruggs, who had clung to the hope that Clinton would endorse the proposals and restore momentum. Outside the White House, Moore suggested the president should ask Congress to stay in session beyond October to push the legislation along, but the answer came back: "No."

The industry was upset, as well. In a frosty statement, Philip Morris, R. J. Reynolds, Lorillard, and the United States Tobacco Company said they stood by the June 20 plan and would do their part to meet its "ambitious goals." In a separate statement, Brown & Williamson objected to vice president Al Gore's calling the June 20 plan "half a loaf." Such a remark "trivialize[d] its considerable achievements," said B&W. For a while, it seemed the deal might never come off.

IN THE END, Clinton had adopted much of what Drs. Kessler and Koop's special commission had asked for—with one important exception. He made no mention of U.S. sales abroad—the fastest-growing markets and the key to the industry's long-term profitability. More than 1.1 billion people smoke; about one-fifth of the world's population. In developed countries, the habit is declining by 1.4 percent a year, but in the developing nations it is growing by 1.7 percent, according to the World Health Organization. Revenue from overseas sales of Philip Morris and R. J. Reynolds leaped from $5 to $27 billion between 1984 and 1996. In 1997, as legal fees and settlements bit into tobacco profits at home, international cigarette sales climbed 7.3 percent.

With home consumption falling faster than in other developed countries, the U.S. companies had started looking at foreign markets well before the era of the Third Wave. New markets were opening up in Eastern Europe (with the heaviest smokers in the world), in Latin

America, and in the Far East. Threatening severe economic sanctions, the Reagan administration had helped the industry pry open markets in Japan, South Korea, Taiwan, and China.

As barriers in Asia came tumbling down, Philip Morris targeted Japanese women with Virginia Slims. Japanese female college students obliged. One study showed they were four times more likely to smoke than their mothers. RJR sought young smokers with Joe Camel. In South Korea, the U.S. cigarette invasion happened so fast that by the late '80s students, antismoking activists, and local retailers staged protests against "tobacco imperialism," and boycotted American cigarettes. In Taiwan, imported brands, most of them American, grew from 1 to 20 percent in less than two years.

In China, with its 350 million smokers, there was a Marlboro soccer league and Marlboro music hour, a Kent billiards contest, and a Salem tennis tournament. In the Philippines, Asia's most Catholic nation, U.S. brands could be found on promotional calendars under a picture of the Virgin Mary.

Even before the collapse of the Soviet Union, Philip Morris and R. J. Reynolds happily responded to an emergency request from Mikhail Gorbachev when Soviet cigarette factories failed to meet demand. The U.S. companies delivered 34 billion cigarettes, the single biggest order in their export history. A pack of Marlboros became standard barter for a cab fare in Moscow. When the Soviet Union collapsed at the end of 1991, Western tobacco companies rushed to buy up dilapidated Russian cigarette enterprises and quickly became the largest investors in the former communist bloc. Philip Morris, RJR, the German tobacco conglomerate Reemstma, and BAT, the British tobacco giant, all snapped up shares. The Marlboro Man was among the first Western ads to appear on Gorky Street. Britain's former prime minister Margaret Thatcher teamed up with Philip Morris (for a reported $1 million) to help the U.S. company establish a foothold in Kazakhstan, among other things. In the Ukraine, American companies outspent health ministry lobbying in the Rada, the national legislature, to reverse a ban on cigarette billboards and other outdoor advertising.

The U.S. global invasion was so crude it sometimes backfired. In Europe, Philip Morris sought to counter moves for antismoking legislation by launching an ad campaign that suggested inhaling secondhand smoke was less dangerous than eating cookies or drinking milk. "Life is full of risks," declared one headline above a picture of three cookies. "But they're not all equal." France's health ministry complained; so did Belgian cookie makers, who said the ads defamed their product. Philip Morris dropped the ads.

The unprecedented legal assault on the U.S. tobacco industry at home stimulated antismoking efforts abroad—especially in Britain, Canada, Australia, and Israel. The American antitobacco forces gave support to the strongest of these legal challenges—in Britain where Tony Blair's new Labor government promised a new antismoking drive. A young environmental lawyer named Martyn Day launched Britain's first smoking class action of forty-seven lung cancer victims against the two biggest cigarette companies, Imperial and Gallahers, which together control 80 percent of the British market. The claim was a simple one: that the manufacturers have known since the 1960s how to make less dangerous cigarettes and had failed to do so, despite their duty under British common law. Day had learned a lot from his U.S. counterparts and from the Merrell Williams documents. Elsewhere in Europe, legal action was minimal. In France, where smoking bans in public places are simply ignored, two individual cancer cases were pending. In Italy, one such case was recently lost against the state's cigarette distribution monopoly. In Germany, there were moves to regulate secondhand smoke. In Asia, two class actions in Japan called on the government to end the state cigarette-manufacturing monopoly. In Brazil, the industry settled two lawsuits by agreeing to put tar and nicotine levels on cigarette packs. But nowhere outside the United States was government as supportive of antismoking measures; nowhere did the legal system present such opportunities to the plaintiffs' bar to confront the tobacco industry.

In 1998, as Congress begins to draft legislation, it has become clear that the legal system had reached its limits in the tobacco wars. It had been used effectively to expose a rogue industry. It could recoup government funds for Medicaid programs, and possibly also nonprofit health-care trusts, but it could not easily, or fairly, provide recovery for the tens of millions of smoking victims. There were simply too many of them and their illnesses and afflictions too diverse. For the courts, the national health epidemic of tobacco was like the national health disaster of asbestos, only worse because the number of victims was greater. Facing the asbestos litigation crisis, the Supreme Court had ruled on the fundamental distinction between courts and legislatures. In the Georgine asbestos class action, the court had turned down Ron Motley's plan for a "global" settlement of current and future claims, ruling instead that such claims were more sensibly a matter for Congress to resolve. The problem was that Congress had done nothing, as it had done nothing about the greater public health calamity of tobacco. Now was the time.

The small band of liability lawyers who had launched the Third Wave would now take a backseat—except for those who had yet to have their day in court—in Texas, in Minnesota, in a New York "son of Castano" case, and, of course, in the repeat performances of Woody Wilner in Jacksonville, Florida. (Wilner lost his third trial against R. J. Reynolds. The jury found the company was not negligent and its cigarettes were not "unreasonably dangerous and defective" in the case of a Jacksonville woman who had smoked for thirty years and developed lung cancer.)

Together the plaintiffs' lawyers had performed the civic duty that Dick Scruggs had spoken of three years earlier. They had pooled their resources to take on Big Tobacco's "organized money," to borrow Justice Hugo Black's wonderful populist phrase for the funds of domineering corporations, and they had cornered the enemy sooner than anyone had thought possible. They had forced a truce on which the state attorneys general had been only too willing, after much huffing and puffing, to lay their imprint. The first two Medicaid suits, in Mississippi and Florida, were settled for $3 billion and $11.3 billion, more than they had dreamed of and in line with the June 20 proposal. At the next $14 billion battleground, in Texas, the industry vowed to stand and fight, but their past policy seemed to belie such valor. Each time they were confronted with a show trial and weeks of exposure in court, the companies had backed down. They settled the Broin secondhand smoke case brought by flight attendants in Florida. And at year's end, the industry was making overtures to "Skip" Humphrey in Minneapolis to settle the Minnesota suit, but it still looked like it would be the first legal engagement of the new year.

As the politicians set out to engineer the peace, the exhausted to-

bacco lawyers looked forward to a rest—or, as David Kentoff, the Arnold & Porter national coordinating counsel for Philip Morris, put it, to
the day when the "exotic, bizarre and maverick" tort claims of the
Third Wave would give way to a "more orderly and predictable environment." That was how the old white-shoe campaigners, such as
Kentoff, excused their outflanking at the hands of the guerrillas of the
plaintiffs' bar. But the battle would continue, of course. As Elizabeth
Cabraser had said, after the smoke of the Third Wave had cleared there
remained a body of plaintiffs' lawyers with the same perpetual existence
as the legal armies of Big Tobacco. They would be lining up at the field
of dreams.

NOTES

In the spring of 1994, the Third Wave of tobacco litigation burst onto the front pages of American national newspapers, in news magazines, and on television—first on ABC News. For the next four years, the tobacco industry would receive the most concentrated media examination in more than a century of existence. Key reports appeared in *The New York Times* [NYT], *The Wall Street Journal* (WSJ), *The Los Angeles Times* (LAT), and *The Washington Post* (WP). Among the professional publications, *The Journal of the American Medical Association* (JAMA), the *New England Journal of Medicine* (NEJM), *The National Law Journal* (NLJ), and *American Lawyer* (AL) ran prominent articles.

Among congressional reports, legal and medical conference reports, and independent surveys are:

Regulation of Tobacco Products: Hearings before the Subcommittee on Health and Environment of the Committee on Energy and Commerce, House of Representatives, Part 1, March 25 and April 14, 1994; Part 2, April 28, May 17, and 26; Part 3, June 21 and 23.

The Tobacco Products Liability Project at Northeastern University 3-vol set: Cipollone and Related Document Packet #7-15-92.

Annual Conferences of the Tobacco Products Liability Project, 10th annual conference, December 2–4, 1994 onward; also for quick reference, see TPLP's Tobacco on Trial.

Mealey's Tobacco Litigation Conference Reports, Sponsored by Mealey Publications, Wayne, Pennsylvania; October 26–27, 1995; June 1–18, 1996; March 13–14, 1997; September 18–19, 1997; also the excellent bimonthly Mealey's "Litigation Report: Tobacco." The 12-volume submission of the tobacco industry to FDA, "Comments of Brown & Williamson, Liggett Group Inc., Lorillard Tobacco Company, Philip Morris Inc., R. J. Reynolds Tobacco Company, Tobacco Institute, before the United States Food and Drug Administration," Docket no. 95N-0253 and no. 95N-0253J. Reports of the Surgeon General, U.S. Public Health Service, 1964, 1979, 1988, 1989, 1990, 1994.

Among the several Internet sites now available are:

Tobacco BBS (Bulletin Board System). Information on smoking, news stories, and links to other sites. http://www.tobacco.org

Centers for Disease Control information and links to other groups. http://www.cdc.gov/nccdphp/osh/tobacco.htm

National Center for Tobacco Free Kids. http//www.tobaccofreekids.org

RJR Nabisco Inc. company information and news. http://www.rjrnabisco.com

Tobacco Control Resource Center and The Tobacco Products Liability Project. http://www.tobacco.neu.edu

PROLOGUE: DINNER AT ANTOINE'S

This snapshot of the opposing forces in the Third Wave was the author's first meeting with members of the plaintiffs' bar.

CHAPTER 1: A NOVEL OBSERVATION

The story of the Nathan Horton case comes from interviews in Lexington, Mississippi, with Don Barrett, Ella Horton, and Earline Hart, and from contemporary news reports, especially those by Morton Mintz, WP, and Myron Levin, LAT.

The formation of the Mississippi suit comes from the author's interviews with key participants: Dick Scruggs, Mike Moore, Don Barrett, Charles Mikhail, and Professor Laurence Tribe. Profiles of Dick Scruggs, AL, April 1996, and WSJ, March 15, 1996; Mike Moore profile, NYT, April 6, 1997.

Garner, Donald, "Cigarettes and Welfare Reform," *Emory Law Journal*, vol. 26, no. 2, Spring 1977.

CHAPTER 2: A DEATH IN NEW ORLEANS

The birth of the Castano class action was put together from interviews with Castano lawyers beginning in December 1994, especially with Wendell Gauthier, John Coale, Elizabeth Cabraser, Suzy Foulds, Russ Herman, Calvin Fayard, and Danny Becnel.

For a racy introduction to the liability lawyers, see John Jenkins, *The Litigators*, New York: Doubleday, 1989. Stanley Chesley was profiled in AL, Jan–Feb 1994. For a round-up of the ABC case, see Ben Weiser in WP, January 7, 1996. Glenn Collins wrote the most colorful business reports of the Castano lawsuit; see his "A Tobacco Case's Legal Buccaneers," NYT, March 6, 1995.

For background on the Georgine (later Amchem) asbestos class action, see Henry Weinstein's "Debate Rages as Court Gets Plan to Settle Asbestos Cases," LAT, February 21, 1994.

CHAPTER 3: THE DRAMA TEACHER

A series of author interviews with Merrell Williams started in May 1996. The author also interviewed Fox DeMoisey in Louisville, Kentucky. Phil Hilts published the first interview with Williams in NYT, August 8, 1994, and he expanded on the interview in his book *Smokescreen*, infra. Subsequent profiles of Williams appeared in LAT, June 23, 1996; WP, June 23, 1996; AL, Jul–Aug 1996. A key Brown & Williamson deposition of Williams was taken on March 20, 1996, in Pascagoula.

The story of how the Merrell Williams documents became public comes from the Castano lawyers.

The UCSF library incident is from court documents. For B&W surveillance at the library, see Declaration of Florie Berger, acting Head of Archives and Special Collection, in the Superior Court of the State of California for the County of San Francisco, case No. 96728, February 24, 1995.

CHAPTER 4: THE PERFECT PLEASURE

BAT researcher's "all we would want is a larger bag to carry the money to the bank" is from document discovery in the Florida Medicaid suit.

For background on the CEO's statements and industry funding of nicotine research, see the 107-page "Prosecution Memorandum," submitted to Janet Reno by Congressman Martin Meehan, compiled by Clifford Douglas.

For background documents on the changing definition of nicotine, see Congressional transcripts of the Congressman Henry Waxman hearings, Part 1; see also the FDA's Appendices to the ruling on nicotine, August 1995, Appendix 1; "Nicotine Dependence and Cigarette Design: Implications for Research, Treatment, Policy and Litigation," January 27–28, Northeastern University School of Law. For the industry's reply see vol. III and IV of FDA Docket Nos 95N-0253 and 95N-0253J, op cit.

DeNoble told his story in interviews with the author and in congressional testimony, Waxman hearings, op cit, (Part 2).

CHAPTER 5: A FOOL'S MISSION

The story of Lloyd Vernon Jones is from an interview with his widow; also from author interviews with Mitch Zeller, lead counsel on the Y1 investigation. The story of Y1 is told in the Waxman hearings. op. cit., Part 3, pp. 5–31.

Kessler's arrival at the FDA comes from author interviews and newspaper reports; especially a 5,000-word article in *The Chain Drug Review*, vol. 14, no. 18, June 29, 1992. For Kessler's progress at FDA, see CBS *60 Minutes*, "Crusader," December 4, 1994. The breast implant story is in "Science on Trial: The Clash of Medical Evidence and the Law," by Marcia Angell, op cit.

For an overview to the year 1994 of tobacco and disease, see Carl Bartecchi et al., two special articles, "The Human Costs of Tobacco Use," NEJM (Part 1 and 2), vol. 330. No. 13, March 31, 1994.

Origins of the FDA's relationship to tobacco were researched by Nathan Abse in the Library of Congress and the University of Wisconsin. The papers of Harvey Washington Wiley are in the Library of Congress Madison Building's manuscript room.

The background to the FDA challenge comes from author interviews with David Kessler, Jeff Nesbitt, and Mitch Zeller.

CHAPTER 6: THE SWEET SMELL OF GAIN

The life and times of Clarence Cook Little are recorded in a handful of newspaper articles about his jobs at the two universities, Maine and Michigan, at the American Cancer Society, and in publications of the Jackson Memorial Laboratory. The best sources are his papers in the library of the Laboratory in Bar Harbor, Maine, and at the Library of the University of Maine, Special Collections. They include pamphlets, biographies, personal letters, and drafts of several of his CTR reports.

On eugenics, see Daniel Kevles, "In the Name of Eugenics," infra.

For background on Hill & Knowlton's relationship with the industry, see Karen Miller, *Amplifying the Voice of Business: Hill and Knowlton's Influence on Political, Public and Media Discourse in Postwar America*, University of Wisconsin-Madison, 1993.

For a compilation of industry documents referring to CTR, see Cigarette Papers, op cit. Also useful is the 3-volume collection of Cipollone documents put together by TPLP, op cit.

For Jim Green's comments, see BAT Research Conference, Southampton, 1972, p. 29, provided by Green. See also Green's essay "Cigarette Smoking and Causal Relationships," 1976.

CHAPTER 7: KINGS OF CONCEALMENT

Ron Motley practiced his court speeches at plaintiffs' lawyers' tobacco litigation conferences. This is from the Mealey Tobacco Conference, West Palm Beach, June 17–18, 1996; also author interview with Motley.

The lawyer takeover of the industry is well documented in the Merrell Williams papers and analyzed in *The Cigarette Papers,* infra; see also deposition of J. Kendrick Wells in *Burl Butler* v. *Philip Morris*, Circuit Court for the Second Circuit Judicial District of Jones County, Mississippi, February 2, 1996; see also Philip Morris papers unearthed in Minnesota litigation (ref. Chap. 10).

For Shook, Hardy background, see David Margolick, "Kansas City Law Firm Defeats All Attacks on Tobacco Clients This 'Firm' Doesn't Kill Its Associates," NYT, November 11, 1992; "Did Big Tobacco's Barrister Set Up a Smokescreeen?" *Business Week*, September 5, 1994; Myron Levin, "Smoking's Big Guns," LAT, December 15, 1996.

The author interviewed Eysenck in London, September, 1996.

CHAPTER 8: AN ORGY OF BUNCOMBE

Author interview with David Kessler, September 1996.

FDA rules are in the Federal Register, Friday August 11, 1995, Part V.

After their experience with the *Day One* program, ABC shelved a second documentary, "Tobacco Under Fire," for the show *Turning Point.* The network claimed that its Emmy Award–winning producers Martin and Frank Koughan had refused to allow the program to be edited to a shorter length. The film attacked the industry for selling to youth and examined the industry's export drive in markets in less developed countries.

For tobacco industry's response to FDA, see 12 vols, op. cit.

CHAPTER 9: THE SCIENCE TEACHER

The author interviewed Jeff Wigand in May 1996, when he was allowed to talk only about his personal life. Even though he would be given a "pardon" by the tobacco companies in the June 20, 1997, deal, he was still unable to talk about his work at B&W until the spring of 1998.

His deposition was taken in Mississippi on November 29, 1995, and was written up by Alix Freedman in WSJ, January 26, 1996. WSJ put the transcript on the Internet.

For B&W dirty tricks on Wigand see S. L. Hwang and M. Geyelin, "Brown & Williamson Has 500-Page Dossier Attacking Chief Critic," WSJ, February 1, 1996.

For the background to Wigand and CBS see Lawrence Grossman, *Columbia Journalism Review*, January–February 1996; "The Man Who Knew Too Much," Marie Brenner, *Vanity Fair*, May 1996. Profile of John Scanlon, *New York* magazine, July 21, 1997.

CHAPTER 10: VOYAGE OF DISCOVERY

This chapter is based on interviews with Skip Humphrey, Mike Ciresi, and Roberta Walburn. The author was part of the British Channel 4 crew with Ciresi when he visited the BAT document warehouse in Guildford.

For background on Judge Fitzpatrick, see reports by David Phelps of the Minneapolis *Star Tribune*; in particular "Taking on Tobacco," June 16, 1997, and a profile of Fitzpatrick, January 27, 1997.

Walburn argued her motion to include BAT Industries in the lawsuit in the County of Ramsey, state court file no. C1-94-8565, December 15, 1994; see also FDA, August 1995, Appendix 2, op. cit.

CHAPTER 11: THE FORDICE SAGA

For an analysis of the tobacco industry defenses, see Charles Mikhail, "The Tobacco Industry's Imaginative but Risky Defense to State Medicaid Actions"; Mealey's Tobacco Litigation Conference, June 1996; plus Mike Moore's "Memorandum in Support of the State's Motion For Ruling in Limine," to Chancery Court of Jackson County, Mississippi, August 11, 1995; plus the defendants' Opposition Memorandum, August 22, 1996; plus Plaintiff's Reply Memorandum, August 25, 1995.

On the industry's economics, "Does Tobacco Pay Its Way?" *Business Week*, February 19, 1996; Kenneth Warner et al., "Employment Implications of Declining Tobacco Product Sales for the Regional Economies of the United States," JAMA, April 24, 1996, vol. 275, No 16, pp. 1241–6; "Tobacco Industry Employment: A Review of the Price Waterhouse Economic Impact Report and Tobacco Institute Estimates of Economic Losses from Increasing the Federal Excise Tax," Arthur Anderson Economic Consulting, Los Angeles, October 6, 1993.

CHAPTER 12: THE IDES OF MARCH

The story of the 1996 Liggett defection comes from author's interviews with Don Barrett, Bennett LeBow, Dick Scruggs, Woody Wilner, and the Castano lawyers. Once again, WSJ had the scoop; see Alix Freedman, Suein Hwang, Steven Lipin, Milo Geyelin, "Liggett Group Offers First-Ever Settlement of Cigarette Lawsuits," WSJ, March 13, 1996. See also, Glenn Collins, "LeBow Savors a Victory, but the Game Isn't Over," NYT, March 14, 1996.

CHAPTER 13: THE SORCERER'S APPRENTICE

The story of Hatsy Heep comes from Castano lawyers' interviews, plus her 68-page sworn deposition, New Orleans, Friday, April 5, 1996.

The background to the breakup of the original Castano suit comes from interviews with Castano lawyers and contemporary media reports.

The dialogue between Wendell Gauthier and Gary Black is Gauthier's recollection. Black recalled the conversation, but not in detail.

The Gauthier-Motley battle is from author interviews with Castano lawyers.

The author attended the OSHA hearings. Transcripts of the hearings are available from the U.S. Department of Labor. The incident with Mayor Althaus and the withdrawal of Philip Morris witnesses was written up in the proceedings of the 10th Annual Conference of Tobacco Products Liability Project, Boston, December 2–4, 1994, op cit.

Cabraser's critique of the Fifth Circuit's decision is in "The Road Not Taken: Thoughts on the Fifth Circuit's Decertification of the Castano Class," ALI-ABA Course of Study, Civil Practice and Litigation Techniques in the Federal Courts, August 14–16, 1996, Seattle, Washington. The *Harvard Law Review* article is in vol. 110, February 1997, No. 4, p. 977.

CHAPTER 14: THE MAN ON THE PINK BICYCLE

This chapter is based on interviews with Woody Wilner. For Wilner's background, see Piper Lowell, "Florida the main staging area in battles against the tobacco industry," *The Daily Business Review*, December 1, 1995; Maggie Mahar, "Where There's Smoke," *Barron's*, October 14, 1996; Randy Noles, *Jacksonville* magazine, February 1997.

The 130-page transcript of Brown & Williamson's deposition of Irwin Tucker, Louisville, Kentucky, July 28, 1997. The subsequent doctors' reports on Tucker are enclosed in a letter to Wilner from Brown, Todd & Heyburn, of Louisville, September 10, 1997.

For jury analysis of the second Wilner trial see "Jury's Verdict Suggests Tough Times Ahead for the Industry," Huang, Geyelin, and Freedman, WSJ, August 12, 1996.

CHAPTER 15: FIELD OF DREAMS

The title of this chapter comes from a remark made by Meyer Koplow at Harvard Law School seminar, "Should Tort Law Be on the Table," July 31, 1997. This was a particularly useful overview of the proposed settlement because it included industry lawyers.

The story of the negotiations is pieced together from news reports and interviews with the plaintiffs' lawyers who took part. See also, Mealey's Tobacco Conference in Chicago, September 18–19, 1997.

EPILOGUE: AN ILLUSION OF SURRENDER

The attack on Stan Glantz comes from author's interviews with all parties concerned.

For reading on international tobacco interests, see WP series by Glenn Frankel et al., November 17, 18, 19, 20, 1996, and the banned ABC film "Tobacco Under Fire," op cit.; also "U.S. Trade Policy and Cigarette Smoking in Asia," National Bureau of Economic Research, Inc., working paper 5543.

For economic arguments of Jeffrey Harris, see his comments for the American Cancer Society, June 26, 1997, and his remarks at the American Cancer Society's press conference, Washington, D.C., July 24, 1997.

For relevance of Georgine (Amchem) asbestos litigation, see response of Laurence Tribe to questions posed by the U.S. Senate Judiciary Committee, August 12, 1997. Also, for evolution of product liability law to "generic liability," see "War on Common Law: The Struggle at the Center of Products Liability," by Carl Bogus, *Missouri Law Review,* vol. 60, Winter 1995.

SELECTED BIBLIOGRAPHY

Since the Third Wave began, three books have been published on the tobacco industry. The first is an encyclopedic work by Richard Kluger: *Ashes to Ashes* (New York: Alfred A. Knopf, 1996). The second is Stan Glantz et al., *The Cigarette Papers* (University of California Press, 1996). The third is Philip Hilt's *Smokescreen: The Truth behind the Tobacco Industry Cover-up* (New York: Addison-Wesley, 1996).

Kluger's work is a monumental 807 pages of social and scientific history, unique in books about the tobacco industry because the author was given access to Philip Morris executives. Unfortunately, unlike the first generation of tobacco lords—the Dukes of Durham and the Reynolds of Winston in North Carolina—those that followed are not very interesting. They harvested the mammoth profits and retreated behind impenetrable defenses. These executives rejected the one chance of scientific and social progress—to produce a cigarette that gave pleasure without killing people. That scandal is given a full airing in Kluger's book, but, although published in the spring of 1996, his account does not include the Merrell Williams documents. Except for a brief, and curiously dismissive, overview of the Castano and states' Medicaid cases, the book stops at the end of the Cipollone trial.

The Cigarette Papers, by contrast, is solely about the 8,000 pages stolen by Merrell Williams. It represents a meticulously annotated version of the documents and is an extraordinary source for anyone interested in the minutiae of the industry's policies. Much is still left unknown because many of the documents are proposals and conference notes, ideas and recommendations rather than specific policy directives.

Smokescreen records how a *New York Times* medical-science reporter, Phil Hilts, found himself catapulted into the Third Wave in 1994, when he was the first reporter to see the Merrell Williams papers. While *Smokescreen* includes much of the new evidence against the industry, it does not follow the liability lawyers—even to their half-way point.

There are a dozen or so books written before the Third Wave. Three stand out, in my view. The first is Elizabeth Whelan's *A Smoking Gun: How the Industry Gets Away with Murder* (Philadelphia: George Stickley Co., 1984). Despite its sensational title, it contains a comprehensive—and nicely anecdotal—history of the tobacco epidemic. The second is Peter Talyor's *The Smoke Ring* (New York: Pantheon, 1984). Taylor worked for the BBC's news magazine *Panorama* and was the reporter on *Death in the West*, a film about cowboys with cancer and emphysema that Philip Morris succeeded in banning with a lawsuit. Taylor's lucid account was the last book on the tobacco industry to look at the politics and the science before the avalanche of internal documents.

The third is Christopher Buckley's satire *Thank You for Smoking* (New York: Random House, 1995).

OTHER USEFUL VOLUMES INCLUDE:

Rob Cunningham, *Smoke & Mirrors*. Ottawa, Canada: International Development Research Centre, 1996.

Jordan Goodman, *Tobacco in History: The Cultures of Dependence*. London: Routledge, 1993.

Paul Johnson, *The Economics of the Tobacco Industry*. New York: Praeger, 1984.

Daniel Kevles, *In the Name of Eugenics*. Cambridge, Mass.: Harvard University Press, 1985.

Richard Klein, *Cigarettes Are Sublime*. Durham, N.C.: Duke University Press, 1993.

David Krogh, *Smoking: The Artificial Passion.* San Francisco: W. H. Freeman, 1991.

Robert Sobel, *They Satisfy: The Cigarette in American Life.* New York: Anchor Books, 1978.

Larry White, *Merchants of Death: The American Tobacco Industry.* New York: William Morrow, 1988.

INDEX

rules of procedure issue, 258, 259–63

See also Castano case

Clements, Ernie, 73

Clinton, Bill, 5, 10, 95, 113, 163–64, 201, 215
   FDA proposals and, 165–66, 167
   national settlement and, 285–86, 290, 292, 293, 304

Clinton, Hillary Rodham, 165, 287

Coale, John, 4, 9–10, 37–38, 43, 45–47, 48, 198, 200, 250, 253
   national settlement and, 263, 287–290, 292, 294, 297–98, 301
   Tamol documents and, 247
   Waxman hearings, 81
   Williams documents and, 68–69

Coalition on Smoking or Health, 33, 284

Coal Mine Health and Safety Act (1969), 29

Cocteau, Jean, 83

Cohen, Marc, 248

Colorado, 254

"commercial free speech" issue, 169

Committee of Counsel, 148, 157, 242, 243

"common benefits," 299

"common sense" definition, 82–83, 88

comparative fault defense, 27

"compulsive use" criterion, 88

confidential documents, 8–9, 56–76, 171–74. *See also* documents; "privileged" documents; Williams papers

confidentiality agreements, 60, 92, 107, 184–85, 187, 188, 189

Connecticut, 207

Connor, Jean, 296–97

"constitutional hypothesis," 115, 116, 125, 158, 159

consumer fraud charge, 202

"contributory negligence," 219

"Controversy on Smoking and Health—Some Facts and Anomalies, The" (Blackman), 154–55

corticosteroids, 144

coumarin, 181–82, 185, 188, 190

Council for Tobacco Research (CTR), 157, 158, 203, 212, 230, 240

"Counterblaste of Tobacco, A" (James I), 101

Crawford, Joan, 240

"crime-fraud" exception, 212, 230, 240–41. *See also* fraud

Cullman, Joseph, 212

Dalkon Shield, 48, 139, 199

damages and money settlements
   Carter suit in FL wins, 265, 269
   Castano case, two kinds, 42, 52–53
   Horowitz wins in CA, 272
   Liggett pays first, 229
   national settlement and, 283, 285, 290, 298–300, 305

Davis, Judge, 270–71

Daynard, Richard, 6, 16, 18, 54, 61, 74, 206, 209, 238–39, 250, 252, 255, 263, 287, 293

Day One (ABC TV program), 33, 39, 201

"deadwood" memo, 157, 196

Delacroix, Scott, 237

Democratic Party, 4, 45, 96, 105, 214, 286

DeMoisey, Fox, 62–65, 67

DeMoss, Judge Harold, 259

DeNoble, Victor, 90–92

"dependence," 86

flight attendants suit, 243
manufacturer's responsibility and, 268, 270–71
Medicaid law, 55, 219
Florida District Court of Appeal, 54
Florida Medicaid suit, 171, 198, 220, 235, 237, 247, 283, 294
Flowers, Jodi, 255
Food, Drug, and Cosmetic Act (1938), 97, 98
1976 "medical device" amendment, 103, 175–76, 296
Food and Drug Act (1906), 102
Food and Drug Administration (FDA), 52
Clinton and, 164–67, 285–86
DeNoble and, 92
history of, 102
jurisdiction issue and, 165, 294, 298
jurisdiction upheld, 296
Liggett settlement and, 231, 234, 235, 237
national settlement and, 284, 289, 290, 294, 297, 298, 306–7
proposes rules on tobacco regulation, 165–71, 174–76, 284, 290, 297, 305–6
regulating nicotine studied by, 5, 10, 33, 95–101, 103–13
tobacco researchers and, 245–46
safer cigarettes and, 183
Wigand and, 178, 186
Ford, Wendell, 167
Fordice, Kirk, 55, 214–17, 223, 224, 282
Foulds, Suzy, 233
"Frank Statement to Cigarette Smokers, A" (Hill memo), 127, 140, 202, 275

fraud, 68, 127, 239–40, 261. *See also* "crime-fraud" exception
Freedman, Alix, 190

Garner, Donald, 28, 29
Gaskins, Samuel, 264, 265, 270
"gasoline hypothesis," 174
Gauthier, Anne, 37
Gauthier, Wendell "the Goat," 4, 6, 7, 8, 100, 139, 198, 199, 226
background of, 36–38, 47, 48
Castano suit and, 10, 26, 34
Castano suit begun by, 36–38
Castano suit filed by, 52–55
Castano team recruited, 24, 42–51
clash with Motley, 250–51, 253
Coale and, 47, 48
decertification of Castano and, 260, 263
documents and, 41–42
Liggett negotiations and, 228, 233–38, 291
national settlement and, 287–89, 291, 294, 298–99, 300
nicotine addictiveness and, 82, 88
Philip Morris documents and, 247–48
stock analysts and, 248–49
Waxman hearings and, 81
Williams documents and, 68–69, 71, 88
genetic makeup argument, 87–88, 114–17, 125
gentlemen's agreement to suppress research, 153
Georgine, Robert, 50
Gephardt, Richard, 164
Gibson, Sherry, 62, 65, 69
Gingrich, Newt, 100–101, 104
Glantz, Stan, 73–76, 140, 165, 285
Golden, Arthur, 294

secondhand smoke, 54, 71, 74, 104, 168
  OSHA hearings and, 254–58
Seevers, Maurice, 86
Seide, Charles, 173
Seligman, Robert, 210
Seltzer, Carl, 159
Seventh Circuit Court of Appeals, 259
Sheffler, Bruce, 269–70, 270
Sherman Antitrust Act, 205
Shoup, Hal, 168
silicon breast implants, 6, 38, 99–100, 139
60 Minutes (TV program), 45, 105, 178, 185, 187–88
Smith, Anderson, 26, 27
Smith, Gordon, 177, 189, 191
Smith, Judge Jerry, 259, 261–62
Smokescreen (Hilts), 57
"Smoking, Health and Personality" (Eysenck), 159
smoking and cancer link
  admitted by LeBow and Liggett, 242
  Carter trial and, 269–70
  research suppressed by tobacco companies, 148–59
  scientific research on, 115–17, 124–25, 129–31, 133–37
  tobacco industry attack on, 126–37
  Tucker deposition on, 276–80
  Wilner's method and, 274–75
  See also lung cancer
"Smoking and Health" (Royal College of Physicians report of 1962), 133
smoking cessation programs, 235, 298, 299, 305
smoking-related costs, 221
smoking-related deaths, yearly, 101
Smoot, Senator Reed, 176
Snow, John, 118
Sobol, Tom, 241

Solomon, George, 52
South Western Nominees Ltd., 205
Souza Cruz Overseas, 110
"Special Projects" funds, 157–59, 240
Stahl, Lesley, 105
Starr, Kenneth, 260–61
state compensation funds, 297, 298
state Medicaid suits (attorneys general), 7, 10, 51, 55, 219, 230
  Liggett settlement and, 239, 242–44, 268
  Motley and, 51, 263
  origin of, 28–32
  national settlement and, 281, 283–84, 286–87, 289–90, 292, 294–95, 297–303
  "seminal" seminar on, 283
stock analysts, 8, 16, 170, 230, 243, 266, 272
  subpoenaed, 248
"Subjective Coding Project," 59–60
"subrogation" doctrine, 30–31, 203, 219
Surgeon General, U.S., 205
  Report of 1957, 131
  Report of 1964, 19, 83, 85–86, 135–36, 144, 148, 149, 269
  Report of 1988, 86–88
"Survey of Cancer Research with Emphasis Upon Possible Carcinogens From Tobacco" (Teague report), 130, 278–79
Synar, Mike, 96, 98, 113

Taddeo, Joseph, 77
Tamol, Ron, 245–48
tar, 105, 106, 108, 130, 145, 151, 182–85, 190, 206
"target level," 85